C000131667

Democratization in the So

March 2000
Manchester.

PERSPECTIVES ON DEMOCRATIZATION

SHIRIN RAI AND WYN GRANT series editors

forthcoming titles

Globalizing democracy
KATHERINE FRIELBECK

Funding democratization
PETER BURNELL AND ALAN WARE

Democratization in the South
The jagged wave

ROBIN LUCKHAM AND GORDON WHITE editors

MANCHESTER UNIVERSITY PRESS
Manchester and New York

distributed exclusively in the USA by St. Martin's Press

Copyright © Manchester University Press 1996

Whilst copyright in the volume as a whole is vested in Manchester
University Press, copyright in individual chapters belongs to their
respective authors, and no chapter may be reproduced wholly or in
part without the express permission in writing of both author and publisher.

Published by Manchester University Press
Oxford Road, Manchester M13 9NR, UK
and Room 400, 175 Fifth Avenue, New York, NY 10010, USA

Distributed exclusively in the USA
by St. Martin's Press, Inc., 175 Fifth Avenue, New York,
NY 10010, USA

British Library Cataloguing-in-Publication Data

A catalogue record for this book is available from the British Library

Library of Congress Cataloging-in-Publication Data

Democratization in the South : the jagged wave / edited by Robin
    Luckham and Gordon White.
        p.   cm.
    Includes index.
    ISBN 0-7190-4941-5. — ISBN 0-7190-4942-3
    1. Democracy—Developing countries. 2. Developing countries—
Politics and government. I. Luckham, Robin. II. White, Gordon,
1942- .
JF60.D47 1996
321.8'09172'4—dc20   96-18065

ISBN 0 7190 4941 5 *hardback*
     0 7190 4942 3 *paperback*

First published 1996

00 99 98 97 96   10 9 8 7 6 5 4 3 2 1

Set by Graphicraft Typesetters Ltd, Hong Kong
Printed in Great Britain
by Bell & Baim Ltd, Glasgow

Contents

Tables and figures

Tables

Figure

Contributors

Geoffrey Hawthorn teaches Sociology and Politics at Cambridge University.

Robin Luckham is a Research Associate (formerly Fellow) at the Institute of Development Studies, University of Sussex, working on demilitarization and the political role of the military, especially in sub-Saharan Africa.

Mick Moore is a Fellow of the Institute of Development Studies, University of Sussex, working on the politics and political economy of development, with special reference to state capacity and to indigenous capitalism in Asia.

Shirin M. Rai lectures in the Department of Politics and International Studies at the Centre for the Study of Women and Gender at the University of Warwick. She is currently researching on issues of gender, representation and governance.

Mark Robinson is a Fellow at the Institute of Development Studies, University of Sussex, with research interests in the areas of governance and the politics of public policy formulation and implementation.

Gordon White is a Professorial Fellow at the Institute of Development Studies, University of Sussex, working on issues surrounding development and democratization with particular focus on East Asia/China.

Laurence Whitehead is a Fellow of Nuffield College, Oxford University and works on the international dimensions of democratization and Latin American politics.

Acknowledgements

We are grateful to the UK Overseas Development Administration and its Economic and Social Committee for Overseas Research and to the Nuffield Foundation for supporting the research on which this book is based. However they bear no responsibility for our conclusions. For research assistance at various stages in the preparation of the book we would like to thank Mark Adams, Will Campbell, Cathy Green, Jethro Pettit and Charles Williams. Margaret Cornell did an excellent editorial job of tidying up and cutting the manuscript for submission to the publisher. We are also grateful to Annie Jamieson for co-ordinating secretarial work on the book and to Marion Huxley, Julie McWilliam, Glenis Morrison and Dawn Widgery for their valued word-processing skills. In addition to comments from the editors and their colleagues, the authors of individual chapters received useful criticism and advice from the following and would like to thank them: Juha Auvinen, James Blackburn, Jeongkee Kwon, Marc Blecher, Paul Bowles, Kim Kyung Ae, Lisa Rakner.

Abbreviations

AD	Acción Democratica
AFCDR	Armed Forces Committee for the Defence of the Revolution
AFDC	Armed Forces Defence Committee
AFRC	Armed Forces Revolutionary Council
AIC	Army Intelligence Command
ANSP	Agency for National Security Planning
BNI	Bureau of National Intelligence
CDO	Civil Defence Organisation
CDR	Committee for the Defence of the Revolution
CNI	Central Nacional de Informaciones
COPEI	Comité de Organización Política Electoral Independiente
DINA	Dirección Nacional de Inteligencia
DJP	Democratic Justice Party
DRP	Democratic Republic Party
DSC	Defense Security Command
EIU	Economist Intelligence Unit
ERP	Economic recovery programme
EU	European Union
FEER	*Far Eastern Economic Review*
FIS	Islamic Salvation Front
FLN	National Liberation Front
FRB	Forces Reserve Battalion
GATT	General Agreement on Tariffs and Trade
IFIs	International financial institutions
IMF	International Monetary Fund
KCIA	Korean Central Intelligence Agency
KMA	Korean Military Academy
KMT	Kuomintang
LARR-SC	*Latin American Research Report – Southern Cone*
LAWR	*Latin American Weekly Report*
MFJ	Movement for Freedom and Justice
MIA	Armed Islamic Movement
MMD	Movement for Multi-party Democracy

NAFTA	North American Free Trade Area
NCD	National Commission for Democracy
NDC	National Democratic Congress
NGOs	nongovernmental organizations
NIC	Newly industrializing country
NLC	National Liberation Council
NPP	New Patriotic Party
NRC	National Redemption Council
OECD	Organization for Economic Cooperation and Development
PAMSCAD	Program of Action and Measures to Address the Social Costs of Adjustment
PAP	People's Action Party
PDC	People's Defence Committee
PNDC	Provisional National Defence Council
RDP	Reunification and Democratic Party
ROK	Republic of Korea
SAP	Structural adjustment programme
SMC	Supreme Military Council
UNDP	United Nations Development Programme
UNIP	United National Independence Party
UNO	United Nicaraguan Opposition
UP	Unidad Popular
URD	Unión Republicana Democrática
WDC	Workers' Defence Committee
ZCTU	Zambian Congress of Trade Unions

INTRODUCTION

Democratizing the South

ROBIN LUCKHAM AND GORDON WHITE

The 1980s and early 1990s saw a dramatic wave of democratization sweep across the developing world, recalling the similar wave following decolonization in the late 1950s and 1960s. It surged over the three continents and affected both developmentally successful and unsuccessful countries across the political spectrum. Though the wave met resistance at times, most vividly in the Tiananmen Square events of mid-1989 in China, authoritarian regimes toppled in profusion, to be replaced by regimes organized along liberal democratic lines. During these years, the pace of institutional change accelerated as political events took on a headlong dynamic of their own and crossed what had seemed, only a few years earlier, the frontiers of impossibility. Accompanying and reinforcing this transformation was a trend towards new forms of 'political conditionality' on the part of the major national aid donors and international institutions, through which they increasingly linked aid flows to progress towards democracy in the recipient countries. Events became suffused with a triumphalist glow which, at its extreme, announced the 'end of history' (Fukuyama, 1992). For a while, this vision of democracy became entangled with perceptions of its reality as democratization took on some of the familiar characteristics of a millenarian movement.

The wave had already begun to recede by the mid-1990s as entrenched regimes either resisted the trend or merely went through the democratic motions, or as newly democratic regimes succumbed to various forms of authoritarian reversion. The rocky political coastline against which it broke has made this returning wave appear decidedly jagged.[1] Hence it is time to take a sober look at the contemporary scene in order to distinguish the rhetoric from the reality of democratization, to assess the depth, permanence and variability of political transformation and to trace its implications for the developmental futures of the countries of the South.[2] This is important for practical as well as intellectual reasons since, without it, political reform programmes in the developing world and likewise the democratic conditionality of the donors run severe risks of being unrealistic and thus counter-productive.

This book represents a collective effort to understand and in certain respects demystify democratization by a group of political scientists who have spent much of their professional lives analysing the political fortunes of the developing world. Libraries are now awash with books about democracy and democratization. However, we believe ours is distinctive in its approach, methodology and the audience we aim to reach. Our objective has been to produce a book that will interest not just academic readers but also policy-makers in the broadest sense, including those seeking to influence or change the shape of politics and governance in the South as well as in the North. We have sought to do this by going beyond normative discussions of democracy to focus on the practical dynamics of democratization and identify the political conditions which underline more genuine as opposed to merely formal processes of democratic transition. We also seek to identify the complex ways in which changes in political regimes relate to issues of socio-economic reform and development. The developmental effectiveness of fledgling democratic polities is of crucial importance for their political sustainability. Our approach has been broadly comparative, but we have also focused on in-depth case studies of selected national cases, notably in the chapters by Robinson, Luckham and White.

In our different ways, we have each addressed a common set of questions. The first revolves around the precise nature of the *particular institutional form of democracy* being adopted by reformers in the South. In all recent cases of our acquaintance, this has been some form of liberal democracy, a procedural system involving open political competition, with multi-parties, civil and political rights guaranteed by law, and accountability operating through an electoral relationship between citizens and their representatives. This is variously referred to here as 'constitutional democracy', 'representative democracy' or even as a 'bourgeois liberal republic', but we have tried to use the label 'liberal democracy' throughout. We are aware that alternative, 'participatory' forms of democracy have been essayed, either instead of or along with the move towards liberal democracy, but almost without exception such efforts have been either eclipsed or superseded (as in the Ghanaian case analysed by Robinson and Luckham), and the overwhelming procedural reality remains that of liberal democracy.

The notion of liberal democracy has inherent tensions and ambiguities, both in its theory and practice. In this volume, Hawthorn analyses the continuing tensions that have arisen within democratic theory between popular sovereignty and the power of elites, between the representative and the participatory principles, between partial interests and the common interest. Rai goes further and argues that the conceptual bedrock of liberal democratic theory is inherently gendered in ways which perpetuate patterns of patriarchy and gender subordination in both polity and society. In practice, as Luckham argues, as systems of rule in the political communities we call states, democracies almost invariably exempt wide areas of public life from full public scrutiny, most notably in regard to national security. In the real world of democracy, it would seem, too close a proximity to the ideal of democratic participation is sometimes viewed as dangerous and destabilizing.

A highly influential strand in democratic theory holds with Joseph Schumpeter (1943: 284) that 'democracy does not mean and cannot mean that the people actually rule in any obvious sense of the terms "the people" and "rule"'. Rather, it comprises institutions and procedures (in practice those that have grown up in Western liberal democracies) that ensure plural centres of power and competition for office between contending political elites. It is more a technique of government than an ideal to be pursued over the long term; more about government for than of the people.

Yet few people would think democratic institutions worth struggling for, if they did not at least some of the time enable the mass of citizens to exert control over those governing in their name. Nor can the characteristic virtues of democratic governance – transparency, responsiveness, accountability, official propriety and tolerance – be achieved without high levels of public awareness and participation. Hence, we do not see the procedural and participatory notions of democracy as alternatives but as complementary facets of a continuing process of democratization, which goes beyond the characteristic institutions of liberal democracy to embrace the broader practices of participation, social empowerment and popular sovereignty which breathe life into formal institutions. As our case studies show vividly, formal democracy can conceal huge variations in democratic substance, ranging from virtual autocracy through oligarchy to democracy worthy of the name; and one can expect these variations to be particularly wide in a developing world which is increasingly heterogeneous in socio-economic terms. The distinction between formal and substantive democracy also implies that democratization cannot be seen as a one-off event involving the replacement of one set of political institutions and procedures with another, but rather is a prolonged process in which procedural changes are but a crucial first step.

In the aftermath of colonialism in the 1960s it was commonplace to observe that Western political institutions had a distinctive historical and cultural heritage and the 'Westminster' or the 'Washington' model could not be transferred into an alien historical and cultural soil. This commonplace is still valid today, as Parekh (1992) has warned us, to the extent that societies in the South retain distinctive socio-economic and cultural profiles which differ from those in the democratic heartland of Europe and North America. Pre-existing conceptions of power and its purposes, of the boundaries between the public and the private domains, and of the interplay between ethnic, cultural, religious and gender identities on the one hand and democratic citizenship on the other, have vastly complicated the task of constructing liberal democracy, as Hawthorn and Rai both stress.

The end of the Cold War has also prompted greater scrutiny of the ways in which 'models' of democracy operate in their showcase countries. This has led to a keener appreciation of the political variations between advanced democracies (for example, between Japan, the United States and France); and to the revelation of the darker side of democratic politics through corruption scandals in Japan, Italy, France and, increasingly, Britain. Like 'the market', 'civil society' and other such contemporary shibboleths, the idea of 'democracy' contains a good dose of self-congratulatory myth.

Our second area of investigation is concerned with the *causes and context* of democratization in the South. We have found it useful to approach this complex issue from three analytical viewpoints. The first focuses on longer-term, glacial factors such as the basic changes in socio-economic and cultural systems, which sociologists in the tradition of 'modernization theory' have identified in terms of a world-historical transition between 'traditional' and 'modern' societies, or Marxists in terms of a transition from pre-bourgeois to bourgeois societies. These factors are important for understanding the genesis of democracy because of the widespread assumption, explored by Hawthorn and Moore, that democracy, to be effective, requires certain basic preconditions such as material prosperity, mass education and a minimal cultural homogeneity and consensus. But, as Moore emphasizes, this approach has more to say about the historical conditions in which liberal democracy has thrived, than about *why*, or about the circumstances in which *transitions* to democracy are most likely to be embarked upon and to succeed.

Thus the starting point of a second, contrasting, approach, typified by the work of O'Donnell *et al.* (1986a, b and c) and of Przeworski (1991) on transitions in Latin America and in Eastern Europe, has been a microanalysis of the short-term calculations made by political elites and of the bargains struck among them. This has resulted in more emphasis on short-term, conjunctural factors which intervene to influence the character and pace of political change, for example, the impact of the end of the Cold War, the 'demonstration effect' of democratization in country A on country B, or the effects of programmes of economic liberalization. The detailed case studies in this volume show the interaction between these short-term conditions and longer-term causal factors in the specific dynamics of democratization in individual countries. In the South Korean case discussed by Robinson, Luckham and White, for example, the impulse towards democratization in the late 1980s was given force by the long-term effects of a successful programme of industrialization launched in the early 1960s, the shorter-term effects of an economic liberalization programme launched in the early 1980s and still shorter-term popular struggles and political realignments among business, governmental and military elites in the late 1980s and early 1990s.

A third analytical viewpoint, therefore, seeks to identify structural factors which may act as a bridge between the slow-acting, glacial determinants and the more immediate influences on democratization in given historical situations. We find it convenient, following Rueschemeyer *et al.* (1992), to group these into three constellations of power which intersect to condition the character and direction of political change in particular countries at specific times. These are: (a) international factors, such as the distribution of power in inter-state relations, the operation of international financial institutions, the foreign policies of major aid donors, or the impact of the global economic system (covered broadly by Whitehead, although Robinson and Luckham also take up some economic and military dimensions of international 'political conditionality'); (b) the state itself, which is composed of a nexus of powers and interests, such as the ruling political leadership or elite and the different institutional sectors, including economic decision-makers (considered by Robinson), or the military and the security services (dealt with by Luckham); (c) 'civil society', which embodies the power of organized groups and interests in society, addressed by White and Rai.

In any particular case of democratization, these constellations interact in ways which are both general across contexts and also specific to the particular time and context. For example, the impact of an international financial institution such as the World Bank may be crucial for a weak, dependent country such as Zambia but less so for a large and assertive country such as China or a developmental high-performer such as South Korea. Similarly, the military has played a smaller role in constraining democracy in Zambia, where it has been relatively weak in most of the post-independence period, than in South Korea or Chile, where powerful military regimes were entrenched over decades. Likewise, the autonomous power of civil society will be stronger in a society which has experienced a prolonged period of industrialization which has brought about material prosperity, raised educational standards and transformed a nation's class structure (as in South Korea or Taiwan) than in societies where the modern sector of civil society is embryonic and where new and old sectors are at war, as in most of the countries in sub-Saharan Africa. The precise political configuration induced by the operation of these three sets of variables goes a long way towards explaining why democratization does or does not take place, how it takes place, what particular form it takes and what are its future prospects. Given the immense heterogeneity of countries in the South, we would expect tremendous diversity in the causes, character and consequences of democratization.

Our third area of concern is about the prospects for the *sustainability and deepening of democracy* in the countries of the South. We need to be more precise about what we mean by sustainability to avoid any tendency simply to equate it with the maintenance of a formal set of institutional procedures. In certain circumstances these may merely establish what has been called 'low-intensity democracy' (Gills *et al.*, 1993), functioning as a cosmetic cover for continued foreign domination or domestic authoritarianism, generalized corruption or social anarchy. We should also go beyond conceptualizations of sustainability which emphasize merely conservation of a democratic order once established, regardless of its character and imperfections, to consider the idea of deepening, which implies the strengthening of democratic institutions and the extension of democratic processes. Of course, sustainability must include the prevention of authoritarian reversals, such as the military interventions which have twice aborted the restoration of constitutional rule in Nigeria, or the changes in the rules of the political game in Peru, through which the elected President (Fujimori) reconverted a democratic political system into a *de facto* autocracy. But it also requires the consolidation and reconstitution of the state along democratic lines, through the reform of institutions in both the state and political society, and successful experience in operating them: for example, free and fair elections, the formation of political parties capable of government and their willingness to accept electoral defeat, the enforcement of legal restraints on state power, protection of civil rights, the establishment of relatively uncorrupt and effective bureaucracies, or the imposition of democratic control over potentially authoritarian forces such as the military or the security services.

The process of democratic deepening takes consolidation further by infusing formal institutions with the practices commonly deemed essential for the successful operation of a democratic polity: accountability, transparency, participation and equity under the law. It involves measures to prevent the continued dominance of unaccountable elites able to manipulate democratic institutions to their advantage as a result of low levels of popular participation and control. Hence, it also involves the empowerment of associations in civil society (discussed in more detail by White) which are capable of representing the interests of citizens in the political arena, limiting the power of social oligarchies and making democratic institutions serve the interests of broader sections of the population. At its most profound level, democratic deepening implies the democratization not only of the polity, but also of the major institutions of society: the family, the firm and the association.

The fourth and final issue we take up is the complicated and sometimes troubled *relationship between democracy and socio-economic development*. There are many in the South who would concur with President Rawlings of Ghana that 'for us democracy cannot simply mean holding ... elections periodically whilst we continue to endure poverty, misery, illiteracy, hunger and poor health facilities and whilst many of our able-bodied citizens are unable to find employment'.[3] Democratization, in other words, is tied morally and politically to the struggle for development and social justice. Without these it is not likely to mean much to the great mass of citizens, nor to be sustainable. The danger with such arguments, as with the somewhat different contention (analysed by Robinson) that economic liberalization is necessary for political liberalization, is that they might be used (as by President Rawlings) to limit democratic reforms, or to defer them altogether.

Indeed, as Moore points out, until the tide turned in favour of democracy during the 1980s, the conventional wisdom amongst development theorists both of the Left and of the Right seemed to be that strong developmental states, often under authoritarian leadership, could play an important role in facilitating productive investment and rapid economic progress. Western donors were more inclined than they are now to extend assistance to dictatorial regimes. Yet at the same time they shrank from open support for developmental dictatorship, either declaring (like the Bretton Woods institutions) that the form of regime had no bearing on the allocation of assistance, or coding their support in terms of the need for political order or (in the Cold War context) international security. But, unlike developmental dictatorship, the case for democracy can be argued directly because it is a value in its own right, and not because it may or may not be a means to some other end, such as economic growth, social justice or national security.

The jury is still out on whether democratization has any

causal impact one way or the other upon economic progress; as Moore shows, the existing research is evenly split. It certainly seems plausible to argue that policies that make a tangible impact on poverty and inequality would also deepen popular support for and participation in democratic institutions (though there is a counter-argument, put forcefully by Przeworski (1991: 32–4), that democratic institutions must also command the support of rich and powerful elites to survive, at least in capitalist societies). But the need to solve the problem of poverty is no reason for postponing struggles for democracy, especially when the latter can have a positive developmental impact, for instance by mobilizing support for economic reforms, insisting on the accountability and efficiency of public bureaucracies, or making governments more responsive to the needs of the mass of their citizens.

In our view, debates about whether or not democracy is good for development have been conducted in an over-simplified way. Instead we prefer to view the new wave of democracies as a given, and to take a more careful look at the *relationships* between democracy and development in all their complexity, and in a manner that neither reduces development to economic growth, nor democracy to the formal establishment of liberal democratic institutions. This will not only give us a systematic way to estimate the prospects for democracy in particular countries, but also has practical implications for political actors who wish to facilitate both democracy and socio-economic progress.

We can discern three groups of actors here who might find our analysis of some relevance and use. The first are domestic political elites in the South, seeking to learn from the experience of their counterparts in other countries who have confronted the dilemmas which face reformers: for instance, how to co-ordinate political with economic reforms so that they reinforce rather than conflict with each other (discussed by Robinson); or how to persuade recalcitrant military men to give up power without giving them a veto over further democratic progress (considered below by Luckham). The second are politically active sections of civil society (discussed by White), notably the 'peak associations' in different key sectors, which see themselves as having not merely a sectional role as the representatives of particular groups or interests, but also a 'constitutive' role as a force for restructuring the state in a democratic direction. The third are the 'donor community' (dealt with by Whitehead), in national governments, international institutions and international NGOs, which seek to foster democracy through political conditionality but do not know how to go about it, or wish to make sure their efforts do not undermine domestically-generated economic and political reforms.

Notes

1 Hence the metaphor we use in the title of the book, which is partly inspired by Huntington's *The Third Wave* (1991) but reflects more recent research and our own distinctive concerns and perspective.

2 There is no simple and satisfactory way to describe the countries of what used to be referred to as the 'Third' or 'developing' world. The Second World of state socialism has disappeared, and is now itself 'developing' (or not) in a different direction. At the same time, some developing societies in East Asia and Latin America have in many respects now 'developed'. Hence for the purpose of this book, which is to consider liberal democracy in Latin America, Africa and Asia, we refer to the 'South' though we are aware of the limitations of the term.

3 Address to opening seminar of the National Commission for Democracy, Sunyani, Ghana, July 1990, cited in Schmitz and Hutchful (1992).

1

Constitutional democracy in the South

GEOFFREY HAWTHORN

The argument for collective self-rule first appeared in the city-state of Athens in the sixth century BC. It reappeared in an attenuated form in republican Rome, disappeared for a thousand years, and reappeared again in the city-states of central Italy towards the end of the eleventh century, to persist, more as ideal than fact, until the sixteenth century. In the seventeenth and eighteenth centuries, the aspiration to a *res publica* attracted those opposed to God-given kingship and other forms of unchallengeable rule. The idea of the ancient republic inspired the political revolutionaries in France in 1789 and those in the Americas who wanted independence from Britain and Spain. But by the early nineteenth century, it was increasingly argued that the new 'commercial' societies required a republic of a different kind: one in which the rules of government should be defined in law and in which the ultimate authority for that law should lie with the people. It is this constitutional democracy – what, in acknowledgement of its affinity with commercialized societies, some prefer to describe as the 'bourgeois liberal republic' (Dunn, 1994) – that now dominates political debate. Indeed, with the end of state socialism, its most principled competitor in the twentieth century, some are even saying again, as political theorists first began to do two hundred years ago, that it alone can satisfy individual interest and the demands of commerce and science (Fukuyama, 1992). Yet in Latin America, Africa and Asia, many have been sceptical of its virtues, and those who have not have often found it difficult to introduce and sustain. In the South and the North, moreover, what it is and can be, and whether it can meet the demands of modern citizens and the modern state, are still much disputed.

The origins of constitutional democracy

Herodotus may have been right to say that the idea of collective self-rule was prompted in Athens in the late sixth century BC by the aristocrat Kleisthenes' mobilization of support from the villages of Attica to improve his chances in factional in-fighting in the city. It certainly crystallized there. The *polis*, the political community – Solon's gathering of all the citizens, thought by some to be the first democracy, or Kleisthenes' later elected council of five hundred – was the setting in which the citizens or their representatives, variously chosen by lot, rotation and election, decided how to be governed (Hornblower, 1992; Meier, 1990).[1]

The more pragmatic defence of the *polis*, forcefully put by the historian Thucydides, was that it was the only alternative to tyranny. Its overriding merit was that it existed at all. But in his view it was inherently precarious; conflicts were endemic and harmony was not preordained. But the more principled defence, put by philosophers, was that it *was*. The city, Aristotle argued, or collective public life, was a fact of nature and prior to the individual. But individuals realized themselves morally, and morality was irreducibly social. Their interests and those of the whole could thus be aligned in the *polis*. The historian acknowledged the differences between men as they were; the philosophers devised moral psychologies to argue such differences away (Farrar, 1988).

In early modern Europe, this 'civic republicanism', as it came to be called, modelled on Athens and more especially on Rome, was perhaps most elaborately articulated by Machiavelli at the beginning of the sixteenth century (Pocock, 1975; Skinner, 1990). Its practical purpose, as in the two ancient cities, was to counter tyranny. Its more principled defence rested on the conviction that there was a public or common good that was accessible to reason and could accordingly be arrived at in the collective deliberation of the citizens or their representatives, the results of which would secure the liberty of the citizens as a whole and of each individually. But this liberty would always be precarious; it would have to be actively maintained against the recurring hazards of fortune, the temptations of power, and the corruption of civic virtue by wealth. The early modern republic was predicated on the perpetual threat of war and fierce internal discipline.

These republics were not democratic or constitutional. Theorists who urged the virtues of a kind of popular sovereignty assumed that it would be guided by virtue, not interest. Citizenship was generally restricted, civil powers were not well separated, and there were few rights against rulers (Skinner, 1992). In his *Leviathan* in 1651, Hobbes scorned 'the specious name of Libertie' engraved on the city gates in Lucca; it was, he said, merely licence for the rulers, and oppressed the people (Hobbes, 1991: 149–50, 152). Good rule should depend on good laws, not virtuous men (Skinner, 1989). Political economists later pressed the point. The vaunted civility of civic virtue, Adam Smith declared in the 1770s, was in fact 'barbarous'. The necessary ground of liberty was personal independence, and independence could only be assured in the extension of commerce and industry, and made secure in law (Smith, 1976).

None of these later theorists suggested that the people should have the ultimate say on this law. For Hobbes, it was God-given. For the Scottish political economists, who were not the 'liberals' (let alone the libertarians) they have sometimes been taken to be, the good constitution would respect the existing balance of powers and privileges in society and the conventions that guided the relations between them (Forbes, 1975; Winch, 1988). For the French aristocrat Montesquieu, it would be a constitution in which the legislative and executive powers would be bound together in a reciprocal balance; only in a balance of this kind, he argued, whose usual outcome would be 'rest or inaction', could liberty exist (Montesquieu, 1989: 162). All regarded democracy as unbalanced, and potentially tyrannical.

The case for popular sovereignty was not made in Europe until after the French Revolution. But the revolutionaries' model, even though all men would be citizens, was still that of Rome. And their new France collapsed into faction, terror and eventual defeat. Constant, one of the sharpest of its critics, agreed with the Scots. In a modern commercial society, driven by private interests, individuals would be more prudent and public life less passionate.[2] They would also require space for their pursuits. This implied a liberty of a new and distinctively 'modern' kind. And that in turn required, as the Scots had not said, a representative democracy (Constant, 1988). Just such a democracy, for just such a liberty, was being developed for the new United States of America. But in the new America, there was no natural aristocracy, not even among the rich planters of Virginia, to provide the kind of representation and government that classical republicanism prescribed. No one could reliably speak for others. All should therefore be represented by people like themselves, and because the representatives would have interests of their own, they would have to be checked. These arguments were powerful and eventually decisive. Constitutional democracy had arrived (Fontana, 1994).[3]

The inherent strains of democratic theory

Democratic theory starts from the premise that government should respond to interests. Constitutionalists insist that not all interests are acceptable; democrats contest the nature of interests and their proper representation. In more deliberately liberal democracies, it is assumed that interests are particular, and will conflict. Many, however, have argued like Aristotle, that citizens have a common interest which can be discovered and defined, and that it is morally, perhaps even metaphysically, prior to that of any one person or party. Thus Rousseau in the 1760s distinguished between what people wanted as separate and particular individuals, which when aggregated could be thought of as the 'will of all', and what they wanted as citizens, the 'general will', and argued that in politics, the second should take priority over the first (Rousseau, 1968). The Abbé Sieyès recast Rousseau's conception as the will of a single economically connected 'nation' (Furet and Ozouf, 1989: 313–22; Greenfeld, 1992). Marx, whose conception of citizenship was somewhat different, extended the idea of a common interest beyond the bounds of the nation to an international socialism. Popes Leo XIII and Pius IX, whose idea of citizenship was different again, reasserted the Christian picture of a common good ordained by God against 'the deceptive wishes and judgement of the multitude' (Oakeshott, 1938: 49–50).

Even those who agree that interests are particular and will conflict have argued that a containable contest between them needs a common ground. A 'democratic government will work to full advantage', insisted the Austrian economist Schumpeter, 'only if all the interests that matter are practically unanimous not only in their allegiance to the country but also in their allegiance to the structural principles of the existing society' (Schumpeter, 1943: 296). Representative government and its incipient clash of wills was feasible in Britain, John Stuart Mill explained, because in contrast to the 'Magyars, Slovacks, Croats, Serbs, Roumans [and] Germans' in Austria-Hungary, the British were fortunate in sharing a strong sense of nationhood (Mill, 1977: 549).

In the new liberal republics, the virtual or indirect representation of ordinary citizens by their betters, the Roman ideal, was no longer seen as acceptable. In the new United States of America, where there was no established hierarchy, it was also not feasible. But all who debated the new American constitution tacitly accepted that the idea of selection for election meant that those chosen to stand were superior. 'Voting by lot', Montesquieu had rightly remarked, 'is in the nature of democracy; voting by choice is in the nature of aristocracy' (1989: 13). Once they were elected, moreover, representatives had to balance representation with organizing for power. This they have everywhere done by forming political parties. The outcome has varied. 'Countries that use the plurality method of election (almost always applied, at the national level, in single-member districts) are likely to have two-party systems, one-party governments, and executives that are dominant in relation to their legislatures', a dominance arguably enhanced in those constitutions which give wide powers to the president as well as the parliament. Proportional representation, by contrast, 'is likely to be associated with multi-party systems, coalition governments (including, in many cases, broad and inclusive coalitions), and more equal executive–legislative power relations' (Lijphart, 1993: 146–7; Linz, 1993a, b; Horowitz, 1993). For some, however, representation itself remains insufficient. They restate the need for direct participation. But as Rousseau and others, including the French revolutionaries, saw, whatever may have been feasible in cities, the active involvement of citizens in government would be impossible in a large nation-state. Those who urge it now accordingly tend to argue for local assemblies and other forms of decentralized participation (Pateman, 1970; Gould, 1988).

In constitutional democracies, constitutionalists in principle accept popular sovereignty and the view that government must be guided by the people's preferences. In his *Considerations on Representative Government* in 1861, Mill agreed that all (except the illiterate, the untaxed and those receiving welfare) should have the vote; if someone has 'nothing to do for his country, he will not care for it' and each individual 'is the only safe guardian of his rights and interests' (Mill, 1977: 401, 404). But Mill argued that a government directed solely by what the electors wanted would not serve the cause of enlightenment and progress. The initiative for legislation should therefore be in the hands of the enlightened themselves and those of 'national stature'; he referred approvingly to the senate in Rome. More recent constitutionalists have been more relaxed about the suffrage, although in a number of countries in both North and South limitations on it have been lifted only relatively recently. They suggest, however, that many popular preferences might neither be wise nor reflect what those who express them might, in other circumstances or at other times, acknowledge to be their better interests (Sunstein, 1991: 10). They might also oppress minorities. They should be constrained. 'To think that words can constrain power', agrees Murphy, 'seems foolish. Yet a political chemistry may turn sheets of paper into hoops of steel' (Murphy, 1993: 7). And as Przeworski, echoing Madison, suggests:

> Constitutions that are written when the relation of forces [is] still unclear are likely to counteract increasing returns to power, provide insurance to the eventual losers, and reduce the stakes of competition. They are more likely to induce the losers to comply with the outcomes and more likely to induce them to cooperate. They are more likely, therefore, to be stable across a wide range of historical conditions (Przeworski, 1991: 88).

Those constitutions by contrast that merely ratify a passing advantage will last for only so long as the advantage itself. The most prescriptive and substantive are often the least successful. Moreover, time itself can 'have some tendency to impress some degree of respect' (Madison quoted in Murphy, 1993: 7). This is especially likely where the constitution has itself constituted the polity. Although the French may be French, whatever their constitutional arrangements, arguably the same cannot be said of Americans in the United States, or of the citizens of many states in the South. None the less, time can also outdate even the most austerely procedural of agreements. In many constitutional democracies, therefore, although not in all, a judiciary is appointed to interpret the constitution and is protected from other state powers to be able freely to do so.

The fragility of constitutional democracy in the South

The strains in constitutional democracy are clear. But it is also clear why the arguments for it have been persuasive, and why the commitment to it, where it has persisted, has been strong. It has offered comparative security, peace and prosperity, and produced enduring and widely accepted procedures for the representation of interests and effective political debate. Why then should its attractions have been more muted in the South, and why, when it has been attempted there, has it so often proved fragile? The first answer is that pre-existing conceptions of power and its purposes in most of Latin America, Africa and Asia have not sat easily with its central tenets, and have in some cases been openly opposed.

In Latin America, these have been the conceptions of ancient liberty itself (Morse, 1954). Spanish American republicanism, like its ancient model, was aristocratic, exclusionary and bellicose. It presupposed a common good, the liberty and honour of the republic itself, and insisted that the defence of this liberty was the first priority. Other interests, especially those expressing a contrary conception of the good and claiming to embody it, were to be resisted. At first, in the movements for independence from Spain, the liberty at issue was liberty from European empire itself. Later, it was freedom from the new republic of the United States to the north, which could seem itself to be assuming imperial powers. In the Latin American states, it depended for its defence on the army, and since the liberty of the republic was the greatest good and the first priority, armies could claim supreme authority. This explains why in Spanish America in the nineteenth century, civilians – especially those of a professedly liberal inclination, who resisted the military and the Catholic church's support for strong central powers – found it difficult to consolidate their authority. It explains why in the face of what came widely to be seen as a humiliating economic and cultural 'dependence' on the United States, the ancient conception of liberty should have persisted into the twentieth century. It explains why in the conflicts between the landed classes and industrial interests, each side should so often have regarded the other as not merely inconvenient but subversive. And it explains why 'the people' who made demands from outside the political class were either, as in the case of the rural poor, excluded, or on the assumption that the good state is 'organic', caressed, co-opted and then to their dismay often subordinated in a politics of a 'corporatist' kind (Schmitter, 1974; Stepan, 1978).[4]

In the larger countries in southern Latin America, in contrast to the smaller ones in the centre, this pattern of politics was reinforced in the move away from the export of agricultural and other primary products to industry after the onset of the economic recession in the north at the end of the 1920s. In the authoritarian corporatism of Vargas's *Estado Novo* in Brazil between 1937 and 1945, for example, of Perónism in Argentina after 1946, and of similar initiatives elsewhere, the interests of the new industrial and commercial classes were promoted against those of the landed elites and the more patrician liberal constitutionalists, and were guarded by self-consciously progressive (if often nervous) elements in the armed forces. The nationalist inclination in this industrial alliance, defending the protection of the Latin American economies, was challenged increasingly by a growing internationalism. But until the 1980s, when the nationalists lost the argument, this did not change the picture radically. Only (among the larger states) in Mexico, where after the success of the 1920 revolution both the armed forces and the Catholic hierarchy were decisively constrained, did the contest subside. Yet there also, the ruling Institutional Party of the Revolution has found the attractions of the old republicanism difficult to resist. The party has continued to try to incorporate all those who have been willing to be incorporated, and to exclude those who are not.

The inspiration of the Spanish American republicanisms is the idea of a common good, a good for each which is the good for all and thus for the *res publica* itself. In this respect, the sharpest contrast is with sub-Saharan Africa. The outcome there too, however, has been a partial conception of the public interest (Bayart, 1989; Sandbrook, 1993; Hawthorn, 1993). Immediately after independence from colonial rule, there were, it is true, several attempts, in Nkrumah's Ghana, Nyerere's Tanzania, Kaunda's Zambia and Senghor's Senegal, for instance, to construct a single political community. However, these attempts failed in nearly every case. An older view reasserted itself. Political power came more openly to be seen as a private prebend. In conditions of persistent material scarcity, which economic development since independence has, in general, done little to reduce, the object has been to appropriate what surpluses there are and distribute them to those, one's kin or one's *ethnos*, who can be relied upon to keep one in power. Because of the resources it brings with it, state power has been the prize, and competition for it a zero-sum game. This is why armies have repeatedly captured it. Their monopoly of force, which in Latin America has been more incidental, has been decisive in Africa.

Nevertheless, there have been attempts in both continents to introduce constitutional democracies. Soldiers, indeed, have often been prepared to hand over power to them. Over most of the Middle East by contrast, including the Islamic countries in North Africa and South Asia, they have done so far less often. Only in Pakistan and Bangladesh has the transfer of power to democratic governments been attempted, perhaps as a result of their historical connection with British rule.[5] In contrast to India, however, democracies have been unsteady in these two countries, and that is explained by their similarities to Middle Eastern states, which are all exceptionally artificial. Pakistan was hastily conceded after Congress and the Muslim League had failed to agree on the division of powers in an independent India. The countries to its west – apart from Afghanistan and Iran – were divided up in their present boundaries after the defeat of the Ottoman Empire in 1919. Like many states in sub-Saharan Africa, they include a variety of socially and often economically separate groups, and have limited experience of statehood. In many this experience fitted a pattern, first described by Ibn Khaldun, of repeated invasions of the city, the site of what settled political authority there was, by purifying nomads from the desert (Gellner, 1981). The Ottoman administration in those parts of the region over which it was imposed, was distant and loose. Since the end of that empire Islam has continued to be the credal basis of rule in some states, including Saudi Arabia and what are now the small Gulf states. In other countries – Egypt, Yemen, Syria, Iraq, Iran, Afghanistan, Algeria and Pakistan – the *ulema* have had to fight for power with one or more secular parties, and each side, when it has succeeded, has tried to exclude the other. In the great majority of states in the region international interests during the Cold War put large arsenals at the command of whoever controlled the state. Even into the 1990s, external incentives to liberalize the politics of these countries remain slight.

Societies in East Asia and parts of South-East Asia, by contrast, have pre-existing conceptions of politics, and in many cases a pre-existing experience of statehood, which stand in sharp contrast to those in the Middle East, Latin America and sub-Saharan Africa. In China, Korea and Japan, this conception was well developed long before the inception of the modern constitutional state in Europe, as was its practice. In China and Korea, and in Japan after the Meiji restoration in the 1860s, it took the form of a central power whose authority was supreme and whose task, through a usually elaborate and carefully recruited administration, was to maintain order and security and as much prosperity as was consistent with them. Such states were not, it is true, always successful. Central power was constrained in Korea and Japan before the 1860s by a conservative landed aristocracy resistant to directive rule. In China it was preoccupied with the difficulty of exercising control over vast distances. But even when this power collapsed, as it did in Korea in 1905 and in China in 1911, the ancient centralizing aspiration remained. In Japan since the military defeat in 1945, in the two Korean states since their creation in 1948, and in China since the victory of the Communist Party at the end of the civil war in 1949, the resources of the modern state have been used to realize this aspiration. The outcomes, of course, have been very different: Marxist–Leninist states in China and North Korea, military dictatorships in South Korea between 1961 and 1987, constitutionally liberal democracies directed and managed by an exclusive political class and a powerful bureaucracy in Japan (and more recently in South Korea) and a mixture of the last two in Taiwan. In Japan, indeed, as in South Korea since 1988, the constitutions meet all that can formally be required for a bourgeois liberal republic. If the political practice has not always been notably liberal, the political class has maintained the formal rituals of popular sovereignty, and its policies have indisputably been to the benefit of capital.[6]

Of all the regions of the South, it is perhaps only in Hindu South Asia that pre-existing conceptions of politics sit at all easily with the demands of constitutional democracy. Many explanations have been offered for India's success in sustaining such a regime. The British legacy of divided powers between the centre and the states and a highly-trained, cohesive and effective civil service has almost certainly been important.

Together with the exceptional size and heterogeneity of the country, the resultant federalism has offset a concentration of conflict at the centre and the consequent risk of pre-emptive dictatorship. Hinduism itself, however, has played a part (Manor, 1990). There are grounds for the claim, pressed strongly against the British by Hindu intellectuals from the later nineteenth century, that in pre-Mughal as well as pre-British India, morality and power were seen as separate realms. Morality governed private life, and left the rest to statecraft, which was guided by prudence. Priests were responsible for the first and kings for the second. Hinduism, moreover, has no single god and, even in the realm of private morality, no consistent set of precepts. In private as well as in public, it allows a pragmatic pluralism that accommodates easily to the demands of a liberal politics.

All these are particular answers to the question of why constitutional democracy has not been as popular in the South as one might expect. Three others are more general. The first is that, whatever their political preconceptions, political leaders everywhere in modern republics, South and North, have put a high premium on 'national unity'. This is not in itself inimical to democracy. Without it, as Mill and Schumpeter saw, there would not be sufficient community to keep political competition within tolerable limits; to be acceptable, oppositions, as the British constitution has it, must be 'loyal'. But as Sieyès himself sadly agreed after the first few years of revolution in France, unity can also be used to resist opposition altogether. In any event, where there is no 'natural majority', and where the will or skill to construct one is lacking, competitive elections, many have believed, cannot be relied upon. For these reasons alone, although others played a part, one-party states were common in the first decades of post-colonial rule (Anderson, 1991; Low, 1991; Zolberg, 1966).

A second ambition in the South, often connected to this, although never so pervasive, has been towards socialism. The rhetoric was to hand in the first part of the twentieth century – as it was not in the colonial societies of Latin America at the beginning of the nineteenth – and what socialists themselves have often disparagingly referred to as 'the masses' could understand it. It was a convenient way in which to articulate and combine objections to the 'neo-imperialisms', 'dependencies' and other adverse circumstances of the twentieth-century post-colonial world. Even into the 1970s, it could also be seen to make some economic sense.

A third ambition, itself often connected to the other two, has been to construct 'strong states' for the purposes of 'development'. This too, like socialism, had its roots in the North, where governments had escaped from recession in the 1930s and mobilized for war in the 1940s by greatly increasing their directive powers. The colonies that came to political independence between the 1940s and the 1960s did so during a moment in modern history when expectations concerning what the modern state could and should do were unprecedentedly high. Their new rulers' ambition for directive development was also reinforced by the examples of other developing states, at first by what seemed to be the success of the Soviet Union, to some also by the example of the People's Republic of China, later by those of Taiwan, South Korea and Singapore, which, although not socialist, appeared to have succeeded because they had in one way or another resisted the form or substance of modern liberty and popular sovereignty. It was an ambition that acknowledged the distance between the early nineteenth century – when it was assumed that 'commerce' meets the needs of individuals and 'satisfies their desires without the intervention of the authorities', so that the state's responsibilities were for security, law and education alone (Constant, 1988: 315, 328) – and the late twentieth.

These answers to the question of why it should have proved so difficult to establish constitutional democracies in the South are answers to the question of why the aspiration itself should have been muted or absent. They also in part explain why those who have wanted to institute such democracies should so often have found it difficult to do so. In answer to this question, however, political scientists have more usually invoked the absence of what they take to be the necessary economic and social conditions for such rule. In contrast to the prerequisites of a more formal, constitutional and institutional kind, these wider conditions are as Murphy puts it 'wonderfully complex' (1993: 4). Political scientists have nevertheless tended to converge on the importance of physical and material security, the absence of extreme inequalities between sectors, regions and classes, few significant divisions of religion or language or of other kinds of affiliation or identity, adequate education, independent institutions and associations outside the state – what is often described as a 'civil society' (Lipset, 1959; Dahl, 1971). The absence of these conditions, it can be said, makes Schumpeter's 'unanimous allegiance' less likely. Together with the wide scope of politics – against which Schumpeter also warned – and the need for continuity in programmes of 'development', it explains why rulers are reluctant to face the uncertainties of democratic competition.

If only by omission, all these causes and reasons suppose that what is politically desirable and actually feasible is decided within the nation-state itself. But there are also external factors. Until the mid-1980s, perhaps the most important of these was the Cold War. In the years after 1945, the United States was anxious to ensure economically strong allies in Western Europe and Japan. The Truman administration believed that this required the protection of markets and sources of raw materials in the South (Leffler, 1992). It also feared Soviet expansion. And after Stalin's death in 1953, the Soviet Union did begin to seek support in the South. Governments there were ambivalent about the new contest. In principle, many declared their non-alignment at Bandung in 1955, but in practice many accepted the invitation from one side or the other. This gave them material benefits, including arms, and in the interests of 'national security' allowed them to assume the arbitrary and often absolute powers to pursue the domestic purposes that a liberal constitution would have restrained. The political price, however, was often high. After the increased US determination, in reaction to the Cuban revolution in 1960, to contest the Soviet Union in the South, and even more after 1969 in the so-called Nixon Doctrine of intended détente with Moscow – which led Washington to insure against Soviet opportunism in the South by strengthening the military and intelligence capabilities of selected 'intermediate powers' – there were increasingly sharp polarizations both between and within developing countries.[7] Constitutional democracy was subordinated.

The Cold War has ended, but pressures on the South continue. The North's desire for alliance has been replaced by a more discreet insistence on the part of the international financial institutions and some Western bilateral donors, notably the United States, and especially on weaker governments, to improve their 'governance'. In the view of the World Bank, this does not necessarily require constitutional democracy. The effective management of public services, greater accountability (which the Bank believes can be ensured by 'proxies' for constitutional checks), the institution of 'a legal framework for development' and improved information and transparency are all, the Bank claims, technical matters; they can be solved within the administration itself. In the opinion of most bilateral donors, by contrast, who, unlike the Bank, are not formally restrained from saying so, good government is political. They ask for 'democratization' (World Bank, 1992a; Gibbon, 1993; Moore, 1993; Lancaster, 1993).

The conditions for sustaining democratic polities

These answers, cultural, structural and geopolitical, to the question of why constitutional democracy has until recently been less attractive in the South, and where attractive, less easy to sustain, are together suggestive. Thus itemized, however, they are not sufficient. They can indicate where to look for explanations, and can eliminate some; but they cannot provide them, either separately or together.[8] Indeed, the move to a democracy and its consolidation will turn as much on the particularities of circumstance and on will, skill and luck as on any more generalizable cause or sequence of causes (Rustow, 1970; Lijphart, 1977; Hirschman, 1986). For the analyst, therefore, as for any actual protagonist, such explanations and predictions will turn on necessarily indeterminate judgements of what might have happened and might yet happen, judgements of practical rather than theoretical reason (Hawthorn, 1991). In this sense, they will themselves be political.

State socialist countries might seem to controvert this. These appear to be obvious instances of the combined effects of the causes and conditions that political scientists have suggested preclude constitutional democracy. It is certainly the conventional wisdom of the 1980s and 1990s, the political corollary of what has been called 'the Washington consensus', that socialism and constitutional democracy are not compatible.[9] In almost every socialist state in the South, pre-existing conceptions of the nature and purposes of power, the insistence on national unity, the commitment to rapid development, internal structural imbalances, and external pressures have all worked together, it would seem, to produce regimes in which the central features of liberal democracy have been absent. The reality, however, has been more complicated. In many such regimes, the hope that ordinary citizens would be able to elect representatives from amongst themselves was realized to an extent not matched in most liberal democracies. But there was no political competition with the ruling party, the representatives were not able freely to represent the interests of their electors, and their legislatures could not restrain the powers of the executive. In some there were attempts, in the agricultural producers' co-operatives in China, for instance, and their derivatives elsewhere, in neighbourhood associations and women's groups in Cuba, and in other institutional innovations, to introduce a degree of local discretion. But this was always subject to close surveillance and control. In many, one of the lauded consequences of post-1945 liberal democracy, the extension of a minimum welfare to all citizens, was pursued more actively and often achieved more quickly than in regimes of other kinds. But rates of growth in state revenues sufficient to sustain these provisions could not be sustained, and the initial advances under socialism in the provision of what came in the 1970s to be described as 'basic needs' were soon matched elsewhere (Stewart, 1985).[10]

There can be no doubt that, in the South as in the North, the more determinedly Marxist–Leninist regimes have in almost all respects been the antithesis of what would generally be understood as 'constitutional' and 'democratic' (Harding, 1992). But just as it would be wrong to conclude that there was nothing of any kind to be said for these regimes at any point in their history, so it would be wrong to suppose that no kind and degree of socialism can meet the conditions of a constitutional democracy. On the contrary. Schumpeter's model of democracy – a 'method', as he put it, for choosing the most effective leaders by subjecting those contending for power to regular approval or rejection by the popular vote – was in his account a model for a managed economy that would have solved the problems of allocation in capitalism and superseded its recurring crises. For it to work, the only necessary condition was that there should be no fundamental difference of opinion about the general strategy. And as many commentators remarked, it did turn out accurately to describe the postwar 'social democracies' in the North.

It has also, perhaps more surprisingly, been approximated in the South. In India from independence in 1947 to 1991 and in Venezuela since 1958, the political classes have been committed to a degree of economic protection, a considerable public ownership of manufacturing enterprises as well as utilities and services, a security of employment for unionized labour, and an extension of welfare, yet also to competitive democracy under a liberal constitution. India's socialism, it is true, was not comprehensive, and indeed did not touch agriculture at all. And the ruling Congress Party was for the first twenty years or more an oligarchic coalition of farmers, industrialists and public officials (Bardhan, 1984). But the party survived its own government's imposition of emergency rule in 1975 and its first electoral defeat in 1977 to return to power between 1980 and 1989, and formed a government again in 1991. India's pre-existing conceptions of politics and the structure of government under the British have certainly contributed to this, its national identity was not in serious contention, and throughout the Cold War its geopolitical position enabled it to use the interest of both superpowers to its advantage. India's continuing democracy is nevertheless striking.

The Venezuelan political classes, by contrast, scarcely talked of socialism at all. In practice, however, two of their three main parties, Acción Democratica (AD), which was dominant, and the Unión Republicana Democrática (URD), were responsive to the interests of the organizations of urban labour and peasants, and were also committed to extensive public ownership and social welfare. Together with the more conservative Comité de Organización Política Electoral Independiente (COPEI), their leaders agreed at the end of a period of right-wing military rule in 1958 to uphold the Constitution, to compete over a carefully defined range of issues in regular elections to the presidency, and to share Cabinet posts (Ewell, 1984). As in India, national identity was not an issue. But Venezuela's previous political history, in which no regime of this kind had lasted for more than three years, the enduring temper of Spanish American republicanism, and the country's close ties to the United States – which in 1958 led the three parties to agree that the Communists could not also be party to the new pact – could all have been thought not to favour a democracy that was both open and stable. Yet from the first election in 1958 until 1993, the successful presidential candidates – the URD having quickly disappeared – all but alternated between those from AD and COPEI. Between the late 1950s and the late 1980s Venezuela may have been an instance of what the satirists describe – in allusion to the historically more salient *dictaduras* of Latin America – as *democradura*. The terms of the settlement were decided by the leaders of the political class, not the people or their representatives. It nevertheless remained a constitutional democracy.

The conventional wisdom of liberals in the 1980s and 1990s, therefore, is too simple. A sustainable democracy does not require a wholly privatized economy. Yet the combination of democracy and socialism in the South, even if one looks at it historically, can still seem surprising. What had been celebrated in the North in the 1950s as the final political settlement between capital and labour and the consequent 'end of ideology' in one or another kind of social democracy had taken at least a century to achieve (Maier, 1992; Bell, 1988).[11] Some governments did attempt to incorporate the increasing numbers of urban, industrial workers and to control a declining but discontented peasantry, and some succeeded. Others, however, resisted, or failed, and suffered revolutions or coups d'état which caused them to be replaced with regimes of the extreme Left or Right. Where the settlement was eventually made – it was completed in the West with the end of dictatorships in Portugal, Spain and Greece in the 1970s, events that others have preferred to see not as the end of the first series of settlements but as the beginning of a third – it was for one or more of essentially three reasons: the exhaustion of war and the solidarity that followed, rising prosperity and the passage of time.[12]

It is these that together do much to explain the successes in India and Venezuela between the 1950s and the 1980s. In a much-discussed analysis of the different paths to dictatorship and democracy in several now industrial countries and India, Moore (1966) concluded that, for democracy to succeed, a 'revolutionary break' with the past had been decisive. But he was puzzled by the fact that on this count, as on others, India seemed to be the exception. Moore's mistake was perhaps to understate the nature of the break. India suffered a violent and traumatic partition of the largely Hindu from the largely Muslim areas at independence. Venezuela, less dramatically, had suffered a harshly reactive military dictatorship since 1948. As in India after the events of 1947, in 1958 at the end of that dictatorship the mood among civilian politicians, civil associations and those members of the armed forces who had not been implicated in it, was one of determined reconciliation. And they acted, perhaps crucially, with speed (Burton *et al.*, 1992: 15).

More puzzling, at least in the case of India, is the contribution of economic growth and prosperity. In most of the Northern societies that were to arrive at a political settlement in the twentieth century, this had been important. Just as parties of the Right came to see that they could lose much by resisting liberals and the Left, parties of the Left eventually came to see that they could lose as much as they might gain by resisting the interests of capital. In Venezuela also, economic growth played an important part. State revenues from oil provided the parties with revenues for public spending and patronage that they could not otherwise have had. None the less, at a little under 2 per cent a year through the 1950s, 1960s and early 1970s, India did grow; and the increase in agricultural production kept ahead of that in the rural population. Until the mid-1970s, when Mrs Gandhi's promise to 'abolish poverty now' came up against a shortage of money, Congress had managed to satisfy all but its left wing with skilful rhetoric, public ownership and the elements of a real, if modest, material redistribution (Frankel, 1978). What is certainly the case is that in neither country, in contrast to both Brazil and Pakistan, was there, or was there seen to be, flagrant and wilful neglect of the poor in favour of the rich.[13]

It is the importance of time, by contrast, that would seem to present the greater puzzle for Venezuela. Time matters if it can bring an increase in material security. In Venezuela, the rise in the price of oil and loans did bring unprecedented opportunities for investment and prosperity through the 1960s and into the 1970s. But by the mid-1980s the price of oil was falling and debts were growing. In 1989, an AD government had to face urban riots after being asked by the International Monetary Fund to implement a financial stabilization and economic liberalization package, and what had once been accepted as the natural corollary of political patronage was now condemned as financial corruption. In 1992, the army attempted two coups, the president was impeached, and in the run-up to elections to state governorships and the mayorship of Caracas, AD and COPEI both began to collapse.

Time also matters in itself. Sustainable democracy, including pacts to maintain it, depends on interested parties coming to see that they have less to lose by continuing to play the game when out of power than by trying to overturn or subvert democracy itself. To put it another way, it 'requires that governments be strong enough to govern effectively but weak enough not to be able to govern against important interests'. 'Democratic institutions', therefore, 'must remain within narrow limits to be successful', although as Przeworski admits, we do not know how exactly to define what these are (Przeworski, 1991: 37). A moderately high discount on the future in favour of modest gains in the present, a wider social and political trust and strategic and tactical skill, together with the right kind of institutions and the right balance between them, all take time to learn. The Indian Congress learnt the lessons of haste in its defeat after the suspension of emergency rule in 1977; in the unprecedented majority given to Rajiv Gandhi after the assassination of his mother in 1984 and the subsequent disorder, the electorate seems to have recalled the virtues of the system it had begun to reject. And with the fragile mandate it has had in the early 1990s to negotiate the kinds of economic reform that many other countries had to face a decade before, Congress itself seems to be drawing on hitherto untapped reserves of political skill.[14] The AD likewise learnt the lesson of its radical haste in the *trienio* between the army bringing it to power in 1945 and taking it out again in 1948. The Venezuelan Right learnt its lesson in the subsequent dictatorship. Even though AD and COPEI were collapsing, the events of 1992 and 1993 suggest that all had come to see the advantages of the previous thirty years. The election for president in 1993 went ahead and was won by a new coalition of the centre, led ironically by the man in whose house the democratic pact had been agreed in 1958. Faced briefly with the prospect of breakdown and coups, Venezuelans reverted to what they had known could work, however imperfectly.

Time, the simple experience of constitutional democracy, is vital. Important though reconciliation may be after a collectively traumatic dispute, it has certainly not led to such a regime everywhere in the South. Nor has increasing prosperity. The high rates of growth in Brazil in the 1950s and early 1960s, in Côte d'Ivoire in the 1960s, in Saudi Arabia and Kuwait in the 1970s and 1980s, and in Indonesia in the 1980s and 1990s, all either failed to produce one or could not keep it in place. Only in East Asia does growth seem to be having its expected effect. And even there, it is time itself again, and the value that East Asians put on order, that are playing a part.

In Singapore, from its inception an 'administrative state', as one of its ambassadors once put it, in which 'politics disappeared' (quoted in Vogel, 1991: 77), the ruling People's Action Party (PAP) has begun to lose seats. In South Korea, the military's Democratic Justice Party (DJP) was all but forced to concede popular elections to the presidency in 1987 and subsequently to introduce and finally observe a liberal constitution. In Taiwan, the once unapologetically authoritarian Kuomintang (KMT) has had to allow space to an organized opposition. In elections to the lower house of the Japanese Diet in 1993, the ruling Liberal Democrats actually lost their majority. Growing prosperity everywhere in East Asia has created a politically critical 'civil society', and oligarchies have been forced to open themselves to defeat.

Yet, except in Japan, their electors have refused to inflict it. The PAP in Singapore and the KMT in Taiwan have retained a striking degree of support. The DJP in South Korea renamed itself the Democratic Liberal Party with the incorporation of two of the three opposition parties, won the presidential election in 1992 and has begun to remove the less liberal features of the old regime it had itself created. Only in Japan is the future less clear. Yet even there, the objection has been to the politicians rather than their policies; there is no radical break. Experience in East Asia seems to lead the citizens still to favour Tocqueville's view that a democracy of a more openly competitive kind 'finds it difficult to coordinate the details of a great undertaking and to fix on some plan and carry it through with determination' (quoted in Elster, 1988: 94) over his contrary conviction that the discontinuities of such a regime are a price worth paying for the energies it can release and the liberties it allows. Their governments were perhaps right in the 1960s and 1970s to believe that 'future legitimation' required 'present accumulation' (Przeworski, 1985: 157). Or perhaps the electors' experience of stability and prosperity has made them value an imperfect but tolerable continuity.

Democratic politics and developmental efficiency

The time it takes for politicians and electors to accept a constitutional democracy may now be shorter in the South than it was in the North. None the less, as Tocqueville and Schumpeter would have agreed, too much has been expected too soon from the economic reforms of the 1980s (Bruno, 1993; Przeworski, 1993). The delay between the introduction of economic stabilization, liberalization and privatization and the resumption of economic growth tends to be protracted, domestic support for the reforms can fall unless there is compensation for those most adversely affected, and the peremptory way in which they have usually been introduced has in many cases worked against the democratic institutions whose consolidation they are supposed to support. Not only does this deepen the difficulties of democratic politics in countries – like those in Eastern Europe and many that are now subject to structural adjustment in sub-Saharan Africa – where constitutional democracy has not been strong. It can also threaten it, as events in Venezuela between 1989 and 1993 suggest, where it has previously seemed secure. The consequences of such threats may only be offset by the fact that, in the 1990s, those who do not like the reforms have no credible alternative, economic or political, to offer.

None the less, even if constitutional democracy is that form of rule best suited, if now only by default, to the demands of 'free commerce', both cosmopolitan and domestic, one can ask whether Northern governments and the international financial institutions are right to make a move to constitutional democracy a condition of continuing assistance. The answer is qualified. If one assumes that states exist to promote the well-being of their citizens – or more exactly, since not all aspects of well-being can be the province of government, that they exist to enhance the benefits of social co-operation – then governments have an obligation to provide justice and, in so far as they are able, the resources, including the institutions, that the citizens need to improve their well-being (Dasgupta, 1993). If one also assumes that constitutional democracy has proved at least as good as any other kind of regime in meeting these obligations; if one accepts that it is best suited to the economic needs of states in a transnational economy; and if one agrees that the financial institutions and the donors have the same objectives for the states they assist as these states have for themselves; then the condition would seem to be justified. The only qualification would be that each side agrees – or can give no good reason not to agree – that what is being proposed is likely to promote well-being (Hawthorn and Seabright, 1996).

This qualification, however, is crucial. It meets objections to what might otherwise be thought to be an unwarranted interference in the internal affairs of a sovereign state. It allows each side to argue that a constitutional democracy may not in practice be the best way in which to enhance the well-being of the citizens; or, at least, allows that one or another feature of what is now widely taken to be the canonical form of such a democracy should be postponed, omitted, enhanced or adjusted in some other way.[15]

Like all negotiations in the real world, however, those envisaged in such an ideal contract would not be conducted in a vacuum. Other considerations, not least power, would play a part. The People's Republic of China, for example, is far more able to counter external pressure than a small African state. The Chinese leadership does resist a transition to constitutional democracy. One of its reasons for doing so, of course, is that the Communist Party has no wish to give up its recently reduced but still considerable powers. A second is the memory, understandably still alive in the minds of the older revolutionaries, of the disorder that can follow when central power in the country is lost, reinforced, no doubt, by the perception of what has happened in the evidently unsteady transition from firm state control in Russia since 1989. A third is the aspiration, at many levels of the Chinese state and party, to maintain a 'developmental state' to the point at which, as in South Korea – a real model now for many in the economic ministries in Beijing – its successes are such that it seems both safe and prudent to concede the possibility of greater checks on the ruling party's power, even perhaps the possibility of its being voted out altogether. Neither the fear of disorder nor the aspiration to a steady transition to what in China is called a 'new authoritarianism' is absurd. In the circumstances of the 1990s, successful development depends on high levels of private investment from abroad; this will not be forthcoming if potential investors suspect that a country is unstable. And if one of the conditions of a controllable democracy is that a sufficient proportion of citizens are materially secure, it would not be sensible to risk a transition until that is achieved. It does not follow, however, that the Chinese leadership could not soon safely concede more civil rights, including more secure rights to association and debate, and institute a properly independent judiciary to defend such rights against itself.[16] Constitutional democracy, in the South as in the North, is not an all-or-nothing affair. In this more pointedly political respect, the model of South Korea, which remains a national security state, is less telling for China than those of Japan or Singapore.

Yet even if the central features of constitutional democracy were to be in place, and even if these features were to be supported by the necessary institutions, this would not in itself be sufficient to enable a government to meet the obligations of a modern state; it could not in itself provide the revenue and the administrative capacity to deliver what its citizens would need to improve their well-being. This, in sharpest contrast to most of the East Asian states, is the central dilemma of sub-Saharan Africa. Even where the political classes in such poor states are disposed to liberal democracy, and might be able to sustain it under scarcity, they are unlikely to be able to meet the most minimal needs of large parts of their populations. This is why the arguments in Africa for an extension of democracy beyond the election of representatives to a central government are persuasive. A degree of self-provision through local associations that citizens themselves devise and control – associations of producers, for instance, and forms of local government that independently raise many of the resources they need – may be the only answer for many citizens.

This is not to say that the revival and extension of such associations in Africa – or anywhere – would be politically straightforward (Sandbrook, 1993). Despite their declarations to the contrary, the governments of most sub-Saharan states are still largely indifferent to the aim of collective self-reliance. They favour exports over self-sufficiency in food and other consumption goods.[17] They also fear the threat that independent associations might present. Liberal democracies in both North and South that have been attempting the kinds of economic reforms that African states are now having to implement have found it convenient to close themselves off from political demands from below. Independent associations of a local kind will accordingly find it even more difficult – and it is nowhere easy – to press their case through national parties.

Constitutional democracy does not in itself guarantee development. Nor, its critics argue, does it meet the demands of democracy itself. It excludes many interests, and it puts unacceptable and unnecessary limits on the possibilities of politics itself (Dahl, 1989; Held, 1987). The excluded are increasing.

The permeability of all nation-states to the international economy and the consequent social dislocations are exciting interests – and identities with which to capture those interests – that had not existed before. Democracies everywhere are being asked to do more under economic conditions in which they can often do less. In the North as well as in the South, the resulting frustrations have been difficult to accommodate to the organizational constraints and disciplinary inclinations of the mass parties through which governments are formed (Panebianco, 1988; Maier, 1987). New movements emerge and often become new parties; the older ones are torn between competing and trying to reduce the expectations for politics.

The more ambitious critics of orthodox democracy, therefore – like Unger, whose plan to counter the limitations that even the best social democracies put upon 'associational possibility' is the most imaginative and analytically impressive, and for the South, also the most interesting, since it starts from anger about the condition of Brazil – will insist all the more strongly that democracy should be re-thought (Unger, 1987: 67–79; Simon, 1990). Sceptics will reply that the hazards of 'the new world disorder' for national politics make the case for constitutional restraint.[18] Some governments will be struggling to maintain the minimal securities. Most will be short of resources. For all, the sceptics will say, the political aim should be to sustain 'the right' and leave competing conceptions of 'the good' to civil society. The chances of such constitutions now taking hold across the South may be better than at any time since independence. The external incentives are greater, the effective alternatives are fewer, and although there will always be temptations to increase executive direction, the economic constraints on it are now much stronger.

Notes

1 The citizens were exclusively male; political responsibility was held to follow from military obligation, and women did not fight.

2 The pacifying effects of the pursuit of interest had become a commonplace of eighteenth-century argument (Hirschman, 1977). The case was extended to relations between states. Free international trade, truly cosmopolitan economic relations, would encourage peace. Economic protection therefore, let alone the imperial command of foreign territories for economic purposes, was to be deplored (Hont, 1983).

3 But the fear of corruption remained. This was evident in the United States in Jefferson's moralized agrarianism, and is evident still in the distrust of government itself in that country, a distrust which is perhaps stronger than in any other modern bourgeois liberal republic.

4 Schmitter defined Iberian and Latin American corporatism as 'a system of interest representation in which the constituent units are organised into a limited number of singular, compulsory, hierarchically ordered and functionally differentiated categories, recognised or licensed (if not created) by the state and granted a deliberate representational monopoly within their respective categories in exchange for observing certain controls on their selection of leaders and articulation of demands and supports' (Schmitter, 1974: 93–4). Actual corporatisms in Latin America, as elsewhere, have in practice been a good deal less tidy and more unsteady than this.

5 An abortive attempt has been made to introduce a multi-party democracy in Algeria, Morocco has a limited degree of multi-party electoral competition under a centralized monarchy and Tunisia has begun a slow and partial liberalization of its political system. Unlike other Middle Eastern countries, all three were under direct French colonial rule.

6 Indeed, some have seen in post-war Japan the most practically effective resolution yet of the dilemma presented to the modern state by the weakness of constitutional democracy in the face of private economic interests and the desirability of directive economic powers (Vogel, 1979; Tsuru, 1993).

7 The effects of the Kennedy administration's anger and anxiety about the Cuban revolution on its policy towards Latin America are described by Schoultz (1987), the Nixon Doctrine by Litwak (1984). The most favoured of the intermediate powers under the Nixon Doctrine was the Shah's Iran, and it was in the reaction against the Shah and his international patron in 1987–9 that the policy most dramatically backfired. There is a useful account of US policies in Africa to the early 1990s in Schraeder (1994).

8 This is so even when the factors are ordered; for instance in Vanhanen's (1992) distinctions between those which are structural, strategic and tactical, and triggers. For an example of an explanation limited by cross-national correlation, see note 15; for penetrating observations on the different ways in which 'transitions' to democracy have been understood, see Przeworski (1991: 95–9).

9 To Williamson, who coined the phrase, the central tenets of this 'consensus' do not rule out the possibility of the government of a constitutional democracy pursuing a liberal economic policy while also addressing issues of equity. In his first collation of what were generally agreed in Washington to be the economic reforms that were necessary in Latin America, Williamson deliberately excluded 'anything that was primarily redistributive ... because I felt the Washington of the 1980s to be essentially contemptuous of equity concerns' (1993: 1329).

10 In this respect, as in others, the contrast between the two Koreas is particularly illuminating (Halliday, 1987). Kornai (1982) is a standard account of the failures of socialist planning.

11 As Bell remarked, 'there are some books that are better known for their titles than their contents'. *The End of Ideology* was not a defence of the status quo, a plea for technocracy, a demand for consensus, or an instrument of the Cold War. Nor was it refuted by the upsurge of radicalism in the West in the 1960s. Bell regards the 'strongest formulation' of what he was trying to say to have been the Swedish commentator Herbert Tingsten's observation in 1955 that 'the great [ideological] controversies ... have been liquidated in all instances ... Liberalism in the old sense is dead, both among the Conservatives and in the Liberal Party;

Social Democratic thinking has lost nearly all its traits of doctrinaire Marxism ... The actual words "socialism" or "liberalism" are tending to mere honorifics' (Bell, 1988: 409, 418). As Bell now agrees, his mistake was to assume that a 'new liberal' Right would not return, and return to power. He always insisted that ideology was not at an end in the South.

12 The alternative view is that the first wave of democratization, affecting 29 countries, broke between the 1820s and the 1920s; that there was a reverse from the 1920s to the mid-1940s, reducing the number in 1942 to 12; that a second wave, which had increased the number of democracies to 36 by 1962, suffered a further reverse in the 1960s and 1970s; and that a third began in southern Europe in the mid-1970s and is now breaking over the South (Huntington, 1991).

13 In this connection, it is interesting that the one widely canvassed obstacle to democratization that has not – in at least one investigation – been found to stand up to comparative statistical analysis is the distribution of income and wealth (Hadenius, 1992: 98–103). This distribution has been and remains as uneven in India and Venezuela – where it has recently increased – as in many countries in which democracy has not succeeded.

14 It was common in the later 1980s to lament the decline of democracy and political order in India (Brass, 1991; Frankel and Rao, 1989–90; Kohli, 1990; Rudolph and Rudolph, 1987; compare Khilnani, 1992). Disorder there was. My argument here is that it is possible to see the turbulence as a transition to a more truly competitive electoral politics, and, in contrast to the previously comfortable coalition between what Bardhan had called the three 'proprietary classes' of land, capital and the state, the beginning of a more open-ended bargaining by government itself.

15 It may be worth remarking that in the absence of the true 'globalization' of democracy that the more optimistic now hope for (Held, 1993a), less coercive negotiations of this kind would at least constitute an advance.

16 The authoritarian impulse is described by Fu (1993). Nathan (1993) has argued that the Chinese leaders missed a good opportunity for political reform in 1989.

17 This may change with the conclusion of the GATT Uruguay Round. Many African states are net importers of food, and as a result of the agreement in the GATT it is thought that the price of imported foodstuffs might rise by as much as 20 per cent.

18 There is little agreement on the nature and implications of 'the new world disorder'. Jowitt (1993) envisages 'a Third World ridden with rage and wracked with despair' in which the liberal emphasis on individual autonomy and responsibility will have little purchase. Huntington (1993) suggests that it is the cultural differences between the West and 'the Rest', not, as in the Cold War years, any difference of economic fortune or political ideology, that will mark the lines of conflict at the end of this century and the beginning of the next. He nevertheless defines the differences in a misleading way. A 'cultural difference' is often marked as much by 'political ideology' and the political history that has shaped that ideology as by language, religion or other less directly political facts. It is politics, for example, that appears to distinguish his 'Latin American civilisation' from those in Portugal and Spain. The West now has unprecedented powers in relation to the Rest, Huntington observes, and to preserve these, may take the offensive. Buzan (1991) by constrast believes that the Rest will be ignored.

2

Is democracy rooted in material prosperity?

MICK MOORE

Since democratic systems became widespread in the nineteenth century, they have been found much more frequently in the more industrialized and wealthy countries. (Lipset, 1960: 49–50; Rueschemeyer *et al.*, 1992: 4; Przeworski and Limongi, 1993: 51–69; Putnam, 1993: 84) How strong, then, is the connection between democracy and material prosperity? Is the strongest statistical relationship between democracy and wealth, democracy and income, democracy and 'development', or democracy and mass welfare? Does democracy lead to material prosperity? Does material prosperity breed democracy? Or is the statistical connection a by-product, with the real causal connection running between democracy and some other factor that happens to be associated with income levels? Are there other factors that are consistently connected with democracy in a statistical sense?

There are many reasons to be interested in these questions. Those involved in giving and receiving international development aid should be particularly concerned. Donor governments are increasingly making adoption of democratic forms of rule a condition of eligibility for aid. Is this justified? For, if democracy is indeed the consequence of economic development, rather than either a contributor to it or an unrelated phenomenon, then it would be perverse and unreasonable to require that developing countries adopt democracy in order to become eligible for the aid intended to help them develop economically. These are also questions in which statistically-inclined researchers have long been interested. This chapter aims to summarize what is known about the causal connections between democracy and economic development to help us decide whether the official aid donors are, however unwittingly, behaving unreasonably when they ask aid recipients to show their democratic credentials. The main conclusions are as follows:

1 Despite a number of recent research findings that appear to challenge the orthodox view that democratic systems are found most frequently in the most industrialized and wealthy countries, there is a consistent and fairly strong statistical connection, on a cross-sectional basis, between levels of national income and the extent of democracy in national political arrangements. At any moment, wealthier countries are more democratic.

2 There is evidence that the same relationship holds over time: that individual countries tend to become more democratic in proportion to increases in income.

3 There are no consistent connections between types of political regime and national economic growth rates, and thus no support for the idea that democracy leads to higher rates of economic growth.

4 Since the evidence does not support any of the other potential explanations for the statistical connection between democracy and income levels, it appears virtually certain that the direction of causation runs from material prosperity to democracy: wealth, income, development and/or well-being generate democratic rule.

5 It is difficult to measure democracy satisfactorily, partly because of data problems, but also for a more profound reason: we cannot directly measure the essence of democracy, which is the capacity of citizens to exercise control over political elites in an organized fashion. Instead, we are obliged to rely on indirect indicators: measures of the extent of adherence to the institutional *procedures* that are believed to be most conducive to giving citizens this power. There are substantial differences between the many different 'democracy scores' that have been produced. Consequently, it is not possible to give confident answers to those questions that require fine-grained statistical analysis. In particular, we cannot say (a) exactly how closely, in a technical, statistical sense, democracy is associated with income, wealth, development or living standards, (b) to which of these factors it is most closely correlated, or (c) whether there really is a close and consistent statistical association between democracy and some of the other factors that sometimes appear to be associated with it.

6 A range of theories attempt to explain the consistent connection between democracy and material prosperity (income, wealth, development or well-being). It is not possible to evaluate them in a rigorous statistical manner, but several are highly plausible, in particular, those that connect democracy to economic development through the association of development with the emergence of, separately, both educated and articulate middle-class groups and organised working-class populations that actively fight for political representation. It is also likely that thriving market economies 'seduce' political elites into implicit bargains whereby they exchange stable and consensual access to this economy for

revenue purposes (taxation) in return for granting taxpayers formal representation in the policy-making process. It is not difficult to explain why democracy might be associated with material prosperity. It is likely that there are several complementary causal mechanisms at work.

7 The spread of democracy has been associated with rising material prosperity. There is no reason to believe that this will not continue to be the case in the future. Democracy has excellent long-term prospects if economic growth continues.

8 The connection between wealth and democracy is evident when one looks at large samples of countries and adopts a broad historical perspective. It seems almost to disappear when one looks at individual countries and time scales covering years rather than decades. Levels and changes of national income are poor predictors or determinants of whether, for example, Jamaica will remain a democracy or Indonesia will become one before the year 2000. A number of very poor countries, above all, India, have an enviable record of sustained democracy. Citizens campaigning for democracy in such countries need not be intimidated or discouraged by the overall statistical patterns reported here. Neither should aid donors attempting to support democracy; they should simply be aware of the danger of trying to enforce it.

There is no possibility that the kinds of statistical analysis examined here could ever provide an explanation of short-run processes of *democratization* (and 'de-democratization') – the ways in which, for example, Brazil has shifted between various degrees of democracy and various types of military rule over recent decades. A wealth of recent literature emphasizes the role of short-term and intangible factors in such processes, above all the tactical and strategic calculations of various political actors and groups, and the important roles played by political elites and international influences (Bermeo, 1990; Diamond et al., 1988, 1989a, b; Higley and Gunther, 1992; Malloy and Seligson, 1987; and O'Donnell and Schmitter, 1986). The concern here is with the underlying material conditions that make such transitions to and from democracy more or less likely in different categories of countries. We are looking at pieces of research that try to analyse politics by assuming that long-run political processes can be isolated from short-run processes. This assumption is useful, probably necessary, but certainly artificial. It is also rather abstract. Let us begin at a more concrete level: how can we measure democracy?

The early part of this chapter focuses on questions of statistical fact: how closely is democracy associated with income levels? We then shift to questions of interpretation: what causal connections can we infer from statistical associations?

Measuring democracy

To measure democracy, one must have some idea of what it is. In the long tradition of debate about democracy and its many variants, ideal or actual, the common thread seems to be the idea that a polity is democratic to the extent that there exist institutionalized mechanisms through which the mass of the population exercise control over the political elite in an organized fashion – a definition almost equivalent to Dahl's (1971) concept of polyarchy. From this perspective, there is no such thing as 'complete democracy'. Every polity is run by a political elite. Democracy is always a matter of degree: the extent to which this elite is controlled and influenced by citizens. Unfortunately, this definition is not very helpful if one wishes to measure degrees of democracy, for it refers to a power relationship, which we have no means of measuring. To measure democracy, one requires a different, operational definition, which will inevitably be *procedural*, relating to the procedures and institutions established to enable the masses to exercise control over the political elite. It is important to bear in mind that, since all procedures and institutions can be manipulated by powerful groups, any measurement of democracy has the potential to be seriously misleading. For example, virtually all sets of democracy scores for recent decades include Italy and Japan with most other industrial countries at the very top of the scoring range. Yet, as recent events have underlined, the extent of popular control over the governments of these two countries has clearly been far less than, for example, in Australia or Sweden.

The wide range of institutional and procedural indicators of democracy used in research all relate to central government only.[1] Among the most common and plausible are: the proportion of the population eligible to vote and actually voting; the existence of different categories of elections and the extent to which they are judged fair and open; the contribution of elections to the choice of the (chief) executive and the membership of the legislature; the extent to which votes are 'monopolized' by the largest political party; the extent of legislative influence over the executive; the degree of freedom enjoyed by the mass media and allowed for individual and collective political and proto-political activity (e.g. voluntary association); and general absence of state coercion. For reasons explained below, the use of two of these indicators – electoral participation and the degree of 'monopolization' of votes – is controversial. There are different views about the use of particular indicators; these are often resolved pragmatically according to which data are actually available. More important, there are problems in assigning weights to the indicators used. How can one decide, for example, that it is reasonable to allocate up to 5 points out of a total of 20 to a measure of the extent of civil liberties, and a maximum of only 3 points to a measure of the degree of legislative control over the executive? The procedures used by the more careful researchers each require several pages of explanation. There is no standard approach, and no standard way of testing the validity of the choices made.

Several researchers have examined democracy scores constructed in alternative ways to see how consistent they are with one another. The most common means for this is to correlate the final scores produced by various researchers for the same set of countries (Arat, 1991; Bollen, 1980: 381; Inkeles, 1990: 5–6). The essence of correlation is to see how reliably the democracy score for a particular country appearing in one index can predict the score for the same country, at the same time, in someone else's index. There is a tendency to draw comfort from the fact that the correlations are usually high. The very best do not quite hit the 90 per cent target, however: less than 90 per cent of variations in one scale are predicted by the measures in the other scale. Many correlations are much lower. We are thus some way from measures of democracy that are sufficiently authoritative to make possible fine-grained statistical analysis of its causes and correlates.

Contradictory evidence?

The debate about the material basis of democracy has been conducted through statistical analysis of data from large samples of countries, almost all cross-sectional, comparing countries at different income levels at the same point in time. There are a few time series data, which are examined later in this chapter. They have, however, been available only recently. It is convenient to ignore them for the present, and to focus on the apparently simple matter of fact: is there a consistent statistical association, on a cross-sectional basis, between democracy and one or more of the indices of material prosperity?

The cross-sectional evidence has been examined recently

by Diamond, who summarizes the results of ten major statistical exercises conducted between 1963 and 1991, covering a range of time periods since the 1920s, and country samples numbering between 28 and 115 from all regions of the world. Every one of these studies indicated a positive and statistically significant relation between the extent of democracy and one or more measures of the level of economic development (Diamond, 1992: table 3), the two dominant ones being GNP and energy consumption per capita.

Yet there appears to be some counter-evidence. During 1990– 2, four new English-language books appeared on the subject of democracy and development, each constructed around large-scale exercises in creating and analysing statistical series (Arat, 1991; Hadenius, 1992; Pourgerami, 1991; Vanhanen, 1990). Three of the authors – Arat, Hadenius and Vanhanen – find little connection between democracy and material conditions.[2] Do we have here the beginnings of a new, revisionist school that seriously challenges the old orthodoxy?[3] The answer is negative, because their apparent findings that democracy is not closely connected to income are not valid. There are particular problems with the ways in which each has, separately, reached this conclusion, which we shall briefly explore because they illustrate the dangers of relying uncritically on individual results that appear to be backed by all the authority of large series of statistical data and complex sets of statistical analysis.

Hadenius, *Democracy and Development*

Hadenius's work is in most respects excellent. There is one relatively minor quibble about his method. He constructs a democracy score for 132 developing countries that relates to late 1988 only. To measure democracy reliably for the kinds of purposes dealt with here, one needs to filter out short-term changes – especially the rapid changes that were occurring in many parts of the world in the later 1980s – by constructing an average score covering several years. For present purposes, it is the presentation and interpretation of his results that requires special attention. Hadenius finds a less close statistical association between democracy and income levels than do most researchers – although the connection remains positive and statistically highly significant (Hadenius, 1992: chapter 4). The reason lies in his unusually comprehensive coverage of countries. Most researchers in this field exclude very small countries from their sample, partly because they are often not covered in standard data series. However, Hadenius took as his sample every 'sovereign state' in the South he could identify: a total of 132 countries. The reason for the low apparent association between the extent of democracy and income levels can be found by looking at the 28 countries that scored very high (9 or more) on his 0–10 democracy scale. Of these, 15 had populations of less than half a million in 1988 – indeed, a combined population of only 1.8 million. They are: Belize, Antigua and Barbuda, Bahamas, Barbados, Dominica, Grenada, St Kitts-Nevis, St Lucia, St Vincent and the Grenadines, Kiribati, Marshall Islands, Federated States of Micronesia, Nauru, Solomon Islands and Tuvalu. All but one are island states, and most are poor. Exclude them from the analysis, and the statistical connection between income and democracy would be within the 'normal' ranges.

It is not that the experiences of these micro-states should be ignored. They are indeed interesting, and raise important questions. Democracy originated, after all, in the very small city-states of classical Greece. Is democracy especially suited to micro-states, because it is easier for citizens to participate, to understand the issues and to feel that their votes count? There is very little research to guide us. Hadenius finds that being an island is itself associated with democracy, as well as having a tiny population (Hadenius, 1992: 124–6). But the real explanation may lie, in whole or in part, in external factors. These island micro-states are politically and militarily dependent on one or two of the three big Anglophone democracies with a history of colonial conquest in the Caribbean and the Pacific: Britain, the United States and Australia. Democracy may reflect this dependence.

Hadenius's attention to micro-states raises a less tangible and more technical question about the basic research method of cross-national statistical analysis: what do we mean by 'country'? Is Tuvalu a country in the same way as Iran? Clearly not. What, then, should be the criteria for including a formally sovereign state in a sample of countries that is intended to represent 'the world'? There are no easy answers to this question. Let us simply note here a deeper implication for research techniques: all theories about the income–democracy connection deal exclusively with the way in which 'internal' processes shape 'national' political systems. We know that theories of this type are incomplete. Democracy is brought to some countries by visible – and sometimes rather muscular – international

influences; the reverse is also true, that such influences sometimes restrict democracy (see Chomsky, 1992; Muller, 1985).
Yet we are unable to make allowance for them in statistical
analysis because we are unclear about exactly what they are
or how they operate.[4]

There are clearly no fully satisfactory solutions to this sam-
pling problem. Since the combined populations of these micro-
states are so small, statistical analysis that excludes them might
be said validly to capture the representative experience of the
world's population of people, if not its population of countries. The more straightforward point is that different country
samples can produce different statistical results.

Arat, *Democracy and Human Rights in Developing Countries*

The central concern of Arat's work is precisely to challenge
the idea that democracy is closely associated with income.
She does not, however, deal with all dimensions of this argument, but only with the particular perspective on which most
statistical research is based: the notion from 1960s 'modernization theory' that socio-economic 'modernization' – 'development'
in more current jargon – generates increases in democracy. She
covers 150 independent countries, developing and developed,
over the period 1948–82, and attempts to construct a democracy score for each country for each year. However, because
some of the countries were not independent throughout this
period, and because of gaps in data, over a quarter of the potential observations are missing. She tends to undertake statistical
analysis with whatever maximal amount of data is available;
this raises some technical questions about the statistical
method that need not be explored here.

Arat's method at first looks promising. She is attempting
time series analysis, looking at changes over time in individual countries in the degree of democracy and the degree of
socio-economic 'modernization'. While her cross-sectional data
do indicate a connection between income and democracy, she
finds no evidence that changes over time in the degree of
democracy are shaped by changes in the degree of 'modernization'. The statistical techniques used are quite sophisticated;
the definition and measurement of the key variables are, however, very questionable.

Only one indicator of socio-economic 'modernization' – per

capita consumption of commercial energy – is used, on the grounds that this was the indicator often used by the 1960s modernization theorists themselves. At that time it was available for most countries and generally found to be more closely correlated with GNP per head than any other proxy measure of income. That situation is history, however. National income figures are now available for most countries, are being continuously improved and are preferable to an indicator no longer regarded as a reasonable proxy for income.

More important, Arat's measure of democracy is unreliable. It is striking that Communist countries consistently score much higher than one would expect. The data from which her democracy scores are presented are not given; one cannot therefore appraise in detail the method used to construct them. The problem seems to lie in the fact that she uses the degree of government coerciveness as one of the major (inverse) subcomponents of the democracy score, and ultimately derives a measure of coerciveness, through an extremely complex and itself questionable route, from (a) the extent to which there is overt 'social unrest' (demonstrations, assassinations, guerrilla war, riots, general strikes, deaths from violence) and (b) the 'appropriateness' of the governmental response to these events (Arat, 1991: 26 and footnotes).[5] One presumes that governments able to suppress or hide such social unrest score abnormally well on a democracy score; this would account for the high democracy scores for Communist countries. In sum, Arat does sophisticated statistical analysis with unreliable data.

Vanhanen, *The Process of Democratization*

Like Arat, Vanhanen attempts to do time series analysis, also on the basis of a set of democracy scores that cannot be trusted. He deals with 147 countries, developing and developed, excluding only countries with a population of less than 200,000 in 1980. He is essentially concerned with the democratization process between 1980 and 1988; he constructs a democracy score for each country for each year over this period, and examines changes over time. This is time series analysis, but over a very short period. In one respect the method is innovative and worth further work. His main hypothesis is that democracy stems from a relatively equal social distribution of power; the variable he uses to explain changes in levels of democracy is a composite Index of Power Resources made up of other indices (Occupational Diversity, Knowledge Distribution and Economic Power Resources). Unfortunately, one can put no faith in his overall results, because his method of measuring democracy is unacceptable. He constructs a very simple measure fashioned from the two most controversial of the many indicators used in this business: changes in the share of votes cast for the largest party; and electoral participation.

The use of the first indicator has a clear rationale in principle: in a genuine democracy, there will be sufficient competition among political parties for none ever to reach a position of substantial (permanent) dominance, let alone 'monopoly'. There are, however, two problems. First, the dominance of one party could simply reflect voter satisfaction. Second, perhaps of more practical significance, the use of the vote share index can easily generate misleading figures about short-term changes. For example, an electoral landslide in favour of one party automatically reduces the democracy score for that country. And Vanhanen has used the vote share index precisely to produce a very short-term measure of year-to-year changes in democracy over an eight-year period.

The case against using electoral participation – the proportion of voters who actually vote – as an indicator of the extent of democracy is made by Bollen (1980: 373–4). There are two arguments: that high electoral turnouts may reflect no more than the power of the political elite to ensure the semblance of democracy in circumstances where there is no real electoral contest; and that, in genuinely democratic systems, low turnouts may simply reflect that voters are satisfied with their political leadership and government. These are powerful arguments.[6] But so too are the arguments on the other side: there are many cases where high or increased voter turnouts clearly do reflect an increase in democracy; and statistics on voter turnout are easily available and can be translated directly and easily into a component of a democracy score. It may be acceptable to use levels of turnout as one of several components of a democracy score. To use it with only one other, equally unsatisfactory measure is not acceptable. Close examination of annual changes in Vanhanen's democracy scores for individual countries reveals the kind of quirky random-seeming changes that one would expect given the measurement techniques used.

None of the three authors poses a serious challenge to

the orthodox view that there is a clear and consistent cross-sectional relationship between democracy and income levels. Their work serves instead to illustrate the costs of failing to build on existing research and of ignoring professional norms of scientific procedure. The mainstream researchers, by contrast, have generally adhered to these norms admirably. Particularly impressive is the effort put into clarifying the statistical and measurement procedures used, comparing results with those of other researchers, and attempting to develop more accurate and refined measures of democracy and related concepts (see especially the collection edited by Inkeles, 1990). We can be confident that the statistical association between democracy and income is robust and consistent. No other feature of society or economy is associated with democracy in any significant or consistent way.[7] The next challenge is to sort out cause and effect.

Democracy and material prosperity: cause and effect

Let us temporarily suspend belief in our conclusion that material prosperity does indeed lead to democracy. There are three plausible alternative explanations of the fact that these two variables are consistently associated with one another on a cross-sectional basis:

1 The first potential explanation is that the causation is direct and strong, but runs from democracy to income levels, i.e. that democratically governed countries are so much more successful in achieving economic growth that, had the original distribution of democracy been entirely random or shaped by some other factor(s) unconnected with income and economic performance, one would over time find democracy concentrated in the wealthier countries. There is no need to discuss in detail here the causal mechanisms which might lead democratic countries to perform better economically (or, as many people have suggested, to perform worse).[8] For there is unambiguous evidence that there is no such consistent connection. One can argue the point historically: it is clear that the pioneer democracies (in North America and northern Europe) were relatively wealthy at the time they embarked on the system; they did not become richer than other countries as a consequence of first becoming democratic. Readers will, however, be more interested in the more contemporary evidence about the relationship between regime type and economic performance since the Second World War. Two recent major reviews of the research, between them covering 22 studies, both

conclude that there are no consistent observable connections between regime type and economic performance (Inkeles, 1990; Przeworski and Limongi, 1993). Many of the individual studies that they review are inconclusive; those that do identify some connection between democracy and good economic performance are precisely balanced by others which find the opposite. Adding two other recent studies (Chatterji *et al.*, 1993; Dasgupta, 1990) not covered by these two reviews yields a total of 24 studies; 9 of them find democracy associated with higher economic growth rates, 9 find the opposite and 6 find no clear pattern. A perfect stalemate![9]

2 The second possible linkage runs through the effect of varying levels of economic performance on the survival prospects of different types of regime. Suppose that two variables – the degree of democracy and national economic performance – were randomly distributed among countries, but that one type of regime was consistently more robust – i.e. less likely to be replaced by another type – in the face of relatively poor economic performance. Provided that there were no strong tendency for 'failed' regimes of one type to be replaced by others of the same type, this would in the long run generate an association between regime type and wealth levels. What do we know of the robustness of different political regimes in the face of economic 'failure'? Przeworski and Limongi (1993: 63) suggest that 'authoritarian regimes are less likely than democracies to survive when they perform badly'. This is plausible because, in the modern world, non-democratic regimes are generally forced to legitimate themselves in terms of the results of their governance; compared with democratically elected governments, they find it difficult to justify their continuation in power on the grounds that they are the properly constituted authority. The evidence for such a connection is limited and not very supportive, however.[10] If it were abundant and of the expected kind, we should have a very perverse outcome: non-democracy would over time become relatively concentrated in the better-performing economies, and therefore in the wealthier countries. Since this is the opposite of what we observe in practice, it appears that we can reject the idea that 'selective regime survival' plays a significant role in explaining the association between democracy and material prosperity.

3 The third suggestion has its roots in the dependency perspective on societal development that was prominent in the 1960s and 1970s. It has been argued that, at the point in history when the now wealthy countries began to develop or industrialize, conditions were conducive to their being or becoming democracies. 'National bourgeoisies' play a central role in such theories: they spearheaded the drive for economic development and used parliamentary democracy to establish their political authority. Once

institutionalized, democracy has persisted. By contrast, the 'late developers' have faced an environment which is hostile to democracy. The links of political and economic dependency between indigenous elites and those of the North tend to undermine the prospects for democracy within the South. And authoritarian rule may be needed if these links are to be broken and development achieved. These are all plausible arguments, but the evidence does not back them. Bollen (1979), looking at 99 countries over a long time scale, found no connection between the timing of the development 'take-off' and the degree of democracy. Our earlier discussion of Hadenius's work tells us that, in the contemporary world, the opposite tends to be true: some of the most dependent countries are also democracies (Diamond, 1992: table 3).

Given the failure of these alternative explanations of the cross-sectional association between income and democracy, we are left with the conclusion that material prosperity must in some way or another generate or support democracy. This conclusion would be all the more convincing if it were supported by time series analysis of the association between changes in national income and changes in political systems. There are few studies of this kind because we have few reliable data series on democracy of any great historical depth. A few recent pieces of time series evidence do, however, support the idea of material prosperity as a significant causal factor.

Time series data

The first piece of time series evidence comes from Samuel Huntington's work on what he has called 'the third wave': the big increase in the number of democratic regimes in the period 1974–89 (Huntington, 1991).[11] The relevant figures are summarized in Table 2.1. In both 1974 and 1989, the association between democracy and national income was very strong. But the new point is the strong connection between GNP per capita in 1976 and the likelihood of non-democratic countries making the transition to democracy as part of the 'third wave': the wealthier the non-democracies were in the 1970s, the more likely they were to become democracies by 1989. Those with a per capita income of more than $1,000 in 1976 had almost a 50–50 chance of making the transition; those with an income of less than $250 had a 6 per cent chance. The successful

Table 2.1 Democratization and GNP levels during the 'third wave', 1974–89[a]

1976 per capita GNP (US$)	Below 250	250–1,000	1,000–3,000	3,000+	Total
Number of countries	34	41	26	23	124
% of countries that were democratic in 1974	3	7	19	78	22
% of countries that were non-democratic in 1974 and democratized during 1974–89	6	26	52	40[b]	26
% of countries that were democratic at the end of 1989	9	34	62	87	42

Source: Adapted from Huntington (1991, tables 1.2 and 3.1).
Notes:
[a] Huntington's table 2.1 includes 6 countries that 'liberalized' politically over this period, but did not democratize on the criteria Huntington used elsewhere in the book. These have been excluded from this table for the sake of consistency. The sample appears to comprise all countries except those with a population of less than one million (p. 26).
[b] There were only 5 non-democracies in this income category in 1974; 2 of them democratized.

transitions were largely made by 'middle-income' countries in Latin America and Eastern Europe.

Huntington uses a simple binary classification of countries: they are either democratic or not. This is not satisfactory. Democracy is clearly a continuous concept: we talk, and wish to talk, of countries becoming more or less democratic in an incremental fashion. It is also unfortunate that Huntington does not explain in detail the procedure he used to classify countries; it is not easy to assess his conclusions independently. Those reservations aside, his data provide powerful additional evidence, of a quasi-time-series nature, for the 'prosperity theory of democracy'. His is not a full time series analysis. The figures measure only the effect of differential income levels in 1976 on the chances that countries would make the transition to democracy by 1989. They do not seek to test for a relationship between *changes* in income over some period of time and subsequent *changes* in the degree of democracy.

There is no published research that attempts this over long time periods for a large sample of countries. Making the best of the sparse and imperfect data available, two separate statistical exercises of this nature were undertaken; they are described in detail in Annexe 2.1. The first relates to a sample of 50 developing countries, where changes in both income and democracy are measured over the period 1960-2 to 1980-2. The second relates to two samples, of 61 and 72 developing countries respectively, where income changes are measured over the same period and democracy is measured in terms of changes between the early 1960s and 1988. The democracy measures are in several respects highly deficient. The income figures are not available for as long a time period as one would wish. It was not possible to introduce adequate time lags between changes in income levels and changes in democracy. Any real statistical relationship that exists between democracy and income is for these reasons likely to be reduced or obscured. Yet the relationship turns out to be positive and statistically very significant in each case: the greater the increases in GDP per capita between the early 1960s and the early 1980s, the greater the positive shifts on the democracy scale. Recalling the evidence presented above that the form of government does not appear to affect economic growth rates in any consistent way, these results and Huntington's work together provide very strong evidence that income growth causes increases in democracy within countries over time.

Why does statistical analysis not tell us more?

It is helpful to know that there certainly is a causal connection running from income to democracy. It would be more helpful if one could be more definite about the strength of that connection. Is income the dominant explanation of varying levels of democracy, or is it simply one factor among others? Unfortunately, we can say little more than that the connection appears to be 'definite' but far from complete. The relationship appears consistently in statistical analysis, but the strength of the association appears to vary so much that one cannot put a figure on it.[12]

Why do we not know more? And when, if ever, will we know more? We can at least throw some light on these questions by taking stock of the research effort. Two general conclusions emerge. On the positive side, techniques for measuring democracy and income have improved, and should continue to do so. If adequate resources are put into accurately measuring the various dimensions of democracy in a wide range of countries, more reliable statistical estimates of its correlates should be possible. On the negative side, the method of multi-country statistical analysis has several inherent and intractable limitations. The main ones, already mentioned above, are:

1 Measures of democracy are assumed to be unaffected by more short-term political struggles over forms of government. This is a useful but imperfect assumption.
2 Many of the factors influencing the outcome of political conflicts about forms of government are highly intangible, such as beliefs about what is right or strategic calculations by key political actors about what they should best do in particular circumstances to advance their own interests. It is virtually impossible to quantify them.
3 Given that the very small countries that (a) contain very few people and (b) tend not to enjoy 'full' sovereignty are on average unusually democratic in relation to income levels, there is no satisfactory way of resolving differences of view about whether they should be included in a 'representative' selection of countries.
4 We have no way of incorporating effectively into statistical analysis the external and international influences that bear on states' 'internal' politics. All models of the income–democracy connection assessed here assume that countries' political arrangements reflect 'internal' factors only.

More research would certainly be useful. Some ideas, such as Vanhanen's attempt to measure the social distribution of power and see if this explains varying degrees of democracy, merit more attention. But research will never answer our questions fully.

Can we explain how material prosperity generates democracy?

Why and how does prosperity generate democracy? There is certainly an abundance of theory, dating back to Aristotle (Lipset, 1960: 50), to explain why this relation should exist – and relatively little to the contrary.[13] Our problem is not to find theory but to try to dispose of an excess, sorting out the more plausible. In doing so, we have to pay more attention to the different dimensions of the concept of 'material prosperity':

wealth, income, mass welfare and the kind of structural socio-economic change that is often labelled (economic) 'development'. Unfortunately, the reservoir of statistics does not allow a rigorous comparison of the degree to which each of these is associated with democracy. We have substantial, reliable data series only on per capita GNP, a concept that measures both wealth and income. There are no reliable measures of the other dimensions for a large number of countries. Judgements about the plausibility of competing theories have to be made on a less formal basis.

Space only permits me to sketch here the main mechanisms through which material prosperity has been argued to generate democracy, using my own categorization of the theories and neglecting to pay full obeisance to the names of the scholars with whom they are associated.[14] None of the theories posits a direct causal influence running from prosperity to democracy; the connection is, to varying degrees, indirect. There are three broad sets of suggested mediating factors: the social, economic and political relationships associated with the competitive market economy; the connection between material prosperity and socio-economic structure; and the association of prosperity with distinctive values and attitudes. Some theories combine elements from these different approaches.

1 The most abstract and doctrinaire argument is that there is a natural affinity between the competitive or free market economy and the competitive (democratic) polity (e.g. Friedman and Friedman, 1980). A free market helps prevent the political power which is inevitably accumulated in the state or political arena from being extended into the economic arena. Keeping the two arenas separate helps maintain political pluralism, which enables private economic agents to resist attempts by the state to 'interfere' in the market. Since the free market generates superior economic results, democracy is closely associated with wealth and capitalism. There is unlikely ever to be agreement about this theory. It is certainly grossly oversimplified, and does not accord closely with observed experiences. It is either partly true, very much at a background level, or false.

2 Equally abstract is the idea from modernization theory that the association between democracy and material prosperity (or modernity, or development) stems from the fact that modernization involves a broad process of social and economic differentiation. A more pluralistic social structure has an affinity with a political structure that is predicated on pluralism: democracy (e.g. Cutright, 1963; Cutright and Wiley, 1969). This theory is difficult to test

empirically; the kinds of variables to which attention is drawn are in practice much the same as those treated by the class theories of democracy (see below).

3 Modernization theory also generated another set of propositions about the causal connection between democracy and prosperity or modernity – that it stems from the tendency of a 'modern' social structure to foster 'democratic' personality types: people who feel comfortable in a variety of situations because exposed to socio-economic diversity and change, and who therefore practise the tolerance essential to successful democratic institutions. Lipset, one of the prominent modernization theorists working in this field, paid particular attention to the way in which formal education appeared to foster tolerance and thus democracy. His interpretation of the survey evidence that the educated espoused more tolerance and democratic values (Lipset, 1960: 56) is open to challenge, however. It could, for example, equally reflect higher levels of political capacity, interest and participation by the more educated: people active and influential in politics are likely to evaluate participation highly. Various measures of education and literacy are associated with the degree of democracy on a cross-national basis, albeit inconsistently (Diamond, 1992: table 3; Hadenius, 1992: 88 and 144; Pourgerami, 1991: 55). We are, however, unable to undertake the fine-grained statistical analysis that could tell us how far (a) education causes democracy; (b) democracy leads to higher education levels through greater government attention to popular needs; or (c) education only appears to be associated with democracy because it is so closely correlated with average income levels. The problems in interpreting the evidence mirror those of assessing 'modernization theory' arguments more generally. They may not be empirically testable.

4 The concept of 'tolerance' is also brought into a rather more specific theory: that democracy is unlikely to thrive in conditions of high socio-economic inequality, because the stakes are simply too high, especially for the wealthy. Inequality is generally higher in less developed countries. The argument is very plausible and is supported by some research (Muller, 1988). Unfortunately, the statistics available on income distribution in developing countries are so unreliable (Moll, 1992) that it is impossible at this point to draw firm conclusions.

5 The most promising set of theories are the 'class theories': those that attribute the prosperity–democracy connection to the way in which income growth is associated with changing occupational patterns, and changing socio-economic structure more generally. There are a variety of specific interpretations of the links between, first, economic growth (capitalist or not) and social structure, and second, social structure and politics. For present purposes, one can identify three main lines of argu-

ment, each holding up a particular class as the main bearer of democracy.

The first is the classic argument, inspired originally by Karl Marx, about the affinity between capitalist development and bourgeois (parliamentary) democracy. The key bearer of democracy is the *'haute bourgeoisie'*, the property-owning middle classes. They support democracy for two related reasons: it is a system that privileges them above other potential elite claimants to power; and they can 'manage' democracy, ensuring that it does not lead to radical attacks on their own position. Their management resources include: ideological control, using the mass media and such 'state apparatuses' as the education system; the power of finance to sway elections, voters and legislators; and the need for any government in a capitalist economy to maintain the 'confidence' of capitalists lest it is faced with capital flight, investment cuts and thus mass unemployment, impoverishment and political unrest or electoral unpopularity (Lindblom, 1977: chapter 13).

The second 'class' argument focuses on the white-collar middle classes, who have considerable latent political power by virtue of education and urban location, and support democracy for both instrumental reasons (to establish governments that will pay more attention to their problems) and, increasingly in the modern world, for 'expressive' reasons: because they wish to feel involved in their own governance. These white-collar middle classes played a major role in recent democratization processes in East and South-East Asia and in Eastern Europe. The East Asian experience is perhaps the most striking. Three countries in particular – South Korea, Taiwan and Thailand – have undergone sustained economic growth, made steady progress from authoritarian to democratic or near-democratic rule, and been propelled along this route at key points by the willingness of the white-collar middle classes to come on to the streets in support of democracy. A frequent component of this general line of argument is that white-collar middle-class employees increasingly work in environments where they are given considerable autonomy from direct supervision, and that this encourages them to claim equivalent responsibility in national politics. (For a succinct statement of this case see *The Economist* (London), 29 June 1991, pp. 17–20.)

The third putative bearer of democracy is the organized working class. One of the major recent contributions to the study of democracy convincingly argues that the role of organized working classes in advancing and sustaining democracy has been understated, in favour of 'middle-class' theories. Organized working classes – mainly urban and industrial, but, in exceptional circumstances, plantation proletariats also – have the capacity to organize to promote democracy and the greatest interest in governments that will respond to the expressed needs of the masses (Huber *et al.*, 1993; Rueschemeyer *et al.*, 1992).[15] One can interpret both this argument and the previous one about the white-collar middle classes as dimensions of a broader theory that contemporary socio-economic development tends rather consistently to promote the empowerment of large organized groups, and thus democracy. Diamond summarizes the argument:

> From Taiwan to China, from the Soviet Union to South Africa, from Brazil to Thailand, economic development has some strikingly similar effects: physically concentrating people into more populous areas of residence while at the same time dispersing them into wider, more diverse networks of interaction; decentralising control over information and increasing alternative sources of information; dispersing literacy, knowledge, income and other organisational resources across wider segments of the population; and increasing functional specialisation and interdependence and so the potential for functionally specific protests (e.g. transit strikes) to disrupt the entire system. These effects would figure to be, and probably are, more rapidly experienced within the context of a market economy, but they have registered intensely in communist systems as well with the expansion of education, industry, and mass communications (Diamond, 1992: 484–5).

The work of Rueschemeyer and his colleagues (1992), representing the conclusions of a great volume of social research, emphasizes the importance of the obverse of the same coin: that contemporary economic growth and associated structural change tend rather consistently to weaken the two main social classes that have historically impeded democracy. Most significant have been agrarian landlords, especially those whose incomes have depended on the mobilization of large numbers of unskilled labourers (including tenants). The relationship between these two classes is generally so conflictual and so clearly perceived on both sides to be a zero-sum relationship (one side can only gain at the expense of the other) that landlords see any kind of political representation for the poor as a direct threat to their own incomes and status. The other social class that has impeded democracy has done so more by omission than by commission: in conditions of poverty, smallholders or peasant populations have rarely been able to sustain effective political organization of any kind above the local level. The 'transactions costs' are just too high. In politics, peasant populations have variously been passive; briefly and under provocation, insurrectionary; and almost always dependent on external organization and leadership. They have rarely played a major role in shaping the political agenda, or in installing and protecting democracy.[16]

There is thus no scarcity of theories linking the emergence of democracy with the societal and socio-economic changes associated with some combination of wealth, high incomes, the market economy and economic development. We are unable to assess the plausibility of these alternative theories on the basis of the kind of statistical analysis reviewed here. Other evidence – and especially that which comes closest to statistical testing by looking at large samples of countries over long time periods (Huber *et al.*, 1993; Rueschemeyer *et al.*, 1992) – indicates that class theory is likely to prove the most fruitful explanation of why prosperity and democracy are associated.[17] The role of different classes varies over time, and class and political conflicts can lead both middle and working classes to adopt anti-democratic positions at particular moments. But the general tendency of capitalist economic growth – and of economic growth in state socialist countries within the capitalist world system – has been to strengthen, numerically and organizationally, the social classes likely to support democracy, and to weaken those opposed or unsupportive.

New theoretical insights?

Given that we have more theory than we can adequately appraise, additional supplies may not be universally welcome. Yet the apparent abundance of the mainstream theory summarized above is in one respect illusory: it is narrow in scope. All these theories are 'society-centric': they explain politics (the incidence of democracy) in terms of variables relating to society and socio-economic relations (in this case, the changes in those relations induced by economic growth). What about the more directly political causes of political phenomena, and the role of states? There are in recent scholarly work the outlines of an approach to the relationship between state forms and economies that provides an alternative explanation of the statistical association between democracy and material prosperity.

One can start from the simple historical point that modern democracy originated in bargaining between political elites and wealthier citizens over state revenue. In the most literal sense, elites in Britain and elsewhere in Europe agreed to grant the elected representatives of wealth some influence over state policy by agreeing to give them a degree of control over state revenue. Parliaments represented the institutionalization of a bargain. The elites secured agreement over the means used to raise revenue and the rates and amounts involved. This provided them with a degree of security and predictability in revenue raising, and reduced the costs, since the wealthy were to some degree co-operative in observing and policing arrangements to which they had consented. The wealthy in turn obtained predictability, freedom from arbitrary exactions, and some say over how money was to be spent – in particular, influence over the recurrent question of whether to go to war, and with whom (Bates and Lien, 1985).

Let us turn next to Charles Tilly's path-breaking work on the history of state formation in Europe (Tilly, 1992). Tilly uses the idea of a continuum of patterns of state formation, from 'coercion-intensive' to 'capital-intensive'. 'Coercion-intensive' states relied heavily on simple physical coercion to obtain the resources they needed from their subjects and to ensure compliance. By contrast, the 'capital-intensive' relationship was more one of state–citizen than state–subject. States obtained their revenues through regularized taxes on economic activities or wealth, permitted those who paid the taxes some say in their imposition, purchased goods and services through the market more than they 'commanded' them, and permitted a substantial devolution of power to municipal governments controlled by the wealthy.[18]

The central point is the finding that the 'capital-intensive' strategy was most common in wealthier areas with substantial trade (Tilly, 1992: 15), and the 'coercion-intensive' strategy the norm in the poorer, agricultural areas. This makes sense: where there is trade, merchants and wealth, state elites face incentives to make bargains with their citizens. Were they to fail to do so, and act coercively and arbitrarily, wealth, trade and merchants would migrate to some other jurisdiction (Bates and Lien, 1985). Conversely, in the poorer agrarian areas with little trade, states found coercion more effective.

Tilly's work thus gives a historical explanation for the association of wealth and trade not only with democracy in the narrow sense, but also with the kinds of non-coercive and 'bargained' state–society relations that tend to underlie pluralist and democratic political systems. Does this pattern have any contemporary relevance? Is one of the mechanisms behind the association between democracy and high levels of economic development the (implicit) calculation of state elites overseeing prosperous market economies that they can best meet their own revenue needs by permitting actual and potential taxpayers some control over state policy? Such a hypothesis seems to fit squarely with the fact that the extent of democracy is far less in oil-rich economies than one would predict on the basis of average income levels (Huntington, 1991: 313). It seems plausible that state elites enjoying such 'windfall' sources of income as oil wells would in fact be 'liberated' from any need to bargain with their subjects. However, this is not the only potential explanation for the low democracy ratings of oil-rich states. The 'society-centric' theories also offer an explanation: oil exports generate high incomes but not the organized middle and proletarian classes who are the bearers of democracy in more normal high-income conditions.

Given the information requirements and the inherent problems in testing this 'revenue-bargaining' theory of democracy, it is fruitless to pursue it further at a general level. It is introduced here for two main reasons:

1 One is to indicate a possible mechanism specific to the poorest contemporary developing countries, that depend heavily on foreign aid. For many countries in sub-Saharan Africa in particular, foreign aid is not only the main source of public revenue, but a major component of measured GNP. The idea that this liberates states from any dependence on, and therefore from any kind of bargaining relationship with, their subjects/citizens is not new. It was a lesson learned by, among others, American counter-insurgency experts working in Vietnam in the 1960s. Given the extent of this aid dependence in much of contemporary sub-Saharan Africa, and the irony that the promotion of democracy is increasingly the justification for aid, we have to take seriously the possibility that the first undermines the second (Guyer, 1992). One reason for the association between wealth and democracy at the global level may be that, in the poorest countries, states freed from dependence on their subjects for revenue need not take seriously any relationship of accountability with these subjects, and will therefore score unusually low on any measure of democracy.

2 The second reason for introducing the 'revenue-bargaining' theory of democracy is to indicate the wide range of mechanisms through which material prosperity, especially that stemming from

economic development as we conventionally understand it, might generate democracy. It seems likely that several mutually reinforcing mechanisms may be at work.

Concluding comments

The original statistical research in the 1960s on the correlates of democracy was partly inspired by, and also contributed to, a perspective on socio-economic development, labelled 'modernization theory', which expected societal 'goodies' to go together: increased incomes, more modern and positive social values, enterprise, socio-economic diversity, income equality and democracy. After a period when ideas about development policy tended to be couched more in terms of 'hard choices' and 'alternative strategies', the core ideas of modernization theory are again dominant. Our concepts have been modified and updated: we are, for example, more likely now to be concerned with mass welfare and indices of human development than with 'value change'. But the central idea that most good things go together is again in the ascendant. Socio-economic research reflects this changing perspective. Much of the current cross-national research on democracy also involves attempts to find positive connections between a range of good things: democracy, equality, economic growth, education and literacy, relative gender equality and high life expectancy.

To look at the full range of this research is beyond the scope of this chapter. It has already been explained that there is no apparent connection between democracy and national economic growth rates, and good reason to be sceptical of the rash of recent research that claims such connections exist. Not all good things go together all the time. But several may do. Democracy does go hand-in-hand with economic development. And it seems likely – although the statistical evidence is inadequate to justify firm assertions – that the two are also associated with 'welfarist' public policies and relatively good performance on the components of human development indices – education, literacy, mortality, etc. Such positive interactions are claimed by, among others, Dasgupta (1990) and Pourgerami (1991). We must reserve judgement because the reliable statistical evidence needed to test such propositions is not available on a large scale. In particular, demographic and literacy measures are often rather crude in developing countries, such that reliable measures of changes over time do not exist. If there are positive relationships between democracy and mass welfare, then this is likely to be (largely) because, for obvious reasons, democratic regimes spend relatively more on popular welfare – and less on the armed forces – than other regimes. There is some good evidence for this (Habibi, 1994).

If the overall message from statistical analysis is rosy for most of the world in the long run, it is distinctly gloomy for particular parts of it in the medium term. This is especially true for most of sub-Saharan Africa, and applicable also to parts of the former Soviet Union. Here we find high concentrations of conditions that are clearly unpromising for democratic rule: (a) low incomes; (b) governments that are heavily dependent for revenue on aid donors, and therefore freed even from the requirement to treat their citizens well so that they might thrive and better 'feed' the state treasury; (c) ethnically divided societies, that rarely sustain democracy, perhaps because effective democracies are almost by definition stable, and ethnic divisiveness tends to militate against political stability (Hadenius, 1992: 112–18; Rueschemeyer *et al.*, 1992: 9 and 19); (d) unstable political systems more generally. Democracy has historically been closely associated with the effective consolidation of (central) government power (Rueschemeyer *et al.*, 1992: 9). This comes close to a truism: democracy represents the institutionalization of procedures for citizens to influence the government and to change its composition. Without a stable and effective political system, democracy becomes impossible or meaningless.

It would be unreasonable, and unkind, for aid donors to try to insist on democratic rule in such conditions. It is understandable that they should gently encourage it, but unlikely that their encouragement would be very effective. We know that international influences, of the kind that Whitehead discusses in Chapter 7, can play a part in the transfer of democratic rule. But the argument that international pressures have played a major historical role is not proven. In social science jargon, it lacks a counterfactual. We may be presented with a long list of countries that have apparently become democratic through international pressures. That tells us nothing until we have examined the other side of the picture: the countries that (might) have been subjected to equivalent international influences, but have failed to become democratic. To test the theory properly would be very difficult, for we have no satisfactory means of measuring international pressures. Until that is done, we cannot reject the proposition that international pressures work (only) where internal conditions are conducive to the establishment of democracy. Arat (1991: 60–3) illustrates the point vividly in relation to the widespread claim that the British Empire has been a major force in establishing democracy world-wide. The existence of a large number of former British colonies that are currently democracies does not itself signify a great deal, because Britain once ruled a high proportion of all current developing countries. It is proportions that matter; and, once they are examined, Arat claims, the British democratic legacy appears unimpressive. Whatever the truth on that particular point, the argument about the power of international influences to extend democracy remains open. By contrast, we can be very confident in claiming that poverty makes democracy difficult.

Annexe 2.1: Time series analysis of the connection between democracy and income

Data are the main constraint on undertaking time series analysis. I was able to find sufficient data to measure changes in democracy over time in two separate ways, and thus do two separate pieces of analysis.

The most comprehensive set of democracy scores is that produced by Arat (1991: appendix B). She provides annual democracy scores for between 65 and 150 countries over the period 1948–82. The scores range between 29 and 109 points. This data source, however, is not quite as rich as it first sounds:

1 The coverage is incomplete (see main text). The series also terminates in 1982. This becomes restrictive in part because, to measure income, I have used only the most reliable figures, the 'purchasing power parity' series, developed originally by Summers and Heston, that adjust earlier national income series to reflect real local purchasing power.[19] However, these figures are not

available for many (developing) countries for the years before 1960. The maximum period over which one can measure both income and democracy for a large sample of countries using Arat's democracy score is 1960–82. I have taken the averages of the years 1960–2 and 1980–2 as the initial and terminal points for measuring changes in both income and democracy. Given that this is a short period of time for historical analysis, I did not introduce any time lags (see below), although these are implied in the underlying theories which attempt to explain why income growth produces democracy.

2 Because most industrial countries score very close to the maximum scores for democracy in the early 1960s, it was barely possible for any growth in democracy to appear in the measures. Industrial countries are therefore excluded.

3 Many of the individual country scores for democracy appear suspiciously high. As explained in the main text, the procedure Arat used to construct the democracy index is very questionable, and tends to yield unjustifiably high scores for effective authoritarian regimes, especially Communist regimes. All Communist countries are therefore excluded.

This left a sample of 50 developing countries: 24 from Africa, 11 from Asia and 15 from Latin America and the Caribbean. Using ordinary least squares regression analysis, the statistical results are as follows:

Y, the dependent variable, defined as changes in the degree of democracy, is measured as movements along the democracy scale (number of points on Arat's scale) between 1960–2 (average) and 1980–2 (average).
X, the independent variable, defined as changes in per capita income, is measured as the ratio of average per capita GDP in 1980–2 to average per capita GDP in 1960–2.
Result: $Y = -23.52 + 14.20 X$ $R^2 = 0.19$, $p = 0.0014$.

Only 19 per cent of changes in democracy can be 'explained' by changes in income levels. This is not high, but is very consequential, given that a poor database will tend to obscure such actual relationships as may exist. The finding is highly significant in a statistical sense: there is one possibility in 714 that it would arise by chance.

A similar analysis can be undertaken on a larger sample of countries over a longer time scale using two independent indices of democracy, one set referring to the early 1960s, and the other to 1988. This is because two scholars – Bollen and

Hadenius – happened to classify overlapping samples of countries, each using a democracy scale of 0 to 100.[20] The earlier set, produced by Kenneth Bollen (1980; 1990), are probably the most reliable available for a large sample of countries (124). The figures for his two series for 1960 and 1965 have been averaged, and are described here as referring to the 'early 1960s'. The second series relates to all developing countries – 132 – at a single point in time: late 1988 (Hadenius, 1992: 61–2). There are 72 countries common to both data sets; these therefore constitute our sample for time series analysis.

The procedures used by Hadenius to construct his democracy scores seem quite acceptable (see main text). However, Bollen and Hadenius applied different standards of judgement to similar basic data. Hadenius was less generous in his marks for democracy than Bollen: his mean democracy score for the 72 countries in 1988 is 43, while Bollen's mean score for the early 1960s is 57. But this does not affect the statistical analysis. Of more concern is the very different distribution of countries on the two scales. Bollen distributes them fairly evenly (only 32 (45 per cent) in the extreme ranges 0–29 and 70–100 points), while Hadenius concentrates 63 countries (88 per cent) in the same ranges. It is very unlikely that these different distributions reflect changes in the real world.

The democracy measures are also questionable for another reason: Hadenius's figures for the terminal period relate to a single point in time, whereas, for long-run historical analysis, some kind of average figure relating to a longer time span is less likely to be misleading. There are cases where countries can switch between high and low democracy scores over brief periods of time, and there was indeed a great deal of movement world-wide in the later 1980s. Real underlying relationships might well not emerge from analysis based on these figures.

Income is measured as above, using the 'purchasing power parity' data. Once again, their non-availability for many developing countries before 1960 restricts the extent to which one can test for time lags between income changes and changes in the degree of democracy. I again measured income growth from 1960–2 (average of three years) to 1980–2 (average of three years). Since the changes in democracy are measured over the period from 'the early 1960s' to 1988, there is an implicit allowance here for changes in income levels to affect them.[21]

The statistical analysis (ordinary least squares regression) was conducted for two samples of countries: the 'full sample' of 72 countries; and a 'small sample' of 61 countries, excluding 11 with a population of less than a million. The results were positive and statistically very significant in both cases:

Y, the dependent variable, defined as proportionate changes in the degree of democracy, is measured as the ratio between the 1988 democracy score (Hadenius) and the 'early 1960s' democracy score (Bollen).

X, the independent variable, defined as proportionate changes in per capita income, is measured as the ratio of average per capita GDP in 1980–2 to average per capita GDP in 1960–2.

Full sample $(n=72)$: $Y = 0.31 + 0.29 X$ $R^2 = 0.12$, $p = 0.0032$.

Small sample $(n=61)$: $Y = 0.21 + 0.38 X$ $R^2 = 0.16$, $p = 0.0015$.

As expected, the analysis using the small sample produces a higher level of explanation. It is also predictable that the proportion of measured changes in democracy that is 'explained' by changes in income levels is less than in the earlier equation using Arat's democracy scores: for the democracy scores used here are not very comparable.

Notes

1 There are excellent pragmatic reasons why local government should be ignored: the conceptual and data problems are much simplified. However, the result is a consistent bias. Putnam's recent finding that, for Italian regional governments, the extent of democratic effectiveness is closely correlated with regional levels of socio-economic development is perhaps an indicator of future research directions (Putnam, 1993: chapter 4).

2 The exception is Pourgerami (1991). His book is, however, devoted to detecting and displaying patterns of statistical connection between all kinds of variables, with scant regard for their statistical significance. He is not in the business of trying to deny statistical connections.

3 Such challenges are not new. Challengers, however, appear generally to have been claiming that the statistical connections between democracy and wealth are weak, rather than denying them entirely (e.g. Neubauer, 1967).

4 From a purist point of view, any attempt to undertake cross-national analysis of the causes of democracy violates an assumption behind the construction of the statistical techniques used: that the cases be independent of one another in a statistical sense.

5 The degree of 'appropriateness' is scored by first using cross-sectional statistical analysis to identify the normal responses of governments to social unrest, and then measuring the extent to which particular governments deviated from the norm. This raises questions.

6 Bollen bolsters his case against using electoral turnout by demonstrating statistically that this figure does not correlate at all closely with other measures of democracy. The point is useful but not fully convincing: the notion that the best indices of democracy should all correlate highly with one another is questionable on the grounds that it implies a narrow range of types of democracy.

7 All statistical exercises find some other variables correlated with democracy to some degree. The problem is to trace the causes of the correlation. There is not the space here to discuss these other variables in detail. The extent of ethnic division and religion are among the non-material factors often believed to influence the prospects for democracy. *Ceteris paribus*, democracy has not thrived in ethnically divided polities (Hadenius, 1992: 112–18; Rueschemeyer *et al.*, 1992: 9 and 19). It has generally been found to be positively associated with, especially Protestant, Christianity, and negatively with Islam. The extent to which these associations reflect causation is, however, in dispute. The 'Protestant connection' may be a by-product of the high dependence of many democratic micro-states on the UK, the USA or Australia (Hadenius, 1992: chapter 6). Equally, in larger states, the extent of Protestantism is anyway correlated with the level of economic development (Bollen, 1979: 582). The negative association of Islam is certainly in part related to the growth of state power in West Asia on the basis of external support and oil revenues, and the consequent very limited degree of accountability of any kind between states and citizens. Further, the role of particular religions or sects in relation to democracy can change over time. Having earlier seen Catholicism as a generic obstacle to democracy, Huntington (1991: 77) has more recently argued that, after 1970, the Catholic church has become a force for democracy. In sum, we have no evidence that religion plays any important or consistent role.

8 See, for example, Dick (1974), Healey *et al.* (1992), Przeworski and Limongi (1993), Sirowy and Inkeles (1990). In short, there are two common arguments why democracies should perform better economically, and two why non-democracies should do so. One suggestion is that democracy leads to higher levels of private investment and private economic activity generally because democratic governments will respect the property rights of citizens, and not subject them to arbitrary exactions or confiscation. Citizens will therefore invest their capital in productive enterprise. The other is that economic policy-making will be more open, considered, flexible and responsive in democracies; policies will be more appropriate, leading to faster growth. The counter-arguments both relate to investment. One is that non-democratic governments are less subject to mass pressures to boost current material consumption, and will therefore be better placed to generate higher levels of investment. The second concerns the direction of investment. Non-democratic governments will have more autonomy to act as 'developmental states': to direct resources into activities of long-term benefit to the national economy, rather than into those favoured by 'market forces' or the short-term profit motives which govern private capitalists.

9 Przeworski and Limongi (1993: 60) note that most studies published up to 1987 either find that non-democratic regimes performed better economically or find no clear pattern, while studies published in 1988 or later nearly all find that democracy leads to faster economic growth. The same pattern is found when one looks at the more recent studies that they did not review. This reversal is far too sudden and complete to be a reflection of actual changes over time in the relationships between types of political regime and economic growth rates. Since there was in the 1980s, even more in the realm of 'development' than more generally, a marked shift of opinion in favour of democracy, one has to share their suspicions (Przeworski and Limongi, 1993: 61) about 'the relation between statistics and ideology'.

10 Przeworski reports in a private communication that his evidence shows this to be 'true of 10 South American countries between 1946 and 1988, but not for the world as a whole, 1951–88'.

11 He dates the first wave as 1828–1926, and the second as 1943–62 (Huntington, 1991: 10).

12 The strongest statistical connections imply that, on a cross-sectional basis, about half the variations in democracy levels can be attributed to variations in income levels. Many of the apparent connections are much weaker. Some researchers find that the association is much stronger over some ranges of income than others: in technical terms, the relationship is not linear. I am not convinced that our measures of democracy are yet sufficiently reliable to permit us to pass judgement on such issues.

13 There are four main theoretical traditions that link economic development (or wealth, or capitalism) and democracy in a negative way. Two of them, summarized in note 8 above, focus on the adverse effects of democracy on economic policy and performance. Two others see wealth and capitalism as undermining democracy, especially 'genuine' as opposed to formal democracy. Social scientists have paid most attention to the ways in which the socio-economic inequalities inherent in capitalism and markets carry through to the political sphere; see Almond (1991). Science fiction has focused rather on the scope inherent in advanced technology for centralized surveillance and control of individual thought and action, and thus for the subversion of democracy by the state apparatus. This is not a misplaced concern. It can, however, be placed in context if one views it as an aspect of one of the two long-term processes central to the evolution of contemporary polities: the increasing concentration of logistical power in the hands of large-scale organizations, especially states; and the secular growth of democratic mechanisms for the control of those organizations. The number of democracies has been expanding relatively steadily for well over a century (Huntington, 1991). These two processes of political concentration and democratization are inter-related in complex ways, and are mutually supportive as well as mutually antagonistic. History suggests that 'Consolidation of state power was an essential prerequisite for democratisation' (Rueschemeyer et al., 1992: 9).

14 Discussions of these theories abound in the literature; for a brief and relatively comprehensive sample which also provides a flavour of changing approaches to the issues, the classic original statement and exploration of the income–democracy connection within 'modernization theory' (Lipset, 1959 and 1960: chapter 2) could be combined with a major recent work that advances a contrary view focused on the centrality of class conflict (Rueschemeyer et al., 1992: especially chapter 1).

15 While Rueschemeyer et al. (1992) are militant in asserting the key role of organized proletariats in the achievement of democracy, in their detailed historical work they effectively attribute a considerable role to other classes.

16 The research backing for these generalizations is vast. Karl Marx's famous comment likening the French peasantry to a 'sack of potatoes' is often seen as the original point of reference for later research. Some of the recent scholarly landmarks, all written from different disciplinary and doctrinal perspectives, include Bates (1977), Lipton (1976) and Moore (1966).

17 The spread of formal education is so closely associated with economic development that it is very difficult to assess the education-based theories of democracy separately from the class-based theories.

18 In the more extreme cases of the Mediterranean and north European city states – Venice, Milan, Genoa, the early Dutch Republic, the Hanseatic League

– municipality and state were virtually merged, and both were controlled by coalitions of trading oligarchs.

19 The actual figures used in all my analysis reported in this paper are from the Penn World Tables, and measure per capita GDP in US$ at 1985 international prices (Laspeyres index).

20 Hadenius actually uses a scale of 0 to 10, but with a decimal place.

21 It was possible to make small adjustments in the length of this lag by varying the reference periods for the income data. Unsurprisingly, this did not affect the statistical results. The details are therefore not given here.

3

Economic reform and the transition to democracy

MARK ROBINSON

Economic reform and political liberalization

The 1990s have witnessed the ascendancy of a challenging new orthodoxy in aid policy circles, hinging on the assertion of a positive and complementary relationship between democracy and development. In an extension of this line of reasoning, it is argued that economic reform and political liberalization are mutually reinforcing because a more inclusive and consultative style of decision-making generates broader support for reform and newly-elected governments are able to capitalize on past policy failures associated with authoritarian regimes. This shift in thinking is a reflection of both the re-installation of democratic regimes in large parts of the developing world and of problems encountered in sustaining the momentum of economic reform under authoritarianism. Aid donors have willingly embraced the new orthodoxy, believing that it offers a conceptual justification for an agenda defined by neo-liberal economic reforms and 'good government' (see Moore, 1993).

As with most orthodoxies, empirical evidence to support the view that there is a positive relationship between processes of political and economic liberalization is both partial and contradictory. On the one hand, evidence can be marshalled from the experience of countries like Taiwan and South Korea showing that authoritarian rule helped to bring about sustained economic progress. At the same time, there are many examples of authoritarian regimes in Africa and Latin America which have presided over economic decline (Sørensen, 1993b). On the other hand, there are comparatively few examples of democracies in the developing world which have managed to achieve a consistent record of economic growth, even if there is a strong correlation between democracy and economic wealth (see the preceding chapter).

Despite this rather inconclusive evidence, the general trend towards political liberalization, especially in countries attempting to adjust their economies, has led to renewed interest in the relationship between economic and political reform. A distinction can be made between three broad types of relationship: (a) sustained economic reform followed by political liberalization; (b) political liberalization followed by economic reform; and (c) simultaneous transition. The first type is prevalent in sub-Saharan Africa, where many countries embarked on structural adjustment and economic liberalization in the early 1980s under the auspices of military dictatorships and one-party rule, later succumbing to pressures for political reform towards the end of the decade. A similar pattern prevailed in many Latin American countries a decade earlier, although the momentum of political reform now shows signs of faltering. Senegal provides a rare example of the second type, although there was some degree of overlap between both sets of reforms. Long-standing democracies which have embarked on economic reforms at a later stage of their development, such as India and Venezuela, constitute a separate category in their own right. The third type is illustrated by Mexico, the Philippines and Zambia.

In this analysis political liberalization refers to the dismantling of authoritarian institutions by means of reforms entailing the progressive relaxation of state controls over political expression and organization, and the granting of civil and political liberties previously denied or suppressed. Democratization involves the deliberate construction of new political institutions and the development of a pluralistic political culture actively favouring participation and contestation. Elections are usually integral to the process of transition linking these two phases of reform, but the holding of elections is not analogous to the achievement of full democracy. This process is in turn divided into several phases beginning with a transition from authoritarian rule, which can take various forms, and democratic consolidation, where the rules and procedures governing fundamental rights and freedoms, the election of rulers by universal suffrage, party competition and government accountability, are agreed and accepted by all concerned (Healey and Robinson, 1992: 129).

Economic reform embraces both macroeconomic stabilization

through monetary and fiscal measures, and structural adjustment, which includes a range of supply-side policies designed to promote sustained economic growth. Economic liberalization refers to moves towards greater market orientation, and the lessening or removal of state controls over prices, foreign exchange, trade, credit and interest rates.[1] As such, it may form part of structural adjustment programmes, but it can also be promoted as part of a long-term process of economic reform.

In reviewing the three types of transition outlined above, Haggard and Kaufman (1992a) argue that countries which attempt simultaneous political and economic reform encounter major problems due to the tensions generated in the process, with the result that they have generally failed to achieve either strong democracies or economic recovery. They also suggest that newly installed democratic regimes which then attempt to introduce wide-ranging economic reforms are likely to encounter formidable problems in accommodating popular expectations and maintaining political stability. By comparison, they claim that authoritarian regimes which introduce economic reforms (often over an extended period) prior to ceding political liberalization stand a greater chance of consolidating both sets of reforms over the longer term. However, not all countries which pursue this strategy will be successful since reform outcomes will depend on the strength of interest-group opposition and the ability of the successor regime to cope with political and distributive conflicts.

This chapter explores the validity of this last assertion in relation to countries which have first embarked on a programme of economic reform, and then at a later stage permitted a gradual process of political liberalization. In particular, it is concerned with regimes which are associated with effective economic management and the successful implementation of economic reforms. This requires identifying common ingredients in the political management of the economic reform package, and analysing how these change under conditions of political liberalization, with a view to understanding the potential for sustaining the momentum of economic reform with the development of a more open and inclusive political culture.

These concerns can be framed as four interrelated sets of questions. First we examine whether there is a set of institutional characteristics common to authoritarian regimes which have presided over sustained economic reform. Second, we examine whether the process of economic reform, when managed by this type of regime, creates the conditions in which political liberalization becomes possible. Third, we look at the extent to which the institutional characteristics associated with economic management under authoritarian rule will need to adapt and change as democracy takes root, in order to sustain economic reform. And finally, we consider whether changes will be required in the economic policy package, in order to ensure the political sustainability of economic reforms under conditions of competitive politics.

The conventional wisdom suggests that pragmatic authoritarian rule provides a firm (but politically undesirable) foundation for the successful implementation of liberal economic policy reforms. East Asian experience supports this type of assumption, although it was also popular among adherents of neo-liberal economic reforms in sub-Saharan Africa in the early 1980s.[2] The key characteristics of this type of regime from the point of view of effective economic management are threefold: (a) strong commitment from the political leadership; (b) the existence of an economic policy team which is insulated from mass political pressure; and (c) the use of repression to quell opposition to economic reforms. While it is not our intention to demonstrate that authoritarian rule is necessary to achieve economically desirable outcomes, we do explore the applicability of this set of institutional characteristics to successful reformers.

Coming to the second question, it is our contention that the process of economic reform, especially when it takes place over a protracted period and achieves the desired economic objectives, creates the conditions in which political liberalization becomes possible. In the short term, it may provoke adverse political reaction from organized interest groups who stand to lose out, from bureaucrats with fewer opportunities for rent-seeking behaviour, from urban workers who fear an erosion of living standards, and from businessmen who may be vulnerable to international competition. In time, new interest groups, such as export lobbies and farmers' organizations, may emerge to press for further reforms or to protect the gains they have made. These responses may develop into demands for greater involvement in the policy-making process and give succour to a process of political liberalization. Over the longer term, structural changes in the economy contribute to the process of class formation, manifest in the growth of the middle classes and the industrial working class, and the consequent reduction in the size of the agricultural sector. These groups might be expected to press for political reform once they perceive the old system to have outlived its usefulness or by virtue of their numerical strength.

A rather different set of institutional attributes might then be required to sustain the momentum of economic reform. The existence of a competent economic bureaucracy is likely to remain key to the continued success of economic reforms, although mechanisms may need to be introduced to encourage increased consultation and policy dialogue, without exposing economic policy-makers unduly to interest-group pressures or political interference. Politically committed leadership is cited as one of the factors underlying successful economic reforms, but such commitment may be more difficult to attain when a democratically elected government depends on diverse sources of political support. The most obvious difference lies in the reduced capacity of the regime to rely on the use of force to contain opposition to unpopular policies. Political liberalization requires the government to find consensual means of accommodating adverse political reactions. The need to replace force by consent will invariably entail the construction of a political alliance in support of continued economic reforms.

This leads us on to the fourth question, namely what changes will be required in the basic package of economic reforms to ensure the political sustainability of the reform process? One way of broadening support for or mitigating opposition to the reforms is to spread the benefits more widely, either by compensating losers, or by creating a policy environment conducive to an enhanced supply-side response which may in turn increase the credibility of the reforms.

The recent experience of three countries – South Korea, Chile and Ghana – provides a backdrop for a critical examination of these questions. All three can be viewed as successful adjusters in the sense that the policy prescriptions associated with macroeconomic stabilization and structural adjustment produced recovery and economic growth, although not without heavy social costs.[3] In addition, each has been undergoing a process of political liberalization since the late 1980s in response to a combination of internal and external circumstances. Despite similarities in regime type and policy mix, there are also differences between the three. Korea was consistently ruled by authoritarian regimes, whereas Ghana and Chile have experienced both military and civilian rule, and has pursued a consistent economic growth strategy from the early 1960s, while Chile and Ghana have experienced major changes in economic policy in accordance with the ideological colouring of successive military and civilian governments. Chile and Korea are more urbanized and are classified as middle-income developing countries; Ghana was in the same league in the 1960s, but years of economic decline have reversed its fortunes and it is now in the least developed grouping.

South Korea

South Korea (henceforth 'Korea') differs from both Chile and Ghana in that it has experienced a sustained period of economic growth since the mid-1960s when it embarked on a series of trade and exchange-rate reforms. There was no formal structural adjustment programme negotiated with the World Bank and IMF, nor has there been a steady process of economic liberalization, since the role of the state remained pivotal over much of the past three decades. Driven by a process of export-led industrialization, Korea achieved an average real GNP growth rate of 8.5 per cent per year between 1962 and 1993. A significant degree of political continuity has existed over this period, and changes in leadership preserved the military and authoritarian character until the democratic reforms of the late 1980s. At the same time, there has been a long record of opposition to authoritarian rule stretching back to the 1950s, but it was only in 1987 that the military-backed regime conceded major democratic reforms in the face of broad-based popular pressure. Korea is currently trying to consolidate its nascent democracy and at the same time liberalize the economy further.

What is of interest for our purposes is not so much the reasons for Korea's economic success, but the relationship between economic policy reform and political liberalization. Why was it not until the late 1980s that there was a concerted political challenge to authoritarian rule? Where did the impetus for democratization come from? How was this related to social changes induced by economic transformation? How is Korea currently managing a transition to democracy and further liberalization of the economy? We begin by reviewing economic policy under authoritarian rule, which provides a backdrop to understanding the political reforms of the 1980s.

Economic policy under authoritarian rule

Two factors are integral to Korea's economic success over the past three decades: the central role of the state in determining an overall economic strategy, and the formation of a relatively autonomous economic bureaucracy to formulate and implement policies to achieve strategic economic objectives. Korea has also benefited from a fortuitous set of historical circumstances and its strategic geographical location in the East Asian region, especially its close proximity to Japan, which has provided ready markets for its exports and exerted an important influence over policy choice.

From 1953 to 1961 Korea followed a conventional import-substitution policy backed to a substantial degree by the United States. During this period the USA financed nearly 70 per cent of Korea's imports and 75 per cent of fixed capital formation. However, this strategy was not particularly successful, due to the poor performance of the agricultural and services sectors (Haggard et al., 1991). In the early 1960s there was a shift to a gradual and selective state-led process of liberalization and industrialization, largely at the instigation of the USA which continued to support capital investment. This hinged on exchange-rate reforms and a drive towards export promotion. The currency was devalued by 100 per cent in 1964, followed by further large devaluations and the adoption of a unitary exchange-rate system. The interest rate on bank deposits and loans was doubled in 1965 to increase voluntary savings and discourage the unproductive use of bank credits. Exporters were provided with a range of fiscal incentives and subsidies to allow them tariff-free access to the imported intermediate products essential for export production, and unhindered access to bank loans for the necessary working capital. Selective tariff reform in 1967 reallocated resources to the export sector, while continuing to protect nascent export industries (Ahn, 1990: 34–5; Kim and Geisse, 1988: 52–4).

The successful implementation of the reforms was made possible by the restructuring of the economic bureaucracy under military rule. This centred on the creation in 1961 of the

Economic Planning Board which assumed responsibility for preparing the budget framework and for planning and co-ordination functions (Evans, 1992: 156). In addition, a more systematic approach to planning and implementation was introduced and civil service recruitment procedures and personnel administration were rationalized (Haggard *et al.*, 1991: 861). The development of a more technocratic economic policy-making apparatus has been highlighted as the key to Korea's subsequent economic success (Amsden, 1989; Wade, 1990). As Lee (1991: 83) has noted, 'the separation of the meritocratic bureaucracy from the military has helped the state function more consistently and efficiently'.

The export-oriented strategy devised in the mid-1960s proved remarkably successful. In the period 1965–73 exports grew at an average annual rate of 31.7 per cent and manufacturing by 21.1 per cent (Kim and Geisse, 1988: 37–9). Manufactured goods as a proportion of total exports rose from 27 per cent in 1962 to 62 per cent in 1965 and 88 per cent by 1975. At the same time, manufacturing export promotion was import-intensive and raw materials and oil imports created large current account deficits. However, with the oil price shocks of the 1970s the annual rate of growth of exports and manufacturing growth declined (Chowdhury, 1993: 58–9). A subsequent boom in the period 1976–8, which produced a 38 per cent increase in real GDP, ended in overheating, an explosion in wages and a loss of export competitiveness. GDP actually fell by 3 per cent in 1980, spurring the government into a gradual process of trade liberalization. From 1979 Korea opened up its economy more to market forces and international competition. Trade liber-alization helped to bring about an average annual growth of GNP of 9.2 per cent between 1980 and 1988. A current account deficit of US$5 billion was transformed into a surplus of $14 billion over this period, mainly due to a 13.6 per cent growth in the volume of exports (Economist Intelligence Unit (EIU), 1994a: 15).

At the same time, economic policy continued to be inter-ventionist as it sought to develop capital-intensive heavy (especially steel, shipbuilding and transportation equipment) and chemical industries. There was dramatic industrial concen-tration, and the development of a close relationship between the large diversified business conglomerates (*chaebol*) and the government. The state's discretionary allocation of credit

Table 3.1 Korea: selected macroeconomic indicators, 1965–93

Year	Average real % growth in GDP	Unemployment* (%)	Average rate of inflation (%)	Index of real wages	Budget deficit/ surplus (%GDP)
1965–70	10.4	5.5	12.5	2.4	−0.8
1970–75	7.1	4.2	15.6	6.5	−1.8
1975–80	7.6	4.0	17.4	24.8	−1.7
1980–85	8.4	4.2	7.3	45.6	−1.9
1985–90	10.0	2.9	5.4	100.0	0.3
1991	9.1	2.3	9.3	116.9	−1.6
1992	5.1	2.4	6.2	135.1	−0.8
1993	5.5	–	4.8	153.6	–

Source: IMF International Financial Statistics.
* UN Statistical Yearbook.

underpinned this concentration of economic power. The importance of conglomerates in Korea's industrialization is evident from the fact that the top ten *chaebol* accounted for 70 per cent of GNP in the mid-1980s (Amsden, 1989: 136).

Proponents of the strong-interventionist-state argument to explain Korea's economic success (Amsden, 1989; Wade, 1990; Evans, 1992) emphasize the centrality of state institutions in directing the economy. Despite an outward orientation the state has been heavily involved in planning and investment, and in devising short-term stabilization policies to overcome external shocks and to facilitate export growth (Chowdhury, 1993). This was made possible by a relatively autonomous economic bureaucracy and a high degree of state control over the financial system, both of which are inherent features of the East Asian NICs (newly industrializing countries). In contrast, the neo-classical interpretation stresses the government's success in maintaining a fairly stable macroeconomic environment, characterized by low inflation and a flexible exchange-rate policy. A World Bank study conducted in the early 1990s acknowledged that, while government has a role to play in ensuring adequate investment in human resources and stable macroeconomic management, economic success occurred irrespective of state intervention (World Bank, 1993: 84–6). These conflicting viewpoints suggest that successive authoritarian regimes judiciously combined selective state intervention with a pragmatic approach to macroeconomic policy formulation, which was sustained for more than three decades.

Economic and political reform in the late 1980s

Pressures on the Korean state to liberalize the economy in the 1980s were both internal and external. The younger technocrats were increasingly aware that the prevailing interventionist model could not continue unchanged. While the *chaebol* wanted to preserve their access to cheap credit, they also favoured liberalization of the financial system to give them greater control over capital and investment. There was also pressure from the USA to liberalize access to the domestic market and reduce the trade surplus.

What finally prompted reform was a drying up of credit for industrial expansion and a steep rise in real interest rates. Partial liberalization of the financial sector brought a shift from foreign to domestic finance, and increased emphasis on corporate bonds and equity rather than bank finance (Amsden and Euh, 1993: 380). In 1989 a more comprehensive trade liberalization policy was adopted which sought to free 97.3 per cent of all imports (Kihl, 1990: 72). Despite these reforms, the growth rate began to falter from 1989. Although there was a healthy current account surplus, exports dropped by 6 per cent in volume terms and the growth rate of real GNP was halved, reflecting the inflationary pressure generated by a 60 per cent increase in wages, currency appreciation and the growing incidence of labour disputes. Poor economic performance was attributed to unprecedented structural problems caused by flagging private investment and a sharp rise in domestic demand. Cumulative trade surpluses acted as a disincentive to adjustment and wages were rising sharply in relation to productivity (Ahn, 1990: 29).

Changes in economic policy in the late 1980s need to be viewed against a backdrop of gradual political reform. A succession of authoritarian regimes with strong links with the military rested on a highly centralized security apparatus and the manipulation of popular fears of Communist threat from the North (Han, 1989). Despite changes of leadership and variations in the intensity of authoritarianism (which became most repressive under the Yushin Constitution promulgated by President Park Chung Lee in 1972), this pattern prevailed until the populist upsurge in the late 1980s.

Authoritarian rule began to unravel during the tenure of General Chun Doo Hwan, who had come to power after the assassination of President Park in 1979. The struggle for political reform was largely waged by extra-parliamentary forces consisting of student activists, middle-class professionals and progressive Christians opposed to authoritarian rule, backed by pressure from the United States on the Chun government to accept constitutional change. Having originally planned to step down at the end of his seven-year term in 1988, the President decided in February 1986 that the Constitution would be revised prior to this. Debate then centred on the appropriate form of government for the country; the opposition wanted direct elections for the presidency while the ruling party proposed that the president should be elected by the legislature (Han, 1989: 283–5). In the face of mounting opposition, an eight-point pledge promising direct presidential elections based on a new constitution, free and fair election procedures, release of political prisoners, enhancement of human rights, press freedom, and competitive party politics was announced by the ruling party's presidential candidate Roh Tae Woo in June 1987 (Lee, 1991: 80). In the first direct presidential election for 17 years Roh was elected in December 1987 on a minority vote, against a hopelessly divided opposition. Although this marked the formal end of authoritarian rule it was only five years later, with the victory of the moderate opposition leader Kim Young Sam in presidential elections in December 1992, that a process of democratic consolidation finally got under way (Paik, 1994).

The transition from authoritarian rule

At this point we return to the questions posed at the beginning of this section concerning the relationship between economic policy reform and political liberalization. Two main questions arise from the political reforms of the late 1980s. Why did they occur at this juncture? And what have been their economic consequences?

The first question concerns the social and political implications of economic reform. Under authoritarian rule the Korean state presided over two and a half decades of export-led economic growth and structural transformation. The reforms have been gradual, rather than sudden, and have moved between an emphasis on stabilization measures and policies designed to promote growth. The social and political effects are therefore of a long-term structural nature rather than short-term responses to radical economic liberalization as in the neo-liberal reforms introduced in Chile and Ghana.

A concerted export-oriented industrialization effort has produced a major shift in the class structure since the 1960s with an expansion of the industrial working class and middle classes. The middle classes, which prospered from economic growth and benefited from heavy state investment in tertiary education, became increasingly politically conscious and assertive during the 1980s. Despite positive public perceptions of economic achievements, negative views about the political and human rights situation increasingly prevailed in the minds of middle-class Koreans. Indeed, contrary to arguments suggesting that good economic performance confers political legitimacy, the Korean public was dissatisfied with the government's political standing despite its economic success (Park, 1991). Despite a rapid growth in union membership in the 1980s, organized labour failed to play a significant role in the struggle for democracy. The reasons given for this apparent lack of militancy are the absence of a labour-based political party and the stifling of any reformist bent by rapid increases in real wages, as well as repressive government labour policies (Lee, 1991: 88–93).

Among the reasons why the democratization movement did not get off the ground until the 1980s were the repressive policies of the Park and Chun regimes, the existence of a solid core of support for the government in the rural areas and the political insecurity of the middle classes, who were unwilling to sacrifice economic gains by becoming involved in the struggle for political reform.[4] Moreover, the authoritarian regimes had the implicit support of the US government, which wanted to maintain a reliable bulwark against Communism during the Cold War. When this form of political rule outlived its usefulness the USA pressured the Chun government to capitulate to opposition demands for constitutional reform and to encourage restraint on the part of the military, in the hope that a peaceful transition would produce a democratically elected government which would continue to uphold its interests.

It remains to be seen whether Korea can maintain a commitment to a new phase of economic liberalization designed to re-establish a competitive edge, and at the same time manage the stresses and strains of democratic consolidation. Soon after gaining office President Kim Young Sam initiated a series of reform measures designed to induce greater accountability in government and contain the influence of the military, including a law requiring all public servants to register their assets with the government and promising prosecution of high-ranking civil servants and military officials found guilty of corruption. In March 1994 the Kim regime sought to institutionalize the process of democratization through a series of electoral reform laws which reduced the permitted campaigning period, introduced stricter spending limits for political parties, and paved the way for elections to local-level authorities. In the June 1995 local elections, which were the first to be held since the 1961 military coup, the opposition parties won a majority share of the local assembly seats and won control of many major towns and cities, including Seoul. These reforms have strengthened the foundations of democracy in Korea, by investing the political system with a greater measure of accountability and legitimacy. At the same time, the military is still very powerful and the business class predominates in the governing coalition, leading some commentators to conclude that Korea remains a 'low-intensity democracy' (Gills, 1993).

On the economic front, the new government has sought to further reduce controls on the credit system, and eliminate rules and regulations governing the activities of private enterprises and foreign investment (Lee and Sohn, 1994). Plans are under way to sell off government stock in 70 companies and a further 60 state corporations are scheduled for privatization. Other state monopolies are in the process of being broken up into smaller units in advance of privatization to make them more saleable to potential buyers other than the business conglomerates that continue to dominate the economy. Changes in economic policy have been accompanied by institutional reforms, the most far-reaching of which was the abolition of the Economic Planning Board and its amalgamation into the Ministry of Finance. These changes not only mark a decisive break with the state-centred approach to economic management that was the hallmark of South Korea's approach to development policy for three decades, but they also signal a desire on the part of the Kim regime to challenge the old political order, characterized by tightly-knit relations between the *chaebol*, government officials and managers of state banks and corporations.

Now that Korea has achieved a high level of economic development it may have a firmer base to sustain democratic politics. But if economic growth were to falter and efforts to open the internal market failed to generate the expected dividend in terms of restoring competitiveness, political turbulence might result, especially if this had an adverse impact on the living standards of ordinary Koreans. The Kim regime is openly challenging the old order, in the process creating frictions between bureaucrats seeking to retain control over economic policy and businesses trying to make the most of new-found economic and political freedoms. Such developments would be unlikely to provide the basis for the return of authoritarian rule, however, since the foundations for democracy are by now well grounded and have been shown to be compatible with economic prosperity.

Chile

Prior to 1973 Chile had a history of constitutional government and democratic politics dating almost uninterruptedly back to the late nineteenth century. By the early 1970s Chilean society had become highly urbanized, with a well-developed industrial base which gave it a class and occupational structure similar to that of Western Europe. But there were significant disparities of wealth, especially in the agricultural sector, where a small landowning class controlled most of the land. There was also substantial foreign domination over the natural resource base, notably in copper, which was largely under the control of foreign capital.

These disparities formed the background to the sharp swings in macroeconomic policy Chile has experienced over the past three decades. In the period 1970–3 a minority socialist government introduced a series of radical reforms designed to alter the fundamental balance of economic and political power. Following a bloody coup in 1973 an authoritarian military government under General Pinochet reversed many of these reforms and took Chile down the road of economic orthodoxy. After a return to democracy in 1989, two successive Christian Democrat-led governments have retained the macroeconomic programme inherited from the military regime, but with greater emphasis on the redressal of economic inequalities and the elimination of mass poverty. The relationship between economic liberalization and democratization is complex, however, and merits further examination.

It is important to note that economic reforms in the Pinochet years took a variety of forms in response to changing economic and political realities. Within this sixteen-year period three main phases of economic policy can be distinguished: the rolling back of reforms introduced by previous democratic governments and the imposition of neo-liberal orthodoxy from 1973 to 1981; managing the recession through heterodox measures in the early 1980s; and structural adjustment followed by sustained economic growth from the mid-1980s. Each was associated with changes in the system of political rule: the early period was characterized by harsh repression and de-institutionalization; this was followed by a short period of partial political liberalization, growing public protest and the re-emergence of a political opposition; and the final period was essentially one of re-institutionalization in which the military laid the groundwork for a managed transition to democratic rule against a backdrop of increasing popular opposition and international pressure.

Chile is held up as one of the most successful examples of structural adjustment in Latin America, but did it require a sophisticated system of authoritarian rule to see it through to a successful outcome? In what ways did economic reforms lay the basis for a successful transition to democracy and are these likely to be sustained under democratic rule?

Economic liberalization under Pinochet, 1973–81

Salvador Allende's minority socialist government was elected to power in 1970 on a radical platform of comprehensive agrarian reforms, centring on land redistribution to co-operatives, and the nationalization of most of the mineral sector, the financial system, large enterprises and strategic industries.[5] Wage increases and substantial expenditure on health, education and housing resulted in a 113 per cent increase in the money supply and a growth in the fiscal deficit from 2.8 per cent to 7.9 per cent of GDP from 1970 to 1971. Although this expansionary policy resulted in GDP growth of 9.0 per cent in 1971 it was not sustainable; the fiscal deficit increased to 12.8 per cent of GDP

Table 3.2 Chile: selected macroeconomic indicators, 1970–92

Year	Growth in GDP (%)	Unemployment* (%)	Inflation (%)	Index of real wages	Deficit/ surplus (%GDP)
1970	2.1	4.1	32.4	–	–2.8
1971	9.0	4.2	20.0	–	–7.9
1972	–1.2	3.3	74.8	59.4	–12.8
1973	–5.6	4.8	361.5	42.2	–7.3
1974	1.0	8.3	504.7	52.9	–5.4
1975	–12.9	15.0	374.7	52.0	0.1
1976	3.5	17.1	211.8	61.6	1.4
1977	9.9	13.9	91.9	66.2	–1.1
1978	8.2	13.7	40.1	78.5	–0.1
1979	8.3	13.6	33.4	91.3	4.8
1980	7.8	10.4	35.1	101.7	5.4
1981	5.5	11.3	19.7	122.6	2.6
1982	–14.1	19.6	9.9	126.5	–1.0
1983	–0.7	14.6	27.3	114.3	–2.6
1984	6.4	13.9	19.9	107.1	–3.0
1985	2.5	12.1	30.7	98.2	–2.3
1986	5.6	8.8	19.5	99.8	–0.9
1987	6.6	7.9	19.9	100.0	0.4
1988	7.3	6.3	14.7	104.7	–0.2
1989	10.2	5.3	17.0	107.5	1.8
1990	3.0	5.6	26.0	107.7	0.8
1991	6.1	5.3	21.8	–	1.6
1992	10.3	4.4	15.4	–	2.3

Source: IMF International Financial Statistics.
* International Labour Organisation.

in 1973 and inflation soared, reaching an annual rate of 505 per cent in 1974 (see Table 3.2). These policies and their resultant macroeconomic effects provoked widespread political opposition from landowners and industrialists threatened with expropriation and a middle class impoverished by runaway inflation.

Political polarization and economic chaos provided the excuse the military needed for the coup d'état in September 1973 which deposed the Allende government. Retribution was swift and bloody; left-wing politicians, trade unionists and leaders of mass organizations were murdered or detained, and many fled into exile. The Congress was closed, political parties were banned, press censorship was introduced, and freedom of expression and association was severely curtailed.

Although the military government had no clear economic programme when it took over, its immediate objectives were to reverse the measures introduced by Allende and to re-establish macroeconomic stability. This later found expression in an export-oriented development strategy followed by an orthodox stabilization programme to combat a growing balance-of-payments crisis. Moves towards an open market economy centred on a progressive reduction of import tariffs and the abolition of controls over foreign exchange, prices, credit, interest rates in favour of market determination and a process of privatization to reverse the Allende expropriations (Ritter, 1990: 171–3). In the agricultural sector requisitioned land which had been distributed to co-operatives was sold off to individual smallholders with the aim of strengthening the family farm sector (Diaz and Korovin, 1990).

Despite these changes, the delayed impact of the oil price hike of 1973 and a 50 per cent reduction in the price of copper in early 1975 combined to create an acute balance-of-payments crisis and economic recession in the mid-1970s. The military regime responded by abandoning its relatively gradualist approach to reducing inflation, opting instead for a policy of orthodox demand management, entailing drastic cuts in real wages, social expenditures and capital outlays, the pruning of subsidies, and a large reduction in public sector employment.[6] Unemployment climbed steeply to over 17 per cent at the height of the recession, and inflation remained persistently high at over 370 per cent in 1975, primarily as a result of the government's failure to control the money supply. Exchange-rate policy became the main weapon in the successful counter-inflationary strategy which brought economic recovery after 1976, though with only a slight fall in the level of unemployment, largely because growth took place in the financial rather than the directly productive sectors (see Table 3.2).

Economic policy in this early period of military rule was under the direction of a team of neo-liberal technocrats who had received much of their training in the United States – the so-called 'Chicago boys' – who were able to operate without any of the usual constraints of accountability and consultation. As a result the business community had little influence over the formulation of policy, even though it had for the most part supported military intervention (Valenzuela, 1989: 194). Technocratic advisers had become increasingly influential in the Frei and Allende governments, but never before had they been granted such autonomy. Indeed, the neo-liberal technocrats not only designed and executed economic policy but 'they were the intellectual brokers between the government and international capital, and symbols of the government's determination to rationalize its rule primarily in terms of economic objectives' (Kaufman quoted in Silva, 1991: 394). This style of decision-making prevailed until the economic crisis of the early 1980s, when a more inclusive approach based on consultation with business interests became necessary to sustain the political momentum of the neo-liberal reforms.

Encouraged by the economic boom in the late 1970s, the military developed a political rationale to carry forward the neo-liberal economic project and guarantee the future stability of the regime. This was achieved through partial political liberalization under a model of 'protected' democracy enshrined in the 1980 Constitution (Jilberto, 1991: 50–3). This provided for a bi-cameral legislature in which the senators in the upper chamber would be hand-picked by Pinochet. Political parties which professed the doctrine of class struggle were banned. Most importantly it provided for a plebiscite to be held in 1988/9 to decide whether military rule should continue.

Economic recession and popular resistance
in the early 1980s

The apparent success of this outward-oriented development strategy was dubbed the 'Chilean economic miracle' by those sympathetic to the regime. But it was not to last for long. In 1981 Chile suffered its worst economic crisis for fifty years, with the largest fall in GDP of any country in Latin America the following year (Ffrench-Davis, 1993: 10). With the move to a fixed exchange rate in June 1979, came a 26 per cent deterioration in the terms of trade over the next four years and a fourfold increase in interest payments on outstanding debt (Jilberto, 1991: 40).[7] Unemployment, which had fallen to 11.3 per cent in 1981, climbed to 19.6 per cent a year later (see Table 3.2). The working class and the urban poor bore the brunt of the crisis, with trade unions powerless to defend their interests as a result of the ban on organized union activity. High unemployment was compounded by adverse trends in real wage rates and by sharp cutbacks in government spending on social services. Public sector workers were especially hard hit; already among the lowest paid in the Chilean workforce, they experienced a decline in real wages of over 20 per cent over the period 1982–7, compounded by a fall in public employment during the adjustment period. The unemployed were forced to adopt extreme survival strategies to cope, pooling resources between households, and supplementing household income from informal sector activity.[8] To quell social discontent, the government created two special unemployment subsidy programmes, involving expenditures equivalent to 1.5 per cent of GDP. But only half the unemployed received benefits under these programmes and those who did were paid benefits well below the minimum wage level.

There was also growing poverty in the rural areas: in 1982 57 per cent of the rural population was below the poverty line compared with 27 per cent in 1970, while rural wages were only 85 per cent of their 1965 level. As a result of the reversal of the Frei and Allende land reforms a trend towards casualization led to a continuous search for temporary employment, while smallholders who had been unable to take advantage of the export boom of the late 1970s became impoverished (Diaz and Korovin, 1990).

Yet while the poor endured excessive hardship during this period, the higher income groups were protected from the worst effects of the recession, and the very richest actually gained. For example, the highest income quintile received more than 42 per cent of all social security transfers, whereas the two lowest quintiles received just 19 per cent. The purchasing power of middle- and upper-income groups also fell proportionately less than that of lower-income groups following devaluation in the mid-1980s. Finally, the regressive nature of the government's policies was most obviously revealed in the fact that fewer than 2,000 individuals with unsecured private debts benefited from central bank subsidies totalling US$6 billion in the period 1982–5, ostensibly to avert widespread bankruptcies and economic and financial collapse (Meller, 1991: 1555–9).

The real hardship caused by the recession and the subsequent adjustment measures provoked a powerful response from the working class and popular organizations. Grassroots organizations initially founded in urban working-class communities for economic survival now mobilized popular resentment in a series of street protests. Transitions to democracy in neighbouring Latin American countries compounded the insecurity of the regime and gave succour to the opposition. Beginning with a national day of action at the instigation of the Copper Workers' Federation in May 1983 there followed a series of mass protests, rallies and demonstrations at monthly intervals, involving Chileans from all walks of life, against the negative effects of economic policies and human rights abuses, which then developed into demands for wide-ranging political reform (Garretón, 1989a: 266–7). More worrying in terms of the support base of the regime, business interests became alienated by its ill-thought-out economic policies. Farmers and small businessmen began to demand changes to prevent a growing number of bankruptcies; they held a series of public demonstrations to press their demands and forcibly prevented banks from taking over bankrupt businesses (Stallings, 1990: 131–2).

The limited political opening created by the 1980 Constitution did not represent the beginning of a transition to democracy in any real sense, particularly since repressive tactics were once again employed with the declaration of a state of siege at the end of 1984 to quell the growing popular opposition. Nevertheless, it did lay the institutional framework for the transition in 1989 and allowed the opposition more room for manoeuvre and for popular discontent to surface. It also provided a firmer platform for the emergence of a centrist alliance to develop later and carry forward a transitional programme (Garretón, 1989b: 150–5).

Economic adjustment and the transition to democracy

The government responded to the crisis by appointing a new team in February 1985 headed by a young technocrat, Hernàn Büchi, as Finance Minister, charged with devising a structural adjustment programme (SAP) to lift the economy out of recession and into sustained export-led growth. Following negotiations with the IMF, the World Bank and other creditors the key measures adopted were devaluation of the exchange rate, monetary restraint involving cutbacks in government expenditure, tax reductions, a major privatization programme, the creation of a copper stabilization fund to control windfall foreign earnings, export promotion and diversification, tariff reductions and debt renegotiations (Ritter, 1990: 179; Stallings, 1990: 137–41). These were backed up by three successive Structural Adjustment Loans totalling US$850 million which compensated in part for the drying up of private bank loans in the early 1980s.

The SAP did not represent a fundamental change of direction but rather a reversion to the neo-liberal orthodoxy that had predominated in the period prior to the 1981 recession, with increased external support. However, it was accompanied by a qualitative change in the style of decision-making. Unlike his predecessors, Büchi actively canvassed support from the business community for his economic policies. In particular, policies designed to increase the rate of investment (which in 1983 had declined to the level of a decade earlier) and to reorient production towards exports found favour among business groups previously critical of government policy. The privatization programme was reinvigorated, with 28 major companies being put up for sale by 1988 through share issues on the stock market, and sale of the equity to private pension funds and public sector workers. This had the advantage of creating a potential base of support for the government among small property owners and reducing the room for manoeuvre of any successor government, whatever the outcome of the 1988 plebiscite.

The SAP is widely held to have been a success. Macroeconomic stability was certainly achieved relatively quickly, with a progressive reduction in the fiscal deficit from 1985–7, and a halving in the rate of inflation over the same period. GDP growth accelerated from 2.5 per cent in 1985 to 10.2 per cent in 1989, fuelled in part by an increase in gross fixed capital formation from 12 per cent in 1983 to 20.3 per cent in 1989. Agricultural and industrial exports grew by 67 and 50 per cent respectively from 1985 to 1988. This favourable economic performance was aided by high copper prices after 1988 and an improvement in the terms of trade, while a significant growth in non-traditional exports and the setting-up of the copper stabilization fund reduced the vulnerability of the economy to fluctuations in international copper prices.

Despite success on the macroeconomic front, the adjustment programme entailed heavy social costs. As part of the campaign to cut government expenditure public sector wages were held down with the result that real wages declined by an average of 3.7 per cent per year between 1982 and 1987. Average wages in 1989 were 8 per cent lower than in 1970 and fewer categories of workers were covered by minimum wage legislation, although unemployment at the end of 1989 was only 5.3 per cent, the lowest since 1973 (Ffrench-Davis, 1993: 13). Moreover, minimum wages and remuneration on government employment programmes failed to keep pace with inflation (Stallings, 1990: 137). Survey data point to a growing maldistribution of income between 1978 and 1988, with that of the top 10 per cent increasing more relative to other income groups, and its share of total income increasing from 40.9 to 48.4 per cent over the decade, mainly at the expense of middle-income groups (Ritter, 1990: 184). At the same time, social indicators continued to improve, largely as a result of increased spending on targeted feeding programmes for the most vulnerable groups, notably pregnant mothers and children. Consequently while poverty and income distribution worsened, infant mortality rates declined during the period of adjustment. And despite cutbacks in social spending, secondary school enrolment continued to rise and illiteracy decreased (Ffrench-Davis, 1993: 12).

On the political front, popular mobilization in the mid-1980s failed to achieve major concessions. However, as a result of participating in the mass protests, people became less fearful of the military. The protests also stimulated the revitalization of political parties and their regrouping into larger blocs. But the opposition lacked a coherent strategy and there was no consensus among the various parties on the way forward. The middle classes weakened in their resolve to engage in open protest against the regime, partly as a result of minor concessions to the professional white-collar unions and the expectation that the government would enter into negotiations with the opposition, but also because they had begun to benefit from the adjustment measures being introduced by Büchi and his team (Garretón, 1989a: 269–70).

The turning point in the transition to democracy came with the plebiscite of October 1988 on the continuation of Pinochet's presidency for a further eight years, as provided for in the 1980 Constitution. By this time, the USA had withdrawn its support for the military regime with the realization that a democratic government could now assume power without threatening political stability or US strategic interests in the region. Despite a campaign dominated by the state-controlled media, the plebiscite resulted in a 55 per cent vote against continued military rule. This marked the beginning of the transition to democracy and the gradual withdrawal of the military from active politics. Pinochet and his immediate supporters concentrated on preserving the corporate autonomy and political influence of the military in a future democratically elected

regime, within the limits of the constitutional reforms negotiated with the opposition and approved by plebiscite in July
1989 (for details see Chapter 4). Pinochet appointees in the
senate, the civil service, municipal government, the univer-
sities, the judiciary, and above all, the military high command,
ensured that the legacy of authoritarian rule would continue
to frustrate the reformist ambitions of a future democratic
regime (Garretón, 1990: 66).

The presidential and parliamentary elections of December
1989 resulted in the defeat of Pinochet's party and presidential
candidate, Hernàn Büchi, who, despite his economic achievements and intellectual flamboyance, was regarded as too closely
associated with the military regime. The victors were a coalition of centre-left parties (principally the former Socialists and
Christian Democrats) whose successful presidential candidate was Patricio Aylwin. The coalition government, which
was formally installed in March 1990, had the good fortune to
inherit an economy which was in relatively good shape following the adjustment programme of 1983–9. There was broad
agreement among the coalition partners on the need to continue with the macroeconomic policies of the previous regime
but to focus attention on income redistribution and poverty
alleviation measures financed by tax increases, since many of
the gains of the adjustment period had been at the expense of
the poor. In a reflection of this change of emphasis, spending
on health, education, housing and welfare increased by more
than 30 per cent in real terms between 1989 and 1993 (Angell
and Graham, 1995: 207). At the same time, the government
aimed at avoiding an unsustainable expansion in government
expenditure and therefore pursued a relatively conservative
fiscal and monetary policy (Ffrench-Davis, 1993; Sunkel, 1993).[9]
These policies did bear fruit, with the overall level of poverty
falling from 40 to 33 per cent from 1990 to 1992; as for macroeconomic indicators, growth averaged an annual 6.5 per cent
in 1990–2, inflation was reduced from 26 to 15 per cent over
the same period (see Table 3.2), and a modest fiscal surplus
was achieved in 1992 and 1993 (Latin American Weekly Report,
25 November 1993).

Democracy and adjustment in the 1990s
The neo-liberal project in Chile had two main objectives: to
transform the economy and to demobilize the opposition. The

long-term objective was for individuals to act exclusively through the market and for market transactions to take the place of collective action. The Pinochet regime certainly succeeded in its bid for economic transformation, but it was unable to prolong authoritarian rule once it had conceded the principle of a plebiscite. This raises the question of the linkages between the economic reforms introduced over a sixteen-year period and subsequent moves towards political liberalization.

Economic liberalization and state contraction in the late 1970s and 1980s gave rise to significant changes in class and interest-group configurations which in turn impacted on subsequent political developments. The working class was fragmented by the sharp downturn in living standards and the growth of unemployment, which led many to seek work as casual labourers or petty traders and producers in the growing informal sector, as reflected in the drop in the proportion of wage earners in the economically active population from 53 per cent in 1971 to 38 per cent in 1982. Many – 36 per cent of the economically active in 1982 – were forced to rely on state handouts and special employment programmes (Garretón, 1989a: 274).

In the agricultural sector a new rural middle class came into being as a result of the break-up of the co-operatives and the transfer of land to individual ownership; this went hand-in-hand with a process of proletarianization among smallholders too poor to take advantage of export opportunities (Diaz and Korovin, 1990). Ironically, the Allende government's land reforms probably had the unintended effect of galvanizing the unproductive landlord sector into a more commercial approach to farming. Among the middle classes, there was reduced scope for employment in the state sector and a commensurate expansion of employment in the financial and service sectors. This accompanied a shift within the business community away from traditional industries to the financial sector where liberalization had created ample opportunities for rapid self-enrichment. A new technocratic elite, typified by the Büchi team, came into prominence and from the early 1980s worked closely with business leaders, particularly those in the financial sector. Finally, the military itself was transformed into a new political class in which the commanders-in-chief of the armed forces came to represent the executive and legislative branches of the state (Jilberto, 1991: 48).

These changes induced by a sustained period of economic liberalization did not bring about class polarization in the conventional Marxist sense. Political repression reduced the scope for collective action and the capacity of workers to defend wage levels and conditions of work, and, as we have seen, the working class became increasingly atomized and impoverished. As Garretón (1989a: 274) has argued, the economic changes produced a shift in the bases of political mobilization from the organized and formal sectors to the amorphous and marginalized popular sectors, with women and young people playing active roles in the opposition movement in the early 1980s. With this, the principal terrain of struggle against the dictatorship moved from the workplace to neighbourhood and community organizations. On the one hand, the fragmentation of the popular classes led to a situation where each group pursued differing and sometimes contradictory agendas, which undermined efforts to bring about unity of opposition. On the other hand, it also provided a basis for closer collaboration between the middle classes (small and medium business people, professional groups and university students) and the popular opposition in the urban shanty towns, since there was less polarization of economic interests. Arguably, this broad coalition of interests provided for a smoother political transition and a higher degree of consensus on economic and political objectives after the transition, making the task of democratic consolidation easier to achieve.

A further issue which merits attention is the extent to which an authoritarian political system was necessary for the successful pursuit of far-reaching economic reforms. Reviewing the economic policies pursued by the Pinochet regime, many commentators hold the view that it would have been impossible for a democratic government to have been re-elected following the policy errors that were a major contributory factor to the recession of the early 1980s. In this respect Stallings (1990: 166) suggests that 'Chile's model was viable only under an authoritarian state', since union activity was suppressed and there was little scope for organized resistance to the regime's determination to depress real wages and reduce social spending in its attempt to create the conditions for renewed growth. According to Jilberto (1991: 42) the authoritarian project aimed at 'granting governability and stability to a political system in which the establishment of democracy could guarantee the survival of the neo-liberal economic transformations'. The authoritarian character of the regime gave the economic team substantial autonomy in working out its development strategy. It would therefore be tempting to conclude that successful adjustment was possible only within an authoritarian political framework, with an insulated and technically competent technocracy responsible for drawing up and implementing a programme of economic adjustment, since it is unlikely that a democratic regime could have weathered the social costs and political opposition that the reforms generated. At the same time, it is clear that many policy errors were committed in the first phase of the military regime, possibly because the economic team had excessive policy discretion and was over-zealous in its efforts to reverse the changes introduced by previous civilian regimes. The new team put in place by the regime in the mid-1980s was certainly more consultative in policy-making and this may help to explain why the adjustment measures that it implemented may now prove more politically acceptable and economically sustainable under democratic rule.

But the immediate political requirements of the SAP do not in themselves explain why it was necessary to prolong military rule beyond the mid-1980s (and through to the late 1990s if Pinochet had won the plebiscite). The Pinochet regime was averse to a more consensual approach to economic reforms for fear of eroding its political power base, although it encouraged limited consultation in the formulation of the SAP in order to appease business interests. This would suggest that the military's political project was ultimately a far more powerful factor in explaining the continuity of authoritarian rule than the functional requirements of successful adjustment.

However, it remains to be seen whether it will be possible for the Christian Democrat government of President Eduardo Frei, which came to power in the December 1993 elections, to sustain the momentum of economic reform while spreading the fruits of growth more widely. The eradication of poverty is the overriding objective of the Frei regime, with the focus on maintaining a high rate of growth (there was an annual average growth rate of 7.6 per cent in the period 1989–93) as a means of generating increased tax revenues to finance higher levels of spending on health, education and welfare provision. Despite the economic achievements of the regime (inflation of 8.9 per cent in 1994 was the lowest since 1960), there is widespread dissatisfaction with the quality of services and a perception that improvements have primarily benefited better-off sections of the population, which has contributed to an erosion in the regime's popularity since the elections.

Pent-up frustrations among social groups who lost out as a result of the reforms clearly require attention, since many of them were actively involved in the struggle for political reform, although there is a strong indifference to politics among a large segment of the population, which to many commentators is the enduring legacy of the Pinochet regime. As the new democratic regime can ill afford to alienate the armed forces, it has to tread a tightrope between adhering to the reforms introduced under the military regime and at the same time ensuring that the poor and the marginalized are brought back into the economic mainstream. The fact that political transition in Chile was carried through by a broad-based coalition may bode well for democratic consolidation but it can also pose difficult choices for a reformist government which has to be responsive to the needs of disparate constituencies.

Ghana

The tenacity of the Rawlings regime in implementing a sustained programme of structural adjustment has attracted considerable acclaim from proponents of neo-liberal economic reforms in Africa. Further plaudits were conferred on it for introducing multi-party democracy and holding presidential and legislative elections in late 1992. This combination of successful adjustment followed by democratic reforms is virtually unique in sub-Saharan Africa. What is significant about the Rawlings regime is its apparent ability to accomplish both economic and political liberalization whilst maintaining some degree of political popularity. However, two qualifications should be made at this point. First, the extent to which Ghana's SAP has been a success is open to dispute, although macroeconomic indicators paint a convincing picture of economic recovery in the 1980s. Second, the results of the 1992 presidential elections, which returned Rawlings to power with a democratic mandate, are also contested, especially by opposition groups who boycotted subsequent legislative elections on the grounds that there had been massive vote-rigging during the poll.

This is not the first time that economic liberalization has been attempted in Ghana. Market-oriented reforms were introduced by the National Liberation Council in the late 1960s and accelerated under the civilian government of Dr Kofi Busia in the period 1969–72, although these were brought to an abrupt end by a military coup inspired by a major currency devaluation. The short-lived government of Lieutenant-General Akuffo from 1978 to 1979 attempted to introduce stabilization measures whilst at the same time negotiating a return to civilian rule, but these were cut short by a military uprising led by Flight-Lieutenant Rawlings. In contrast, the failure of the civilian Limann Government that took office in 1979 to heed IMF/World Bank advice in the face of growing economic crisis brought political turmoil and paved the way for renewed military intervention by Rawlings and his supporters in 1981. However, none of these initiatives was sustained; until the advent of the Provisional National Defence Council (PNDC) government in 1981 civilian and military governments alike succumbed to the strains and stresses of economic management and popular discontent, seemingly unable to carry through a programme of economic liberalization whilst retaining a modicum of political legitimacy.

The present regime has gone through several distinct phases in its political evolution: the first is best characterized as one of radical populism from 1981 to 1983; the second, from 1983–9, by pragmatic authoritarianism and political decentralization; the third, by political liberalization beginning with Rawlings's decision to accede to the demand for multi-party democracy through to the 1992 elections; and the fourth current phase following his victory in the presidential elections and the installation of a limited democracy. Each can be further distinguished by the nature of the economic policies pursued. These have been associated with a process of cumulative liberalization, preceded by populist anti-corruption drives and administrative controls, and then moving through stages of stabilization, structural adjustment and institutional reforms, accompanied by measures designed to mitigate the effects of adjustment on the poor and substantial aid flows in support of the reform programme. The current phase is marked by uncertainty in the reform process and renewed macroeconomic difficulties as the elected government adjusts to new political circumstances.

When Flight-Lieutenant Rawlings took power for a second time in a military coup on 31 December 1981, few commentators could have predicted that, within two short years, anti-imperialist rhetoric would have given way to economic orthodoxy and negotiations with the IMF. How was this accomplished and why did Rawlings decide on this course of action? What implications did this have for the political complexion of the regime and what effect on the underlying class composition and political alliances in Ghanaian society? How have the institutional arrangements of the PNDC regime adapted to a more democratic political environment, and what changes have taken place in the basic economic policy package since the elections? These questions are examined for each of the various phases of the Rawlings regime identified above.

Radical populism, 1981–3

Rampant corruption and catastrophic economic mismanagement were the principal reasons for the 1981 coup, and the policies pursued by the Rawlings PNDC government from 1982 were very much a reaction to these.[10] Leading members of the PNDC advocated a self-reliant socialist development strategy characterized by the imposition of price and import controls, curbs on luxury consumption and severe anti-corruption measures. A system of popular democracy in the form of People's (PDCs) and Workers' Defence Committees (WDCs), inspired by Cuban and Libyan models, was designed to build a strong organizational base for the military regime and to promote anti-corruption drives and root out illegal trading activities. There were excesses in the form of attacks on churches, physical abuse of market traders, and destruction of property, but the government at first made no attempt to rein in the activities of the PDCs and WDCs (Haynes, 1991a: 149–52).

The first year of PNDC rule did little to alleviate existing economic problems; if anything it made matters worse. By 1983 the economy was in a state of near collapse. Price and import controls contributed to a 16 per cent decline in exports and a 36 per cent decline in imports in 1982, while inflation soared. In 1983 real GDP fell to 0.7 per cent and real GDP per capita declined by 3.1 per cent (see Table 3.3). The 1983/4 cocoa crop was just 16 per cent of what it had been in the record year of 1964/5.

A combination of factors exacerbated an already worsening

Table 3.3 Ghana: selected macroeconomic indicators, 1983–92

Year	1983	1984	1985	1986	1987	1988	1989	1990	1991
Real GDP (% change)	0.7	2.6	5.1	5.2	4.8	5.6	5.1	3.3	5.3
Real per capita GDP (% change)	–3.1	–1.3	2.4	2.5	2.1	0.0	2.0	0.2	2.2
Savings/GDP (%)	3.3	6.6	7.6	8.0	7.2	8.3	7.9	5.8	7.9
Investment/ GDP (%)	3.7	6.9	9.6	9.4	10.4	10.9	13.5	12.3	12.7
Inflation (CPI, %)	122.9	39.7	10.3	24.6	39.8	31.4	25.2	37.3	18.0
Money supply (M2, %)	56.8	37.9	43.2	49.8	52.6	44.0	50.8	29.7	4.3
Revenue/GDP (%)	8.0	9.9	13.3	13.8	13.7	13.7	15.1	13.2	15.0
Expenditure/ GDP (%)	5.5	8.0	11.3	13.6	14.1	13.5	14.4	13.0	13.7
Deficit/surplus (%)	–2.7	–1.8	–2.2	0.1	0.5	0.4	–	–	–

Sources: IMF International Financial Statistics. Ministry of Finance, Ghana.

trend. A severe drought brought severe food shortages and led to power shortages by sharply reducing the country's hydro-electric generating capacity. Forest fires destroyed one-third of the cocoa-growing areas. Foreign-exchange shortages reduced food and fuel imports, causing transportation difficulties and scarcities of essential foods and spare parts. The expulsion of up to one million Ghanaian workers from Nigeria imposed a further burden on a ravaged economy (Leith and Lofchie, 1993: 260–1).

As the situation grew increasingly critical, the government sought financial help from Libya and the Soviet Union, but with little success. Ghanaian Marxists sympathetic to the regime failed to come up with any viable policies to deal with the economic crisis (Ahiakpor, 1991: 590). Economic difficulties were compounded by political problems culminating in a series of coup attempts by disaffected junior officers and militant organizations opposed to attempts to clamp down on populist excesses. All these factors encouraged Rawlings to consider radical solutions to fill the policy vacuum (Ninsin, 1987: 28–9). In September 1982 the former law lecturer and newly appointed secretary for Finance and Economic Planning,

Kwesi Botchwey, and a small team of economic advisers began to put together a far-reaching economic recovery plan as a precursor to reopening negotiations with the IMF. This provided the basis for the signing of an agreement with the IMF for an orthodox recovery package in April 1983.[11] Some commentators suggest that the severity of the crisis left the government with little choice but to turn to the IMF. Others attribute the decision to Rawlings's pragmatism and good sense, whereas radical critics of the programme portrayed it as a betrayal of the thrust of the 1981 revolution. Whatever the motives, the reality of the situation was the adoption of an Economic Recovery Programme (ERP) which had all the ingredients of a standard IMF stabilization programme.

Economic orthodoxy and authoritarian rule, 1983–9

The first (1983–6) phase of the ERP concentrated on halting the decline in industrial production and commodity exports, and increasing import capacity with the assistance of concessional finance. A major currency devaluation was followed by a series of progressive exchange-rate adjustments. Cocoa producer prices were increased to promote exports, while price controls on most other goods were abolished. Government spending was slashed and a restrictive monetary policy introduced to hold down domestic credit and achieve positive interest rates to promote domestic savings. Rehabilitation of the physical infrastructure and investment in energy and industrial production were largely financed by concessional aid, and were designed to restore productive capacity to the levels attained five years before. The second phase (1987–9) focused on structural reforms and efforts to rebuild the country's productive base. This entailed a relaxation of quantitative trade restrictions, the removal of price distortions in the production and marketing of domestic and tradeable goods, the phasing-out of public monopolies in production and distribution through a comprehensive privatization programme, and rationalization of public sector concerns (Frimpong-Ansah, 1991: 147).

In macroeconomic terms the ERP was a success and the decline in the country's economic situation was halted. Real GDP rose by 5.1 per cent in 1985, and for the period 1985–9 averaged annual growth of 5.2 per cent (see Table 3.3). The budget deficit was virtually eliminated by 1986 and a realistic exchange rate was restored. Boosted by increased producer prices and currency devaluation, cocoa exports recovered to reach 300,000 tons by 1988/9 – double the low point of 1983/4 and 60 per cent higher than the 1981–6 average. Clearly, as Green (1988) has noted, these achievements were due as much to the recovery of food and cocoa production after the 1983 drought, as to the beneficial effects of the stabilization measures.

Not everyone benefited from the reforms, however. Indeed, the economic gains did not result in improved living standards for most Ghanaians. The absolute position of food crop producers, especially northern farmers and women food producers in the south of the country, worsened under the ERP due to a neglect of non-cocoa agriculture (Toye, 1991). Petty retail traders also lost out as wholesale and retail prices came closer into line; their profit margins were squeezed as the informal sector expanded with a corresponding increase in competition. Civil servants and workers in state-owned enterprises who lost their jobs in the process of retrenchment were a further casualty of the recovery programme.[12] The poor were adversely affected by the introduction of cost recovery mechanisms and the removal of subsidies in health and education. Measures introduced from 1988 to mitigate the social costs of adjustment had minimal impact on the welfare of lower-income groups, many of whom turned to the informal sector for employment or sought work in agriculture.[13] According to Jeffries (1992: 207) the urban poor gained least from the ERP:

> The economic gains realised since the inception of the programme have undoubtedly benefited quite large sections of the population, particularly in the rural areas. In the urban areas also, there are at least superficial signs of progress ... It is equally clear, however, that the majority of urban inhabitants in the lower income groups have experienced very little, if any, improvements in real incomes, and that some ... are probably worse off than they were six or seven years ago.

On a more positive note, the incomes of cocoa farmers improved quite significantly, especially those who were able to produce for the export market. Minimum wages were also raised above the rate of inflation and real wages doubled between 1983 and 1987 to the benefit of employees in the formal sector, although this was not achieved without concerted trade union pressure. While this represented an improvement over the situation in 1982 when real wages were 84 per cent lower than they had been in 1975, unskilled workers continued to find it difficult to make ends meet (Kraus, 1991a: 144–7).

The ERP came under mounting opposition from 1986 onwards, especially in the urban areas, as a result of the combined effects of retrenchment in employment, low incomes, high prices, the ending of subsidies and the introduction of user fees for education and health services. There were outbursts of popular resentment, and labour unions, students and left-wing opponents of the PNDC attempted to mobilize opposition to the regime, which increasingly found expression in demands for political liberalization and the creation of a democratically elected constituent assembly. Local business interests sought protection from the ERP's import liberalization which threatened the economic viability of producing for the domestic market. They were lukewarm in their response to the reforms and distrustful of the government which had been stridently anti-business in the period immediately following the coup. According to Tangri (1992: 102):

> The generally negative reaction of the PNDC to the plight of indigenous enterprises brought it into sharp conflict with members of the business community. The regime was not perceived as sufficiently supportive of the economic interests of domestic capital, let alone aiding those hurt by the operational consequences of the ERP policy reforms.

The government, which had become increasingly authoritarian during the adjustment period, responded by repressing outbreaks of discontent and arresting its leading critics. Herbst (1991: 184) points out that, while organized workers agitated about the impact of the reforms, 'union leaders clearly recognised that, given the nature and history of the PNDC regime, there were real limits to the regime's patience in confronting actual protests'. Opposition was therefore sporadic and easily suppressed.

In 1987 bilateral donors came to the assistance of the government which, until that point, had relied almost exclusively on IMF and World Bank credit to finance the recovery programme. At the Consultative Group meeting in May $800m was pledged over four years, some 30 per cent more than the government had hoped for, followed by a further $90m in 1988 in support of the Program of Action and Measures to Address the Social Costs of Adjustment (PAMSCAD), devised in consultation with UNICEF. This inflow of capital helped to offset a decline in cocoa prices on the world market and to compensate for low levels of direct foreign investment. It also boosted the adjustment programme as it was beginning to flag, and allowed the regime to relax its stringent budgetary controls and increase social spending which had been run down during the course of economic stabilization. The infusion of aid played an important role not only in sustaining the ERP but also in conditioning the pace and direction of political reform.

Amidst growing discontent with the PNDC and its economic policies the government declared its intention to hold elections to District Assemblies and sub-district bodies in December 1988 and February 1989. Some commentators saw this as an attempt to enlist rural support in the face of its unpopularity in urban areas rather than as a genuine concession to political reform (Martin, 1991: 243). Nevertheless, it did provide the first test of the government's standing and created some scope for organized political activity. The plan announced in July 1987 envisaged the creation of a four-tier structure of local government focused on 110 District Assemblies, two-thirds of whose members were to be elected by popular vote on a non-party basis, with the remainder nominated by the government. The proposed structure was framed in terms of advancing 'participatory democracy and collective decision-making at the grassroots' (Haynes, 1991b: 291). However, this occurred to only a limited extent, since the District Assemblies were at best only quasi-democratic and not genuinely representative of the popular will (Crook, 1994). While they had responsibility for a range of administrative functions such as tax collection, agricultural development, transport, industry and construction, they were obliged to operate in accordance with central government policies and PNDC-appointed District Secretaries remained in place to oversee their operations. Those elected and appointed to the Assemblies were for the most part local notables (a fifth of the PNDC nominees were traditional chiefs) and people who had benefited from the economic reforms, namely large cocoa farmers and businessmen involved in construction, transport and trade (Haynes, 1991b: 297). Hence with their formation, the PNDC reinforced its institutional base at the local level and consolidated a new class alliance supportive of the regime and its economic strategy.

Institutional and political reforms in the early 1990s

From 1989 the government laid greater stress on structural and institutional reforms, to create a more favourable investment climate and to promote sustained economic growth. These reforms were principally in the financial sector with a view to improving the efficiency of the banking system, while institutional reforms were aimed at restructuring the parastatals and improving the calibre and effectiveness of the civil service. There was slow but steady progress on privatization; in January 1994, President Rawlings announced that 49 enterprises had been liquidated, 33 sold outright and a further 14 reconstituted as joint ventures or leased to private management, with a further 221 enterprises targeted for attention (EIU, 1994b). As noted earlier, a significant feature of the economy in the late 1980s was its heavy dependence on foreign aid, although Ghana ceased to rely on IMF balance-of-payments support in 1991. Despite this high level of dependence, real GDP growth averaged 4.7 per cent per year from 1986 to 1992, and industry and services each grew on average by more than 7 per cent per year in the period 1986–90. As a result, the share of GDP accounted for by industry more than doubled over the same period, and cocoa's contribution also reflected a marked improvement in production levels.

In the early 1990s political debate increasingly centred on the national stage. Administrative decentralization failed to assuage critics of the regime who wanted the creation of a genuine multi-party democracy. Disparate groupings launched the Movement for Freedom and Justice (MFJ) in August 1990, at a time when the regime was calling for a wider debate on an appropriate political framework. There were none of the mass anti-government demonstrations that were taking place in many other African states at the time, partly because of the fear of suppression, but also because of the relative absence of corruption and economic mismanagement that had galvanized protests elsewhere (Jeffries, 1992: 224). The MFJ, while representing a sizeable current of opinion, failed to establish a strong organizational base; nor did it develop a distinctive set of alternative policies, largely because there was broad agreement on the need to persevere with the economic reforms. Opposition demands therefore centred on reforms in the political sphere and improved human rights.

Although he accepted the need to set up some kind of representative national assembly at the apex of the political system, Rawlings had consistently resisted opposition calls for a return to multi-party democracy, fearing a resurgence of the elite corruption that had consistently marred democratic politics in the past and the prospect of ethnic or regional fragmentation (Jeffries, 1992: 224–5). There was also concern that a rapid transition to representative democracy would undermine the achievements of the ERP.[14] Nevertheless, he did announce a series of measures designed to promote greater political participation, but without initially making a commitment to reintroducing multi-party politics. The first such measure was the publication in May 1991 of a report on the future of the Constitution by the National Commission for Democracy, to which the PNDC responded by signalling its intention to set up a committee of experts to formulate proposals to be debated by a consultative assembly of elected District Assembly members, representatives of various civic associations and government nominees. At the formal inauguration of the Consultative Assembly in August 1991, Rawlings announced that there would be a national referendum on the draft constitution early in 1992, followed by presidential and parliamentary elections on a multi-party basis at the end of the year.

The PNDC decision to return the country to civilian rule was clearly influenced by the new political conditionality of aid. This policy had already hastened the pace of political liberalization in other West African states and there was a distinct possibility that donors would exert this type of pressure on Ghana (Robinson, 1993). In view of the critical role of foreign aid in the second phase of Ghana's adjustment programme the PNDC did not want to jeopardize its relationship with the donors. Nevertheless, while the prospect of political conditionality undoubtedly influenced the thinking of the PNDC on this matter, it confirmed a course of action that had already been decided on. As Jeffries (1992: 225) has observed, Rawlings probably calculated that he stood a reasonable chance of winning the elections since the opposition was still relatively weak and poorly organized and the PNDC had established a firm base of support in the District Assemblies.

The transitional process began with a referendum on a new multi-party constitution in April 1992 which was overwhelmingly supported by over 90 per cent of the electorate. A number of controversial Transitional Provisions protected the previous government from prosecution and from attempts to reverse its measures. The eleven-year ban on political parties was lifted in May, although 21 old parties were proscribed and the use

of their names or symbols declared illegal. The PNDC reconstituted itself as the National Democratic Congress (NDC),
drawing its support from a coalition of clubs and membership organizations sympathetic to the government. Rawlings
accepted an invitation to stand as the NDC presidential candidate and duly won an outright victory in the November
1992 elections. Despite charges of malpractice the elections
were pronounced free and fair by the Commonwealth and
Carter Center observer groups. Victory for Rawlings was backed
up the following month by a landslide win for the NDC in
parliamentary elections, which were boycotted by the opposition parties (Adjei, 1993: 312–17). The Fourth Republic was
formally inaugurated on 7 January 1993 with Rawlings as president, this time with a mantle of democratic legitimacy.

Sustaining economic reform under civilian rule

The post-election period was characterized by political uncertainty and some degree of slippage in the country's macroeconomic performance. Pre-election fiscal excesses and generous
pay awards to public sector workers, many of whom secured
increases of 75 per cent, increased government expenditure
from 13.7 per cent of GDP in 1991 to 17.0 per cent in 1992
and forced up inflation, from 10.9 per cent in 1992 to 24.9 per
cent a year later. Real GDP growth, down to 3.9 per cent in
1992, recovered to 4.8 per cent in 1993, largely as a result
of a large increase in gold production and cocoa output, but
macroeconomic stability was undermined by fiscal profligacy
in the pre-election period (EIU, 1994b).

The 1993 budget sought to reduce the large deficit through
tough corrective measures centred on a 60 per cent increase in
petrol tax. Predictably it met with a hostile response from the
opposition parties, who criticized it as being anti-poor, though
this stance was belied by their general support for market-
oriented policies designed to boost the private sector. Nevertheless, the president adopted a more conciliatory stance at
the opening of the second session of parliament by inviting
opposition representatives to submit their views on the budget to the Speaker. The Trades Union Congress was even more
hostile, threatening an escalation of the wave of strikes that
had begun in the run-up to the presidential elections. A further wave of labour unrest was unleashed during the latter half
of 1993 over planned redundancies in the Cocoa Board, with

threats to block cocoa shipments. Despite a decline in numbers in the TUC membership and repression by the PNDC government in the 1980s, the unions had the potential to undermine the economic reform programme. The government was able to mollify them to some extent with its acceptance of the recommendations of the Salary Review Commission in June 1994 for a 20 per cent salary increase for civil servants and agreement to negotiate two-year pay deals with public sector unions.

The most significant feature of the government's economic programme was a strong commitment to private sector development. Improvements in the investment climate resulting from attempts to liberalize the economy and privatize inefficient state enterprises were cited as evidence of this, underpinned by a budget proposal to lower corporate taxes. The government was also planning to introduce a new investment code centred on a package of tax incentives, depreciation allowances and a reduction in the categories of business reserved for Ghanaians. By way of response, there were signs of increased business confidence with a 75 per cent increase in investment applications in 1993. But the new-found willingness of the government to give active support to the private sector encouraged calls from local industries for protection against cheap foreign imports. While the government maintained its opposition to blanket protectionism, it set up a Business Assistance Fund in early 1994 funded by privatization receipts to assist potentially viable domestic enterprises.

These moves indicate an acknowledgement of the potential political dividends that could result from a strategy of courting the private sector, as well as signalling a more pragmatic outlook among the NDC leadership. In the past, the credibility of the PNDC government had been dented by the revolutionary fervour of the early 1980s and the anti-business sentiments expressed by Rawlings and his colleagues. Many exiled political leaders hailed from the business community and retained a deep suspicion of the regime and its political leanings. Hence, the new pragmatism was motivated in part by a desire to promote sustained economic growth, but also by a need to broaden the political base of the NDC.

On the eve of the Fourth Republic, the four major opposition parties constituted themselves into a shadow cabinet to act as an extra-parliamentary watchdog, but tension was eased somewhat by a call to their supporters to 'give the NDC-led government a chance to prove that it is genuinely interested in the restoration of democracy' (*West Africa*, 18–24 January 1993). In response, the government adopted a strategy of political accommodation designed to bring leading opposition figures into the decision-making process, beginning with the formation of a 25-member Council of State in May 1993, which included traditional leaders as well as opposition representatives. By the end of the year, discussions were begun between government officials and opposition representatives which resulted in the formation of two committees to review the electoral system and registration procedures, and to look into the political situation in general. The opposition's willingness to participate was strengthened by two Supreme Court rulings guaranteeing them airtime on state-owned television and abolishing the requirement of police permission for processions and demonstrations. A further indication that the political climate was maturing was the decision of three of the four Nkrumahist factions to merge into a single political party in late 1993, which is expected to attract support from the labour movement and act as a significant third force in Ghanaian politics. Despite attempts to unify the disparate factions in advance of the 1996 elections, the opposition remains divided and incumbent leaders are being challenged by younger politicians from within their own parties.

Relations with the press continued to be a source of friction, however, especially over the issue of civil liberties, allegations of official corruption and delays over deregulation of the media, although more than thirty companies have now been licensed to operate private TV and radio stations. There have also been several outbreaks of localized ethnic unrest in the northern region since early 1993 which have resulted in more than 1,000 deaths and more than 150,000 people displaced from their homes.

Economic policy has become a divisive issue, with several opposition parties calling for a thorough review of the economic reform programme and restrictions on the sale of public enterprises to foreign investors. The government's decision to replace sales tax with a higher Value Added Tax in May 1995, in order to correct a large and growing fiscal imbalance, provoked a strong political reaction from the trade unions and opposition parties, who organized a series of large demonstrations to capitalize on wider resentment over the government's economic record. The shooting dead of five protestors at an opposition rally led the government to rescind the tax within two weeks of its introduction. This was later followed by the resignation of the finance minister, Kwesi Botchwey, who had been responsible for the Economic Recovery Programme since the early 1980s, but had found it increasingly difficult to keep public spending under control in the face of political imperatives. These events were indicative of the stresses and strains accompanying political liberalization, and demonstrated that the transitional process would be plagued with difficulties as civil and political liberties were gradually restored and new expectations generated in the process.

Economic reform and political liberalization under Rawlings

It is tempting to describe the Ghanaian political economy in the 1980s and early 1990s as the successful implementation of adjustment measures by a pragmatic authoritarian regime which, with the legitimacy conferred by economic success, successfully fought and won an electoral contest in order to maintain itself in power by democratic means. The reality is not so simple. A close examination of this period reveals a complex interaction between the twin prerogatives of economic reform and political liberalization. The former did not give rise to the latter in any mechanical or preordained manner. Rather, it is more accurately viewed as a protracted period of deft political manoeuvring by an astute leader, committed both to economic progress and to political survival. At the same time, sustained reform has clearly helped to bring about significant changes in the structure of the economy and the relative well-being of the various social classes, even though thirteen years is too short a time for fundamental revision of the class structure to occur. This in turn provides a backdrop to the shifting pattern of class alliances that took place under the Rawlings regime and helped to guarantee both political continuity and the sustainability of the adjustment programme.

The PNDC regime was authoritarian in that it banned political parties, suppressed popular opposition and had an unelected executive. However, it differed from most other authoritarian regimes in sub-Saharan Africa in that it successfully implemented an economic recovery programme and was relatively free of corruption. Ghana under the PNDC was in many ways the closest approximation to a 'developmental dictatorship' that Africa has seen in the post-colonial period.

The Rawlings government was able to maintain its commitment to policy reform not only by suppressing dissent and securing external support, but also by investing considerable autonomy in the small economic team led by Finance Secretary Kwesi Botchwey. According to Callaghy (1990: 275): 'The coherence, continuity, and ongoing political insulation of this economic team explains a good deal of the sustainability of the economic reform effort in Ghana'.

Although the team lacked support staff and financial and technical resources, it was highly competent and its ability to negotiate and implement policies grew with experience. It was assisted in its work by foreign consultants and advisers, usually paid by the World Bank and the IMF, although the initial motivation and the subsequent momentum of the reforms emanated from the shared commitment of the economic technocrats and the political leadership (Martin, 1991: 241). A high degree of insulation certainly contributed to the success and coherence of the ERP but it also inured the regime to criticism from those adversely affected by the reforms. As noted by Tangri (1992: 109): 'Public debate on the ERP has hardly been permitted, the press is by no means free, and opportunities to question key decisions are virtually non-existent.'[15]

Though the 1981 coup met with widespread popular approval, the PNDC came to power with a base of political support largely confined to junior officers, organized labour, student activists and left-wing intellectuals. Over time many of these became disenchanted as a result of the deleterious impact of adjustment measures on the urban working class and public sector employees. Rawlings sought to build a new class coalition to provide a firmer political foundation. Senior civil servants, a new technocratic element which had gained considerable power in the course of the reform process, and increasingly the officer corps of the military constituted its core (Kraus, 1991a: 148-9). Rawlings also retained the backing of a clutch of trade union activists by means of co-option and the use of divide-and-rule tactics (see Gyimah-Boadi and Essuman-Johnson, 1993). From the mid-1980s he had cultivated support from among the traditional chiefs, many of whom had been alienated by the radical populism of the pre-adjustment period, but responded well to the regime's overtures.

As regards mass support for the reform programme, Rawlings increasingly looked to the rural areas, and in particular the big commercial farmers who profited from the drive to increase the export of cocoa and higher producer prices. There is relatively high land concentration in the cocoa sector, with the larger farmers drawing a disproportionate share of the income from cocoa production (Anyemedu, 1993: 37–8), and of the benefit from subsidized inputs in the early years of reform. These farmers now play an important part in the District Assemblies, a role denied to the majority of small cocoa producers who are precluded from active political participation by the need for continuous attention to their holdings (Jacobeit, 1991). Farmers producing for subsistence or for the domestic market have received little benefit from the economic reforms. Moreover, their ranks have been swollen by retrenched public sector workers returning to work on the land. These changes in the agricultural economy do not amount to a major upheaval in the rural class structure but they do highlight the increased economic and political clout of the commercial farmers, whose ability to mobilize rural voters was probably instrumental in returning Rawlings to power in the 1992 presidential election.[16]

Although the reforms had an adverse impact on the living standards of some Ghanaians, especially those living in the urban areas, there is some evidence to suggest that the counterfactual argument deployed by the regime (i.e. that things would have been far worse if the reforms had not been implemented) had a degree of popular resonance.[17] It would appear that the reforms did provide the PNDC with an element of political legitimacy, although this was attributable more to the absence of economic mismanagement rather than to active popular support for the recovery programme (Anyemedu, 1993). However, this view is not shared by all analysts of Ghana's recent political history. According to Chazan (1992: 139):

> Economic liberalisation ... while sharpening political sensitivities, did not provide guarantees for orderly political change. Indeed, the case of Ghana verifies Hyden's assertion that economic improvement is an insufficient precondition for the assertion of legitimate authority.

Hence the regime did not actively seek to build a proadjustment coalition but instead relied on a centralized style of decision-making combined with the selective use of repressive measures to silence dissent and as a means of forcing through its chosen policy package.

This helps to explain the political pressures for liberalization. Key interest groups were systematically excluded from the decision-making process and the reforms failed to generate significant improvements in the living standards of ordinary Ghanaians. Urban workers and low-ranking civil servants were among those most adversely affected. The PNDC never commanded much support from the business community or from middle-class professionals, especially lawyers, who objected to its flagrant abuse of civil and political liberties. These groups were in the forefront of the struggle for political reform in the late 1980s and early 1990s, in conjunction with trade unionists and former PNDC supporters.

Without a functioning opposition in Parliament, democracy in Ghana has its limitations and the government will have to find ways of encouraging the opposition to take part in the political process without prejudicing its own mandate to rule. A major challenge in the years ahead will be for the government to sustain its commitment to reform and economic growth, while at the same time allowing for greater consultation with business leaders, trade unions and other interest groups who were excluded from the decision-making process during the PNDC period but are now organized into an influential network of voluntary and professional organizations. It also remains to be seen whether the NDC government can reconcile pressures for increased accountability and transparency in decision-making while preserving a measure of autonomy for the economic policy team. Finally, it will have to make serious efforts to tackle urban poverty and unemployment which were not addressed systematically in the 1980s. Failure to do so could create serious problems when it comes to subsequent elections, but also represents a potential source of instability during the interim period since the government will be unable to employ the repressive tactics that it relied on in the past.

Conclusion

Chile, Ghana and South Korea have successfully introduced economic reform programmes over varying periods of time and are now engaged in a process of political liberalization. The source of pressure to democratize was different in each case, and was related to economic reform in disparate ways. While there was a similar sequence of economic reform followed by political liberalization in all three cases, it was conditioned by the political calculations of the incumbent regime, the power of the opposition and external pressure. The fact that political liberalization followed economic reform rather than vice versa is significant from the point of view of the sustainability of the reform process, and there are lessons from this experience which might have wider application.

However, it should not be concluded from the case studies that there will always be a direct relationship between economic reform and political liberalization, since a highly specific set of circumstances prevailed in each of the three countries under review. The causal link is not as obvious as proponents of a complementary relationship might wish to claim, and there were a number of conjunctural factors at work which permitted countries which had undergone economic reform subsequently to liberalize their polities. Moreover, too little time has elapsed since the political reforms were initiated to form a judgement about the ability of the new regimes to sustain the momentum of the adjustment process over the longer term, while at the same time attempting to consolidate a fledgling democracy.

At this point we return to the four issues raised at the outset, namely, whether there is a common set of institutional characteristics which contributed to the successful implementation of economic reforms under authoritarian rule, the extent to which the economic reforms create the conditions in which political liberalization becomes possible, the need for institutional adaptation under democratic rule to sustain economic reforms, and the changes in economic policy required to ensure their political sustainability.

Despite differences in the content and implementation of the economic reform agendas the three countries under review shared three key institutional characteristics: the decision to reform was taken by authoritarian regimes headed by pragmatic political leaders, policies were formulated and implemented by an insulated and technically competent economic team, and dissent was met with repression.[18] The three authoritarian regimes were committed to achieving high rates of economic growth and, in the cases of Ghana and Chile, reversing economic mismanagement and decline. In short, they were wedded to a developmental state as the vehicle for promoting neo-liberal economic reforms. This sounds like a contradiction in terms, in that neo-liberal reforms are generally premised on a much reduced role for the state in economic affairs. In practice, this was achieved by strengthening some elements of state power, while at the same time cutting back its unproductive functions. In all three cases the coercive capacity of the state was reinforced, to enable it to suppress dissent and force through unpopular measures (the removal of subsidies, restrictions on trade union activity, etc.), and its policy-making capacity was strengthened and insulated from both popular pressure and political interference. Military regimes in Ghana and Chile, although they differed in their ideological complexion, slashed civil service payrolls, closed or privatized inefficient state enterprises, and removed price controls, in the process reducing the direct involvement of the state in production and regulation. Successful economic adjustment was carried through by leaner and more sophisticated state apparatuses and driven by political elites committed to economic recovery and sustained growth. But, despite the institutional similarities outlined above, economic reforms in South Korea were introduced in the context of a relatively efficient state sector and effective public administration.

There is evidence from the case studies to support the contention that the process of economic reform can in itself generate pressures for political liberalization, through its differential social impact and changes in the underlying class structure. In Korea, where the reform process was protracted, a major change in the class structure resulted from state-guided industrialization and rapid wealth creation. The middle class and, to a lesser extent, the industrial working class, who accounted for a significant majority of the population by the late 1980s, played a central role in the struggle for democracy. This emanated in part from a realization among the middle classes that the authoritarian state no longer served their interests, whereas the industrial working class was able to make more effective use of its numerical dominance in political struggle. In both Ghana and Chile, military regimes came under pressure from groups who were alienated from the economic reform process, from urban workers and civil servants who were adversely affected by the reforms, and in Ghana from domestic business groups who perceived the regime to be unsympathetic to the private sector.

On the face of it, an authoritarian state structure would not appear conducive to subsequent moves towards political liberalization, even though democratic transitions did take place in all three countries. While the process of economic reform certainly helped to create the conditions in which domestic pressure for political reform could take root, other factors played a role. In Ghana and Chile there was strong external pressure, though this did not force immediate political concessions, since aid donors wanted to avoid undermining the continuity of the economic reforms. Hence the regimes in power were able to dictate the timing of the political reforms and prepare the ground for a transition to civilian rule in order to maximize their influence on the electoral outcomes. While there was opposition to authoritarian rule at various points in all three countries, which challenged the legitimacy of the regime, this was easily suppressed. In Chile and Ghana popular opposition to authoritarian rule was often synonymous with opposition to structural adjustment, and it was only when the mainstream opposition forces accepted the need to persevere with the economic reform programme that the prospect of political liberalization became more likely. In all three cases, the authoritarian regimes conceded the principle of political reform once they were confident of the success of the economic reform efforts. At this point they were prepared to adopt a more inclusive approach to policy-making if this was likely to prove conducive to the longer-term sustainability of the economic reforms.

This leads into the question about the way in which the successor regime had to adapt its style of economic policy management and implementation to fit in with a democratic political environment. Clearly, it was no longer possible for an elected government to rely on repressive means to contain political opposition; force had to be replaced by consent achieved via the broadening of political support for the regime, for the most part through the creation of a pro-reform coalition. A key objective of the authoritarian political project in Chile and Korea was to maintain the existing balance of power through the formation of class coalitions which would support the continuation of the economic reform programme. However,

this strategy was only partially successful, since active political support was not always forthcoming from the benefici-
aries of the reform process, either because they were poorly
organized or because they were in a minority. This failure to
build a pro-reform coalition helps to explain why incumbent
regimes were unable to hold on to the reins of power in elections. Nevertheless, they incorporated institutional safeguards
into the political system to protect their interests long after
the formal handover of power. In Ghana President Rawlings's
ability to remain in power despite the failure of the PNDC
to build a pro-adjustment coalition owes more to his skilful
political manoeuvring and the opposition's boycott of the legislative elections. Although the opposition has no formal presence in the legislature, a more liberal political environment
has forced the government to seek a wider mandate for its
economic policies.

This introduces the fourth concern that underpins the analysis, namely what changes in economic policy were made by
the successor regime to ensure the political sustainability of
the reforms? There was a remarkable consistency in the economic policies favoured by the newly elected governments in
all three countries. In Chile the coalition government wanted
to avoid abrupt policy reversals which might have had an unfa-
vourable impact on business confidence and macroeconomic
stability, and to avoid giving the military a pretext for renewed
intervention. The main policy innovation was to devote more
attention to those marginalized by the economic reforms
and previously excluded from the benefits of liberalization,
through increased expenditure on targeted social welfare programmes but without creating unsustainable demands on the
public purse. In South Korea the new government was committed to further liberalization of the economy, but conceded
a series of generous wage increases in response to a wave of
strikes which greeted its accession to power in order to avoid
alienating working class support. In Ghana, where the former
regime remained in power, it continued to adhere to the essential tenets of the Economic Recovery Programme. However,
in the lead-up to the elections, public servants and workers in
government enterprises were given generous salary awards, in
the expectation that this would generate electoral dividends.
In the post-election period the government made efforts to
consult business representatives and the trade unions over

budgetary proposals and other aspects of economic policy. This was backed up by concessions on corporate taxation and generous severance payments to retrenched public sector workers, although efforts to mobilize revenue through a revamped system of indirect taxation provoked a political backlash.

All this appears to support the conclusion that successful economic reform can pave the way for political liberalization, once the outcome of the reform process is certain and likely to be sustained. The three case studies suggest that authoritarian regimes which have pursued a programme of structural adjustment and economic liberalization prior to embarking on political reform have been successful on both fronts. By comparison, countries where regimes have introduced economic and political reforms simultaneously, such as Nigeria and Mexico, have generally failed to achieve either strong democracies or sustained economic recovery. Similarly, countries which have first sought to democratize and then attempted to introduce economic reform programmes (for example, Brazil, the Philippines and Zambia) have proved markedly unsuccessful in generating sustained economic growth (Haggard and Kaufman, 1992a).

One should not conclude from the foregoing that authoritarian rule is a precondition for the successful implementation of economic reforms and that economic reform should always precede political liberalization. Rather, it suggests that economic reform may be the best starting point for regimes that happen to be authoritarian, assuming they exhibit the institutional characteristics associated with the three regimes examined in this chapter. While democratic rule is certainly desirable as an objective in its own right, it is probably unrealistic to expect authoritarian regimes which have been economically successful to attempt simultaneous economic and political reform without encountering major problems of implementation or political legitimacy. For this reason, advocates of rapid political liberalization should consider the implications of forcing the pace of political reform at a time when pragmatic authoritarian regimes are in the process of consolidating economic reforms, and should concentrate their efforts on the latter until such time as a democratic transition can be successfully negotiated and sustained. Once the process of political reform is under way, aid donors can play a supportive role in helping transitional regimes to accommodate the institutional characteristics associated with the successful implementation of economic reforms to the political requirements of democratic rule, and in assisting efforts to extend the fruits of economic reform to disadvantaged groups in order to ensure their political sustainability.

Notes

1 According to Fukuyama (1992: 44) economic liberalism 'is the recognition of the right of free economic activity and economic exchange based on private property and markets', and hence is synonymous with capitalism. Neo-liberal reforms operate on the premise that market-oriented principles and policies provide the best foundation for long-term economic growth and development, and short-run allocative efficiency is preferable to state-led intervention. Neo-liberal policy prescriptions invariably aim at minimizing the role of the state and promoting market-based solutions.

2 Although neo-liberal adherents of this type of thinking would argue that (at least until recently), while the form of regime is critical to reform outcomes, economic success is ultimately contingent on the adoption of the right mix of policies, centred on market-led growth and a much diminished role for the state. Conversely, critics of the neo-liberal view, drawing on the experience of Korea and Taiwan, highlight the centrality of the state, not only in economic policy management, but also as an economic actor in its own right. Where these two points of view converge is over the contention that authoritarian rule was in some way conducive to successful reform outcomes.

3 In the case of Korea, a partial economic liberalization was introduced in the 1960s and extended in the early 1980s, although it would be incorrect to view subsequent policy initiatives as directed towards this goal alone since selective state intervention continued to play an important role.

4 This is not to say that it lacked popular support. As noted by White, there were strong traditions of social protest and widespread labour unrest in the 1970s, although they were unable to effect any changes in the political system until the mid-1980s.

5 By September 1973 the public sector share of industry accounted for 69 per cent of the capital stock, 32 per cent of sales and 24 per cent of employment (Ritter, 1990: 170).

6 Between 1975 and 1981 there was a 31.5 per cent fall in the number of public employees; in the period 1970–86 public expenditure on housing and health dropped by more than 60 per cent and on education by a third (Lomnitz and Melnick, 1991: 4).

7 Chile's debt to private banks increased at a rate of 57 per cent per year between 1977 and 1981, reaching $15.5 billion in December 1981, compared with just $4.9 billion in December 1975 (Griffith-Jones, 1987: 27).

8 Thirty per cent of the economically active population in Greater Santiago was involved in the informal sector in 1988, many of whom were from the middle class who had lost jobs in the public and private sectors (Lomintz and Melnick, 1991: 6).

9 For a detailed account of the government's decision to continue with the trade, exchange rate and macroeconomic policies of the previous government see

Arriagada Herrera and Graham (1994: 271–3). For a more critical account of economic policy under the Aylwin government see Petras and Leiva (1994: 167–82).

10 There had been consistent economic decline from the early 1970s. By 1981, real GDP was 15 per cent lower than in 1974 (Rothchild, 1991: 5).

11 According to Jeffries (1991: 164), Botchwey played a key role in persuading Rawlings of the need for a radical change of course, by demonstrating how past policies had primarily benefited a small privileged urban elite to the detriment of rural small-holders who would gain from a market-determined pricing policy.

12 The size of the Cocoa Board's payroll fell from 100,000 to 50,000 employees (half of these were allegedly 'ghost workers') in the mid-1980s, and 29,000 public sector workers and civil servants had been laid off by mid-1989 (Kraus, 1991a: 147).

13 Kraus (1991b: 33) reports that by the mid-1980s the informal sector accounted for 85 per cent of employment in Ghana.

14 This was reflected in a speech by Rawlings to activists of the Committees for the Defence of the Revolution in March 1991, when he accused donors of failing to acknowledge that a viable economy was a central prerequisite for sustaining democracy (Africa Confidential, 19 April 1991).

15 Herbst (1991: 188) quotes a senior trade union official from an interview in 1989 which attests to this lack of consultation, even with groups putatively aligned with the regime: 'The impression given is that the TUC is part of the planning process but it is not. Since 1983 the TUC has not been consulted. We are not in a position to participate.'

16 The election results indicated that the NDC performed poorly in Ashanti prov-ince, which is the main cocoa-growing region. Although it won all 33 seats in the legislative elections, the 20 per cent voter turnout was one of the lowest in the country (West Africa, 11–17 January 1993). This paradox could partly be attrib-uted to ethnic factors, as the Rawlings regime was popularly perceived to be Ewe-dominated, indicating that the economic gains received by cocoa farmers were not translated directly into political support.

17 Jeffries (1992: 223) found that over half the respondents in a survey conducted among lower-income groups in three urban areas in 1990–1 feared that a handover of power in multi-party elections would reverse the economic gains under the ERP and waste the sacrifices that many of them had endured.

18 This is somewhat at variance with the view that structural adjustment and stabilization programmes will only succeed if they are deliberated and ratified by representative political institutions rather than imposed in the form of techno-cratic blueprints (Bresser Pereira et al., 1993). Of course, the regimes which pre-sided over economic reform in South Korea, Ghana and Chile were very different from authoritarian governments elsewhere in Africa and Latin America, many of which were corrupt, extractive and incapable of promoting economic growth.

4

Faustian bargains: democratic control over military and security establishments

ROBIN LUCKHAM

Introduction: the military factor in transitions to democracy

The contradictory relationship between democracy and military power

The military and repressive apparatuses of the state may not seem the best vantage point from which to study democratization. Some would question whether they belong to the story of democracy at all, except as its antithesis. However, as Tilly (1985) has argued, the emergence of liberal democracy in the West was linked historically to the industrialization of warfare and the creation of professional military establishments in modern nation-states. It was partly because rulers had to persuade emerging bourgeoisies to fund wars and colonial conquests, and conscripts to risk their lives, that they became accountable to parliaments and electorates. This historical compact became the basis of what Huntington (1957) calls 'objective' civilian control over professional military establishments. It worked because in Europe and North America military force was used to serve the purposes of expanding imperial states, more than to coerce domestic opponents. Hence the temptation to politicize military establishments was less, and they were more easily subordinated to the civilian executive; in exchange, they were conceded considerable institutional and professional autonomy. Thus, major concentrations of corporate power developed around Western military–industrial complexes, reaching their apogee during the Cold War, without coming into conflict with democratic institutions.

The contradictory relationship between these arrangements and democracy is revealed in the theory and practice of 'national security'. The discourse of security holds that the safety of the state, that of the political community and that of its citizens are necessarily connected. What gives it ideological force is the idea that all citizens are protected, in the same way that all enjoy democratic rights and freedoms. Security is supposedly a public good, and the state uses force on behalf of the collectivity of citizens. Yet the basic fact is that the means of coercion are controlled exclusively by the state, and are deployed by the most secretive and least accountable of all its bureaucracies, usually in defence of established interests.

In the South, durable accommodations between democracy and military power have been even harder to achieve. Authoritarian or military regimes, rather than democracies, have until recently been the most common form of governance. Partly this has reflected a basic feature of politics in the South, namely that the social product tends to be allocated through extra-economic means (including coercion) rather than the capitalist market-place (Sangmpam, 1993). Partly it is because states and ruling classes have acquired advanced technologies of warfare and repression from industrial countries, assuring them a capacity to use force that bears little relation to their real ability to govern or to win the consent of their citizens (Tilly, 1985). And partly it is the result of the specific historical conditions of the Cold War era, in which military aid and arms supplied by major world powers sustained authoritarian regimes and equipped them for 'low-intensity conflict' against their opponents.

Moreover, until recently authoritarian regimes could garner international respectability from the presumption that 'strong' or 'hard' states were required for rapid material progress: a diagnosis shared not only by conservative theorists of 'political order' (Huntington, 1968), but also by analysts of the 'bureaucratic-authoritarian' (O'Donnell, 1978) or 'developmental' (Gregor, 1979) state and by Leninist proponents of the command economy. Such views had an important influence on policies: directly upon those of individual donors such as the United States or France, which justified provision of military and economic aid to authoritarian regimes in terms of alleged links between 'security' and 'development' (Commission on Security and Economic Assistance, 1983; Luckham, 1982 and 1990); and implicitly on those of international financial institutions, like the IMF and the World Bank, even though their official mandate does not permit them to consider the political credentials of regimes.

The reasons, including the termination of the Cold War, for the paradigm shift from authoritarianism to democracy are discussed elsewhere in this volume. Most actual transitions to democracy have been protracted, contested, contradictory and incomplete. They have usually started with the opening up of democratic opportunities and spaces under authoritarian rule – what Sklar (1987) calls 'democracy in parts' and others 'political liberalization'[1] – precipitating crises, from which regimes must either retreat by reconsolidating dictatorship, or move forward by conceding a transition to democracy. According to the liberal democratic story, the transition is complete when power is transferred to a government chosen in fair and freely contested elections. But this does not mean that the struggle for democracy is over, except in a purely formal sense. Military and security establishments in most new democracies remain formidably equipped to reintervene if they fear that their privileges are threatened, or that the new government might jettison the policies (like neo-liberal economic reform, or containment of the revolutionary Left) instituted under authoritarian rule. Once acquired, their habits of power, practices of repression and capacities for political surveillance are not lightly surrendered. Nor can it be assumed that elected governments, themselves not necessarily free from authoritarian tendencies, will be willing or able to bring them to heel.

The uncertainties of democratic transition

Recent analytical models of democratization have concentrated on 'pacted' transitions, usually involving complex negotiations between military hardliners and reformers and civilian moderates and radicals (O'Donnell and Schmitter, 1986; Przeworski, 1991). These models are seriously incomplete. In many instances, bargains among elites are improvised in the context of crises precipitated by events over which they have little control. Authoritarian governments themselves have varied in their willingness and ability to manage their own demise. The final outcome of any process of political reform is often hard to predict, and does not necessarily resemble the initial plans of the reformers, all the more so where regimes and their military structures are liable to fracture or implode.

Figure 4.1 presents a stylized categorization of possible

Figure 4.1 Different paths to uncertain democracies

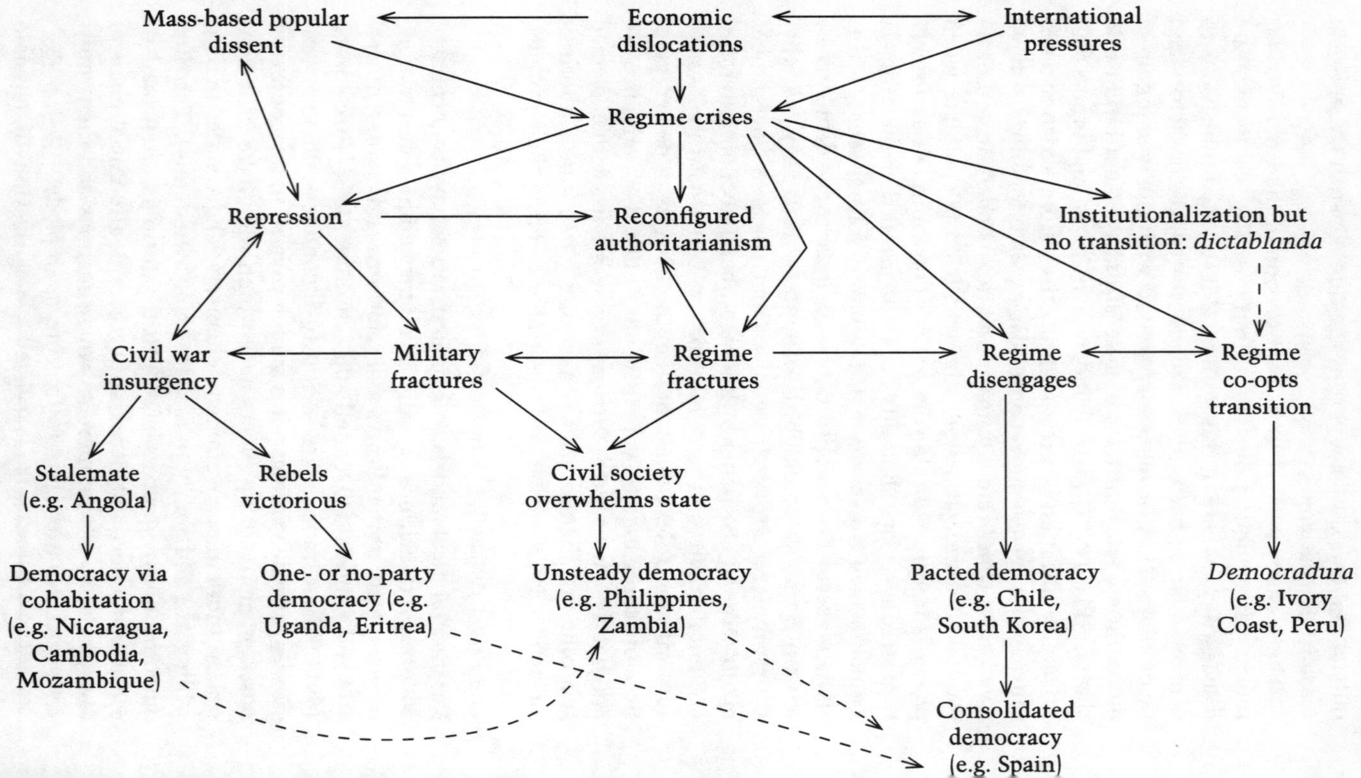

outcomes, and of the various factors producing them. To summarize, international pressures, economic dislocations (like, for instance, those created by structural adjustment) and popular protests combine to generate crises that undermine regimes (lines 1 and 2). The latter may respond (line 3) in a number of ways, and it is here that the political calculations of elites come into play: by simply repressing dissent; by reconfiguring authoritarian regimes, for instance through palace coups against the existing leaders; by attempting to 'institutionalize' themselves through ruling parties or corporate links with civilian elites; or by disengaging and initiating some kind of transition to a more democratic political system. Whether any of these succeeds depends on circumstances the regime may or may not be able to control (line 4). Repression may generate further mass protest, leading to armed revolt or civil war. Military establishments may fracture, resulting in counter-coups, revolutions and political instability. Regimes may also decompose, sometimes opening up the space for liberalization, at other times merely aggravating instability. The possibilities categorized in Figure 4.1 include fully consolidated liberal democracy, as in Spain or Greece; pacted or partially consolidated liberal democracy, encumbered with exclusions or limits, as in Chile or South Korea; *democradura*, or quasi-authoritarian regimes in a democratic shell, as in Ghana or Peru; varieties of unsteady democracy, as in the Philippines or Zambia; revolutionary or populist one- or no-party 'democracies' established after successful uprisings or wars of liberation, as in Uganda or Eritrea; and democracies based on uneasy cohabitations between formerly warring parties, as in Nicaragua, Cambodia or Mozambique.

Such categories are by no means exhaustive,[2] and they classify situations which are in reality highly ambiguous and fluid. Moreover, they do not exclude further progression to more consolidated democracy or regression back to limited democracy, reconfigured authoritarianism or outright military rule.

Consolidating democratic control in new democracies

The remainder of this chapter will focus on just one of the possibilities sketched in Figure 4.1, namely 'pacted' transitions in which military-based authoritarian regimes negotiate a transfer of power to elected civilians under a liberal democratic constitution. This is partly because most countries where transitions to democracy have so far succeeded have in fact followed such a path. At the same time, the problems of controlling military and security establishments have manifested themselves even in such apparently 'successful' transitions, raising wider issues about military power and its relationship to democracy, that are relevant in all new democracies. These issues can be discussed under five main headings:

(1) The first and most obvious question is how the military can be prevented from intervening or reintervening, or from using the threat to do so, to shape the new political order in accordance with its interests. Clearly this is not a problem that can easily be resolved by constitutional and legal bans against coups. Much of the answer lies beyond military establishments themselves: in democratic institutions that function effectively and remain legitimate; in an active civil society in which social and political forces remain strong enough to deter military intervention; in economies that grow and redistribute resources so as to minimize discontent and conflict; and in an international environment that supports democratic institutions. But even the more prosperous Southern democracies cannot entirely discount the possibility of military intervention during periods of political upheaval; all the more so in the great majority of developing countries, where conditions are far less propitious.

Nevertheless, a sizeable minority of developing countries have never experienced military rule (e.g. India, Côte d'Ivoire, Malaysia, Senegal, Zambia or Zimbabwe) or have enjoyed long periods of civilian rule after periods of military dictatorship (e.g. Chile before 1973 or Venezuela since 1958). Those who have tried to explain military *non*-intervention (Goldsworthy, 1981 and 1986; Decalo, 1989 and 1991) in such countries have come up with long lists of factors that may be individually plausible, but scarcely add up to a parsimonious general explanation (Luckham, 1994). Moreover, not all the techniques of civilian control they enumerate – such as bribing the armed forces with higher salaries and more weapons, giving officers access to the spoils of office, ethnic manipulation of appointments and promotions, penetration of the officer corps by the intelligence services and the ruling party, or the use of parallel security structures to counterbalance the regular forces – can be considered conducive to *democracy*. Often they simply stabilize one variety or another of civilian autocracy. Hence, even if civilian rule is a necessary condition for the consolidation of democracy, it is by no means sufficient.

(2) A second set of problems relates to the prerogatives and structure of military bureaucracies themselves. The relationship between democracy and military professionalism is difficult enough in advanced democracies. In countries emerging from authoritarian rule it tends to be yet more contradictory. Dangers come from two directions. In countries like Chile or South Korea, the armed forces have often taken advantage of their control of the state to push forward the boundaries of professional autonomy (column 1 of Table 4.1). However, there have been risks in too little as well as too much professionalism, especially in the weaker military structures that have emerged in other parts of the South. Whilst military factionalism and indiscipline have brought down many an authoritarian regime, they have often proved just as destabilizing to the civilian governments succeeding them. Indeed in sub-Saharan Africa, almost all the 'returns to civilian rule', before the recent round of transitions, were aborted, most of them by factional coups or revolts originating in the ranks[3] (as in Ghana during 1979–81).

(3) Military establishments tend to acquire new political as well as professional prerogatives under authoritarian rule (column 2 of Table 4.1) that they are often reluctant to give up. In some new democracies like Brazil and Pakistan, Faustian bargains have been struck, with military and security establishments granted powers to police the political order, and to continue as virtual states within the state. Elsewhere incoming democratic governments have attempted to compress the military's privileges into the professional sphere, against resistance from the elites most deeply implicated in the 'military as government', but not necessarily from the entire profession. As we shall see in the case studies, some members of the officer corps may oppose political involvement, either because they have not shared in its perks and benefits, or because they believe it diminishes their professional competence.

(4) Further issues arise in relation to the prerogatives of the shadowy security bureaucracies (column 3 of Table 4.1), which can give them immense leverage. Unlike the military, they cannot usually stage coups. But they can make life extremely difficult for incoming governments which try to restrict their influence and activities.

Table 4.1 Prerogatives of military and security establishments

1. Military professional prerogatives	2. Military political prerogatives	3. Prerogatives of security bureaucracies	4. Authoritarian residues in state and regime
No overall Defence Ministry	Active-duty officers in cabinet	Peak intelligence agencies insulated from political control by civilian executive	Perpetuation of national security state/ ideology
De facto command by service chiefs, not the civilian executive	Active and retired officers in many government posts	Lack of routine parliamentary oversight of intelligence matters	Heavy burden of military spending
Absence of routine legislative hearings on defence/military matters	AF in command of police or gendarmerie units	Continued existence of special security agencies	Resort to states of emergency during crises
Armed Forces (AF) still control top military appointments	AF in control of national intelligence agencies	Continued existence of paramilitaries and terror squads	Secrecy paramount in defence and security affairs
AF set standards for appointments and promotions	AF have autonomous role in internal security operations/ surveillance of dissent	Special courts/ legal procedures for security matters	Absence of parliamentary/ media debate of defence and security issues
Substantial AF control over military organization, doctrine, education and reform	AF maintain independent links with sympathetic political groups/ parties	Security bureaucracies exempt from judicial scrutiny in regard to human rights abuses	Extensive corporate ties between military, security, state and economic elites
AF effectively control own budgets, procurement and force levels	AF have access to independent sources of finance	Intelligence agencies involved in efforts to manipulate media and public opinion	Weak legal and political protections against human rights abuses
Military insulated from civil society and governed by different standards (e.g.	Military participation in 'strategic' economic activities including defence industries	Extensive covert links between	

Table 4.1 Cont'd

1. Military professional prerogatives	2. Military political prerogatives	3. Prerogatives of security bureaucracies	4. Authoritarian residues in state and regime
in regard to labour rights) Military personnel largely exempt from civilian justice	Active-duty or retired officers manage many state enterprises AF keep independent links with external suppliers of arms/military assistance	security bureaucracies and foreign powers	

Sources: Adapted from Pion-Berlin (1992); Stepan (1988, chapter 7); Zaverucha (1993).

(5) The final set of issues relates to the political behaviour and commitment to democracy of the new governments themselves (column 4 of Table 4.1). Many of the new regimes now being installed in the South are 'restricted' (Rueschemeyer *et al.*, 1992), 'exclusionary' (Remmer, 1985–6), 'low-intensity' (Gills *et al.*, 1993) or 'delegative' (O'Donnell, 1994) versions of democracy. Some, like the present government of President Rawlings in Ghana, directly continue the outgoing authoritarian regimes in a more democratic guise. In others, the ruling parties may have been initiated by the old regime, financed by its intelligence agencies (as in South Korea), or have become vehicles for the political ambitions of retired officers. Even when not beholden to their predecessors, democratically elected presidents or prime ministers have on many occasions declared states of emergency, suspended rights, dismissed legislatures, locked up opponents and called the military and police out in their support, like President Fujimori in Peru. In other words, the dangers of authoritarian regression within a formally democratic shell may be as great as, and certainly are more insidious and difficult to detect than, those of direct military reintervention.

Hence the government's capacity to control powerful, non-accountable security bureaucracies remains a major danger to democracy even in nominally 'democratic' polities. This is why it is vital that there be established procedures for *demo-cratic* accountability with respect to the military and security establishments, not merely civilian control. In other words, democratization requires a systematic reduction of many of the military's professional prerogatives and of most, if not all, of its political prerogatives; of the special powers of security and intelligence agencies; and of many other authoritarian residues entrenched at the heart of the state. The list is comprehensive (see Table 4.1) and covers matters given too little attention in advanced democracies, let alone in the fragile democracies of the South.

The case studies

The case studies in this chapter will consider the lessons of three apparently 'successful' transitions, in South Korea, Chile and Ghana, in each of which different forms of democracy have been 'pacted'. Each was until recently ruled by a strong and effective authoritarian government, heavily reliant on its military, police and intelligence establishments. But, contrary to appearances, neither the regimes nor their military and security apparatuses were entirely monolithic, nor could they indefinitely suppress political protest, in the face of increased international as well as domestic pressure to democratize. And in all three, they did so pre-emptively: organizing their retreat from power so as to ensure continuity in economic policy, protect established socio-economic interests and preserve their own military power base.

These are defensible reasons for concentrating on these three countries, rather than those where the course of political and economic reforms may not have been quite as smooth. In the first place, other countries may have something to learn from the way in which reductions in military powers and prerogatives have been brought about. Secondly, they each in different ways illustrate the limited and provisional nature of the democracies that have been installed, and the pitfalls that lie in the path to democracy, even in these apparent paradigm cases. Thirdly, the three embody pertinent variations in development, political structure and military organization, ranging from South Korea with its relatively advanced capitalist economy and massive military machine at one end of the scale, to Ghana with its less prosperous economy, weaker military structures and more fragile democracy at the other.

South Korea: democratization within a garrison state

Before 1987 South Korea was a virtual model case of developmental dictatorship; run by a strong government, backed by large, well-equipped military and security bureaucracies, it had enjoyed almost unprecedented rates of economic growth since the early 1960s. Over the next five or six years it made an apparently successful transition to democracy. The military retired to barracks, and the economic expansion barely faltered. What went right, and what, if any, are the lessons for other developing countries?

The consolidation of developmental dictatorship

South Korea's historical circumstances have been in several respects unique. Its position at one of the epicentres of the Cold War encouraged the build-up of immense military and repressive apparatuses and their entrenchment at the heart of the state and the political process. From the initial US-supported build-up of the 1950s, the active-duty strength of the armed forces has been maintained more or less continuously at more than 600,000 (mainly conscript) men with around 60,000 officers, constituting the sixth or seventh largest military force in the world. Added to these have been part-time reserves of up to 4.5 million, a paramilitary civilian defence corps of 3.5 million, and large police and intelligence establishments (the Korean Central Intelligence Agency (KCIA) alone numbering more than 370,000 within three years of its creation in 1961 (Kim, 1990: 136)). Military spending has been correspondingly high, averaging around 30 per cent of the budget (Park, 1993: 80), more than keeping pace with the country's remarkable 9.5 per cent annual real GNP growth (Kim, 1984: 18), and pushing the military share of GNP to a peak of over 6 per cent in 1980 falling to around 4 per cent of GDP by 1990 (SIPRI, 1992). There has been massive investment in sophisticated weapons-systems, and in building up the defence-industrial base, so that by 1991 the proportion of the defence budget spent on arms and equipment had risen to 35 per cent, compared with 38 per cent for personnel (*Far Eastern Economic Review (FEER)*, 26 September 1991). In sum, the South Korean state was, and to a significant extent remains, a national security or garrison state; in permanent confrontation with an even more heavily garrisoned North Korea; locked into an alliance system with the United States; presiding over a highly militarized society; and linked to an economy in which militarization has been 'at the core of economic transformation' (Hamilton and Tanter, 1987: 80).

This militarization has been reflected in its political arrangements (see Table 4.2). From Major-General Park Chung Hee's transformation into a 'civilian' presidential candidate in 1963, the governments up to 1988 were neither strictly speaking military, nor in every particular dictatorships. As Han (1990: 319–20) has observed, 'even during the height of political repression, opposition parties, elections, policy debates and the subsystem autonomy of various non-official groups and institutions have existed and been meaningful, although only to a limited extent'. Yet at the same time, 'despite appearances, the denial of democracy . . . was a systematic policy', and political rights and freedoms were narrowly restricted under the national security and anti-Communist laws at the 'juridical core of the authoritarian state' (Gills, 1993: 226 and 230). But even if only lip service was paid to democracy, this still kept limited spaces open for dissent, and helped preserve political values and practices (of voting and party organization, etc.) that could be re-activated when the political system was eventually liberalized.

The ruling bloc constructed itself upon impressively solid foundations, namely the military establishment, the security and intelligence services, the state bureaucracy, Korean capital (in particular the *chaebol* or large capitalist conglomerates) and the US alliance system. Yet Park and his successors maintained a clear separation between the military government and the military as an institution, partly by constituting a new political class of ex-officers, who retired on taking up political or administrative positions. These ex-military men dominated the Cabinet, comprising some 46 per cent of Park's ministers during 1961–71, 31 per cent of those serving under the 1972–9 Yushin Constitution, 33 per cent of Chun's Cabinet during 1980–7 (Kim, 1990: 123) and 28 per cent of Roh's administration in 1988 (Cotton, 1991: 214). They were similarly prominent in top administrative and parastatal positions. In theory the military establishment itself was 'constitutionally mandated to be politically neutral and to maintain professionalism', but at the same time it was the power base of the regime. The discordance between these two roles 'resulted in the development

Table 4.2 South Korea: a profile of regimes and their economic and military policies

Dates	Government	Type	Economic policies	Military control
1945–48	US military government	Foreign occupation	Foreign military and economic aid subsidizes economy	By occupying power
1948–60	President Rhee	Authoritarian presidential rule under democratic constitution	Continued foreign subsidies; with import-substituting industrialization (ISI)	Through patronage and corruption; backed by US military guarantee
1960–61	Prime Minister Chang	Fragile democracy	External subsidies; with ISI	Government fails to reform or control military
1961–63	Junta headed by General Park	Military rule	Transition from ISI and reduction of external aid	Military and political hierarchies fused
1963–71	President Park	Democratic forms, authoritarian substance	Export-oriented industrialization (EOI), promoted by active state	Military as institution differentiated from military as government; controlled through adroit combination of professionalism, patronage and surveillance by intelligence services
1972–79	President Park (Yushin Constitution)	Authoritarian form and substance	EOI with industrial deepening, promoted by state	
1980–88	President Chun	Authoritarian; limited liberalization after 1985	EOI with pressures to liberalize economy	
1988–92	President Roh	Partial democratization in both form and substance	EOI with partial economic liberalization	Slow military disengagement from political roles
1993–	President Kim	Liberal presidential-type democracy; single-party dominance protects ruling-class interests	EOI with partial economic liberalization	Military and security bureaucracies further professionalized and subordinated to civilian executive

of an informal network of control and an untenable and uncertain locus of power', which was held in place by personal patronage and a criss-crossing surveillance network (Kim, 1984: 24).

Much of the day-to-day business of political control was in the hands of the intelligence bureaucracies, notably the KCIA, established soon after the 1961 coup. The latter not only undertook surveillance and repression against Communists and others believed to threaten the security of the state; under its first Director, Kim Jong-Pil (later to be Park's Prime Minister), it organized and funded electoral victory for the ruling Democratic Republic Party (DRP), which, like the Democratic Justice Party (DJP) under Chun, was palpably the party of the state security apparatus and its business allies. Although under Chun the KCIA (or Agency for National Security Planning (ANSP) as it was renamed) became less powerful, sharing its influence with other agencies, like the Defense Security Command (DSC) and the Army Intelligence Command (AIC), the deep involvement of the security bureaucracies in every area of political and economic life remained.

The regime was consolidated not simply through these techniques of political control, but also by its delivery of material progress in the form of sustained expansion in the economy. Yet broad categorizations of the South Korean state as 'bureaucratic-authoritarian' (Cumings, 1989) or as a 'neo-mercantile security state' (Kim, 1990) obscure certain important differences from other developmental dictatorships, notably in Latin America, with which it is commonly compared (Cotton, 1992). Moreover, although the economy was reformed to make it highly competitive in the global capitalist market-place, it was never restructured on neo-liberal principles as in Chile (Kim and Geisse, 1988).

The state's leading role in promoting export-oriented industrialization and in subsequent moves towards economic liberalization was described in Chapter 3. A crucial reason for its interventionism is to be found in the background and national security interests of its military leaders. Park and the generation of officers who served under the Japanese military occupation were peculiarly conscious of the connection between industrial and military strength. Moreover, they wanted to reduce Korea's strategic and economic dependence upon the United States, especially after the latter started cutting its support during the 1960s and 1970s. The Five-Year Economic

Development Plans instituted during the 1960s were followed up by five-year Force Improvement Plans to re-equip the armed forces. The *chaebol* were given inducements to build up defence industries, mainly on the basis of licensed production of US weapons-systems. Massive surveillance by the security agencies of all forms of radical politics and trade union activity tilted the political balance in favour of capitalist employers and exerted downward pressure on wage costs. In sum, whilst the national security state emerged from Cold War confrontation and the US alliance to become the instrument of the military elite's nationalist ambitions, it was also inseparable from the country's model of capitalist development.

Cracks in the monolith

The above characterization of a strong militarized state orchestrating rapid capitalist growth requires qualification in three major respects. First, though domestically strong, the Korean state and its military establishment have remained laterally dependent, especially upon the United States. After the Korean War, that dependence was immense, but by the late 1960s most of the US subventions had been phased out, and by the late 1980s the US Congress was insisting on Korea contributing to the costs of its own protection under 'burden-sharing' arrangements. Nevertheless its defence is still to a large extent managed by the United States under the complex arrangements of the UN and US–Korea Combined Forces Command, with its network of bureaucratic and intelligence linkages. It participates in a wider regional division of strategic and economic labour, under which, on the one hand, 'the coercive capacities of the South Korean state function as the *completion* of the Japanese state: that is, without the ROK [Republic of Korea] Army, Japan would have to reconsider its entire military posture' (Cumings, 1989: 14); and on the other hand the Korean economy benefits from easy access to Japanese and US markets and finance. Though these arrangements have been modified as the economy has grown stronger, and as defence ties with the United States have been renegotiated, Korea's domestic politics have remained extremely sensitive to changes in US–Korean relations. On the US side, there has been a gradual switch from *de facto* support of the regime to open promotion of democracy in the late 1980s. On the Korean side, nationalism and anti-Americanism have surfaced not only in the opposition, but also in the military elite's own desire for an industrially and militarily strong state, able eventually to disengage from the United States.

Secondly, the authoritarian regime was never entirely monolithic or completely stable. There was not only massive state repression, but also limited constitutional government, kept alive against all the odds by prolonged opposition from the far from submissive *chaeya seryok* ('forces in the field'): dissident students, intellectuals, Christians, urban workers, and other civil society groups described in Chapter 5. The country has passed through prolonged periods of upheaval (in 1945–52; 1958–62; 1969–72; 1978–82; and 1986–90), each of which, except the last, was followed by authoritarian reconsolidation. These crises kept alive the promise of democratic politics under authoritarian conditions.

Thirdly, despite their professionalism and esprit de corps, the military and security establishments have never been completely united. Both Presidents Park and Chun were brought to power by coups carried out by relatively small groups of officers, who directly challenged the existing military command, Park indeed dying in 1979 at the hands of his own security chief. Both Park and Chun in theory insulated the active-duty military establishment from politics, but in practice relied on personal followings, including serving as well as retired Army officers. Officer factions based on graduating classes of the Korean Military Academy (KMA), regional cliques like the so-called TK mafia, and secret societies, like the Hanahoe ('One Society'), have dominated the micropolitics of the armed forces and of the regime. The eighth graduating class led the 1961 coup, and its members held leading government positions under Park. A secretive faction in the eleventh class (to which Chun and Roh belonged) formed the Hanahoe society which a select few from each subsequent class were invited to join. Hanahoe members from the eleventh, seventeenth and nineteenth classes formed the core of Chun's conspiratorial group in 1979 and of his subsequent government. Whilst factional divisions have complicated the problems of bringing the military under political control, they have also fostered political pluralism. Indeed, some former officers have joined (often conservative) opposition parties: like Kim Jong Pil who took the rump of Park's DRP into opposition under Chun; or General Chong Sung-hwa, the former Army Chief of Staff dismissed by Chun in 1979, who was elected to the National Assembly in 1987 as a member of Kim Young Sam's Reunification and Democratic Party (RDP).

At different times, professionalism has both encouraged and discouraged military involvement in politics. It was a factor in the original 1961 coup, when middle-ranking officers criticized the democratic government's failure to reform a military hierarchy that had become politically subservient, corrupt and inefficient under Rhee. There was strong corporate military support for the policies of containing Communism and building a powerful developmental state, and it was fear of their dilution that swung the military establishment behind Park's authoritarian Yushin Constitution in 1971–2 and Chun's seizure of power in 1979–80. Yet by the late 1980s much of the officer corps seemed to have come round to the view that further resistance to political liberalization would damage its professional interests, reopen internal divisions and compromise the strategic relationship with the USA, especially now that the latter was openly pushing for democracy.

In so doing, it was responding to economic transformations that had created an economy too complex to be managed by the directive methods of the past, a business class starting to detach itself from the regime, and assertive groups in civil society. Even so, the military establishment itself has remained (despite acquiring advanced armaments) a huge hierarchical, labour-intensive, Fordist structure. It can no longer claim to be 'a leading engine of economic growth as it was during the 1960s. It has lost the edge in managerial and industrial skills to the private sector' (*FEER*, 14 March 1991). And this is now reflected in low military pay levels relative to other occupations, falling numbers of well-educated candidates applying to the service academies, and low prestige in opinion polls relative to other professions.[4]

Bringing the military and security establishments under control

It was such 'antinomies of success' (Hamilton and Tanter, 1987) that ultimately undermined the military elite's faith in its capacity to rule, and gave its opponents political space in which to organize. To begin with, it seemed as if the transition to the 'low-intensity' democracy outlined in Chapter 3 might leave the fundamentals of a militarized state intact (Cumings, 1989).

Even after President Roh Tae Woo purged his Cabinet of Chun appointees in December 1988, 7 of his 25 ministers were former army officers; and many members of the ex-military elite remained entrenched in the party and state apparatuses. Military spending continued rising, at least until 1991 when it declined for the first time in three decades. Draconian national security and anti-Communist laws remained in force, and were used against opposition figures who initiated contacts with North Korea. The strikes and labour unrest that spread during 1987–9 were dealt with severely by phalanxes of national combat police and the *kusadae* ('save the company corps') of the large corporations.

Nevertheless the Roh, and far more decisively the Kim Young Sam administration elected in December 1992, initiated efforts to bring the military and security establishments under firm civilian control, as well as to renegotiate their ties with the United States. In 1990 the previously autonomous armed services were placed under an Armed Forces Chief of Staff responsible to the Minister of Defense. Senior promotion procedures were reformed so as to emphasize professional criteria and diminish political manipulation. Soon after assuming office in 1993, President Kim Young Sam shocked the military establishment by appointing a relatively junior former Major-General as his Defense Minister, and by replacing the Army Chief of Staff and the commander of the DSC, both members of the Hanahoe society, which he now denounced openly (*FEER*, 1 April 1993: 25). This was followed by the arrest of senior Navy, Marine Corps and Air Force officers, including the retired heads of all three services, for alleged corruption in regard to officer promotions.

Even more controversially, President Kim castigated Chun and Roh's mobilization of troops after Park's 1979 assassination as 'tantamount to a coup d'état in which lower ranking officers disobeyed the orders of superior officers' (*FEER*, 27 May 1993: 15), removing four generals, including the chairman of the Joint Chiefs of Staff, for having participated (Lee and Sohn, 1994: 3–4). He praised the Kwangju uprising of 1980 as a 'pro-democracy movement' and declared its anniversary a public holiday and (in 1995) initiated the prosecution of Chun, Roh and other military figures for suppressing it.

The political activities of the intelligence and security services were also cut back. After it was revealed in 1990 that the

DSC was monitoring opposition politicians, President Roh dismissed its head, shut its interrogation bureau and reduced the number of agents. More restrictions were imposed by President Kim in 1993, when he stripped the DSC of all powers unrelated to military affairs, and made it responsible to the Minister of Defense. The ANSP was similarly cut down to size, being forbidden to participate in the ruling party's 1992 election strategy meetings, monitor journalists, 'advise' editors, and tap the phones of the opposition parties. As Kim put it, the ANSP 'has to change from being a Savak to a Mossad' (*FEER*, 15 October 1992), an analogy those familiar with the latter's operations might not find entirely reassuring. Yet the agency still reports direct to the President, is controlled through special legislation, largely escapes parliamentary scrutiny, and still continues to enforce the country's draconian National Security Law.

The military budget became another target of reform. In 1991 a major public debate developed after the Defense Ministry proposed large increases in military spending, to hold it at a constant 4.5 per cent of GNP. Not only the opposition parties and reform groups like the Citizens' Coalition for Economic Justice, but also the Federation of Korean Industries, called for deep cuts, revealing a serious decline in business support for the military (*FEER*, 26 September 1991). More rifts were exposed by the long-running dispute over the Korean Fighter Program, under which a military aircraft industry was being created on the basis of licensed production of US-designed planes. The competition between rival bids was characterized by vicious in-fighting within the *chaebol*, the military and the bureaucracy, peppered with allegations of corruption and undue political influence. The McDonnell Douglas–Samsung Aerospace F/A 18 consortium appeared to have won the competition in 1989, but the decision was reversed in favour of the General Dynamics–Daewoo Industries F16 in 1991, only for the issue to be reopened by President Kim in 1993, when two former defence ministers, the former chiefs of staff of the Air Force and Navy and a former presidential security adviser were prosecuted for alleged corruption.

At the same time the military relationship with the United States came under renegotiation, with agreements reached on reductions in US troops and bases, 'burden-sharing' of US military costs and increased Koreanization of the Joint Command structure, but not so far withdrawal of US nuclear weapons. The main obstacles to further US disengagement have been slow progress in negotiations with North Korea and fears regarding the latter's possible development of nuclear weapons. Hence military changes have tended to lag behind other transformations in the special relationship between the two countries, including US pressures to liberalize Korea's neo-mercantilist trade policies, and to democratize its polity.

Evaluation: has democratic control over the military been consolidated?

In the late 1980s it still appeared as if South Korea had liberalized its political system without yet democratizing; the ex-military elite was still in charge; its repressive apparatuses were still in place; and there remained a real danger that military reintervention might reverse even the limited progress that had been achieved. By 1993, however, democracy of the Western liberal variety had effectively been consolidated, and a civilian politician was installed as President for the first time since 1961. Moreover, President Kim has surprised everyone by the boldness of the steps he has taken to break the grip of the old military elite, to attack corruption (including indictments against former Presidents Chun and Roh and several influential business leaders) and to liberalize the economy.

Nevertheless, it may be misleading to overemphasize the suddenness and scale of the political transformation. First, it must be remembered that it has been linked to far longer-term transformations in the economy and the social structure, discussed at length in Chapters 3 and 5. Secondly, it developed out of struggles waged by democratic forces throughout the period of authoritarian rule to keep open and expand the limited spaces that still existed. Thirdly, one should not forget the inherent limits and constraints of a democracy still managed by a political party (the former DLP, now renamed the New Korea Party (NKP)) brought into being with the express purpose of preserving the hegemony of the country's state, military and corporate elites.

Both the scale of the changes and their limits are epitomized in the military and security establishments. The latter have been stripped of many of the political prerogatives they possessed under authoritarian rule and of some professional prerogatives as well, and they have put up less resistance to these losses than their counterparts in some other democratizing countries, like Chile. This lack of resistance partly reflects their long-term decline in influence relative to other elites in a fast-growing capitalist economy; and partly the corruption scandals which have tainted their reputation for governmental competence. However, it is also because they have retained much of their professional and bureaucratic autonomy in exchange for giving up direct claims on political power, a bargain welcomed by some of the more professional elements in the officer corps. They still retain a significant share of the national budget, and remain linked to the industrial sector through an expanding military–industrial complex, within a continued national security state. So far, however, there has been little visible progress in the direction of *democratic* control, in terms, for example, of greater accountability to the legislature, relaxation of state secrecy, or open and informed public debate about defence and security policy. But in these respects many Western democracies also fall short by the standards of democratic theory.

Chile: military prerogatives within a liberal democracy

Chile, like South Korea, is another seeming paradigm of progress from developmental dictatorship to democracy. But the two countries' transitions differ in crucial respects. Unlike Korea, Chile had an established tradition of democratic governance before the military seized power in 1973. Yet General Pinochet ruled with an even heavier hand than his Korean counterparts. By no stretch of the imagination could Chile's authoritarianism be characterized as 'plural', even though its military and security apparatuses never disposed of the immense resources commanded by South Korea's national security state.

Differences in economic and political strategy have also been striking. In Chile the Pinochet regime's economic policies were unequivocally neo-liberal, in contrast to the state-led capitalism of Korea. Yet they failed to achieve comparably rapid and sustained economic progress; although the incoming civilian regime of 1990 inherited a restructured and burgeoning economy. Moreover, Pinochet failed to broaden his conservative political support-base sufficiently to win freely contested elections like Roh in Korea. Instead, he was beaten by a pro-democracy coalition in the 1988 referendum and the 1990 election. He then turned to the 1980 Constitution – originally meant to institutionalize an authoritarian or 'protected' democracy – to preserve the military's (and his own) prerogatives. Thus military rule has left behind even deeper 'institutional traces' than in Korea, and this has complicated the task of consolidating democracy.

The transition from civilian rule and the mechanisms of military dictatorship

Until the military's dramatic intervention in 1973, Chile had been unusual among Latin American countries in having a functioning parliamentary democracy and an apparently pro-fessional, non-political military establishment, firmly under the control of the civilian authorities since the last period of civilian–military instability in 1925–32. It has been argued that it was the armed forces' very professionalism and isola-tion from the rest of society (epitomized in the high proportion of officers drawn from military families) that encouraged their intervention in politics. Their former subordination to civilian authority 'was due not to the assimilation of democratic val-ues, but to obedience to a political imperative. [It] was accepted as part of an inherited tradition, not as a result of reasoned and firm adherence to principle' (Arriagada Herrera, 1988: 82). Neither the armed forces' long-standing ties with the Prussian and German armies (Remmer, 1988: 8), nor their anti-Marxist national security doctrines acquired from France and the USA, nor their links with US military advisers and the CIA were hospitable to democracy. Furthermore, military subordination to the civil power had been nurtured in a polity where the practice of democracy had been relatively oligarchic, at least prior to the opening of the political system to the 'popular sectors', which culminated in the election of President Allende at the head of the Unidad Popular (UP) government in 1970 (Remmer, 1985–6).

Moreover, the Allende government hastened its own demise by adopting a disastrous 'macro-populist' economic programme (Dornbusch and Edwards, 1990) and attempting a revolution-ary transformation of society, with minority electoral and par-liamentary support. The ensuing crisis was deepened because the right-wing opposition, joined later by parts of the Christian Democrat centre, campaigned to destabilize the government and pressed openly for a coup, aided and abetted (through the

CIA) by the United States. But there were clear signs of military discontent – including a 1969 revolt over pay and promotions and the assassination of General Schneider, the Army commander, by right-wing officers – even before Allende became President. The UP government's efforts to win back the support of the armed forces, including substantial increases in military spending (Scheetz, 1992: 186), proved counter-productive. Although the Army commander, General Prats, initiated consultations among his colleagues through a new Commission of General Officers, his peers assailed him for aligning the Army with the government, and shamed him into resignation after a public protest by officers' wives. By the time General Pinochet was appointed to replace him in 1973, a group of Army generals, with confrères in the Navy, Air Force and *Carabineros* (the paramilitary police), was already planning a coup, bringing Pinochet in at the last minute as 'swing man', to ensure the broad support of the officer corps.

To start with, the new military regime claimed that it had intervened to restore Chile's traditions of constitutionalism and democracy. But it soon proved itself to be highly repressive even by the harsh standards of Latin American military governments, ruling through a mixture of terror, surveillance and ideological control. The Dirección Nacional de Inteligencia (DINA), formed in 1974 to unify the secret services, became in many respects the backbone of the government, used not only to control the populace, but also to watch over the armed forces.

The centralization of military and state power did not occur automatically, or all at once. Indeed, the junta started as a partnership among the heads of the four services, with General Pinochet as their titular head. The latter moved swiftly to consolidate both his own personal control and the institutional pre-eminence of the Army. For this, he made good use of DINA, dominated by former Army intelligence officers who reported directly to him as head of state. He methodically built up personal control over the careers of officers in all four services, informally to start with, but later through statutes governing appointments, promotions and retirements (Arriagada Herrera, 1988: part III). With the removal in 1978 of General Leigh, the Air Force commander, who opposed the perpetuation of military rule, his domination of the junta and the armed forces was complete, and was institutionalized in the 1980 Constitution, which nominated him personally as President for the next ten years.

Table 4.3 A profile of Chile's governments after 1970

Dates	Government	Type	Economic policies	Control of military
1970–73	President Allende (Unidad Popular)	Left-wing civilian presidency with minority parliamentary support	'Macro-populist', socialist, inward-looking policies; growing economic crisis	Professional tradition, with increasing military participation in government
1973–75	General Pinochet (Phase I)	Military junta	'Normalization'; dismantling of socialist economic model	Broad-based support of all Armed Forces (AF) for junta
1975–77	General Pinochet (Phase II)	Transition from junta to military dictatorship	Neo-liberal 'shock treatment'; externally oriented	Pinochet uses DINA and career patronage to ensure personal control of AF
1978–81	General Pinochet (Phase III)	Military dictatorship, institutional-ized under 1980 Constitution	Neo-liberal reforms extended to virtually all policy areas; high financial concentration under Chilean conglomerates	As above, but with more emphasis on professionalism

[1981–83 – Financial and economic crisis initiates widespread protest against military rule, 1983–86]

Dates	Government	Type	Economic policies	Control of military
1982–87	General Pinochet (Phase IV)	Military dictatorship, with very limited 'decompression' in response to protest	A more pragmatic neo-liberalism after 1983, guided by IMF/World Bank, restoring growth	As above
1988–90	General Pinochet, transitional government	Interregnum between military and civilian rule after referendum	Continuity in pragmatic neo-liberal policies	Consolidation of AF prerogatives in preparation for withdrawal from government
1990–	Presidents Aylwin (1990–4) and Frei (1994–)	Presidential-style democracy, backed by pro-democracy coalition (Concertación)	Pragmatic neo-liberalism, tempered by measures against poverty/ inequality	Limited civilian control in professional and intelligence matters; but diminished likelihood of reintervention

Sources: Adapted and updated from Remmer (1988) and Oppenheim (1993).

The concentration of personal, state and military power achieved by Pinochet was probably greater than in any other recent Latin American military regime. Remmer (1989: chapter 5) characterizes his rule as 'personal', 'patrimonial' and even 'sultanistic'; and Arriagada Herrera (1988) and Valenzuela (1990) make similar appraisals. The military and civilian bureaucracies became politicized, with personal loyalty counting as much as professional competence; lines of influence radiated directly from the President, superseding regular bureaucratic channels (Remmer, 1989: 137–42). In the armed forces a 'tarnished professionalism' dominated, that had 'as its basis the abusive use, the manipulation in a dictatorial political context of a highly developed professional military tradition and of the values associated with it – i.e. subordination to political power, obedience, non-deliberation, hierarchy and discipline' (Arriagada Herrera, 1986: 123).

There is truth in these assertions.[5] However, Pinochet's rule, though personal, was effective, sharply contrasting with the corrupt patrimonial autocracies of many other Southern countries, such as Nicaragua under Somoza or Zaïre under Mobutu. It was more comparable to the governance of other developmental dictators, such as Suharto in Indonesia or Park in South Korea. But it also differed from the latter in constituting itself as a more corporately *military* government. Pinochet kept (and still retains) his military position as Captain General of the Army, also appointing himself *Generalissimo* of the armed forces. Between 1973 and 1986 around half of all Cabinet ministers, 87 per cent of university rectors and 45 per cent of ambassadors were retired or serving officers, as were 46 per cent of the members of the four commissions that functioned as the country's legislature between 1980 and 1986. Regional superintendents and provincial governors were almost invariably serving officers in direct command of troops. Many directors of state enterprises (36 per cent in 1986) were military men. Hence senior officers became members of two distinct hierarchies, one political, the other military, and were shuffled between them, to prevent their accumulating too much influence in either, and to integrate the power groups to which they belonged (Arriagada Herrera, 1988: 167–72; Hunneus, 1987: 116–18). Unlike Korea, officers allocated political or administrative jobs were not expected to resign from the forces, and Pinochet amended military regulations to allow those reaching retirement age to keep their military status so long as they stayed on in government positions.

In sum, there was less separation between the military-as-institution and military-as-regime than in South Korea. Yet, as one Chilean commentator (Hunneus, 1987: 120) has argued, this system 'has not politicised the military institutions, nor has it weakened their professionalism', whilst 'giving the regime and head of state enormous power'. Pinochet himself claimed, in his 1979 Presidential Message, that 'our armed forces are not politicized, because they have understood that the power of the state lies in their Chiefs of Staff' (Arriagada Herrera, 1986: 122). Thus the debate about whether the forces were 'politicized' or remained 'professional' is partly semantic. In practice the Pinochet regime played the professional card both ways. It asserted traditional ideas about military discipline and subordination to the government, to ensure its uncontested control of the armed forces. At the same time it redefined professionalism under the broad canopy of the new national security doctrines of the Cold War era, to justify an expanded military role in politics. This enlarged conception of professionalism was written into the 1980 Constitution, which guaranteed the armed forces corporate and professional autonomy and entrenched them as 'non-political' guardians of the state and the Constitution.

Authoritarian rule and capitalist restructuring

The regime's highly coercive and exclusionary character has often been explained in functional terms by both critics and apologists. According to the critics, military or bureaucratic-authoritarian rule was a response to a crisis of hegemony, resulting from the breakdown of Chilean capitalism and the UP government's opening of the political system to the 'popular sectors', threatening dominant class interests (Garretón, 1989: chapters 3 and 6). According to apologists, the coup and the 'state of exception' were 'necessary' to avert revolution, and to protect 'national security' from the threats posed by Communism and civil war (the argument the military elite has used to justify its human rights abuses). A 'hard' authoritarian state was also 'required', so it is argued, to force through the neo-liberal restructuring of the economy during the late 1970s and 1980s.

However, the counterfactuals implicit in these assertions

are open to question. Did the crisis of 1970–3 have to be resolved by military intervention and authoritarian rule, or were other political outcomes possible? Did the situation remain so unstable *after* the coup, that political activity had to be banned and opposition brutally repressed? Why was it not possible to hand power back to civilian politicians when the crisis was over and order restored? Was neo-liberal economic reform the only way of renewing growth in the economy; did it 'require' the shock treatment administered by the regime?

Even if a plausible case for some kind of authoritarian rule could be made, it would still not constitute a *sufficient* explanation of why and how Chile's military rulers established and consolidated an exclusionary dictatorship; nor of why they committed themselves to a project of economic, social and political restructuring, that went much further than restoring the status quo. The 'foundational logic' of the regime (Garretón, 1989: part III) cannot just be assumed from the crises that brought it into being. Rather, this logic emerged *after* the coup, when the new military rulers began to seek political formulas under which to govern and policy instruments to manage a crisis-torn economy. Like Park in Korea, Pinochet's concentration of power enabled him to install a new economic model (see Chapter 3). But in contrast to Korea, the emphasis from the start was on neo-liberal, market-led capitalist restructuring of the economy, which furthermore never produced anything comparable to the Korean economic 'miracle' (Kim and Geisse, 1988). To the extent that the more or less constant expansion of the economy since 1984 can be considered a success, it is attributable to the specific adjustment measures introduced (with IMF/World Bank assistance) after 1982–3, not to a neo-liberal approach, still less authoritarianism, in general.

Thus how far Pinochet's dictatorship was 'developmental', even in narrow growth terms, is a matter for dispute. What arguably distinguished it from most other Latin American regimes was the scale and depth of capitalist restructuring. This had three principal goals: first, to demobilize the 'popular sectors', which had sustained the previous revolutionary regime, by banning political parties, and maintaining surveillance over a wide range of groups in civil society; second, to shift the economic and political balance from labour to capital; and third, to reorder social life on market-oriented principles, notably under the 'seven modernizations' proposed by the government's civilian advisers in the late 1970s, including trade union reform, scaling back the social security system and the partial privatisation of health and education. But despite the rhetoric, the size of the state (in terms of its share of GDP) was not much cut back, although its contours changed, with its repressive capacity expanding and its welfare functions declining, as measured by changes in the shares of military and social spending in the budget (Scheetz, 1992: 180–3).

It is of some significance that the first moves towards an *apertura* were made when the military government was at the peak of its powers. The 1980 Constitution, endorsed by the electorate in a carefully orchestrated referendum, aimed to install what was termed a 'protected' democracy: i.e. to institutionalize the authoritarian regime, rather than replace it by a liberal democracy. In principle, the Constitution subordinated the government and the armed forces to the rule of law; but in no meaningful way were they made accountable to the mass of citizens. Its one major concession to democracy – whose significance was not appreciated until later – was to schedule a referendum for 1988, when the electorate would choose between continuing for a further ten years under the President chosen by the government (i.e. Pinochet), or holding elections for a new administration.

Soon after the Constitution was enacted, the regime's authority was shaken by the near collapse of the economy in 1981–3, and a wave of strikes and political protests during 1983–6. The latter were an impressive demonstration of the renewal of civil society, but were harshly suppressed. Pinochet brushed aside attempts by the churches and other groups to broker negotiations with the 'legitimate' opposition of former political elites, who were themselves divided over whether to support mass action by the popular sectors. Indeed, the clearest lesson of this period seemed to be that the ruling military bloc remained cohesive and willing to confront resistance with overwhelming force, whilst a divided opposition was in no position to compel it to renounce power.

How, then, was Pinochet prevailed on to permit the dismantling of the regime during the late 1980s? The standard explanations found in the literature on transitions are of limited relevance. The economy was expanding again, and the mass protests of 1983–6 had largely subsided. The government and the armed forces were more united than other Latin

American military governments and overwhelmingly supported the continuation of Pinochet's leadership (Garretón, 1989: 128). Nevertheless, the *apertura* of the mid-1980s had begun a slow erosion of the regime's capacity to govern. The 1981–3 crisis tarnished its reputation for competent economic management, and economic recovery did not halt the steady erosion of business support. Spaces had opened for a range of groups in civil society to organize politically; political parties too had started to re-emerge, though they were not legalized until 1987. The costs of repression were increasing, internationally as well as domestically: in addition to arms embargoes and US congressional investigations, the regime faced unexpected pressure from the Reagan administration for democratization, later to be castigated in Pinochet's memoirs as 'US interventionism' (*Latin American Weekly Report* (*LAWR*), 23 September 1993: 443).

Hence the military regime badly needed to reinstitutionalize its rule, even if full return to democracy was not exactly what it had in mind. The opposition too changed its tactics, ceasing to confront Pinochet head on. Instead, it decided to negotiate within the framework of the 1980 Constitution, stitched together a broadly based coalition of Centre and Left parties, the Concertación por el No, and campaigned against the continuation of military rule in the 1988 referendum. Despite electoral manipulation and governmental intimidation the Concertación won and (as the Concertación de Partidos para la Democracia) triumphed in the December 1989 presidential and congressional elections. Pinochet's defeat reflected the narrowness of his power-base outside the military and state security apparatuses. Even though his regime controlled the bureaucracy and most of the media, and sponsored the creation of right-wing political parties, it was unable to transform its genuine middle-class support into a conservative political bloc broadly enough based to win at the polls.

The rules Pinochet had himself inserted in the 1980 Constitution obliged him to accept defeat. Not only would the costs of reneging – international sanctions, capital flight and protests in the streets – have been enormous; the regime would have been able to maintain itself in power only through a repression even more severe than in 1973–5, but it would now have been bereft of legitimacy, so that its capacity to repress would have been a diminishing asset. Moreover, it is not certain that the corporate unity and discipline of the armed forces would have held, as was emphasized by (among others) the Air Force commander, General Matthei, who went to the Moneda Palace on the night of the referendum to 'pull out the detonators' and make Pinochet admit defeat (*Latin American Research Report – Southern Cone (LARR-SC)*, 15 March 1990: 9; Oppenheim, 1993: 192).

Pinochet's plan of retreat

Pinochet made a defiant exit, stressing that the armed forces were going with their 'mission accomplished' (Loveman, 1991: 35). Moreover, he did so only after carefully preparing his retreat. One of the major objectives was to make it impossible to prosecute members of the regime, the armed forces and the security services for acts of repression and abuses of human rights carried out under military rule. Another was to preserve the extensive professional prerogatives that the military establishment had acquired during its period in office. A third was to protect its political prerogatives as self-appointed arbiter of the Constitution and guardian of the state. A final, and still broader, objective was to ensure the continuity of Chile's market-oriented model of development and preclude the re-emergence of socialism. To a large extent this battle was already won by the time the military regime handed over power. Although the Concertación insisted on repeal of the notorious Article 8 of the Constitution banning political parties adhering to the concept of class conflict, the regime's willingness to give way was indicative of the shift that had taken place within the political debate. As a consequence of the altered policy environment in the 1980s, there was broad consensus that any elected government would continue on the path of economic reform, based on agreements already entered into with the IMF and the World Bank.

Pinochet thus concentrated his efforts on preserving a number of authoritarian enclaves that would protect the political and military legacies of the regime (Arriagada Herrera and Graham, 1994: 250–5). Between the October 1988 referendum and the transfer of power in March 1990, he followed a two-track policy: negotiating with the Concertación over constitutional changes needed to put an elected government in place, whilst simultaneously legislating to ensure that (in his words) Chile was 'tied, and tied well' (Loveman, 1991: 42). The end result was the transformation of a framework originally designed to enhance the power of the state, and within it the president and the military establishment, into a straitjacket constraining both the executive and the legislature, whilst assuring the military establishment substantial autonomy from both, as a virtual 'fourth branch' of government.

The impediments placed in the way of civilian control of the military were of five main kinds (see Loveman, 1991 for details). First, the Constitution preserved elements of the military regime at the heart of the new democratic state, most notably by guaranteeing Pinochet's personal status as Army commander until 1997. Second, a high wall of protection was placed around the military command and its career structure, making it virtually impossible to promote officers not already closely identified with Pinochet to command over the four military services, or to dismiss them during their four-year terms of service. Third, the military establishment largely retained the privileged legal status it had acquired during the dictatorship, including wide-ranging special powers, exemptions from prosecution in the civil courts and jurisdiction of military courts over civilians in security matters (including trial of members of the public for threatening or insulting the armed forces). Fourth were the provisions providing amnesty from prosecution for human rights abuses committed before 1978 and putting difficulties in the way of prosecution for later abuses. Finally, the armed forces kept a direct and autonomous role in the political process as guarantors of the 'institutional order' and of 'national security' under Article 90 of the Constitution. Among other things, the commanders of each military service have remained *ex officio* members of the National Security Council, and former commanders belong to the block of nine nominated members of the Senate, whom the conservative parties have used to vote down constitutional amendments.

A slow and incomplete demilitarization

The Concertación's programme committed it to diminishing the political role of the military establishment, and restoring the authority over it of a civilian-controlled Ministry of Defence. However, President Aylwin's government proceeded with extreme caution. It attempted to drive a wedge between Pinochet and the military establishment, highlighting his personal responsibility for corruption and abuse of power, for instance

by starting criminal investigations into dubious business deal-
ings with the armed forces by Pinochet's son and daughter. To
the extent that an embryonic constituency of officers opposed
to the military's political involvement emerged, it was better
represented in the Air Force than the other services. But the
Air Force controlled few troops on the ground and was not well
placed to assert itself politically. Moreover, officers opposing
military involvement in politics, or looking forward to Pinochet's retirement, did not necessarily want to see the military's entrenched privileges reduced, or their colleagues tried
for human rights abuses.

President Aylwin demanded that 'that all members of the
Armed Forces, from the top to the bottom, perform strictly
their constitutional and legal duties' (independence day speech
1990, cited in *LARR-SC*, 18 October 1990), and in a number of
public confrontations tried to make Pinochet submit to his
authority as President and to the Minister of Defence. Pinochet
for his part was prepared to test to the limit his view that the
armed forces were 'not deliberative, but not mentally castrated
either' (*LAWR*, 23 September 1993: 443). Twice he went so far
as to bring the Army out into the streets, first on a 'security,
readiness and co-ordination exercise' in December 1990, and
the second time in May 1993, when a contingent of special
forces in full battle equipment stood guard outside the Armed
Forces headquarters, whilst the generals held an emergency
meeting. That both episodes took the government by surprise
was sufficient testimonial to the Army's continued control of
the intelligence apparatus. Pinochet had formally abolished the
CNI shortly before the transfer of power, supposedly in response
to public condemnation of its activities, but, in reality, had
transferred its personnel and records more or less intact to the
Army's own intelligence branch. The latter continued its dirty
tricks and surveillance of Concertación politicians, though it
almost came unstuck in 1992, when a phone-tapping scandal
revealed that it was also involved in political in-fighting on
the Right.

One reason the military establishment was able to fight its
own corner was its relative financial independence, partly
assured by its guaranteed 10 per cent share of the country's
copper export revenues (around $300m) to underwrite its arms
purchases.[6] Also under the Armed Forces law entrenched by

Pinochet, the military budget was index-linked to a floor no less than the 1988 level of some $700m. In the course of time, however, this ceased to be an advantage, since the increases above this limit needed to modernize equipment and improve salaries could still be blocked, giving the President and Congress a degree of financial leverage that could be used to wear away at the ramparts of military privilege.

President Aylwin asserted his constitutional powers as Commander in Chief to reject a number of Pinochet's proposals to promote and reassign senior generals, one of the issues that precipitated the December 1990 demonstration of military strength. Legal reforms (the *Leyes Cumplido*) were enacted to modify the draconian laws on security offences and to confine the jurisdiction of military courts. Draft constitutional changes were introduced to restore the President's ability to appoint and replace the commanders in chief of the armed forces and do away with the nominated senators, who made up part of the blocking vote in the Senate; but these measures were ferociously opposed by the military and in any case stood little chance of receiving the necessary two-thirds Senate majority.

The issue which perhaps more than anything made it difficult to stabilize civil–military relations was the unresolved legacy of repression and human rights abuse under the military regime. One of the Aylwin government's first acts on assuming power in 1990 was to establish a non-partisan Commission for Truth and Reconciliation (the Rettig Commission) to investigate these violations, and recommend ways of making moral and material reparation. The purpose was not to assign guilt, since the inquiry was into victims, not perpetrators; rather, it was to compile an accurate historical record, enquire into the role of the military and security services, and if possible secure a pledge it would not happen again. Pinochet did his best to obstruct the investigations, and in March 1991 openly attacked the published report. Bringing the perpetrators to book was still more problematic, not only because of the Army's refusal to co-operate, but also because of the attitude of the judiciary. The Supreme Court attacked the Rettig Report as 'impassioned, reckless and biased', particularly in its criticisms of the judiciary's own failure to protect human rights under military rule. It insisted on transferring several cases from civilian to military courts, and impeached magistrates attempting to try cases antedating the military regime's 1978 amnesty.

An attempted compromise, the proposed *Ley Aylwin*, submitted to Congress in 1993, would have involved rapid trials held in secret by a panel of specially appointed judges; amnesty for crimes committed before 1978, after guilt had first been established in court; and special places of confinement for military prisoners convicted of crimes committed after that date. However, human rights groups and the two main left-wing parties in the Concertación were opposed, arguing that secret trials by special courts would defeat the purpose of providing public examples; that the judiciary could not be trusted if it met behind closed doors; and that the special procedures would be tantamount to creating a new jurisdiction for offences committed with the backing of state power.

In the end, the President withdrew the bill, leaving the issue unresolved when his successor Eduardo Frei took office in 1994.[7] Frei's election manifesto committed him to accelerate constitutional and military reform, but he found himself obstructed in the Senate on precisely the same issues as his predecessor. He pressed unsuccessfully for the resignation of General Stange, the Director-General of the *Carabineros*, accused of complicity in covering-up police murders of Communist militants in 1985. Nevertheless a handful of officers were tried and imprisoned for abuses under the military regime, including the former head of DINA, General Contreras, for his role in the assassination of Orlando Letelier in the USA. A 1994 court ruling circumventing the Pinochet regime's 1978 amnesty apparently opened the way for more prosecutions (*LAWR*, 13 October 1994); prompting (thus far inconclusive) government horse trading with the armed forces and conservative parties over a possible moratorium on future trials, in exchange for military acquiescence in reform.

The government's failure to sort out these outstanding issues has been disappointing, but not fatal to democracy. The armed forces have grudgingly come to accept that outright military reintervention is no longer on the cards, and begun to accommodate themselves to civilian control. Admittedly they have continued, with the support of the right-wing parties, to insist on their special prerogatives, claiming they are needed to buttress the constitutional order and a market-oriented development strategy. But the civilian government's success in managing the economy has deprived such claims of some of their sting. At the same time it has begun to pay more attention to reducing poverty and inequality (Silva, 1993), as reflected in the Concertación's espousal of a modified social democracy in its 1993 election manifesto. Political polarization has declined (Oxhorn, 1994), though opinion polls during an uninspiring election campaign testified to widespread disillusion with politics (Garretón, 1995: 154–6). The revolutionary Left and the anti-communist Right remain active but politically marginalized, and the old political dynasties are largely back in control.

Evaluation: consolidation of democracy but not civilian control?

To conclude, with private capital restored to control of the economy, growth on course, political stability assured under a liberal democracy, and good relations with the United States and the international financial institutions, who in Chile now needs the military's protection? These political and economic considerations, rather than constitutional provisions or military professionalism, remain the best safeguards against military reintervention. In the meantime, Pinochet and his generals have manipulated the Constitution, the courts and professional doctrine to preserve a wide sphere of military autonomy, within which they are not accountable to the government, still less to the legislature or the public. Whilst this autonomy remains a major impediment to full democratic control of the military establishment, it is unlikely to endanger democracy itself, short of a major economic breakdown or hegemonic crisis, of which there is less apparent risk than almost anywhere else in Latin America. Meanwhile, the government's problem is how to continue its campaign of attrition against Pinochet and his colleagues until they retire in March 1997, without provoking retaliation; how to pick more flexible successors to them (not easy whilst the military elite still controls the nomination process); and how to build bridges with new generations of officers, whose professionalism is less tarnished by the legacy of military dictatorship. Chile's transition to a fully institutionalized democratic regime will not be fully complete until the remaining authoritarian enclaves have been eliminated.

Ghana: from populist authoritarianism to limited democracy

Democracy, military rule and state collapse, 1957–81

Ghana's present transition to democracy is more recent, and its future more uncertain, than those in Chile and South Korea. Yet it is only the latest episode in no less than four ventures into democracy: the 1957 post-independence government headed by Kwame Nkrumah; two aborted democratic restorations in 1969–72 and 1979–81 (the Busia and Limann governments); and the self-transformation since 1993 of the former Provisional National Defence Council (PNDC) headed by Flight Lieutenant (now President) Jerry Rawlings into the elected government of the Fourth Republic, armed with all the formal attributes of parliamentary democracy. The obverse side of the story has been frequent regressions to authoritarian rule: under Nkrumah between 1961 and 1966; three standard-issue military governments in 1966–9, 1972–8, and 1978–9; and the two 'revolutionary' military regimes of 1979 and 1981–93.

All this reinforces the need for caution in attaching labels and consequences to regimes (Table 4.4). Not only were the content and extent of democracy under each of Ghana's 'democratic' governments far from the same. The country's military regimes have also differed from each other in almost every significant respect. The National Liberation Council (NLC) of 1966–9 was a classic junta of senior soldiers, committed from the start to returning power to civilians after dismantling the legacy of Nkrumah. The National Redemption Council (NRC) which seized power in 1972 also began as a junta. Its head, Colonel (later General) Acheampong, purportedly transformed it – in the form of the Supreme Military Council (SMC) – into the most hierarchical and 'military' of Ghana's regimes; but in practice it degenerated into an ineffective and corrupt personal autocracy. The Akuffo (SMC II) government was a weak junta of Acheampong's former colleagues, whose main goal was to withdraw from power, whilst retaining as much as possible of the military elite's accumulated wealth and privileges. The Armed Forces Revolutionary Council (AFRC) that overthrew it in 1979 and tore down the military hierarchy was a committee of junior officers and NCOs, chaired by Flight Lieutenant Rawlings, who saw their role as purely short-term and 'corrective'. Its revolutionary descendant, the PNDC, which

Table 4.4 Ghana: a political and economic profile, 1957–94

Dates	Government	Type	Economic policies	Control of the military
1957–66	K. Nkrumah, Convention People's Party (CPP)	Presidential-style democracy; becoming (by 1964) single-party authoritarian rule	State socialist, protectionist, high public expenditure	Divide and rule; reliance on parallel security structures
1966–69	National Liberation Council (NLC)	Military junta, preparing return to constitutional rule	Renounced socialism; adopted economic liberalization and austerity	Return to professionalism
1969–72	K.A. Busia, Progress Party (PP)	Multi-party parliamentary democracy	Continued liberalization with elements of economic nationalism	Professionalism with some political and ethnic manipulation
1972–75	Col. (later Gen.) I.K. Acheampong, National Redemption Council (NRC)	Military junta	Protectionist, reversed Busia's devaluation; 'self-reliance'	Increasingly based on personal patronage. Tensions middle ranks/senior officers
1975–78	Gen. I.K. Acheampong, Supreme Military Council (SMC)	Military dictatorship	Protectionist and increasingly kleptocratic	Patronage and corruption prevalent. Armed Forces (AF) discipline suffered
1978–79	Gen. F.W.K. Akuffo (SMC II)	Military junta preparing return to constitutional rule	No real change from above	No real change from above, military falling apart
1979	Flt. Lt. J.J. Rawlings, Armed Forces Revolutionary Council (AFRC)	Revolutionary committee of junior officers/NCOs	Anti-corruption, tightening of economic controls	Final collapse of discipline; 'health purge' of officer corps by AFRC

Table 4.4 Cont'd

Dates	Government	Type	Economic policies	Control of the military
1979–81	H. Limann	Presidential-style multi-party democracy	Failure to abandon protectionism or to implement proposed liberalization. Economy in tail-spin	Reprofessional-ization thwarted by continued politicization and dissent in ranks
1981–83	Flt. Lt. J.J. Rawlings, Provisional National Defence Council (PNDC)	Revolutionary/ populist military dictatorship	Radical/grass-roots economic programme fails to halt collapse of economy	Formation of Armed Forces Defence Committees (AFDCs) in ranks; but partial restoration of hierarchy
1983–93	Flt. Lt. J.J. Rawlings, PNDC	Populist military dictatorship	Stabilization and structural adjustment under market-oriented Economic Recovery Programme (ERP)	Slow reprofessional-ization of AF, but continued reliance on AFDCs and on parallel security structures
1993	President J.J. Rawlings, National Democratic Congress (NDC)	Presidential and single-party dominant multi-party democracy	Continuation of ERP, but pressures to relax fiscal discipline	Emphasis on professionalism; but *de facto* retention of parallel security structures

took power under Rawlings in 1981, included civilians as well as soldiers, declared it was not a 'military' regime, and undertook to reverse Ghana's economic and political decline.

Nor does Ghana's post-independence history permit facile generalizations concerning developmental dictatorship (or indeed democracy), or concerning military regimes as the enforcers of capitalist interests. Having set out in the late 1950s with a prosperous agricultural economy generating surpluses for investment by an interventionist state, Ghana became a graveyard for almost every variety of developmental orthodoxy. It was ruled by socialist and conservative civilian governments and by radical as well as right-wing military regimes. Before it became an IMF/World Bank structural adjustment 'success story' in the 1980s, it had tried out almost every conceivable economic strategy: state socialism under Nkrumah; market-oriented reform under the NLC and Busia; economic 'self-reliance' under Acheampong; and a quickly abandoned experiment in grass-roots socialism in 1982 during the first few months of the Rawlings revolution. Behind these diverse political and economic experiments, there occurred a long-run decline. Between 1960 and the early 1980s, Ghana became an African paradigm of the 'development of underdevelopment'. GDP per head (at constant prices) declined at an average annual rate of 1.2 per cent between 1960 and 1966, 2 per cent between 1972 and 1979 and 5.3 per cent between 1979 and 1981 (Ahiakpor, 1991: 598–9).[8] And the decline was as much political as economic. Not only was Ghana one of the most unstable and coup-prone countries in the African continent prior to 1981 (Ravenhill, 1980; Luckham, 1985). Economic decline was reinforced by a slow breakdown in state institutions, and erosion of their capacity to manage development (Chazan, 1983). This did not simply reduce the state's ability to get things done, it undermined its ability to reproduce itself; i.e. to maintain its revenue base, control the means of coercion and assure a modicum of political stability.

Two interrelated aspects of this erosion of the state were crucial for civilian–military relations. First, the inability of successive governments, whether civilian or military, to count on the loyalty of their armed forces, and hence stabilize their own political existence. Second, the breakdown of command and control in the military establishment, fatally reducing its ability to act as a professional disciplined body and to carry out its basic security functions. The reasons for this breakdown have been documented in detail by Hutchful (1979 and 1993) and Baynham (1988 and 1984–5): inheritance of rigid colonial military structures; the accelerated promotions of the post-independence era; the consequent dislocation of careers and lines of command; increasing antagonism between officers at different ranks, and between officers and subaltern groups at the bottom of the hierarchy (i.e. NCOs and men in the ranks); and ethnic and regional antagonisms (not, however, as acute as in some other African armies).

These institutional dislocations were magnified by the efforts of successive governments to manipulate the armed forces politically, together with the military's own interventions in politics. Their most visible manifestation was military intervention, including not only five successful coups, but many more coup attempts. None was staged by the military command as such; instead groups of officers or soldiers acted on their own initiative, the organizers coming from ever descending levels of the hierarchy.[9] At the same time, there was a steady erosion of the boundaries between military institutions and civil society, so that in 1979 and 1981 soldiers and junior officers acted not only in their military capacities, but also expressed the rage of subaltern groups throughout Ghanaian society against the venal elites they blamed for the country's decline.

Military regimes were as much at risk from coups as civilian governments. Indeed, to describe any of the authoritarian governments prior to the advent of Rawlings as 'developmental dictatorships' would be highly misleading. Quite simply, most of them were not sufficiently interested in development, and were too weak and inefficient to dictate. As the economy declined, military and police spending declined also. In practical terms this meant that military wages and salaries ceased to be enough to live on: the military elite could perhaps survive or even prosper through predatory accumulation, but ordinary soldiers and policemen were unable to feed their families, except by moonlighting, informal trading or engaging in various forms of extortion and banditry.

The military establishment was finally broken apart by a revolt from the ranks on 4 June 1979, which brought to power the AFRC to carry out what its chairman Flight Lieutenant Rawlings called a 'health purge' (Folson, 1993: 78) in the government and armed forces, culminating in the trial and execution of eight senior military figures, including three former heads of state. The AFRC allowed scheduled national elections to go ahead, and handed over power to a civilian government headed by Dr Hilla Limann in September 1979. But the military establishment remained in turmoil, worsened by the government's clumsy attempts to neutralize Rawlings and his associates. At the same time, the government was too weak to take the difficult decisions needed to reverse the collapse of the economy. Both structures simply fell apart when Rawlings and a tiny band of some 35 serving and former soldiers moved against them on 31 December 1981.

Populist authoritarianism and structural adjustment

Rawlings's 'second coming' at the end of 1981 is the point at which the standard narrative of Ghana's 'success story' normally begins (Callaghy, 1990). It tells how he came to power committed to 'nothing less than a revolution, something that would transform the social and economic power of the country' (Rawlings's broadcast of 1 January 1982, cited by Folson, 1993: 79); how his pragmatic economic advisers (the functional but maybe not ideological equivalent of Chile's 'Chicago boys') then persuaded him to change economic course, negotiate with the IMF and the World Bank and implement an Economic Recovery Programme (ERP) to stabilize and structurally adjust the economy; and how, to impose these changes, he broke with the revolutionary Left, brought mass organs under central control, curbed the trade unions, and turned to coercive and corporatist methods of political management.

This characterization is broadly accurate, but does not fully explain the 'foundational logic' of his regime: *why* it made this momentous shift in strategy; and *how*, having done so, it managed to carry it through with a success that had eluded earlier governments. Part of the explanation is to be found in Rawlings's and the PNDC's contradictory relations to the military establishment and the two 'revolutions' inside it in 1979 and 1981. As we have seen, the latter were both institutional rebellions by the ranks against the command structure, and armed risings against the ruling elite by military revolutionaries claiming to act on behalf of Ghana's 'popular sectors'. They swept away not only the corrupt SMC military dictatorship, but also the liberal democracy of the 1979–81 Third Republic, contending that the latter had merely introduced 'a new constitution of slavery' for the 'productive majority' of the population (Rawlings's broadcast of 5 January 1982, cited by Ahiakpor, 1991: 588). Rawlings himself emerged (not unlike other military populists, such as Perón in Argentina) as the charismatic interlocutor of these subaltern groups, both inside and outside the armed forces. In his first broadcast after the 31 December 1981 revolution, he asserted that he was not staging a coup but restoring power to the people; and he has continued to deny ever since that the AFRC and PNDC were 'military' governments (Hutchful, 1987).

Yet from the onset he also pursued a more narrowly military and étatist agenda, dictated by the changing calculus of power. He moved as quickly as he could to restore command and control in the armed forces and the police, under officers many of whom had initially been arrested by men in the ranks. Whilst he endorsed the formation of Armed Forces Defence Committees (AFDCs) alongside the mass organizations emerging in civil society, he intervened to block radical proposals for military reform. The decisive break with the radicals came in late 1982, when the three most prominent left-wing members of the PNDC (two ex-NCOs and a former student leader) and other activists were arrested or forced into exile after an attempted coup. This followed Rawlings's support for the Secretary of Finance and Economic Planning, Dr Kwesi Botchwey, and the Economic Policy Review Committee, who insisted on negotiating a stabilization programme direct with the IMF, in preference to more radical proposals to negotiate with the IMF whilst attempting to fit stabilization into a less market-driven framework (Hansen, 1991: chapter 5). The Economic Recovery Programme (ERP) which eventually emerged is discussed in Chapter 3. Rather than cutting the overall size of the state, the ERP restored its revenue base and substantially increased public expenditures, including annual (constant price) rises during 1982–8 of 6 per cent in defence spending and of 44 per cent in spending on arms, military buildings and equipment (Fosu, 1993: 50–2).[10]

A crucial corollary of the restoration of the state's strength, and of its capacity to coerce, was the reimposition of labour discipline. The IMF and the World Bank made little secret of their view that the Workers' Defence Committees (WDCs) and trade unions should be brought to heel and labour unrest brought under control (Haynes, 1991a: 450). The PNDC skilfully combined divide-and-rule tactics among workers' organizations with outright repression, including bans on strikes, deployment of armed security personnel to control protesting workers and detention of ring-leaders. The result, as Gyimah-Boadi and Essuman-Johnson (1993: 205–6) observe, was that, unlike earlier periods of economic austerity 'when wage freezes, price increases and especially devaluation had been met by a wave of strikes ... only an average of 16 strikes per year were recorded between 1983 and 1989, when a more thorough and consistent version of such policies was being pursued'.

Hence there is at least a *prima facie* case that the consolidation of a strong authoritarian state under Rawlings and the restarting of capitalist growth in the economy were mutually and causally interlinked. Yet this leaves one little the wiser about why the PNDC alone among Ghana's authoritarian governments was *effective*: not just in managing the economy, but also in enforcing political stability, in redisciplining the armed forces and in reinventing itself in 1993 as a 'democratic' government. A number of outside observers (Callaghy, 1990; Chazan, 1989; Jeffries, 1993) attribute these successes to the political astuteness, managerial competence and economic skills of Rawlings and his small group of advisers. Here at last was a Ghanaian government that 'got its policies right'. A more cynical view is that international financial institutions and donors needed an African 'success story' and were prepared to provide the large-scale injections of finance to back it. If so, their choice of a radical military regime to deliver success was remarkable, all the more since it did not depart significantly from its non-aligned and Pan-Africanist foreign policy, continued to receive assistance from Cuba and Eastern Europe and had poor relations with the United States (Boafo-Arthur, 1993).

In sum, what needs to be explained is what made the Rawlings/PNDC government a *developmental* dictatorship, or an 'adjusted state' (Green, 1991: 70), in marked contrast to the patrimonial authoritarianism of many other African regimes. A crucial, but contradictory, factor was its distinctive populism, which survived its alleged betrayal of the revolution that brought it to power. Though most of the Left saw the ERP as a betrayal of the PNDC's original mandate, there remained, as Ahiakpor (1991: 584) suggests,

> a considerable consistency [behind Rawlings's] search for means to alleviate the plight of the poor in Ghana, and this explains why he decided to alter course so significantly after the original repression of the market only made matters worse (in 1982–3) than they had been previously.

Admittedly once he chose this course, poverty alleviation took second place to the requirements of structural adjustment and market efficiency; and how far the poor, and which groups among them, have actually benefited, has remained a matter of controversy (Green, 1988). In a 1990/1 survey of urban attitudes, Jeffries found that, despite believing that their own real incomes had declined during the preceding five years, most of the sample thought that the country's and their own economic plight would have been worse without the ERP: a tribute to Rawlings's ability to persuade at least some of the populace that, in the words of a respondent, 'he always puts the interest of the country first' (Jeffries, 1992: 215 and 218).[11]

Rawlings's populist–authoritarian style also influenced how he handled another central structural problem: that his regime was of military origin, but did not enjoy full support from the professional military establishment during much of its period of rule. Some other African military rulers facing this dilemma (including the Acheampong regime in Ghana) have attempted to control the armed forces by giving them opportunities to enrich themselves through the state. Rawlings, in contrast, insisted on an institutional separation between the armed forces and the PNDC government of which he was Chairman, and which included more civilians than soldiers.[12] He pointedly kept his original rank of Flight Lieutenant, and delegated operational control of the armed forces to his General Officers Commanding (GOCs). The military and police establishments were removed from the purview of the PNDC in late 1982, and made directly answerable (via their commanders) to Rawlings, his Head of Security, Kojo Tsikata (in charge of the Bureau of National Intelligence (BNI)), and the National Security Council.

The regime also turned its attention to reprofessionalizing the military establishment. It needed simultaneously to re-establish its authority over a traumatized and hostile officer corps and to restore discipline among radicals in the AFDCs and lower ranks. Not only was each of these goals problematic in itself, they also potentially conflicted, as, once the officers were back in control of their men, they might be tempted to move against the government. Rawlings's solution (described in fascinating detail by Hutchful, 1996) was to put his GOC, Lieutenant-General Quainoo, in charge of re-equipping and reprofessionalizing the armed forces, but to integrate the AFDCs (or Armed Forces Committees for the Defence of the Revolution (AFCDRs) as they became in 1984) as consultative and advisory bodies within the formal military structure. Their class character was diluted by opening them to officers as well as the ranks, and by cutting their links with civilian mass organizations, whose personnel were banned from barracks. A counter-revolution was thus carried out within the armed forces, so as to restore the former command system. All the same, Rawlings insisted on retaining the AFCDRs, against the advice of his senior commanders. Not only were they a safeguard against coups, since officers could not draw weapons, nor move troops, without alerting them. They arguably contributed to increased morale by reducing the social distance between officers and men, a feature commented on when Ghanaian units served in peacekeeping forces elsewhere in Africa, but above all, they remained an important focal point for Rawlings's own populist–authoritarian leadership within the armed forces.

Rawlings relied on a small cadre of politicized officers, NCOs and security personnel to watch over the military hierarchy. Through their efforts the PNDC built up a formidable array of special military and paramilitary units and security organizations including the BNI, the so-called 'commandos' of the Forces Reserve Battalion (FRB) and the Civil Defence Organisation (CDO) with its Mobisquads and militias, not dissimilar to the parallel security structures Nkrumah attempted to establish in the 1960s (Baynham, 1985). But whereas the regular forces frustrated Nkrumah's efforts to bypass them by staging a coup in 1966, under the PNDC the professional military establishment was too divided and demoralized to act pre-emptively.

The purpose of these reorganizations was not just to stabilize the regime against coups, but also to control civilian dissent. In this there was some continuity with the regime's early and more radical phase, from which much of the government's repressive legislation dated, and when human rights abuses had been aggravated by the PNDC's inability to control the revolutionary excesses of its supporters (Gyimah-Boadi and Rothchild, 1982; Haynes, 1991c). As Rawlings consolidated his authority, the machinery of repression was brought under firmer political direction. The investigatory or quasi-judicial bodies that had probed illegal acquisition of wealth and abuse of power were slowly allowed to fall into disuse, or were used to silence political opponents. The secret services (notably the BNI) were expanded, and surveillance of potential dissenters was stepped up. The judiciary was intimidated, or circumvented by extra-judicial bodies like the Special Military Tribunal, which investigated and prosecuted alleged security offences by civilians as well as soldiers.

The path from 'true' to liberal bourgeois democracy

Whilst there is little doubt that the PNDC regime was repressive, deploying force both to stabilize its rule and to push through the ERP, it never entirely abandoned its original populist project. Flight Lieutenant Rawlings continued to hold himself up as a democrat and a man of the people, by emphasizing that he did not envisage 'a democracy with a hollow political content but one rooted in our economic realities' (Rawlings, 1986: 80). However, his attitude to democracy was shot through with contradictions. Having staged the 1979 and 1981 revolutions on behalf of 'the people', he clipped the wings of the mass organizations, and scorned radical solutions to the country's economic difficulties as 'populist nonsense', in effect making GDP growth the touchstone of the general will. He complained about the 'culture of silence' surrounding the government, yet refused to engage in serious dialogue with his critics (Boahen, 1989: 54). Nevertheless, he commanded enough public support to create his own political machine, orchestrate the regime's transition to a multi-party democracy in 1993, and secure his own election as President: precisely what Pinochet failed to achieve in Chile.

In the process Rawlings's vision of 'true' or popular democracy was transformed and ultimately abandoned. The mass organizations were purged after the break with the Left in late 1982. In 1984 their national directorate (the National Defence Committee) was disbanded and the People's and Workers' Defence Committees were reorganized as 'Committees for the Defence of the Revolution' (CDRs). At the same time, the regime began to redefine its original conception of 'the people': forming corporatist ties with a wide range of groups in civil society (chiefs, women, businessmen, unions, etc.), which did not always belong to the 'masses' in whose name it had carried out the 31 December revolution. It did so selectively: giving political and financial backing to groups supporting it; downgrading more neutral bodies; intimidating those that were critical; and heavily censoring the media. In late 1984 it put its democratization strategy into the hands of the National Commission for Democracy (NCD), headed by a former judge, Justice D.F. Annan, who also became Vice-Chairman of the

PNDC. The emphasis shifted to rebuilding popular participation through a series of reforms in local and regional government, leading to a grass-roots-based 'Ghanaian form of
democracy' at the national level. As discussed in Chapter 3,
what ultimately emerged was a Constitution not very different from that overturned by Rawlings in 1981. Little remained
of Rawlings's original aspirations for a more 'Ghanaian' constitutional framework. Nor was the political position of the armed
forces entrenched, except in a vaguely worded provision of the
Constitution (Article 210) that gave them a role in national
development.

Why did the PNDC change its mind and embrace Western-
style liberal democracy? The end of the Cold War, the 'good
government' agenda of international financial institutions and
the advocacy of multi-party democracy by Western donors (notably the UK) all played their part.[13] Yet domestic political and
economic considerations were also crucial (Jeffries and Thomas,
1993: 336), including the social and economic stresses generated by the ERP, continued doubts about the sustainability of
economic recovery, and growing protests from a range of civil
society groups that the regime had never been able entirely to
suppress. The latter, notably the established churches under
the Christian Council of Ghana and the Catholic Bishops' Conference, and the Ghana Bar Association, had begun to breach
the 'culture of silence' before regional forums were held on
constitutional reform in 1990. Thereafter, the pro-democracy
movement emerged into the open, with the formation of the
Movement for Freedom and Justice (MFJ), bringing together
politicians from all the major political parties of Ghana's first
three Republics.

The protests organized by this emergent opposition were by
no means as large or as violent as the upheavals that shook
Chile between 1983 and 1986. Yet, with the crucial exception
of the Transitional Provisions, which the PNDC pushed through
to ensure members of its government comprehensive immun-
ity from prosecution for actions taken since 1979, Ghana's
new Constitution was less restrictive than the constitutional
settlement 'pacted' by Pinochet. Partly this was because public pressures emboldened the NCD, the constitutional drafting
committee and the Consultative Assembly to be more independent than anyone had expected them to be. Partly it arose
from a division of opinion within the PNDC, some of whose

influential members persuaded Rawlings that a no-party constitution might provoke a hostile public reaction. And partly, it reflected the growing confidence of Rawlings's political advisers that they could use their political machine to ensure victory, even in contested elections.

Another element in the PNDC's calculations was that it could not necessarily count on the indefinite loyalty of the military and security establishments. Since it was not (like the Pinochet regime) a regime of the military hierarchy as a whole, it could not discount the possibility that elements in the officer corps might move against it. There had been major coup attempts in 1982 and 1983, and a number of subsequent plots, the most recent in 1989, for which over 60 soldiers and civilians had been shot or imprisoned since 1982. An uncontrolled democratization resulting from a military revolt or a civilian uprising, as in Benin, Mali or the Congo Republic, would certainly have exposed members of the regime to retribution for the deaths, torture and detention inflicted on their opponents.

Having taken the basic decision to proceed with a multi-party constitution, Rawlings and his advisers were better placed to capitalize on their political assets, once again in contrast to Pinochet in Chile. They soon recaptured the political initiative from the opposition, by taking over many of the latter's reform proposals; dismantling parts of the PNDC's repressive legislation, including the decrees relating to suspension of *habeas corpus*, detention and newspaper registration; and pressing ahead with the new Constitution and the 1992 elections. Rawlings's decision to stand seems to have been informed by two interlinked calculations: first (based on informal soundings up and down the country by his advisers), that he had a good chance of organizing a victory; and second, that if he did *not* stand, the National Democratic Congress (NDC), formed to defend the regime's interests, risked losing at the polls.

In the event Rawlings won the presidential election by a comfortable majority of 58 per cent of the vote, compared with 30 per cent for his nearest rival, Professor Adu Boahen, standing on the opposition New Patriotic Party (NPP) ticket. The four main opposition parties immediately challenged the result, alleging serious voting irregularities and intimidation of their supporters, and then proceeded to boycott the subsequent parliamentary elections. Their non-participation guaranteed the NDC an overwhelming majority of 189 out of 200 parliamentary seats, the remaining 11 seats going to other pro-Rawlings parties and independents.

The reasons why Rawlings and the NDC won the elections so decisively remain controversial (see New Patriotic Party, 1993; Jeffries and Thomas, 1993: 349–54). The opposition contends it was robbed of victory by electoral fraud, although teams of Commonwealth and American observers monitoring the elections did not consider this took place on a large enough scale to affect the result. Perhaps more important than actual fraud was the PNDC's ability to dictate the scheduling of the democratization process and the elections; its decision to proceed on the basis of a flawed and incomplete electoral roll; manipulation of electoral procedures; Rawlings's ability to campaign unofficially several months before the opposition was permitted to do so; use of official resources, such as government transport, in the NDC's campaigning; use of government patronage to influence local opinion-makers; and widespread deployment of the CDRs and paramilitaries to intimidate wavering voters.[14] Rawlings's majority was cumulatively enhanced by these advantages of incumbency. Whether he would have lost without them is harder to say. He campaigned effectively, and made full use of his popular appeal, especially among rural voters. He was also able to claim some credit for the ERP, all the more so as the opposition parties did not propose serious alternatives to it. Also important was the fact that the PNDC could count on the political support structures established during its period in office – the CDRs and other 'revolutionary organs', the 31st December Women's Movement, and, via the District Secretaries, sections of the local government machinery – to bring out the vote. Rawlings profited from the opposition's failure to turn the MFJ, or the Alliance of Democratic Forces (ADF) as it later became, into a coalition putting forward a single opposition presidential candidate. Unlike the Concertación in Chile, it became split between the NPP representing the Danquah-Busia tendency, and four other parties, all claiming the mantle of Nkrumah's CPP (a fifth Nkrumahist party, the National Convention Party (NCP), was manoeuvred into an electoral alliance with the NDC). Moreover, it is arguable that the opposition parties made a major tactical error in refusing to participate in the parliamentary elections, in which they might conceivably have gained a larger share of the vote, as Rawlings's personal popularity exceeded that of the NDC.[15]

Democracy or electoral authoritarianism?

Transition to multi-party democracy seemed on the face of it to have produced the result the opposition most feared: namely the resurrection of the PNDC in the form of an electoral dictatorship under President Rawlings, comparable to 'low-intensity' democracies in other parts of the South. Not only was Rawlings the first sub-Saharan African military ruler to transform himself into the head of a civilian government through contested multi-party elections;[16] under the Constitution of the Fourth Republic he became the elected Head of State as well as of government, disposing of wide executive powers, and remaining Commander in Chief of the armed forces. Eleven of the seventeen Ministers of State in his first cabinet were ex-PNDC members or former Secretaries; and less than half were MPs (*West Africa*, 10–16 January 1993: 17–18; also 22–8 March and 5–11 April 1993). Furthermore, President Rawlings came in on a Bonapartist platform of continuity in economic policy based on 'stability, discipline, efficiency and unity of purpose' as the 'general condition' of economic recovery (*West Africa*, 10–16 January 1993: 15). In practice, as discussed in Chapter 3, this meant continuing with the economic mixture as before, of austerity, market liberalization, support for privatization and the containment of labour unrest.

The temptation to revert to the authoritarian methods of the past remains powerful. That democratization remains on the agenda is partly because of discreet donor pressure, partly because of constitutional protection, partly because Parliament is by no means the cypher it was widely expected to be, but most of all because the opposition has remained vocal. In early 1993, the opposition parties announced that they would work within 'the present institutional arrangements', despite their objections to the conduct of the election and their non-representation in Parliament. They have attempted to challenge the government by making full use of the flourishing independent press, supporting peaceful demonstrations and strikes, and bringing constitutional cases before the courts. The latter tactic has been especially effective, reviving Ghana's long-established tradition of an independent judiciary and legal profession (Luckham, 1978), the Court of Appeal ruling against the government in a series of constitutional cases, including one in which it ruled that the anniversary of the 31 December revolution could no longer be celebrated as a public holiday. President Rawlings's response, that although his administration would 'respect the constitutional position of the Supreme Court, we cannot allow that arm of the government to stage a coup d'état against the other organs',[17] was a thinly veiled threat that no tampering would be permitted with the protections enjoyed by former members of the AFRC and PNDC regimes under the Transitional Provisions of the Constitution. Nor, whilst Rawlings and his associates hold office, is there any possibility of even a non-judicial enquiry into past human rights abuses, comparable to the Commission for Truth and Reconciliation in Chile.

However, many of the structures that supported repressive governance under the PNDC have been reformed or abolished. The Constitution provides for the integration of the Public Tribunals into the regular hierarchy of courts, and for new bodies to protect rights and increase governmental accountability. In theory the PNDC's shadowy parallel security apparatuses, notably the Forces Reserve Battalion, have been disbanded and their men integrated into the armed forces or elsewhere, though in fact they keep their operational independence. State support for the CDRs and other revolutionary organs is forbidden under the Constitution; instead, they are co-ordinated through a non-official 'Association of CDRs'. The BNI remains in place as the government's prime intelligence agency, but shares its responsibilities with a resurrected Department of Military Intelligence (see *Africa Confidential*, 21 January 1994). But what all this means in terms of the willingness and capacity of the government to cease spying on and intimidating its opponents, and to rein in its security bureaucracies, is still uncertain. Parliament has a Sub-committee on Defence and the Interior, but it is too early to judge whether it will be able to ensure effective legislative oversight over the military and security bureaucracies.

The Constitution vests responsibility for the armed forces in a National Security Council, an Armed Forces Council and a Ministry of Defence. In reality, however, most of the major decisions are taken, as before, by President Rawlings and a small circle of advisers, to a considerable degree bypassing the official machinery. In the military establishment itself, there exist broadly two main bodies of opinion: on the one hand, those who regard the return to constitutional rule as an opportunity to depoliticize, reprofessionalize and re-equip the armed forces as a more effective military force,[18] and on the other, those who continue to hold the view that 'the military has now become a major power bloc and is therefore a *de facto* political constituency' which should still be involved in the 'political administration of the country' (National Commission for Democracy, 1991: 84). The differences between them should not be exaggerated, however. For example, both groups resented the criticism and abuse levelled against the armed forces by the opposition during the transition process and the election campaigns. The Ghanaian military establishment is by no means as powerful and cohesive a corporate interest as that of Chile, nor as resistant to efforts to bring it under greater control. But neither can its interests and role in the consolidation (or otherwise) of democracy be ignored.

Ghana's new democracy, as we have seen, is still a long way from being consolidated. The most optimistic scenario would see the opposition being slowly reintegrated into the political process, contesting fair and free elections in 1996 (to ensure which the donor community is already offering various forms of support) and emerging as at the very least an effective parliamentary opposition, keeping the government on its toes, if not necessarily replacing it; whilst economic reforms (which have support from both government and opposition) continue to sustain growth in the economy.

This scenario could come under threat from a number of different directions, two of which are especially pertinent to this discussion. On the one hand, the government itself might call a halt to further political liberalization, or even reverse it, re-establishing some form of authoritarian governance behind a carapace of democratic institutions (a *democradura*). President Rawlings and his administration have already warned against 'irresponsible' press and opposition criticism, and been critical of the new-found independence of the judiciary. A more serious test of their respect for democratic procedures would come if there were a hiatus in the Economic Recovery Programme and/or major social unrest (both of which seemed rather more likely after demonstrations and strikes in early 1995 forced the government to postpone plans to introduce Value Added Tax, than they did at the time of transition in

1993). Another issue that could conceivably arise when the next elections are held in 1996 is whether President Rawlings would tolerate the prospect of electoral defeat. This is not an entirely hypothetical question, given his contemptuous remarks during the 1992 election about the ability of the opposition parties to run the country or carry through the ERP.

Were there such a crisis – caused either by election-rigging or by government refusal to accept defeat – the risks of military reintervention would be heightened. But this time it could conceivably be *against* the Rawlings government, to install another tutelary military regime, or to set in motion yet another attempted 'restoration of democracy'. The government may have increased its vulnerability to such intervention by partially dismantling the parallel repressive apparatuses and support structures (like the AFDCs) that protected the PNDC. To the extent that it becomes more reliant on a reprofessionalized officer corps, members of the latter are more likely to uphold the *Constitution* in a crisis, rather than the present government.[19] For this reason it probably continues to be in the government's best interest to respect the Constitution, and to ensure that the opposition is given opportunities to work within it, however much it may be tempted to do otherwise.

Conclusions

Contrary to the first impression that South Korea, Chile and Ghana have progressed along similar paths from developmental dictatorship to multi-party electoral democracy, despite wide variations in development, socio-economic structure and military power, more detailed analysis reveals important and sometimes unexpected differences (summarized in Table 4.5).

Chile is where most progress has been made in consolidating democracy and opening the system to political and social forces excluded under authoritarian governance. Yet its armed forces have clung tenaciously to their prerogatives, more so than in almost any other new democracy. But the wave of change has swept around the lonely military promontory they guard to the hinterland of civil and political society beyond. Return to military rule is more or less unthinkable; citizens enjoy substantial protections of their rights and freedoms; and executive accountability to the legislature is assured. Yet the

Table 4.5 Military and authoritarian residues after transition to democracy in South Korea, Chile and Ghana

	South Korea	Chile	Ghana
Military professional prerogatives	High	Very high	Medium
Military political prerogatives	Low	High	Medium
Prerogatives of security bureaucracies	Medium	High	High
Authoritarian residues elsewhere in state/regime	Medium	Low	High
Consolidation of democracy	Becoming consolidated	Becoming consolidated	Still in balance

governments of Presidents Aylwin and Frei have enjoyed very limited control over their military and security establishments because of the Faustian bargains made during the handover of power.

In South Korea there has been more *political* continuity between the outgoing and incoming regimes, mainly because of the fusion between the former government and opposition parties, which now form the ruling bloc. Indeed, it is arguable that this continuity, together with divisions in the armed forces, has hampered the latter's efforts to dictate their own terms for withdrawal. Presidents Roh and Kim have contrived to remove most of the political prerogatives of the military and security bureaucracies, whilst assuring their continued professional autonomy and centrality in the national security state. The main limitations on democracy remain those inherent in the conservative nature of the hegemonic bloc rather than the veto power of the military as such.

The balance of forces in Ghana is again different. The armed forces *per se* enjoyed less professional autonomy and political influence under authoritarian rule than in the other two countries. They remain less influential under civilian governance, mainly because they are still subordinated to the control structures put in place by the 'revolutionary' government of Flight Lieutenant Rawlings. Insofar as President Rawlings's administration is a democracy at all, it is arguably a 'delegative' (O'Donnell, 1994) not a liberal democracy, in that it bases its claim to govern directly on its mandate from the people and is somewhat resistant to attempts to make it horizontally accountable to parliament, the courts and the other institutions of a liberal state. It is the government's own tendency to reject restraints on its power, the weakness of the opposition, and continued surveillance by the intelligence and security bureaucracies, rather than the prerogatives of the military establishment, that are the main barriers to democratization. Yet even in Ghana, transition to constitutional rule has made a palpable difference to the conduct of government, by ruling out the more obvious forms of repression and by opening up spaces in which demands for further political change can be pressed.

What can democrats elsewhere learn from the experiences of these three countries? There are both broad historical lessons, and conclusions relevant to the political actors identified in the introduction to this volume: namely, political elites (including reformist soldiers); pro-democracy groups in civil society; and democracy promoters in the aid community. The former can be summed up in three broad propositions. First, not even well-consolidated authoritarian structures, of the kind that existed in all three countries under review, can indefinitely resist pressures to democratize. Second, the role of military and security establishments in transitions differs widely, even within the relatively narrow category of 'pacted' democratizations studied here. Third, the formal transfer of power is only the first chapter in a long and complicated story: the struggle *afterwards* to persuade suspicious, embattled military establishments to accept democratic control is every bit as important.

A distinctive feature of all three countries under review was that their ruling elites democratized pre-emptively once they realized repressive governance could no longer contain pressures for a democratic opening. Once pre-empted, pro-democracy groups in all three countries found themselves forced on to the defensive, facing hard choices about whether to co-operate with reform processes that might marginalize them (like the Ghanaian opposition, or South Korea's Left), or leave entrenched authoritarian enclaves (as in Chile). Although they probably had little choice but to collaborate on the best terms possible, the consequences have differed in accordance with their ability to mobilize support around democratic institutions in civil society. In Chile, where they were forced to concede most in terms of formal constitutional limitations, the fact that they were politically united and had strong foundations in civil society enabled them to neutralize Pinochet's constitutional advantages and monopoly of coercion, except in his narrow military domain. Strong civil society movements were also active in South Korea, but were counterbalanced by more conservative groups prepared to co-operate with regime elites to ensure a transition that would protect business and (to a degree) military interests. In contrast, in Ghana problems arising from division and demoralization among the main groups in civil and political society enabled the outgoing PNDC to co-opt the transition.

Pro-democracy groups not only need to empower themselves by remobilizing civil society, they should also have a credible policy for handling the armed forces. There is usually some scope for forging alliances with reformers in the latter, who do not necessarily wish to perpetuate military rule, and may even regard it as harmful to the military *qua* institution and profession. At the very least potential military supporters of democracy should not be alienated, as happened between opposition parties and many otherwise sympathetic soldiers during Ghana's 1992 elections. It is equally vital to wean military and security establishments from the practices of power acquired under dictatorship. Consensus needs to be forged between soldiers and civilians around reforms to reinstall civil supremacy, whilst respecting the military's need to maintain professionalism and have some voice in national security policy. The capacity of political actors, such as human rights groups, party defence spokespersons or legislative committees, to make informed judgements on security issues, to control defence budgets and to monitor abuses of power, needs to be enhanced. Most of all, civilian groupings should resist the temptation to invite the military in to arbitrate in political conflicts, however sorely tempted they might be by the 'undemocratic' behaviour of governments and other political actors.

The lessons for the donor community are fairly limited, especially as regards external military influence as a source of internal political reform. In Chile, the US arms and military aid embargo had little impact on the Pinochet regime, being offset by the inflow of foreign capital and economic support, as well as of arms from other Western sources. South Korea was enmeshed in an alliance with the United States during the entire period of authoritarian rule, yet there was no serious pressure on it to democratize until the late 1980s, and even then, internal developments probably had more effect than the diffuse signals coming from Washington. Western donors, and in particular Britain, provided military and economic assistance to Ghana during almost the whole PNDC period, and only tilted towards the promotion of democracy in the late 1980s. Even then, the change was signalled politically; never at any stage did the donors directly threaten to cut aid if the government failed to comply.

In sum, in all three countries, foreign pressure for democratization was applied inconsistently (if at all) prior to the late 1980s and even after then it was mostly exerted indirectly. Hence not much can be concluded about the efficacy of more direct forms of conditionality, such as curbing arms supplies or military aid, except that donors have tended to be reluctant to use them against regimes which have been show-cases of economic reform. The real test of donor intentions would come if there were an attempted reversion to authoritarian rule. In general, however, the best protection for democracy would still be the countervailing power of groups in civil and political society, rather than the support of a donor community which has lacked consistency, direction and sustained commitment.

Notes

1 I prefer the former term, and to use 'liberalization' more narrowly to refer to increases in constitutionally and legally protected rights and freedoms.

2 O'Donnell (1994) and Weffort (1993), for instance, make a further distinction between liberal and what they call 'delegative' democracy, where the executive has a plebiscitary relationship to the mass of citizens, and is insufficiently accountable to other democratic institutions. Delegative democracies, they argue, may in certain respects be more democratic than liberal democracies, but are normally less liberal.

3 Sierra Leone was the sole exception, where an army revolt from the ranks in 1968 paved the way for an elected government (that of President Siaka Stevens) which then turned itself into a civilian autocracy, only for the country to come under military rule again in 1992.

4 According to one poll held in 1991 (*FEER*, 14 March 1991), generals were ranked fourth from bottom in ethical and moral standards, compared with other high-level professionals (though Members of Parliament and senior police officers were even more poorly regarded!).

5 However, they may attach too much significance to the alleged incompatibility between personal and rational-legal forms of domination. Studies of military organizations suggest that (unlike classic Weberian bureaucracies) they are normally based on unique fusions of *both* kinds of domination (Luckham, 1971 and 1994). Most military regimes are likewise characterized by varying amalgams between personal and institutional sources of power.

6 A 10 per cent military levy on profits from the copper industry had been in existence since the 1920s, which the military government increased to 10 per cent of gross sales revenues.

7 Even so, individual trials have continued in the courts, though so far only in two cases have the military perpetrators of such crimes been convicted and imprisoned (in both cases for offences committed after 1978): *Guardian*, 2 April 1994.

8 However, the NLC and Busia regimes presided over a limited market-based re-vival, with 1 per cent real growth in GDP per capita between 1966 and 1971.

9 This was the basic pattern, though it is simplified in a number of respects. For example, the core group in 1966 included more middle-level than senior officers, though the latter predominated in the NLC junta. The 1978 'palace coup' by senior officers against Acheampong's colleagues was also a deviation from the pattern, but only a temporary one.

10 However, due to the large overall increases in public expenditure, military spending declined as a proportion of the current budget and increased only slightly as a share of the capital budget.

11 The study used a selected rather than a random sample. Hence its findings about the proportions of people favourable towards Rawlings and the ERP need to be interpreted with much caution.

12 At the beginning, military members included two of Rawlings's radical associates from the lower ranks as well as the GOC of the armed forces. During most of the period after the purges of late 1982, the GOC was the sole military representative, apart from Rawlings himself.

13 In interviews with the author in August 1994, Ghanaian officials claimed there was no specific political conditionality in terms of aid being promised or given in exchange for democratic reforms. Rather it was a case of their reading the political signals, for example in the relevant speeches by the British Foreign Secretary and Minister of Overseas Development.

14 Most of these are documented in Jeffries and Thomas (1993). Nevertheless they contend that the opposition had no real grounds for complaint, as it had been so confident of victory that it assented to fight the election in full knowledge it would do so on an unlevel playing field – an excessively Machiavellian line of reasoning.

15 The NPP's presidential candidate, Adu Boahen, argues that the opposition parties had little choice. Not only would they have faced more intimidation in the parliamentary elections, they would also have had to contend with a mass revolt by party organizers in the constituencies: interview, June 1994.

16 However, African military rulers like Mobutu in Zaïre have civilianized their rule, formed parties and held plebiscitary, but not genuinely contested elections.

17 Speech at state opening of Parliament, cited in *West Africa*, 16–22 May 1994.

18 The view taken by the present Chief of Defence Staff, who is a strong advocate of greater transparency and public discussion of defence and military matters. Interview with the author, August 1994.

19 The same may also be true of men in the ranks; it is widely believed that the opposition won a majority of votes in the Burma Camp in Accra and other military installations during the 1992 presidential election, although this was officially denied, and cannot be verified in the absence of detailed poll breakdowns.

5

Civil society, democratization and development

GORDON WHITE

Together with the market and democracy, 'civil society' is one of the magic trio of developmental panaceas which emerged in the 1980s and now dominate conventional prescriptions for the global ills of the 1990s. As the third element of a comprehensive reaction against the 'dirigisme' of developmental states in the 1960s and 1970s, civil society is a sociological counterpart to the market in the economic sphere and to democracy in the political sphere. As such, it is a valuable analytical complement to the tired old 'state–market' paradigm in discussing broad issues of development. However, while each of these three ideas reflects key historical processes and embodies potentially powerful solutions to the central problems of development, they are commonly used in vague, simplistic or biased ways.[1] This encourages wishful thinking and blunts their practical utility.

Never more so than with the idea of civil society, an idea which has a long and distinguished but highly ambiguous history in Western political theory (see Keane, 1988: part I). Over the past decade it has been dusted off and deodorized to suit a variety of ideological, intellectual and practical needs. The result is that, though there is now a paradigm of thought and discussion about the developmental implications of 'civil society', the term means different things to different people and often degenerates into a vapid political slogan. The resulting confusion could wreak havoc in the real world, given the fact that the civil societies of developing countries have now been recognized as a legitimate area of external intervention by aid donors as part of an ever deepening process of international social engineering (e.g. Blair, 1992; Landell-Mills, 1992).

The central aim of this chapter is to investigate the relationship between civil society and democratization in the context of developing nations. Does civil society contribute to democratization and, if so, how?

The meaning of 'civil society'

The rehabilitation of 'civil society' as a term of political and social scientific discourse can be traced to its role in explaining the crises which have befallen authoritarian developmental states over the past decade, particularly in identifying the social forces which have participated in struggles against overweening state power. The term came to prominence in the late 1970s and early 1980s with the rise of social movements against the Communist states of Eastern Europe, notably Solidarity in Poland and a variety of oppositional groups in Hungary, Czechoslovakia and Yugoslavia (Hann, 1990; Gathy, 1989; Miller, 1992). To the extent that the task of redressing the political balance between overbearing states and repressed societies was an important priority elsewhere, 'civil society' has been a useful intellectual tool in contexts as far apart as South America, sub-Saharan Africa and Taiwan (see Hsiao, 1990). The idea became embroiled in a demonology of the state, often serving as an idealized counter-image, an embodiment of social virtue confronting political vice: the realm of freedom versus that of coercion, of participation versus hierarchy, pluralism versus conformity, spontaneity versus manipulation, purity versus corruption (for an example in the case of South Korea see Ahn, 1991). While this makes the term useful as a rationale for political struggle, it reduces its value as a social scientific concept.

Despite the growth of a cottage industry among political theorists bent on tracing the roots of the idea of 'civil society', its precise meaning remains elusive. It is often used loosely to mean either society as opposed to the state[2] or, more precisely, as an intermediate sphere of social organization or association between the basic units of society – families and firms – and the state.[3] This can include decidedly 'uncivil' entities like the Mafia, 'primordial' nationalist, ethnic or religious fundamentalist organizations, and 'modern' entities such as trade unions, chambers of commerce and professional associations. Faced with this social farrago, some authors try to give the term a more precise meaning. For instance, Lise Rakner (1992: 47) restricts it to organizations which actually interact with the state (as opposed, for example, to 'remote community organisations, kinship groups, some religious societies and self-help groups located in rural communities which stand apart from the state and shun all contact with it'). Jean-François Bayart links it with the notion of antagonism between state and society, restricting it to those social organizations which embody 'society in its relations with the state insofar as it is in confrontation with the state' (1986: 111).[4]

While such attempts at greater precision may reflect the experience of particular regions of the South or a desire for empirical convenience, others have reflected divergent intellectual and political traditions. For example, Hugh Roberts equates civil society with 'political society' in the sense of a particular relationship between state and society based on the principles of citizenship, rights, representation and the rule of law (Roberts, 1987: 4). As such, it becomes virtually indistinguishable from a standard conception of a liberal democratic polity and probably should be described as such. Marxists may equate it with 'bourgeois society' on the grounds that historically the rise of civil society has accompanied the the rise of capitalism and, in Marx's writing, the term *bürgerlich* can be translated as both 'bourgeois' and 'civil'.[5] Others work (in most cases implicitly) within the sociological paradigm of modernization theory, thereby regarding 'traditional' associations as 'pre-civil', limiting civil society to 'modern' organizations such as trade unions, Christian groups, and business or professional associations, and converting 'civil' into a virtual synonym of 'modern' (Rakner, 1992: 46). Analysts in the US tradition of pluralist political analysis tend to see civil society as a field of interest groups, often viewing the political process as a market and political outcomes as representing equilibria resulting from the interplay of social actors in civil society (e.g. see Blair, 1992: 30).

The term 'civil society' has also been hijacked to further various developmental or political projects, each with its own preferred sector of associational life. Neo-populist development theorists and practitioners extol the virtues of grass-roots non-governmental organizations as paradigms of social participation, alternative developmental agencies and potential building blocks of democracy. Economic liberals bolster their case for deregulation and privatization by emphasizing how these policies contribute to the emergence of business interests to counterbalance and discipline wayward states. Treasury-based cost-cutters see devolution of governmental functions to voluntary organizations as an ideologically palatable way of reducing state expenditure. Conservative thinkers see it as a way of preserving traditional social solidarities in the face of the disruptions caused by markets. Radical socialists zero in on the potential role of social organizations based on community, group or issue in transforming society or providing an alternative form of social governance (Hirst, 1993).

Can we disperse this ambiguity and come up with a serviceable notion of civil society which will help us to explore its role in establishing and maintaining democracy? If the concept is so ambiguous and confusing, cannot the issues it raises be analysed more efficiently by talking about changing forms and dynamics of state–society relations? In this framework, civil society could be viewed as but one particular form of the political relationship between state and society, along the lines suggested by those who equate civil society with the liberal notion of political society. In looking at particular societies, one would be seeking to identify and explain the emergence of the social forces which play a political role in establishing such a relationship.

But a selective approach of this kind would probably lead us to espouse one or other of the intellectual paradigms mentioned earlier: 'civil society' as referring only to modern forms of association, or to those which accept the principles of liberal democracy, or to the organizational repercussions of the growth of capitalism. Each approach would select a particular group of social organizations as 'truly civil', the rest being presumably 'uncivil', 'non-civil' or 'pre-civil' because they are traditional, authoritarian or pre-capitalist. Each of these approaches carries with it characteristic biases and limitations and each runs the risk of pressing analysis into a manichean mould, with civil society taking on distinctly 'good' or 'bad' connotations by definition. However, if we are aware of these limitations, each of these approaches to civil society – which in different ways link its growth to the development of liberal democracy – can be converted into a potentially productive empirical inquiry. We could draw up a set of 'democratic' benchmarks against which specific types of social organization can be assessed to see whether or not they merit the term 'civil' and go on to investigate historically the ways in which they have contributed to the emergence and consolidation of democratic institutions.

However, in current development debates 'civil society' is used to denote a much more complex social universe. It makes more practical sense to try to come to terms with this breadth rather than defining it away. The main idea which is common to most current uses of the term is that of *an intermediate associational realm between state and family populated by organizations which are separate from the state, enjoy autonomy in relation to the state and are formed voluntarily by members of society to protect or advance their interests or values.*[6] This approach prompts us to recognize the realities of 'actually existing civil societies'[7] rather than to search for some ideal type. It is more appropriate to the hybrid character of developing societies and can better capture the consequent diversity of their associational life. It would also give us a more complete picture of the social forces which obstruct as well as facilitate democratization.

We would then need to distinguish between different types or sectors of civil society: for example, between 'modern' interest groups such as trade unions or professional associations and 'traditional' ascriptive organizations based on kinship, ethnicity, culture or religion; between formal organizations and informal social networks based on patrimonial or clientelistic allegiances; between those institutions with specifically political roles as pressure or advocacy groups and those whose activities remain largely outside the political system; between legal or open associations and secret or illegal organizations such as the Freemasons, the Mafia or the Triads; between associations which accept the political status quo or those which seek to transform it by changing the political regime (such as a guerrilla movement or a reactionary religious organization) or redefining the nation (as in the former Yugoslavia).[8]

These distinctions are important for understanding the relationship between civil society and democracy because one would expect different sectors of civil society to have different orientations to the prospect or the reality of democratic politics. Depending on the context, some elements of civil society would be politically uninvolved, some tolerant or supportive of authoritarian rule, some working towards an alternative conception of democracy radically different from the liberal version, and some 'progressive' in the sense that they favour and foster a liberal democratic polity. Thus any statement to the effect that a 'strong' civil society is more conducive to democratization would be meaningless unless one went further to identify the specific constellation of politically active social forces which support democratization in a given context. As Bayart (1986: 118) has argued in the African context, 'The advance of a civil society which does not necessarily contain the democratic ideal does not in itself ensure the democratisation of the political system'. Conversely, the statement that a 'weak' civil society is not conducive to democratization would be equally suspect: witness the case of the former Soviet Union where the main thrust towards democratization came from within the Party/state apparatus and not under pressure from civil society. Since we are interested in the role which civil society plays in fostering democracy, we shall concentrate on those particular sectors which can be described as 'democratic'. However, the latter would have to be analysed within the context of a wider civil society which may contain anti-democratic, undemocratic and non-political entities.

If we choose to identify civil society as a distinct, but broadly defined, sphere of intermediate social associations, we should, before proceeding, clarify its relationship to the state on the one side and society on the other. Though the conventional dichotomy between state and civil society is important in identifying the latter as a social sphere separate from and independent of the former, it oversimplifies the relationship. We should take care to distinguish between civil society as an ideal-type concept which embodies the qualities of separation, autonomy and voluntary association in their pure form, and the real world of civil societies composed of associations which embody these principles to varying degrees. In this latter world, the boundaries between state and civil society are often blurred. States may play an important role in shaping civil society as well as vice versa; the two organizational spheres may overlap to varying degrees (for example, the case of public sector unions and professional associations, or intermediate 'quangos' embodying representation from both sides); individuals may play roles in both sectors; and the principle of voluntary association may be infringed through political pressure or legal regulation. In particular, the autonomy of civil society organizations is highly variable – a question of degree rather than either/or.

Turning to the relationship between civil society and society more generally, civil society derives its specific political character from the deeper socio-economic structure of a society and the distribution of interests, social norms and power which it embodies. But note two aspects of this relationship. First, as a separate and distinct sphere of social relations, civil society itself embodies a specific source of social empowerment based on a capacity for association. Second, we cannot regard civil society as a mere reflection of the socio-economic structure because the degrees of organizational representation and associational capacity of different sectors are different. As the theorists of collective action constantly remind us, the capacity for collective action is affected by factors such as the number of participants, or the resources available to them (for example, it is usually easier for a small group of large landowners to organize and exert influence than a large number of small tenants). The sad paradox is that those with greater access to socio-economic resources find it easier to organize effectively and vice versa. Though this may tend to reinforce unequal social relations, it can be contested through strategies aimed at the empowerment of relatively deprived groups through association-building (Landell-Mills (1992) stresses the need for such strategies). In this context, the question is not merely one of building up civil society against the state, but of building up one sector of civil society against another, as, for example, with the clash between unionized rural workers and merchant cartels in parts of rural India (Harriss-White, 1993: 57).

Moreover, when discussing the relationships between civil society and political systems, it is useful to make a further distinction between civil society, political society and the state. Drawing on Stepan (1988: 3–4), one can distinguish between the state, which refers to the apparatus of administrative, judicial, legislative and military organizations,[9] and political society, which refers to a range of institutions and actors which mediate and channel the relationships between civil society and the state. Two crucial elements of political society are political parties and political leaders, both of which can act to strengthen or weaken the democratic or authoritarian potential of a given configuration of civil society. For example, parties may be integrative institutions in that they are able to group together disparate or conflictual elements of civil society into broad and stable political coalitions; alternatively, they may act divisively to intensify the inherent schisms. Political leaders may play similarly varying roles. Even detractors of the former president of Zambia, Kenneth Kaunda, admit that he was very skilled at mitigating potential ethnic antagonisms, whereas his counterpart in Kenya has been accused of fomenting ethnic conflict to stay in power. Indeed, Claude Ake (1991: 34) argues that the main political problem in Africa derives not from ethnic conflict but from bad political leadership.

The relationship between civil society and democratization

Expectations about the role of civil society

The idea of civil society is central to any discussion of democratization since it raises fundamental questions about the role of social forces in defining, controlling and legitimating state power. In current debates about the evolution of developing countries, it is argued that the growth of civil society, in its modern form at least, can play a crucial role not merely by undermining authoritarian governments and fostering a democratic polity, but also by improving the quality of governance within that polity.

We can identify four ways in which this might come about. First, a growing civil society can alter the *balance of power* between state and society in favour of the latter, thereby contributing to the kind of balanced opposition held to be characteristic of developed democratic regimes. In the context of the authoritarian developmental states which pervaded the South from the 1960s to the 1980s, this implies a gradually increasing ability of organized social forces to weaken the capacity of states which have sought, to a greater or lesser extent, 'to administer society, even against itself, and to order it according to the explicit canons of modernity' (Bayart, 1986: 113).

The balance of power between states and civil societies varies widely: from totalist state-socialist regimes where the state is all-pervasive and civil society is either non-existent or marooned on embattled islands, to formerly authoritarian regimes in Latin America and East Asia where the writ of the state was extensive, but certain organized forces of civil society enjoyed some freedom of action, to the situation in many African countries where the state might have been the dominant institution in society, but was itself weak and eroded by particularistic social pressures, a 'Leviathan with feet of clay' (Chabal, 1986a: 15). In this case, both the state and the modern sector of civil society were weak. (For a fascinating analysis of the Algerian bureaucracy in these terms, see Roberts, 1983.)

Second, a strong civil society can play a *disciplinary role* in relation to the state by enforcing standards of public morality and performance and improving the accountability of both politicians and administrators. This role reflects Lord Acton's maxim that 'power tends to corrupt and absolute power corrupts absolutely'; a more powerful civil society will exert greater pressure on state officials to act more responsibly. In the African context, for example, Wraith and Simpkins (1963) made this case by drawing on the experience of changes in the character of British public institutions from the seventeenth to the nineteenth century. Of course, the validity of this argument depends on which sector of civil society one is talking about. In the British case, the key groups in question were the entrepreneurs and professional groups of the new bourgeois order. However, if a currently emerging civil society involves, say, ethnic associations seeking sectional advantage or business groups bent on buying political influence, the result could be forms of public behaviour which, while accountable in some sense, would prove unacceptable to advocates of this argument. It may also rest on over-optimistic assumptions about the moral and political character of civil society in modern capitalist societies.

Third, civil society plays a potentially crucial role as an *intermediary* or (two-way) transmission-belt between state and society in ways which condition the relationship between individual citizens and the formal political system. In an optimistic scenario, an active civil society can serve to improve the performance of democratic polities by articulating the interests of sectors of the population. It can facilitate political communication between state and society, functioning thereby as an alternative principle of representation complementary to periodic elections and as an additional mechanism for strengthening democratic accountability. It can also economize, as it were, on the transaction costs of democracy by identifying, packaging and relaying political demands which otherwise might remain dormant or be expressed in fragmentary or ineffective ways. By so doing, it may exert a disciplinary effect on society by channelling and processing disparate demands and contributing thereby to ameliorating the fundamental contradiction between the state as a (more or less) unitary institution and the citizenry as a collection of atomized individuals. This aspect is emphasized by elitist theories which stress the important role played by the leaders of civil society organizations in underpinning the stability and effectiveness of democratic regimes. In the various forms of corporatism, moreover, this intermediary role takes on an institutionalized form. In a more pessimistic scenario, civil society may act to increase pressures on the state beyond tolerable limits, contributing thereby to a crisis of 'governability'. It may also polarize conflicts between social interests and contribute thereby to political instability and decay, a phenomenon to which we shall return when discussing the issue of social mobilization and 'hyper-mobilization'.

Fourth, civil society can play a *constitutive* role by redefining the rules of the political game along democratic lines. This can be conceived of in pragmatic terms, in the sense that certain organizations of civil society see it as in their interest to observe a set of political rules of the game characteristic of competitive liberal democracy and can therefore agree among themselves to perpetuate these rules. Adam Przeworski argues along these lines when he says that 'democracy is consolidated when compliance – acting within the institutional framework – constitutes the equilibrium of the decentralised strategies of all the relevant political forces' (Przeworski, 1991: 26). There is a slight tautological tinge to this approach (rules are effective because enough social actors want them to be), it tends to rely too heavily on a rather simplistic notion of market equilibrium drawn from economics and it probably begs far more questions than it answers; but it contains an obvious political truth.

While Przeworski tends to analyse the setting up and observance of democratic rules as the result of pragmatic considerations and to discount the role of norms which define political legitimacy, others have argued that the constitutive role of civil society extends beyond organizational interest into the normative sphere, i.e. that civil society creates and sustains a set of new democratic norms which regulate the behaviour of the state and the character of political relations between state and the public sphere of society and individual citizens. As Dwayne Woods argues, 'the public in many African countries is attempting to articulate a principle of political accountability that is binding on the state elite' (1992: 95), a principle characteristic of that found in established Western democracies and radically contradictory to previous forms of accountability based on ethnic, regional or patrimonial principles. Bayart makes a similar point when he refers to the need for a 'new cultural fabric' and a 'conceptual challenge' in the African context (1986: 120). Thus different sectors of civil society can be expected to have different sets of norms about the political relationship between state and society, and the yea or nay of democracy would depend on the interaction between these sectors. For our purposes, it would be sensible to consider both the pragmatic and the normative dimensions of the political impact of civil society.

But a third element, power, is lacking in both these approaches. On the pragmatic side, different sectors of civil society have different power resources at their disposal, and notions of democratic consensus based on market equilibria tend to marginalize these. Just as real markets contain inequalities and exploitation, so civil societies contain inequalities and domination, and the resolution of any competitive game between components of civil society depends heavily on its internal balance of power. In the words of Samuel Bowles and Herbert Gintis, heterogeneous social power 'gives rise to a multiplicity of distinct structures of dominance and subordinacy in social life' (Bowles and Gintis, 1987: 32). Similarly, the capacity of different systems of norms to define and sustain political arrangements depends on the power embodied in or lying behind each system. Rueschemeyer and his colleagues make this point forcefully when they argue that 'it is power relations that most importantly determine whether democracy can emerge, stabilise and then maintain itself even in the face of adverse conditions' (Rueschemeyer *et al.*, 1992: 5). Similarly, Michael Bratton defines the recent transitions to democracy as embodying 'a struggle between incumbent and opposition political interests over both the rules of the political game and the resources with which it is played' (Bratton, 1992: 82). Understanding of these power dimensions in turn requires that civil society must again be considered in terms of its relationship to the broader socio-economic structure in which it is embedded. Thus, the constitution or otherwise of democracy is not merely a contest between state and civil society, but also depends on patterns of conflict and co-operation in these three aspects – interests, norms and power – between the constituent parts of civil society.

Moreover, when assessing the process of and prospects for democratization in any country, the specific cluster of power, interests and norms embedded in civil society/society must be identified as only one among three power clusters, the others being the political forces embedded in the international environment and in the state itself. In any given context of democratization (or its reverse), therefore, the 'civil society factor' may be more or less influential depending on the current and evolving balance of power between these three clusters.

Hypotheses about the historical relationship

In the Pollyanna-ish days of 1960s post-colonialism, it was felt by many that a combination of wise institutional bequests by the colonizers and gradual socio-economic improvement would lead to the consolidation of democracy in the South. However, the ensuing experience of de-democratization, buttressed by sobering studies of the ambiguous relationships between socio-economic and political levels of development, led to a new orthodoxy, crystallized in the seminal work of Samuel Huntington on *Political Order in Changing Societies* (1968). The central thrust of this view was that the excessive political pressures exerted on states in developing countries, resulting from social mobilization in pursuit of rapid improvements in material welfare, would lead to a crisis of governability. In consequence, strong and probably authoritarian states were needed to provide the institutional capacity to control and process these pressures. If we rephrase this argument in the language of civil society, the rapidly growing strength of the latter would pose political problems – not, as today, solutions – since it would intensify the barrage of social demands raining down on hard-pressed states. For example, this kind of hyper-mobilization resulting from a rapid explosion of demands from previously excluded social groups has been adduced as an explanation for the breakdown of Chilean democracy in 1973. (The original argument was by Landsberger and McDaniel, 1976; for a critical response see Rueschemeyer *et al.*, 1992: 332, n. 65).

However, the current paradigm of civil society has returned, implicitly, to the ideas of the 1960s. It rests on historical arguments about the character and political repercussions of socio-economic development. The story of civil society can be told in different analytical languages. In the discourse of modernization theory, the process of modernization leads to greater social differentiation which is the potential basis of political pluralism; to higher levels of education and awareness which lead to greater popular expectations from government and greater ability to comprehend and participate in national-level politics; to a spread of specialized expertise which creates powerful elites increasingly able to enforce their claims in the political arena; and to the diffusion of the kind of secular and universalistic values which are conducive to the operations of modern bureaucracies and democratic polities. These changes provide the underlying conditions for, and impetus towards, liberal democracy which is the unchallenged institutional embodiment of political modernity.

Liberal and Marxist political economists, in their different ways, portray a similar great transformation. This identifies certain momentous social repercussions of the rise of the bourgeoisie which provide the political impetus first for liberalization and then for democratization: the pluralization of social power and the separation of the public and private spheres; the links between the assertion of private ownership rights and the demand for political rights and freedoms; the force of the market in undermining state power; the desire of the dominant classes to tame the state and transform it into an efficient instrument to further their own interests; and the democratizing influence of the other groups brought into existence through successful capitalist development (the professional middle strata and the industrial working class).

The traditions differ in their view of the political end-point. On the liberal side, the 'end of history' is represented by the global triumph of liberal democracy, defined primarily in terms of a set of institutionalized procedures and guarantees. On the Marxist/socialist side, the feasibility of a radically different model, embodied in the theory and practice of Communism and the notion of 'socialist democracy' which it laid claim to, has been dealt a mortal blow by the collapse of the Soviet bloc. Yet radical socialists, Marxist or not, define the nature of democracy and thus the process of democratization in terms which go well beyond the liberal model, stressing the need to democratize society as well as the state (Bowles and Gintis, 1987). As Przeworski argues (in O'Donnell *et al.*, 1986a: 63), 'Democracy restricted to the political realm has historically coexisted with exploitation at the workplace, within the schools, within bureaucracies, and within families.'

Yet, though these two traditions differ in their definitions of democracy, they agree to some extent about the role of civil society organizations themselves as potential microcosms of democracy, practising in their internal relations the kind of 'organizational citizenship' which makes each of them a basic building block in the edifice of a national-level democratic system. For example, in the socialist tradition, Claus Offe and Ulrich Preuss (1991) argue that a 'civilized democratic polity' should be based on a continual process of micropolitical learning within the organizations of civil society. However, in the real world of civil society, the degree of democratic participation within associations varies widely and thus the contribution of the microcosms to the consolidation of a democratic macropolitical system would depend on the specific configuration of different types of association.

To a considerable extent, the current language of 'civil society' represents an eclectic, and often highly confused and undigested, amalgam of disparate ideas used to address pressing political and developmental problems. Implicitly or explicitly, there is an underlying historical hypothesis: of a transition from a previous political situation characterized by state dominance and traditional social relations (pre-modern or pre-capitalist) to an emergent or established situation in which new forms of civil society, reflecting a new pattern of socio-economic relations and institutions, serve to transform the state and their relations with it. If we apply this to any given society, we would need to investigate the extent to which its particular level and pattern of development has led, first, to a shift in the balance of power between the state and emergent socio-economic forces; second, to a basic change in the social character of the associational forms through which these forces articulate and impel their interests in the social and political arenas; and third, to an increasing desire on the part of the latter to consolidate and extend their new-found influence by redesigning the political system along democratic lines. One would expect, for instance, that the shift in the balance of power between state and society, the transformation of civil society itself and the impetus towards democratization would be more pronounced in societies which have undergone a relatively successful process of industrialization. One would also expect, *ceteris paribus*, that the degree of heterogeneity of a given society would not only reflect the extent to which civil society has been transformed (along modern or bourgeois lines), but would also affect the likelihood of its being able to develop the 'organisation principle', in Bayart's words (1986: 117), which would enable it to create and sustain a viable democratic regime.

To summarize these first two sections: we have sought to clarify the main ideas involved in discussing the relationship between civil society and democratization and to identify some central hypotheses about the nature of this relationship. The next step is to use this framework to analyse current processes of democratization in Southern contexts through selected case studies.

Two case studies

Given their evident complexity, the relationships between civil society and democratization can best be explored through case studies of societies undergoing democratic transition, using a configurative approach which looks at the intersection between more general trends and specific national patterns of response. The most important general trends which affected the 'third wave' of democratization in the 1980s and early 1990s were changes in the international environment – notably the collapse of the East and the end of the Cold War, increasing globalization in the world economy, the spread of internally or externally generated economic liberalization, the rise of political conditionality among aid donors and the snowball effect of democratization elsewhere (see Huntington, 1991: 100ff.). These trends have impinged on different regions and countries in different ways and have interacted with the internal dynamics of specific societies to produce distinctive experiences of democratization.

We have chosen two countries in different regions of the developing world: South Korea in East Asia and Zambia in sub-Saharan Africa. This choice also has an historical dimension, since one would expect the character of civil society and the viability of a democratic polity to depend heavily on the level of socio-economic development of a given country. According to the World Bank's basic indicators, Zambia is a 'low-income economy' with a GNP per capita in 1993 of US$380, while South Korea is an 'upper-middle-income' economy with a GNP per capita of $7,660 in 1993 (World Bank, 1995: 162–3). Their developmental trajectories are also very different. South Korea is a classic case of successful late industrialization which has transformed its society and economy in the space of a few decades under a repressive modernizing military regime. Zambia is a failed modernizer whose initial post-independence gains have been eroded by the economic and political crises of the 1980s which destroyed the credibility of its key leader and its hegemonic political institution. The historical approach enables us to situate the rapid democratic transitions of the late 1980s and early 1990s in the context of the more glacial, longer-term socio-economic determinants of democratic durability, of which a transformed civil society is one. The distinction between transition and durability is important because, as Rueschemeyer *et al.* point out (1992: 76), the forces which instal democracy may differ from those which maintain it. In each case study, therefore, we would want to go beyond a mere analysis of the political dynamics of transition to look at the social, economic and political variables which shape the longer-term feasibility of political transformation. Our central questions are thus as follows: why did a transition to democracy take place in a given country, how sustainable is this democracy, and what role does civil society play in both these processes?

South Korea: an emergent civil society

In the mid-1980s, South Korea made a decisive step in the transition from an authoritarian to a democratic regime. The symbolic starting point was in October 1987 when the National Assembly and the electorate approved a new Constitution, heralded as ushering in a new Democratic Era under the leadership of Roh Tae Woo to replace the military regime of Chun Doo Hwan. This followed, and was in considerable part a response to, an unprecedentedly intensive wave of popular protests during 1986 and 1987 involving students, workers and Christian organizations. Official estimates suggest that there were no less than 1,700 protest demonstrations in 1986 alone (Billet, 1990: 300). It seems that certain organizations in civil society played a major role in propelling the transition.

South Korea is one of the four 'little tigers' of East and South-East Asia which have been the most outstanding and consistent economic performers in the erstwhile developing world over the past three decades, with an annual growth rate of GNP per capita of 7.1 per cent between 1965 and 1990. The country has undergone a dramatically successful process of rapid industrialization which catapulted it into the second echelon of global economic powers. The result was a funda-mental transformation of the economic structure, as described in Chapter 3, with major changes in levels of popular well-being. To cite two indices, average life expectancy had reached 71 by 1990 (compared with 76 in Britain) and the infant mor-tality rate had dropped from 62 per thousand live births in 1965 to 17 in 1990. In education, secondary enrolments rose from 35 to 86 per cent of cohort between 1965 and 1989 (with female enrolment rising even faster from 25 to 84 per cent) and tertiary enrolments rose from 6 to 38 per cent of the age cohort (compared with 31 per cent in Japan). The urban popu-lation rose from 32 to 72 per cent of the total population between 1965 and 1990.

This process of industrialization was presided over until the latter part of the 1980s by authoritarian military governments which created a strong and autonomous state bureaucracy to direct economic change and exert social control. The Korean state could be described as 'hard authoritarian' during the 1960s and 1970s, repressing or harassing oppositional activity and intermittently attempting to impose comprehensive corporatist controls over the population (for notions of 'hard' and 'soft' authoritarianism in the East Asian context, see Winckler, 1984). However, there was still an area of social space in which in-dependent associations could operate and some limited scope for political competition. To this extent, a nascent civil soci-ety was able intermittently to mount an organized challenge to authoritarian control.

The core of the ruling elite included senior administrators, legislative and party politicians, military officers and big busi-ness, organized through 'bureaucratic rings' (Kim K.W., 1992). However, the industrialization which it sponsored created new classes and strata which gathered strength during the

1970s and 1980s. There is a good deal of contention about the precise contours of the contemporary Korean social structure (Dong, 1991). One estimate for 1987, based on a sample of the male population, using a composite index of income level, house ownership and educational attainment, produced the following breakdown: capitalists 2 per cent, new intermediate strata 15 per cent (mainly technical and clerical white-collar workers), old intermediate strata 9 per cent (medical and legal professionals and small–medium self-employed), working class 43 per cent, urban semi-proletariat 9 per cent, and farmers and fishermen 22 per cent (Dong, 1991: 271). The figure of around 24 per cent for the middle class is rather low compared with other surveys cited by Dong which place greater reliance on asking people to estimate their own social status. In fact, estimates of the Korean middle class range from 23 per cent to 84 per cent of the population!

On the eve of the surge towards democratization in the mid-1980s, three classes were politically important as the basis of civil society. First, a differentiated capitalist class located in different levels of private enterprise, dominated by a small number of large conglomerates, the *chaebol*, which had been nurtured by the previous authoritarian regime (Kuk, 1988). Second, an urban working class in both labour- and capital-intensive industries, with large concentrations in the *chaebol*. Third, a complex middle class composed of members of the liberal professions, intellectuals and white-collar clerical and technical personnel in the public and private sectors, along with their aspirant successors among the student population. By the mid-1980s, there was already considerable evidence that not only were these groups growing in size and social influence, but they were also becoming increasingly restive under the constraints of authoritarian rule and were attempting to push back the frontiers of political possibility.

The capitalists, particularly their upper stratum, remained heavily dependent on state patronage. In Korea's highly concentrated industrial structure, the business elite was a tiny group, linked, both internally and with state elites, through informal ties based on marriage or regional background. Suh (1989: 132) estimates, for example, that in the case of 15 *chaebol* he studied, each had an average of 2.7 marriage ties with other *chaebol* and 2.3 with ministers or vice-ministerial-level elites. Nevertheless, businessmen were increasingly chafing during the 1980s against what they regarded as unreasonable restrictions or onerous financial exactions on the part of officials and politicians. Moreover, the economic liberalization measures which began in the early 1980s increased their power in both the industrial and the financial sectors (see Chapter 3). By the late 1980s, argues Eckert (1990: 125), the *chaebol* had 'become too important to the economy for the state to ignore their needs and demands'. The main business association, the Federation of Korean Industry, also increased its activity in pursuit of greater corporate autonomy, which was to include more freedom for commercial banks in the mostly state-controlled financial sector.[10]

Turning to industrial labour, the rapid increase in their numbers in the 1970s had already led to disputes which brought organized workers into conflict with the coercive organs of the state and its corporatist labour organizations. Labour activism was facilitated by the relatively high rate of literacy among workers, particularly effective militancy on the part of women workers and outside support, particularly from Christian activists. According to Bianchi (1986), a strike by women workers was a precipitating factor in the struggle within the political elite which culminated in the assassination of President Park in 1979. While labour unrest played a relatively small role in the agitation leading up to the decision by Roh Tae Woo in June 1987 to introduce democratic reforms, the number of unions increased from 2,742 in June, when his announcement was made, to 4,103 by the end of the year (Kim Young Rae, 1992: 6). This proliferation played an important role in maintaining the impetus to democratization.

As for the white-collar middle class, political and social militancy in the 1970s and early 1980s was heavily channelled through Christian bodies which were able to avoid easy classification as political organizations and could depend on support from abroad, particularly the United States. The spread of Christianity during the 1970s was phenomenal, from $4^{1}/_{2}$ million to over 10 million, about one-quarter of the population. Indeed, since socialist forms of radicalism were linked to North Korean Communism and suppressed, Christianity provided the main ideological vehicle for political opposition to the Park regime in the heyday of hard authoritarianism. Christian churches, both Protestant and, increasingly during the 1980s, Catholic, also set up organizations to support the struggling independent workers' movement, notably the Urban Industrial Mission (Bianchi, 1986: 527). Another part of the middle class (in waiting) were university students who maintained their role as the most visible force in the struggle against authoritarian rule which had begun with their unseating of the Syngman Rhee government in 1960. They took the lead in the democratization movement which followed the death of Park Chung Hee, culminating in the bloodily repressed urban revolt in Kwangju in 1980 during which student activists received widespread support across the whole spectrum of the urban population (Eggleston, 1991). This and other popular movements at the turn of the decade were also supported by critical journalists in a press which was seeking to raise its voice. These organized groups expanded during the 1980s and increasingly co-ordinated their activities, strengthened by determined leadership provided by dissidents (known as 'the forces in the field'), who had been victims of previous waves of repression. These middle-class groups were at the forefront of the public agitation which tipped the political balance in 1987.

Historically speaking, there was a dual process at work here. South Korea seems a good example of a historical pattern whereby a developmentally successful authoritarian regime digs its own political grave by sponsoring the rise of ultimately hostile social forces. Successive authoritarian governments were weakened by their unwillingness to allow significant political concessions to these new forces and clung to economic performance as their (increasingly fragile) claim to legitimacy. Though this historical dynamic fits the case, it is too neat and mechanistic to provide a full explanation. Rather, we can detect a double dynamic at work. The first is the longer-term and slower-moving political consequences of industrialization in terms of the growth of private economic power, a changing occupational structure, and higher levels of education and material welfare. The second is the more fluid and volatile arena of politics itself, specifically the persistent and mounting struggles waged by opposition forces in both political and civil society during the previous decade which nagged away at the authority and credibility of the regime, intensified dissensus among the political elite, mobilized international support and generally set the political scene for the change of regime in 1987. Particularly striking is the courage shown by, and the political impact of, organizations of students, workers and Christians, acting both separately and together. The opposition parties also played an important role through their dramatic successes in the 1985 elections (Bedeski 1992: 152–3). The political elite was increasingly harassed, divided and uncertain, increasingly unable to impose its writ even on its own clients, weakened by economic liberalization, pressured into reform by its main external ally, the United States, and further bedevilled by contingent factors such as the example of 'people's power' in the Philippines in 1986 and the prospect of embarrassment during the Seoul Olympics in 1988.

One can also trace a double dynamic in the political role of civil society in the transition. Most of the groups discussed above played a highly visible role in pushing for change; one could call them a 'sunlight civil society'. But it was the business elite which probably played the decisive role in the downfall of the Chun regime, operating informally behind the scenes as a 'shadow civil society'. Their attitude was ambivalent. They increasingly recognized that some form of democratization was ineluctable and that it could bring them certain advantages, yet they were apprehensive about the potential threat to their position posed by majority rule and increased civil rights (notably the right for labour to organize independently). Moreover, since they were tied closely to, and dependent on, the state apparatus and elements of the previous political elite, they had cause to fear any radical challenge to the status quo.

The powerful vested interests of big business partly underlie the fact that the form of democracy which emerged in South Korea in the late 1980s was still relatively restrictive and rested on an accommodation between a small group of political, military and economic elites. Despite these limitations, however, the specific historical and social context of South Korean democratization provided a certain degree of optimism about its future. First, the change in regime could be linked to the fact that South Korean society had reached a relatively mature stage in which the classical historical argument for the progressive role of a civil society emerging from modernization and capitalist industrialization appears to apply. Second, consequent to the role of civil society organizations in pushing for the political transition, the democratic opening of the mid-1980s led to a vast increase in their numbers and an intensification of their activity. By 1990, for example, the number of trade unions had increased to 7,698 (see Kim Y.R., 1992). Even more important, the nature of labour organization began to change as unions arose spontaneously to challenge the Federation of Korean Trade Unions, which was associated with the corporatist efforts of the *ancien régime* (Launius, 1991: 44). The field of civil society also expanded with the entry of organizations representing hitherto unrepresented groups: for example, a National Association of Farmers was established in February 1987, supported by organizations such as the Christian and the Catholic Farmers' Federations, each of the latter having its own newspaper (Christian Institute, 1988: 256–7). There was also a mushrooming of what have been called 'civil society movements', organized around broad social issues such as environmental protection, women's rights, consumer protection and economic justice (Lee S.-H., 1993: 359).

At the same time, however, South Korean democracy at its outset was heavily based on a compact of elites in which state-based elites, notably the military, were still very powerful (Kim K.W., 1992: 109; Gills, 1993). The balance between elites shifted somewhat in the years that followed as the power of the military was reduced and the *chaebol* played a more direct and assertive role in politics (Lee H.Y., 1993; Kihl, 1991). But continuing elite dominance not only imposes limits on the broadening and deepening of the new democracy; it also contains the seeds of future conflict, between the state and social forces and among those forces, which threatens the stability of even this limited form of democracy through 'a seismic fault of social disaffection' (Eckert, 1990: 148). For example, there is a serious prospect of conflict between a capitalist class accustomed to the discipline enforced by authoritarian rule and an increasingly assertive labour movement. The scenario would be as follows: capitalists who feel threatened by increasing labour militancy and radical politics might turn to sections of the state to reimpose authoritarian controls, supported by sections of the urban middle class who yearn for stability or feel threatened themselves (Dong, 1991: 279). The continued menace of the Communist North could be an added rationale for, and impetus to, such a reversion, an intensification of the current tendency to invoke 'national security' as an excuse for clamping down on democratic activity. In this dismal scenario, Chile's past could be Korea's future.

The prospects for optimistic or pessimistic scenarios for

the future depend a great deal on events in political society: the quality of political leaders and institutions and their ability to handle the conflicts evident in the new social and political order. The political elite was responding to this challenge in January 1990 when they combined the governing party with two opposition parties to form a hegemonic institution, the Democratic Liberal Party. A one-party dominant regime along erstwhile Japanese lines is politically attractive because it allows established elites to consolidate their power and incorporate opposition leaders. It can also provide a new institutional matrix for the continuation of the Korean model of development and the networks of elite co-operation underpinning it. In this positive scenario, it is hoped, Japan's past could be Korea's future.

The 'Grand Coalition' scenario also contains certain political dangers, as the Japanese case has shown: schisms and factionalism within the dominant party, the growth of institutionalized corruption and the marginalization of opposition forces which are driven to extra-parliamentary methods and violence. The election of former opposition leader Kim Young Sam as President in 1992 was a positive event, offering the possibility not only of a cleaner break with the authoritarian past than the previous Roh regime, but also of an extension of the democratic process as the political system was opened to a wider range of social forces (Lee and Sohn, 1994). To this extent, South Korea's political society is being reshaped, in terms of both leadership and institutions, to tackle the competing challenges of political cohesion, continued developmental dynamism and further democratization. But the long-standing schisms of South Korean politics – notably political factions based on regional affiliation – are hard to transcend and by 1995 there was a danger that the 'Grand Coalition' would collapse into four regionally-based parties.[11] If this were to occur, it would not only introduce greater instability and incoherence into South Korean politics, but also weaken the process of deepening the country's democracy through a programme of institutional reform introduced by President Kim Young Sam after coming to power.

Zambia: weak civil society and weak state

During 1990–1, Zambia underwent a dramatic transition from the one-party regime of President Kenneth Kaunda and his

United National Independence Party (UNIP) to a multi-party democracy whose first president was the head of the Zambian trade union movement, Frederick Chiluba. This marked a return to competitive politics after nearly two decades of hegemonic one-party rule which began with the adoption in 1972 of a State Constitution which made the UNIP the only legal party. The transition was triggered by large-scale rioting and demonstrations in June 1990 against economic reform measures (particularly an increase in the price of maize), which were part of a structural adjustment programme endorsed by external donors and international financial institutions. The disturbances culminated in a failed military coup in July that year. These events intensified an already evident decline in the authority of Kaunda and the UNIP and stimulated the rise of a political opposition which coalesced to establish the Movement for Multi-party Democracy (MMD) in 1990 and adopted Chiluba as its leader in 1991.

A reluctant Kaunda was pressured into agreeing to the introduction of multi-party politics, a decision ratified by the Zambian Parliament in August 1991. At the presidential and legislative elections held in October that year, the MMD won a sweeping victory, taking 125 of the 150 seats in the National Assembly and the presidency for its candidate, Chiluba, who received 76 per cent of the popular vote on a turnout of 45.4 per cent. It is widely recognized that civil society organizations, notably trade unions and religious and professional associations, played a significant role in this transition.

The events of 1990–1 must be understood in the context of a long period of economic and political decline, beginning as early as the mid-1970s. The record of development in Zambia over the past two decades presents a sharp contrast to that of South Korea, and the two countries differ widely in terms of their social, economic and political profiles. Zambia's GNP per capita actually declined by 1.9 per cent a year between 1965 and 1990. The country still depends heavily on copper as its main source of export earnings (90 per cent in 1993) and had been hard hit by a severe deterioration in the terms of trade since the mid-1970s as copper prices collapsed and oil prices increased. By 1991 the country had run up an external debt of over US$7 billion, equal to twice the value of GDP that year. The structure of production, in terms of the ratio between agriculture and industry as percentages of GDP, had hardly changed since 1965, and although some initial progress had been made in developing labour-intensive manufacturing, particularly for daily necessities, this sector was hard-hit by the economy's mounting external crisis in the 1980s. In terms of popular welfare, though there were gradual long-term improvements, these were eroded alarmingly by the cuts in government spending on welfare programmes as the economy declined. In 1990, the infant mortality rate was 82 per thousand live births and average life expectancy was only 50 years. As of 1989, only 20 per cent of the age cohort were enrolled in secondary education (14 per cent for females) and 2 per cent in tertiary education; the adult illiteracy rate was estimated to be 27 per cent in 1990 (35 per cent for females).

Zambia represents a pattern of development failure common to most countries across the African continent. By the dawn of the 1990s, economic problems had reached crisis proportions as the country experienced massive food shortages, 100 per cent annual inflation and deteriorating social services. Efforts at macroeconomic stabilization and reform were failing and the crisis was exacerbated by a freeze in foreign aid imposed as a penalty for debt default. The widespread discontent provided high-octane political fuel for the opposition.

Comparing Zambia with South Korea at the beginning of the 1990s, the developmental differences are glaring. With the exception of the copper industry, Zambia's industrialization process was in its infancy, efforts at economic diversification and technological improvement in agriculture had failed and the material and educational levels of the population were very low. Compared with other countries in the sub-Saharan region, however, the Zambian social structure has certain distinctive chacteristics which are important in understanding the political strength of civil society. A relatively high percentage of the population is urban (just over 50 per cent in 1990) and there is a large concentration of formal industrial employment in the Copperbelt. Since urban populations can more easily be mobilized for political action and because the copper industry has given rise to a strong trade-union movement, the political potential of Zambia's civil society is greater than that of many of its neighbours. However, the overall proportion of the population working in the formal sector of the economy is low (9.8 per cent in 1990), reflecting the predominance of a large urban informal sector and small-scale agriculture. We can thus expect the modern sector of its civil society to be poorly developed, certainly in comparison with a country like South Korea.

This weakness of the modern sector should be set against the fact that Zambia is a multi-ethnic society with several large ethnic groups located in specific regions, one of which (the Lozi) has threatened some form of secession. Kaunda was careful to balance ethnic divisions (particularly between the Bemba and the Lozi) in forming party or government cabinets and, when faced with demands for multi-party democracy at the end of the 1980s, warned of the prospect of 'stone-age politics' based on ethnic conflicts. This raises the prospect of politically destabilizing conflict between different sectors of civil society, a situation which would not be the case in an ethnically homogeneous society like South Korea.

As to the political context of civil society, Zambia is radically different from a country like South Korea which had a strong and effective developmental state in place from the early 1960s. Zambia shares in what seems to be a pervasive phenomenon in Africa of a state which is simultaneously dominant and weak: in Blair's words, a form of statism in which 'a government tries to regulate everything, but through a combination of corruption, arbitrariness and its own general ineffectiveness ends up controlling virtually nothing at all' (1992: 22). If the relative weakness of African 'soft' states has been a constant aspect of the post-colonial era, the situation deteriorated during the 1980s as states were further weakened by radically worsening economic environments and by their own incapacity to remedy the situation. Those which did try to take strategic action through structural adjustment programmes (SAPs) often found their scant reserves of authority further depleted by the disruptive political consequences of reform measures. Unable to remedy the situation through an alternative strategy, Africa's would-be 'developmental states' became increasingly perceived as the main source of the problem not its solution, and generated mounting domestic as well as international pressures for a change of regime (for a review of political decline in the region see Jeffries, 1993: 21–3).

The history of Zambia in the years immediately preceding the political transition of 1990–1 is a vivid example of this regional malaise. While the deterioration in the economic environment would have tested any government, the UNIP government contributed to the problem and frustrated its solution through its own policies (for example, its neglect of agriculture, unrealistic exchange-rate policies, and maintenance of inefficient parastatals). Attempts at an SAP sparked off food riots and labour unrest in late 1986 and early 1987 which led to the abandonment of the programme in May 1987. Though an indigenous alternative was then attempted – the New Economic Recovery Programme – it soon ran into the sand and the government returned to the SAP approach in mid-1989, setting the context for a renewed round of popular protest in mid-1990. But, as Bates and Collier point out (1993: 429), these protests were very different from their predecessors in 1986–7:

> [While] the food riots of December 1986 had focused on the price of maize, those in June 1990 focused on the political system itself. The rioters attacked the Party and the single-party system. They identified the political system as the source of their economic woes.

It was these protests which ushered in the end of the Kaunda regime.

The one-party state's continuing inability to halt developmental decline and the increasing perception that it was a major contributor to that decline led to the activation of civil society. However, it is important to realize that the political opposition which gathered strength at the end of the 1980s did not arise from nowhere. Zambia's one-party system had allowed elements of opposition in the legislature in the 1970s. Moreover, some of the forces of civil society which provided the impetus for the transition to democracy in 1990–1 – in particular, the trade unions, religious organizations, intellectuals and students – had already been active before the introduction of one-party rule and retained some independent initiative. Kaunda's version of mono-partyism was a relatively soft one, in which attempts to repress, harass or co-opt opposition were combined with efforts at appeasement and accommodation (for analyses of the dynamics of Zambia's one-party system, see Gertzel *et al.*, 1984; Mijere, 1988; Phiri, 1991). This was particularly the case for the trade-union movement, whose power derived from its influential position in the all-important copper sector. For example, Lungu (1986: 402–4) documents the active role of the Zambian Congress of Trade Unions (ZCTU) in opposing the price rises and income restraints imposed in

1983 in connection with an IMF loan, and refers to the labour movement in that period as an 'unofficial opposition party'. Similarly church organizations, Catholic and Protestant, opposed government policies on population control and educational reform in the late 1970s and early 1980s, with considerable effect (Lungu, 1986: 394–401); on the latter issue they were joined in opposition by the labour movement (see Rakner, 1992 for a valuable analysis of the political role of the trade-union movement).

The decline of the Kaunda regime breathed political life into civil society. This was partly the result of its failing ability to dispense resources to client groups (notably to private business, which was thus more inclined to support the opposition in the hope of a better deal), partly of the antagonisms stirred up by attempts to implement the SAPs, partly of growing dissensus within the regime and increasing defections of leaders to the opposition camp, and partly the result of the simple fact that an increasing political vacuum was being created which allowed more space for other political forces. In such a situation, the political representatives of civil society hastily organized in 1990–1 were kicking against a door which was already hanging off its hinges.

The political movement which gathered strength in 1990–1 represented both a resurgence and a strengthening of civil society, involving previously active and newly emergent groups. It rested on the coalescence of a wide variety of urban groups (Chiluba called it a 'rainbow coalition') and was given force by spontaneous or semi-organized expressions of popular dissatisfaction. The MMD, its integrated political expression, embodied a temporary coalition of trade unionists, ex-politicians, professionals, students, intellectuals, businessmen, commercial farmers and religious leaders.[12] The political force of civil society increased as its active membership expanded, as its different components co-ordinated their activities more closely and as they constructed a unified organizational representative in the MMD. The movement was given extra strength by the rise of opposition newspapers and magazines; large sections of the urban population threw in their support by participating in protests and attending opposition rallies; and religious leaders played a particularly cardinal role not only in calling for democratization but also in brokering the dialogue between the regime and the opposition. While it would be accurate to speak of a strengthening of the political influence of civil society during the transition, it is important to bear in mind that this took place in a relatively short period of political crisis and that the shift in the balance of political power occurred against the background of a collapsing regime. In other words, the power of civil society was boosted by immediate circumstances and magnified by a concomitant decline in the power of the state. One could argue that, in the aftermath of the change of regime, both state and civil society remained politically weak in terms of their capacity to establish a coherent political order and tackle the massive problems facing the nation. This situation is very different from that in South Korea where there is a firm socio-economic basis for the emergence of a strong civil society, rooted in successful industrialization, and where the state retains much of its previous institutional integrity and power.

This distinction is crucial if we address the question of whether Zambian democracy is sustainable. Certainly the impetus towards democracy is stronger and more firmly rooted in Zambia than in many, if not most, of its regional neighbours which have attempted or undergone a similar transition (for a regional review, see Tordoff, 1994; Woodward, 1994). The coalition underlying the new polity is weak in that it is historically contingent in the sense that it coalesced to fight against a now defunct regime; it represents a relatively small proportion of the country's population and social interests (overwhelmingly in the urban and formal sector); and it lacks the coherence and authority to carry through the radical programme of economic reform deemed necessary to halt the country's decline. For example, while the trade-union movement played the vanguard role in undermining the Kaunda regime, its relationship to the new democratic regime of its erstwhile leader, Frederick Chiluba, has passed through ambivalence to opposition. The power of the trade unions is overwhelmingly located in the state-run economy, an inefficient sector targeted for major reforms which may strike at the heart of union power. This is but one example of the wider fact that, with the state still the main employer in the formal sector and the main sponsor of private capitalist enterprise, many of the civil society groups which occupied the political vacuum in 1991 are either rooted in or dependent on the state. This reality makes any simple political distinction between state and civil society unhelpful in current circumstances. As Woods points out when discussing the political role of urban middle classes in Africa, 'the degree of socio-economic stratification that exists between Africans arises, largely, from their position in this vast public sector' (Woods, 1992: 89). Paradoxically, the social forces which organized the transition to democracy run the risk of being weakened by the actions of the new regime.

This fundamental fact bodes ill for Zambia's political future. First, continuing conflict can be expected between civil society organizations which are defending the interests of their members and the depredations of an SAP implemented by the Chiluba government. In 1992, for example, there were strikes among local government employees in protest against a cancellation of promised salary increments. Such conflicts are bound up with fundamental issues of political accountability. The Chiluba government, and the democratic system with which it is identified, faces a potential 'accountability dilemma'. On the one hand, it is accountable to foreign donors for the implementation of a radical and politically disruptive SAP which threatens the short-term interests of many of its previous supporters. On the other hand, those supporters demand that the government, as their democratically chosen representative, should take the lead in protecting them from the advent or the consequences of economic reform. As Nolutshungu remarks wrily (1992: 318):

> [political] reform was not always, if ever, identified with the unlimited opening of national economies to foreign penetration, the reduction of public expenditure on social welfare, or the large-scale privatisation of national assets.

The external donor community would be well advised to mitigate its pressures for radical economic reform if it does not wish to undermine the political and institutional capacity to manage the repercussions.

Second, one can also expect further splintering of the coalition of groups which deposed President Kaunda, particularly the already uneasy alliance of trade unions and prominent businessmen, interests which can be expected to view the prospect of economic reform with different eyes. Between 1992 and 1994, Chiluba's government became increasingly dominated by business interests, but they also were divided between more reformist elements committed to the principles of the SAP and more 'cronyist' elements bent on retaining state sponsorship. There is a danger of a political catch-22, all too familiar in the days of the Kaunda regime. If radical economic reforms are implemented, the ensuing conflicts may weaken the institutions of the new democratic polity, particularly the MMD, which will stall the economic reform process and lead to political paralysis or disorder. If the MMD abandons the reforms, the economic crisis remains unresolved, foreign donors remain unforgiving and political paralysis or disorder ensues. There is a temptation to resolve the dilemma through a new form of authoritarianism, a phenomenon which showed itself in President Chiluba's declaration of a state of emergency and arrest of prominent opposition figures in early 1993, and his tendency towards an autocratic style of leadership. But Chiluba's political resources are limited, particularly if his base of support in the labour movement evaporates, and the existent, but increasingly conflictual, elements of civil society may well be enough to checkmate any authoritarian ambitions, albeit at the cost of political paralysis or disorder. There is also a temptation for the MMD to revert to clientelistic means to garner support through various forms of favouritism and corruption, or to manipulate ethnic rivalries to its advantage (Chiluba has already been accused of favouring the Bemba over other ethnic groups and regionalist sentiment has grown among the Lozi in the west). This raises the spectre of potentially destabilizing conflict between the modern and traditional segments of civil society. It also raises the spectre of institutionalized corruption, a phenomenon which has increasingly pervaded the ranks of the MMD and Chiluba's cabinets.[13]

These considerations lead to pessimism about the future of Zambia's fledgling democracy. Yet, at one level, whether or not democracy 'survives' in some minimalist procedural sense may not be the real issue. External pressure may be sufficient to keep it in place regardless of its effectiveness, the degree of participation it embodies and the amount of legitimacy it enjoys. In an earlier era, external pressure helped to keep authoritarian governments in power in various parts of the world regardless of their effectiveness, their repressiveness and their lack of legitimacy. The same may be true in the post-authoritarian order. If one hopes that democracy may go beyond this and entrench itself more deeply in a society such as Zambia, much of the answer lies in the emergent character of political society, the institutions through which the forces of civil society occupy the state and determine its behaviour. Any such post-authoritarian transition, in which disparate and potentially inimical forces of civil society came together temporarily to unseat an unpopular regime, can be expected to be followed by a period of flux and realignment as old coalitions break up and new ones are established. The social base of the MMD was already being seriously eroded during 1992–4 and the institution itself was split as leaders left to form new parties, most notable among them the National Party formed in 1993. The stability and effectiveness of Zambia's fledgling democracy depends heavily on the outcome of these organizational realignments, on the new groupings of social forces which they represent and their capacity to strengthen Zambia's devastated state institutions. There is also the possibility of a regrouping and resurgence of the old hegemonic political force, the UNIP, visible in the return of Kenneth Kaunda to political life in 1994.[14] If the MMD were to retain some political coherence as the party of market reform and the UNIP able to redefine itself – with or without Kaunda – as a left-of-centre but non-hegemonic party, there is a possibility that two-partyism might become the norm, an outcome which would serve to provide much-needed stability within a framework of competitive democratic politics.[15]

Civil society and the sustainability of democracy

In the case studies analysed here, and in many other countries over the past few years, the role of civil society organizations in fostering democratic transitions is a palpable fact. Even in Africa, where the socially modern and politically progressive sector of civil society is in general weak, they have brought about impressive changes and promise much for the future. The question is whether these superficially dramatic changes in the political regime can be sustained and consolidated. As Nolutshungu points out (1992: 324):

> the legitimation of policy in terms of a measure of responsiveness to human rights and domestic democracy lobbies may be a product of irreversible structural developments within states and transnationally, but it may also be merely contingent.

Most commentators agree that 'in the long term' the growth of new forms of intermediate organizations will create inexorable pressures for democratic politics. But a good deal can happen between now and the long term, and the lives and welfare of a lot of people hang on that fact. The image of a 'wave' of democratization over recent years is a good one, because it implies that the wave will recede and reveal a political coastline which is decidedly jagged. What are the key factors which will determine the promontories and bays and, in particular, what role are civil societies likely to play?

It is worthwhile repeating the point made at the outset that civil society is but one cluster of political power among three in the Great Game of democratization, the others being located in the state and the international environment. The power of state actors and interests to impede the extension of democracy varies widely across countries, as we have seen in our case studies. The South Korean state and its constituent strata – a political elite holding over from the *ancien régime* and a powerful coercive and administrative apparatus – still dominate Korean society with ambiguous political effects. They may contribute to stabilizing the new political order at the cost of reducing its participatory potential. In Zambia, by contrast, the state is a disaster area and is in desperate need of reinforcement as an essential part of the process of democratization.[16]

As for international factors, the current stress on democratic conditionality for aid flows can play a role in maintaining democratic rule, but it must be recognized that in many cases the latter may be formal rather than substantive since the necessary internal conditions are lacking. Moreover, intervening directly to foster democratization is a tricky business and can prove counter-productive. The very power of international actors is a problem for new democracies because of the possibility of an 'accountability dilemma', such as we identified in the Zambian case. Democratic accountability requires an irreducible amount of national sovereignty, and if a government, democratic or otherwise, is seen to be at the beck and call of foreign forces, or is reduced to powerlessness by constraints imposed by those forces, the foundations of democratic accountability are put in jeopardy. There is the possibility of an accountability crisis which could give rise to radical nationalist regimes of a populist, religious or military nature.

Though this is a problem which would have particularly strong implications for weak and dependent states such as Zambia, it has growing significance for a far wider range of states, as witnessed by the mounting external pressures for economic liberalization in South Korea in the 1980s and 1990s. Finally, though the pressures of an international 'wave' operate well when the wave is in democracy's favour, if there is a rip-tide of authoritarianism which gathers numerical strength, then the cumulative effect could operate the other way and the costs of enforcing democratic conditionality increase.

Turning to the political role of civil society, our first finding is that it should be analysed in relation to the nature of particular democratic transitions. We should guard against the general assumption, common in the triumphalism of the time but now ebbing, that the forces of civil society supported transition because they wanted a change in regime, rather than merely a change of government. In the African case, for example, Kpundeh and Riley assert that 'authoritarian regimes are being challenged, as political activists and mass publics are converted to pluralism and political choice' and that, in the Zambian case, Chiluba's victory was 'simply a vote for an end to one-party rule' (Kpundeh and Riley, 1992: 265, 270). There is clearly some truth in such statements, but they may sometimes be based on transient impressions, not systematic empirical evidence. They may also obscure important considerations, notably the fact that the political motivations of participants in such transitions are very mixed and may have a lot to do with sectional self-interest rather than preference for political regime. The degree of political 'conversion' to democracy is a murky variable. In the South Korean case, Korean analysts warn about the threat to democracy posed by a deeply-rooted authoritarian political culture which still pervades society and its dominant institutions and threatens an authoritarian reversion if democracy is perceived to become too 'chaotic'.

Our case studies also point to important differences in the political outcomes of particular transitions. In South Korea, the constitutional changes introduced in 1987 overlaid a highly unequal distribution of political power which maintains a good deal of continuity with the previous regime. To a considerable extent, therefore, democratic politics is a game played by a small number of influential elites in both state and civil society.

This form of 'oligarchic democracy' does not trouble certain theorists of liberal democracy because they see successful democracy as relying on the discipline imposed by political elites, since over-mobilization of the masses may strain or break the system. In the context of transition, a stronger case for the role of elites can be made since, though mass mobilization may play a cardinal role at key points (for example, through huge street demonstrations against the *ancien régime*), the design and maintenance of democratic rules of the political game depend on the interests and commitments of political elites. As Blair puts it baldly, '[If] enough key elites support democracy, it will continue; if they desert, it will end' (1992: 13).

If we are interested in the role of civil society in sustaining democracy, then we need to know who these key elites are. If, as in the South Korean case, they are based in the state or on a relatively narrow sliver of civil society (big business), then a significant section of civil society may be excluded or marginalized in the political process. This suggests that the maintenance and deepening of democracy in such circumstances depend on continuing struggle by subordinated sectors of civil society (for example, the independent labour movement in South Korea and Taiwan) to extend their formal rights and increase their influence on the political process. This expansion of the scope of social participation allows civil society to play a disciplinary role not only in relation to the state, notably the military, but also in relation to key social elites, notably the *chaebol* which, many Koreans now believe, 'will be able to use their wealth to buy elections' (Lee H.Y., 1993: 39).

The Zambian situation leads one to an opposite conclusion. Since the nature of the transition is more fragile, the previous hegemonic party has collapsed and the new counter-hegemony of social interests is so fissile, it is reasonable to hope that the main concern of politically active sections of civil society should be to build sturdy social coalitions, coherent political institutions and strong public organizations to underpin the functioning of the new democratic order. This lays a heavy burden on the shoulders of a relatively small number of political and social leaders within the new democratic elite. Large-scale mass mobilization in such a context, whether by members of the democratic coalition or forces outside it, such as regionally based ethnic groups, could paralyse the new polity. In Zambia, therefore, the constitutive role of civil society is currently the most urgent.

In sum, these two cases suggest that the political role of civil society in sustaining democracy may vary systematically across countries. These variations reflect fundamental differences in developmental levels between societies, and it is this factor which will play a key role in drawing the contours of the political shore after the 'third wave' of democratization has receded. The prospects for democratic sustainability depend heavily on the historical timing of the transition within a particular society's developmental trajectory. The relative maturity of South Korean society, which is reflected in an increasingly dense and complex civil society, is more propitious for the future of democracy than the Zambian situation. In the African context, one can agree with Bratton when he argues that the power of associational life, and thus the prospects for sustained democratization, are likely to be greatest in those countries where the level of indigenous industrialization is the most advanced (namely in Kenya, South Africa and Zimbabwe). But even an 'advanced' associational life contains its dangers for democracy, as we shall see below.

The level of socio-economic development affects the political role of civil society in two basic ways: by shifting the balance of power between civil society and the state and by changing the character of civil society. While there is considerable comparative evidence to support the first contention, the case studies show that one must be cautious about assuming linearity in the evolving relationship between state and civil society. There is an important political difference between the case of South Korea, where the state has played a central role in the industrialization process and retains much of its dominance after the advent of democratic institutions, and the case of Zambia, where the state has failed developmentally, and is in critical condition and dire need of reconstitution.

On the second contention, that changes in the character of civil society are brought about by socio-economic development, our cases point to two historical patterns which have different implications for the issue of democratic sustainability – 'early' and 'late' development. In a situation of 'early development', as typified by the Zambian case, socio-economic development is little advanced or highly uneven. The presence of a modern, more democratically-inclined sector of civil society (sponsored in particular by a modern business sector, specialized professions, an industrial labour movement and reformist religious organizations) is still relatively superficial. The society at large still operates on the basis of different political, social, cultural and ideological principles. To a considerable extent, Zambia still fits this pattern.

As development sociologists often point out, one should not counterpose different sectors of civil society (such as the 'modern' and the 'traditional') as totally alien and incompatible. For example, one should not assume that, say, modern business organizations are automatically pro-democratic or that ethnic organizations are inherently anti-democratic. And yet, in a context such as Africa, there are important ways in which the character of civil society is contradictory and the resulting political conflicts can be inimical to the implantation of democracy. Incipient democracies can be threatened by a wave of religious fundamentalism which could restore authoritarian rule itself or provoke the restoration of secular authoritarianism, as in Algeria. It is not surprising, therefore, that analysts of Africa, both local and foreign, tend to counterpose an 'advanced' and a 'backward' sector of civil society and see the issue of successful democratization as resting heavily on the political balance between them (for example, Decalo, 1992; Kpundeh and Riley, 1992).

Lemarchand, for example, argues that older forms of civil society are currently being revived (for example, kinship organizations in Mozambique, religion in Nigeria and Senegal, and millenarian/sorcery cults in a number of countries), that the nature of African civil societies is in consequence highly contradictory and that this makes the institutionalization of democratic governance very problematic because 'the structures of accountability are segmented, syncretistic, and fluid' (Lemarchand, 1992a: 190). In the political process, the key contradiction is between a progressive public sphere sustained by certain modern elements of civil society and the political constraints imposed by 'neo-patrimonialism', in which associational and political ties are based on clientelism, ethnicity and kinship. In particular, political clientelism impedes the emergence of the kind of hands-off institutional separation which underpins the relationship between state and civil society in more advanced forms of democratic polity because, in Lemarchand's words, it leads to a 'structural confusion' between state and society (1992b: 182).

These analysts are no doubt right to point out this contradiction and its dangers for democratization, but just how dangerous is it? Part of the answer depends on how we expect democracy to operate. In particularly poor and dependent countries in which political conditionality means that democracy is the door to the donors, there may be tremendous pressure to maintain some formal appearance of democracy. Some of the resulting regimes may be so far from the usual political requirement of a democratic polity, even defined in minimalist procedural terms, that they can be dismissed as a sham. However, it is worth recalling Parekh's argument (1992) about the 'cultural particularity' of liberal democracy. Just as there are somewhat stereotypically positive expectations about how a democratic polity should operate, based on the (often idealized) experience of Western democracies, so there are stereotyped and idealized expectations about the nature and role of civil society (most visible in the glorification of nongovernmental organizations (NGOs), or the over-optimistic expectations of the democratic character of the bourgeoisie or the working class). While strong grass-roots/community organizations and independent economic interest groups may be a valuable dimension of a democratic society and their relationship with the state may be more distanced or hands-off, this does not exhaust the possibilities of linkages between state and society in a democratic polity. As the recent experience of Japan and Italy suggests, so-called 'advanced' democratic polities are pervaded by neo-patrimonialist practices which may be ethically questionable from a strictly liberal democratic point of view, but which play an important role in linking actors in the state and political society to social constituencies and constituting a principle of accountability between them. Similarly, it is argued that a potentially fissile patchwork of ethnic, religious or regional groups could be co-ordinated through a 'consociational' pattern of democratic representation. Unsurprisingly, this is seen as a suitable way of institutionalizing democratic politics in the African context (for instance, Bayart, 1986), though historical experience shows how difficult this process can be.

To summarize, a democratic polity may rest on a variety of

civil societies and may be linked to them in a variety of ways, only some of which coincide with the more optimistic and narrowly defined expectations of liberal democratic ideologues. In other words, one may expect considerable variation in the patterns of relationship between civil society, political society and state which underpin democratic polities. The latter will vary systematically in consequence.

The other pattern of relationships between development, civil society and democracy is that of late development. Countries such as South Korea and Taiwan which have achieved a considerable measure of socio-economic modernization and in which consequent changes in state–society relations and in the character of civil society have pushed the political system in a democratic direction are two examples of this pattern. To the extent that a transition to democracy does in fact shift the balance of power in favour of the forces of civil society, the terrain of political conflict changes, from a struggle between state and civil society to a struggle between different sections of civil society for control over the state.

This raises questions about the structural fissures present in industrialized societies and enters the debate between liberals and Marxists about the potential for conflict inherent in a capitalist society. There is historical evidence to suggest that the capitalist class – and many of its subalterns in the middle strata – are more interested in the liberal than the democratic component of liberal democracy, in negative rather than positive freedoms and in a more strictly political rather than a socio-economic definition of democracy. Other sections of civil society – poorer sections of the population, the industrial working class, groups representing socially subordinated or politically marginalized groups such as women, neglected regions, and ethnic, racial or religious groups – have an interest not merely in the liberal but also in the democratic potential of liberal democracy in the sense that it opens up new channels for them to articulate their grievances and pressure the state to do something about them. In the case of societies with relatively well-developed capitalist economic systems, such as South Korea, Taiwan or several countries in South America, one can expect the large and increasingly activist working class not only to exercise its new-found rights to social and economic protest, but also to attempt to make its voice heard in the political arena. We have seen this process at work in the South

Korean case. To the extent that this political pressure takes a radical form, the resulting conflict may resolve itself through an authoritarian reversion along the lines of Chile in 1973, as an embattled capitalist class turns to the military to defend its interests.

Here we can see how powerful elements of civil society may sponsor a move *away* from democracy, a phenomenon common enough in the not too distant past of today's advanced democracies (Japan, Germany and France) and another antidote to the current idealization of the democratic character of civil society. One is led to raise questions about the allegedly democratic political roles of certain social classes and strata. In the classic British transition, the liberal component of liberal democracy to a considerable extent preceded the democratic component, and the political range of democratic participation gradually extended to include wider sections of society. By contrast, democratization in the current context delivers a comprehensive package combining civil freedoms and universal electoral representation. In such a context, one can argue that it is the relatively deprived and subordinated sections of civil society which have the most powerful motive for supporting and extending democratic politics, whereas socially privileged and powerful strata have a more ambiguous relationship to democracy and a greater interest in restricting its scope. In this context, a strategy of empowering weaker groups in society, particularly the effectively disenfranchised peasant populations of many poor countries, could play a powerful role in consolidating and deepening the democratic processes.

A final set of conclusions about the sustainability of new democracies concerns the nature of the state and political society and their relationships with civil society. First, the design of state institutions, which defines a particular pattern of access and representation of social forces, may have important implications for the durability of a democratic system. This issue directs our attention, for example, to the precise nature of electoral systems, variations in which may serve to facilitate or undermine the process of democratic governance. It also raises basic constitutional questions about the relative virtues of different institutional variants of democracy: presidential versus parliamentary systems, the political insulation of areas of policy-making (the currently most favoured version of this being an independent central bank), checks and balances between different branches of government, and so on. Second, the precise nature of political society mediates between civil society and the state in ways which have important consequences for the stability and effectiveness of democratic politics. For example, does the political process fragment into a multitude of small, sectionalist parties or into a small number of larger parties embodying broad coalitions? Do parties represent a set of interests or values, or do they represent clientelistic machines, as is the case in contemporary Thai politics? A similar set of questions could be asked about the political commitments and styles of individual leaders. The answers to these questions require us to turn our attention to a study of political society as the next step towards understanding the complex relationships between civil society and democratization.

Notes

1 For example, see White (1993) for a critique of the conventional conception of the 'market' in current discussions on development.

2 For example, Booth (1987: 23) refers to it as 'socio-economic life as distinct from the state'.

3 Uses of the term also vary in their degree of abstraction: for some, civil society is a public *space*, distinct from and autonomous of the state, which is occupied by associational activity; for others, civil society is a wide-ranging *behavioural* phenomenon which not only includes the activity of organizations, but also such 'spontaneous' phenomena as riots, protest demonstrations and parallel markets. Most commonly, however, the term is used to refer to the activity of organized social associations of a voluntary character.

4 In similar vein, Chabal (1992: 83–4) sees civil society as 'a vast ensemble of constantly changing groups and individuals whose only common ground is their exclusion from the state, their consciousness of their externality and their potential opposition to the state ... Its politics ... are the politics of counter-hegemony.'

5 For a critical evaluation of Marx's analysis of civil society, see Gouldner (1980); for a discussion of current Marxist uses of the term, see Wood (1990).

6 The conventional use of 'civil society' usually excludes firms as well as families, but it could be argued that economic institutions, as key matrices of social organization, should also be included within the definition. In my view, this would stretch the term beyond the bounds of analytical utility. Rather one can identify a society's economic institutions and patterns of economic interaction as a distinct realm, akin to 'civil society', which could be dubbed 'economic society' or simply 'economic system', a realm which constitutes one of the basic foundations of 'civil society' in any social system.

7 This term refers to the now fading distinction made by Rudolf Bahro (1978) in describing Communist Eastern Europe between ideal 'socialist' societies and the actual social form taken on by state socialism in the Soviet bloc.

8 We should not exaggerate the separation and distinctness of these differences and sectors of civil society. As Chabal (1992: 87) points out in discussing traditional and modern sectors, they interpenetrate in complex ways.

9 While Stepan would include legislatures and electoral systems under the heading of 'political society', I would see them rather as part of the institutional patterning of the state. For further discussion of the idea of 'political society', see Rueschemeyer *et al.* (1992: 287).

10 Tension between the Chun regime and the *chaebol* surfaced in the case of the Kukje corporation, which was forced into financial collapse as a penalty for supporting an opposition leader, Kim Young Sam. Chun apparently wanted this case to serve as a warning to other businessmen contemplating similar acts of disloyalty.

11 Shim Jae Hoon, 'Bitter Pill', *Far Eastern Economic Review*, 2 February 1995: 17–18.

12 For an analysis of the social and political composition of Chiluba's first cabinet, see Graham (1994: 341).

13 For example, in early 1994 the government lost four ministers who resigned or were sacked amid allegations of corruption and drug-trafficking (*Africa Research Bulletin*, No. 11291, 1–31 January 1994).

14 For an inside account of Kaunda's return, see 'The return of "Super Ken" ', *Africa Confidential* 36 (2) (20 January 1995): 6–7 and 'The market democrats', *ibid.* 36 (10) (12 May 1995): 6.

15 For a detailed analysis of the dynamics of Zambian politics in the mid-1990s, see Burnell, 1995.

16 Many analysts of the African scene, though arguing from different perspectives, agree on the critical problem posed by the weakness of state institutions and the consequent danger of strengthening 'civil society' while ignoring the issue of state capacity (for example, see Jeffries, 1993; Van de Walle, 1994).

6

Gender and democratization: ambiguity and opportunity

SHIRIN M. RAI

To paraphrase Eleanor Roosevelt, 'Where, after all, do democratic rights begin? In small places, close to home ... '.

Democracy is in vogue once again. Both the Left and the Right are concerned about extending, deepening or transforming democracy. In established democracies the emphasis is on making democratic citizenship more meaningful in people's lives. In the generalized euphoria about democracy, however, particular issues tend to be obscured, among them the ambiguous position of women in democratic polities. This chapter examines what democratization means for women in the Third World. The latter is by no means homogeneous, and the issues women face in the political sphere have been shaped by different historical and cultural trajectories. Neither can the category 'women' be seen as homogeneous. Below, I will draw out the importance of these differences and the dilemmas that they pose for women.

The issues

The participants

Two points need to be made about democracy itself. First, democracy has generally been conceived of as pertaining to relations between individuals and institutions in the public domain. Here the public domain would mean the social and political terrain between the spaces occupied by the state and the private sphere. Second, democracy has been given two different meanings. One confines it mainly to representation and the processes by which this may be secured. The other gives more emphasis to participation, including the involvement of citizens in the routine business of regulating the public sphere and holding the state accountable. While liberal democracy has generally functioned within the representational democratic framework, a wide variety of political groups have supported the participatory model.

Given the two different traditions in democratic theory, we have to consider what we mean by democratization. In the political rhetoric of the 1990s, democratization has been linked directly to the process of marketization on the one hand, and representative democracy on the other. It is in this context that we have to consider the gains and losses that women of the Third World are experiencing as this process unfolds. Moreover, when we speak of democratization it is important to establish what sphere of life we are discussing. This is a particularly crucial question for women because their exclusion from one (public) sphere of life is based upon the undemocratic norms and relations operative in the other (private) sphere. For this reason the dichotomy between the public and the private has been rejected by feminists.

They argue that a narrow definition of democracy grounded in the public sphere not only obfuscates the role that women play in the private domain in order that the public may exist, but also endorses a form of political practice that can only exclude women. So while the woman is considered to be in charge of child care and the functioning of the household, and remains dependent on the man's 'family wage', the time and resources at her disposal to enable her to cross the boundary of her private life into the public sphere remain very limited. Furthermore, as political institutions have evolved over the years with men as the major (if not sole) participants, they reflect in their functioning and procedures a male bias that does not allow women to gain easy access to them. Women's absence is thus very much a presence in the public arena of politics. They maintain the private sphere which allows men to organize the public.

Feminists would argue that the conventional understanding of democracy as a set of political arrangements whereby multiple parties contest free and fair elections means very little to most women. In polarizing the public world of universal values and the sexually differentiated one of the private domain, such a definition allows politics and representative democracy to be largely coterminous with the activities of men (Phillips, 1991: 6).

The public and private spheres

Is the distinction between the private and the public an essentially male construction? Should this distinction be maintained or obliterated? Do women only lose by this division or do they also have something to gain by keeping the private domain private? Feminists themselves are not agreed on the goal of, and reasons for, bridging the gap between the public and the private spheres.

Some have criticized the liberal conception of politics, which locates itself explicitly in the public sphere, in that it systematically excludes women; they argue that the social contract that created a political sphere was not only about equality and liberty but also about *fraternity* and therefore clearly about empowering men not women (Pateman, 1989). Others would like to see the values of the (maternal) private sphere 'humanize' the public arena, which is so dominated by masculinist discourse and practice (Elshtain, 1981; Ruddick, 1980). Yet others would want to regard the bridging of the public and the private spheres as transitory – a phase which would allow the entry of women into the public arena as independent and autonomous actors because, together with the democratization of the public, the private sphere would be politicized and thus democratized (Phillips, 1991 and 1992). Others insist on the importance of the autonomy of the public sphere and would argue that, while democratizing the private domain is crucial for women's participation in the public, it ought not to be confused with issues of civic participation and rights (Dietz, 1992; Mouffe, 1992a).

I would argue here that the question of democratization of the public and the private spheres for women needs to bring together the last two perspectives. What we need is not a confused melding together of the private and the public spheres, but a process of simultaneous but parallel democratization of both. It is important to mark a conscious transition that women must make to politicize the issues that affect them personally. While 'the personal is political' has been a long-standing slogan in the women's movement, the *process* through which this can be brought about has to take into account the crossing of boundaries between the private and the public, while acknowledging them as separate spheres.

However, for all the various groups of feminists, democratization of the private sphere would entail not only the redistribution of domestic responsibilities, but also a greater control and say in the financial and resource arrangements within the family. Given the concept of the family wage that has been constructed in the public domain, the difficulty of achieving one without the other becomes apparent. Whatever the debates among feminists, one thing is clear. Challenging the boundaries separating the public and the private spheres has been one of the most important feminist contributions to democratic theory. It is one of the distinctive perspectives that feminism brings to bear on the discussions of democratization.

The state and civil society

In discussing democratization in the lives of women, one needs to address the question of the dichotomy not only between public and private, but also between the state and civil society. This is important because the sphere of state processes is situated in the public domain, even though in its functioning it routinely crosses the boundaries of the public and the private. So, while governments make policies, seek legitimacy through representative institutions, and enforce laws through public agencies and practices situated in the public domain, the limited access of the majority of women to the public sphere means that their ability to influence, oppose and change the policies that affect them is circumscribed. The relationship of the state/civil society distinction to the public/private dichotomy is, of course, not one of easy correspondence.

Western liberal, and even radical, theory has generally taken the position that civil society is 'the space of *uncoerced* human association and also the set of relational networks – formed for the sake of family, faith, interest and ideology – that fill this space' (Walzer, 1992: 89, emphasis added), whilst the state is the sphere of coercion. Hence the suppression of civil society by authoritarian regimes is one of the important issues for democrats. The process of democratization has been one of reinstitution of the autonomy of civil society. However, in societies in the Third World (as well as in the West), civil society, instead of being an uncoerced space, can be one ridden with danger for women who attempt to leave the private sphere of domesticity. Like regulation of dress, policing of language and enforcement of segregation, civil society is implicated in forms of oppression. The impetus for participation in the public sphere on the part of many women in the Third World has come from state-led economic and political reforms rather than civil society. Whether this has led to the democratization of the private sphere is another (not entirely happy) story (see Einhorn, 1993; Rai *et al.*, 1992). I am not suggesting that the state, in the context of the Third World, is an unproblematic 'liberator'; far from it. In most instances patriarchy and the state function well together – supporting and reinforcing each other. Political expediency and social prejudice combine at times to subvert even modest demands made by women (see Jaising, 1987; Kishwar, 1986). However, what I am suggesting is that one of the key features of liberal democratic theory – the characterization of civil society as a benign public space – is deeply suspect, as is the state, in the eyes of many women of the Third World.

If we are prepared to share this scepticism about civil society we are also able to question the next assumption in Western democratic theory: 'only a democratic state can create a democratic civil society; only a democratic civil society can sustain a democratic state' (Walzer, 1992: 104). We come back to the definition of democracy once again. Are we speaking of democracy that takes into account issues of gender? Further, Walzer's formulation does not address the question of which comes first – a democratic state or a democratic civil society– in historical and cultural contexts that diverge significantly from the Western liberal one. As Parekh points out, even in the West, 'liberalism preceded democracy by nearly two centuries and created a world to which the latter had to adjust' (Parekh, 1992: 161). For Walzer, what a democratic civil society needs is 'men and women actively engaged – in state, economy and nation, and also in churches, neighbourhoods and families, and in many other settings too' (Walzer, 1992: 106). How are women to participate in the associational politics of the civil society, the interest-based politics of the state, and the economy, and also bear the burden of domestic work? Further, if the dominant (male) discourse on social relations excludes women, how can a civil society that is open and democratic come about?

Citizenship and radical democracy

Finally, at a time when national boundaries are being rethought and reconstituted, the growing interest in citizenship brings together two different political concerns of democratic theory – rights and participation. 'It restates the centrality of specifically political rights, yet does this in a language of activity and participation', writes Phillips (1991: 76). However, the different basis upon which liberal and radical democracy constructs the model of the citizen is important. Under liberalism, writes Dietz, 'citizenship becomes less a collective, political activity than an individual, economic activity' (1992: 67). It also remains wedded to the ideal of representative government and suspicious of the collective participation of citizens in the public sphere. In studying the process of democratization, the limitations of both the individual and the representative readings of democracy emerge. In emphasizing these limitations radical democratic theory contributes to a feminist critique of liberal democracy.

An important strand of democratic theory has argued for a more active, participative democracy, participation in the public sphere being regarded as good in itself. Radical democracy is one such strand. It allows individuals to become citizens, to gain greater control over their own lives and thus be more empowered, and to rise above their own immediate interests for the general good (Bachrach and Botwinick, 1992). Radical democracy bases itself on the continuous political engagement of citizens in public life: 'the power of democracy rests in its capacity to transform the individual ... into a special sort of political being, a citizen among other citizens' (Dietz, 1992: 75). However, while emphasizing the collective notion of democratic practice (in opposition to the liberal democratic assumptions of individuated democratic practice), radical democracy is more suspicious than liberal theories of democracy of recognizing identity-based political configurations. Further, radical democracy also insists on maintaining the distinction between the public and the private spheres (Canovan, 1992), through redefining the realm of the public as 'human activity' (see Dietz, 1992: 75).

Most feminists welcome the contribution of radical democratic theorists in defining the democratic process as more than representational and individual. At the same time, they criticize them on the basis that democracy 'grounded in the construction of a *specific* sphere of political activity, implicitly depoliticizes social relations within the home, family, workplace, and community' (Cooper, 1993: 163). However, as my discussion of specific case studies will show, the identification and exploitation of distinct spheres of political activity have been as important a part of women's strategies of resistance and mobilization (Mernissi, 1988) as have attempts at narrowing the divide between notions of 'private' and 'public' within democratic discourse.

Culture, authenticity and democracy

Women carry within them multiple identities grounded in class, race and ethnicity. There is no *essential woman* or *womanness* that can be isolated when we scrutinize their lives under any type of regime – democratic or not. As the poet June Jordan comments, 'every single one of us is more than whatever race we represent or embody and more than whatever gender category we fall into' (cited in Amos and Parmar, 1984). However, that does not imply that at certain moments of history, of transition, of aggression, they are not perceived simply as women erased of all other detail. There is an essential woman created where none exists. Here we assume that difference marks all women, but also recognizes their inscribed uniformity.

The individual and the cultural group

For women in the Third World, issues involved in democratization do not simply have to address the question of the public/private dichotomy, or divisions of class, but also of cultural differentiation, in particular, issues relating to their ethnicity, race and religion. Here too, the feminist critique of liberal individualism is relevant. Some feminists have pointed out that, in giving representational voice to the (male) individual, liberalism refuses to recognize the relevance of group differentiation. Gender cannot be regarded as a factor in politics if it is only the individual who is regarded as pertinent in the political process. While feminists are increasingly rejecting the idea of 'women's interests' (Pringle and Watson, 1992), they regard the acknowledgement of gender differentiation as important if the patriarchal character of liberal politics is to be exposed and group difference made part of representational politics. 'Democracy cannot continue to proceed on the assumption of an undifferentiated humanity, or the complacent assertion that voices are equally weighted by their equal right to participate in the vote' (Phillips, 1992: 78).

This critique of liberal democracy raises two different points. First, it points to the continued under-representation of women in liberal democratic politics and suggests that this is because of the initial presumptions made by liberal democracy – the division between the public and the private spheres, and the emphasis on the individual as the legitimate actor in democratic politics. Second, it addresses the question – does liberal democracy have anything to offer women, or should women give up on liberal democracy? Can liberal democracy be modified and made less masculinist? The critique has not led to any easy answers to these questions.

Some political theorists from the Third World have also pointed to the absurdity of universalizing the discourse of *liberal* democracy, as opposed to democracy, on grounds of historical specificity (Parekh, 1992). Taking individuation as the central tenet of liberalism, Parekh points out that 'Individuation is . . . a matter of social convention, and obviously different societies individuate human beings and define the individual differently' (Parekh, 1992: 16). Does this argument against liberalism not take us towards relativism? Parekh denies the charge of cultural relativism by endorsing a 'broad cross-cultural consensus commanding varying degrees of universal support' that would sign up to a 'genuinely universal core, such as respect for human life and dignity, equality before the law, equal protection of the law, fair trial and the protection of minorities'. While he does not suggest what mechanisms would ensure the continued observance of these core values, one can assume that he would endorse representational democratic practices. His quarrel is not with democracy but with liberalism. What I want to emphasize here is not some relativist position that posits cultures without questioning how they have evolved and been defined (most could be shown to be masculinist), but the problems with assuming that liberal democracy is universally applicable in both its assumptions about political values and its institutional forms.

The tension between individualism and cultural context poses particular problems for women. On the one hand, if the individual is spoken of as a gender-neutral human being, history would show that, in effect, it would be the gendered (male) individual that we are normalizing in such a discourse. In the context of *human* rights discourse, for example, women have tended to lose out. Constructed as 'human' rights, this discourse did not until very recently acknowledge the specificity of abuses of *women's* rights. When it did acknowledge certain issues as specific to women – rape, for example – they were considered too specific to be deemed universally human and thus part of the discourse (MacKinnon, 1993: 85; Gibson, 1993). It was only in 1991 that Amnesty International put the violation of women's rights on its agenda. Prior to this, feminist activity was not a recognized 'political' category except when integrated into the programme of a political party or trade union (Ashworth, 1986: 11).

On the other hand, as feminist critiques of Western feminism have shown, normalizing men as individuals has been paralleled in the history of the feminist movement by the normalizing of the 'white' woman as 'the woman' (see Amos and Parmar, 1984; Hooks, 1984; Lorde, 1981; Mohanty *et al.*, 1991; Liddle and Rai, 1993). To understand their own lives, consider options of negotiation and struggle, represent themselves to others in their own society and build coalitions with those outside it, women in the Third World cannot afford to neglect their own culture. If the individual in the political sphere has to be gendered, she has also to be recognized as a culturally-specific individual.

Cultural authenticity and codes of silence

Third World feminists are only too aware that culture has all too often been used to silence them. External threats to a culture have often ensured that a 'code of silence' that may be oppressive to sections within the community (Crenshaw, 1993) is imposed on communities. As Mernissi writes about the Arab culture's imposition of restrictive codes of conduct on women (1988: 37):

> as Arab women calling for change, we threaten the ahistoricity of the Arab identity imposed by society under the guise of authenticity, heritage, and using the past as a reference and a model for the future.

Similarly, Third World feminists tend to be less convinced than some Western ones of the importance of group representation as *opposed* to individual rights. Individuation, as Parekh points out, has occurred only partially in Third World societies. Individuation is, however, what many feminists passionately desire in societies where women are situated only within the family; they want to be citizens as well as believers, without being forced to make a choice.

In Iran, for example, when Khomeini warned women against celebrating International Women's Day on 8 March, women in Tehran organized a demonstration of 20,000, the biggest in Iranian history. However, this act of opposition led not only to attacks upon the women who participated, but also to differentiation between Iranian women on the grounds of cultural authenticity. The demonstrators and their supporters were singled out in official discourse from 'respectable' Muslim women who were good mothers and contributors to the Islamic Revolution (Hendessi, 1990: 13). Here again we witness the signifying of women as other than themselves – they are mothers, wives, even the 'armed angels' of revolution. Women as individuals, however, are not visible, and therefore find it difficult to stand up for their own rights.

The Algerian situation demonstrates the painful complexity of the issue of democratization for women. In October 1988 the socialist state, under the control of the National Liberation Front (FLN) since its independence from France, faced the wrath of its young people. The demonstrations were the 'result of a complex process of internecine power struggles within the body politic, as well as popular rejection of the political and economic monolithism of the system as a whole' (Cheriet, 1992: 9). Though the protesters had not demanded a pluralist democracy, 1989 saw the promulgation of a new Constitution which initiated the process of democratization under the watchful eye of the FLN and the Army. Ironically, the Islamic Salvation Front (FIS), a political party that explicitly rejects democracy as alien and divisive, gathered a formidable opposition to the FLN in the run-up to the elections in January 1992. As a result, the FLN regime cancelled Algeria's first free parliamentary elections. The Western powers did not protest at this violation of the democratic will of the Algerian people, nor did most Algerian feminists, though they themselves had been suppressed by the heavy hand of the FLN's coercive ideology. The reason for supporting the FLN decision given by both democrats and feminists was fear of the establishment of an Islamic fundamentalist state. For Algerian feminists, Iran was an example of how the installation of a populist religious movement had led to the circumscription of women's lives.

The FLN government had long tried to carve out a distinct regional and political identity for itself, and this was reflected in the 1976 Constitution where Islam was proclaimed as the state religion. The National Charter of the same year established socialism as an 'irreversible choice'. This made for an impossible political position in a country where both Islamic and revolutionary traditions were very strong. It created a situation whereby, between 1981 and 1987, the Islamic and feminist challenges to the state could both look to official discourse for legitimacy. Islamicists could cite the 'religion of state' article of the 1976 Constitution, while feminists could assert their citizenship under Articles 39 and 40 (Cheriet, 1992: 13). Though in the pre-1992 period both these groups suffered repression by the state, the crisis triggered by the cancellation of the 1992 elections brought them into conflict with each other. A bitter fight has broken out between the 'fierce individualism and modernism of the feminists [and] the patriarchalism and populism of the Islamists' (Cheriet, 1992: 14). In the aftermath of the cancelled elections more than a thousand members of the anti-fundamentalist intelligentsia and the feminist movement were killed by the Armed Islamic Movement (MIA). On the other hand, the FLN government is continuing mass arrests of suspected FIS and MIA members. Human rights abuses, and the routine use of torture, are widespread. Feminists in Algeria now face a painful dilemma: wanting the democratization of the private sphere, they find themselves unable to support the same process in the public political domain.

So where does the above discussion of democratic practice leave Third World women? To repeat the question that Phillips poses, 'Can women give up on liberal democracy?' Perhaps the way to look at it is to focus not only on the representational but also on the participatory aspects of democracy and the latter's potential for increasing the former. Is increased participation in politics the way forward for women? And further, does representational, liberal democracy provide women with greater opportunities to mobilize, and to articulate their interests? Finally, how best can women of the Third World address the painful dilemmas arising out of conflicts between the democratization of their private spheres, participation in the public domain, and the demands made in the name of the authenticity of cultural identity?

Women in the struggle for democracy

'God have mercy upon democracy and freedom of opinion' (a woman detainee in an Egyptian prison in 1981, cited in el-Saadawi, 1986: 30).

One of the arguments that Samuel Huntington makes for democracy is that life under a democratic regime might be unruly but it is not often politically violent (Huntington, 1991: 28). While doubting whether this assertion is valid in all cases, I would argue that a feature of non-democratic states is that they provide less scope for internal regulation by social forces. We need to distinguish here between different types of non-democratic regimes. There have been military-bureaucratic oligarchies where high levels of corruption and state violence are endemic. And there have been socialist-authoritarian regimes where, while there has been a largely unregulated monopoly of violence by the state or party, political disorder leading to violence has (at least until recently) been rare.

These different types of authoritarian regimes can also be distinguished by their approaches to the question of patriarchy. Complicity with patriarchy leading to restrictions on women's rights has been more likely to be evidenced in the first group of regimes, while state paternalism accompanied by an emphasis on women's mobilization in the public sphere has been more characteristic of the second group (see Kruks et al., 1989; Rai et al., 1992). The problems faced by women in the two different types of regime have therefore been distinct, though in both situations the possibility of women's autonomous participation in public political life has remained extremely limited, if not completely absent. The discourse of individual rights in this context has become important, not as a guarantor of freedom, or of good state practice, but as a starting point for struggle. Individual rights, therefore, however flawed in their conception, have played a useful role in opening up contestation with the state.

A question of rights

The question of rights is a highly contested one in feminist literature. There are those who feel that the power of the law is a structuring power, that the rights it bestows have a price tag that is disempowering to women, and that the language of rights is a male language that claims for itself, like other male-stream knowledges, not only universality but also Truth (see Smart, 1989). This, it is argued, can be seen in the way the family is constructed, not simply through social discourse, but through legal and legislative practice. Assumptions of the family as heterosexual, based upon the institution of marriage, and the best social institution in which to bring up children, are all underpinned by legal arrangements. Tax concessions, property rights and so on are used to validate the normalization of this family and to penalize deviations.

Other feminists regard rights as crucial in the fight against a patriarchal state, and as a form of protection against the daily violence of sexual and racial discrimination. They argue that rights are not stable, though that is what the state and legal institutions would like us to believe. They can be contested and subverted by infusing them with meanings that were not originally intended. Further, they point out that informality of power benefits only those who know the rules of the game; the outsiders of society can only lose by disregarding rights (Williams, 1991). So, while acknowledging the problem with rights, I would argue strongly for taking rights seriously. The struggle women face with the rights discourse is the same as with democracy – the engendering of laws. In many cases women's exclusion from the public sphere is difficult to fight precisely because, while there is a culturally authenticated language legitimizing their invisibility, there is no counter-discourse that allows them recognition as individual women in the public sphere.

Strategies and negotiations

In most struggles to introduce democracy into political systems the presence of women is significant, indicating the importance that they attach to the democratization of the public sphere. The terms of their inclusion in these struggles might be restricted and their role in the struggles carefully edited to conform with the social context, but their presence cannot be denied.

The strategies that women have used to challenge non-democratic regimes are often anchored in existing social relations, and are powerful because of the inability of those in power to counter this subversion without going against the norms which govern their own social rhetoric. As Kandiyoti argues, 'different systems may represent a distinct kind of "patriarchal

bargain" for women with different rules of the game and differing strategies for maximising security and optimising their
life options'. Different systems also determine 'both the potential for and specific forms of women's active or passive resistance in the face of oppression' (Kandiyoti, 1988: 277). While
such a strategy of bargaining could have a hidden political
danger in that women might appear to be acquiescing in the
continued inscription of their traditional roles, the importance
of these movements lies in the fact that the very act of participation, whatever the starting point, has a potential for radical
subversion and challenging the dominant discourses on gender
relations.

Las Madres des Plaza de Mayo (The Mothers of the Plaza de
Mayo) became a powerful symbol of resistance to military rule
in Argentina. At a time when no other oppositional group
found it possible to stand up to the brutal repression of the
military regime, fourteen mothers looking for their children
who had 'disappeared' under the regime took their protest
into the public arena. Their question was a simple one, 'Where
are our children?' This was a question which could not be
answered without bringing the very existence of the military regime into question. Therein lay its huge transformative
potential. In a country where the military junta unleashed a
Process of National Reorganisation in 1976 to 'restore the values
fundamental to the integral management of the state, emphasizing the sense of morality, fitness, and efficiency', housewives
and mothers drew courage from their socially inscribed and
politically validated roles in order to protest (Navarro, 1989:
243).

The National Commission on the Disappearance of Persons
set up by President Alfonsin after Argentina returned to democracy in December 1983, has documented the disappearance
of 8,960 persons during the military rule, an underestimate
according to most analysts. 'Disappearing' people has been,
and continues to be, used by many Latin American states –
Brazil, Chile, El Salvador – but 'the Argentine military per-
fected the weapon, widened its scope, and in fact transformed
it into a policy' (Navarro, 1989: 245). After the first shock of
this form of state terrorism wore off, a few groups began to
organize opposition around the issue of human rights. Las
Madres was one of these groups. It had two distinctive features according to Navarro. First, it was composed exclusively

of women, most of them housewives, all without any political experience. Second, it was committed to a militancy avoided by other groups (Navarro, 1989: 249).

On 30 April 1976 the first fourteen women met in the Plaza outside the Interior Ministry offices, to bring their disappeared children to the notice of the authorities. 'By walking around the pyramid as mothers of children who had disappeared, they transformed their private, personal statement into a public and political act' (Navarro, 1989: 251). At first they used Catholic symbols like a carpenter's nail, but later they started wearing white scarves, and carrying pictures of their children with the dates of their disappearances. These were emotive symbols linked to the history of mothers' sufferings. They were hard to characterize as protest in the macho world of Argentinian politics. The only way the military had of discounting them was to use ridicule; to call them *las locas de Plaza de Mayo* ('the madwomen of the Plaza de Mayo'). The fact that initially the military did not see mothers as political actors, since they could not conceive of mothers being politically active, provided the women with much needed time to mobilize their own strength and begin to develop a network of support that eventually crossed Argentina's borders and became an important factor in isolating the regime internationally. During this period, the women's informal network was transformed into a formal organization which allowed them to formalize their links with other human rights organizations inside and outside Argentina.

Motherhood, that archetypal patriarchal construction of women, served Las Madres and the cause of Argentinian democracy well. It was the same in Chile and El Salvador. 'We are mothers not women ... we are looking for our children. Our fight is for our families not to be forgotten and to reclaim justice from the state', said a Chilean woman involved in the Argupacion de Familiares de Detendidos-desparacidos (cited in Waylen, 1992: 304).

> Their refusal to acquiesce in the loss of their children was not an act out of character, but a coherent expression of their socialisation ... True to themselves, they had no other choice but to act, even if it meant confronting the junta (Navarro, 1989: 257).

Motherhood silenced the military regime and legitimized the women's protest. This also allowed some Latin American and Western feminists to claim that 'there exists a uniquely female political ideology, as shown by the metaphoric and symbolic content of the protests against violence' (Agosin, 1986: 1). While such a view of women's activism as 'essentially' female is challenged by other feminists, the importance of traditional roles to the forms of protest that women can choose to adopt cannot be denied.

In Chile, the involvement of women in protest at the disappearances also led to a re-evaluation by some of the roles of women within the home. *Democracia en Chile y en la casa* became the slogan of the emerging feminist movement in Chile. So, while for many political protest remained anchored in motherhood, for others the questioning of authority in one sphere led to challenges in the other. They realized that a successful struggle leading to the institution of a representative democratic form of government does not necessarily (or very often) bring democracy close to women's lives. In Chile as elsewhere, after the immediate goal was achieved, women have returned to their original roles of private actors, of mothers. A study of the process of democratization and women's involvement in it reveals a painful irony. While institutionalized politics is not operational, women participate in the public arena. With the institution or return of formal democracy, the public stage is reclaimed by men, the 'natural' actors of representative democracy.

Thus it is not surprising that some feminists have argued that, because of the exclusion of women from the public political sphere, women's participation in politics is inversely proportionate to the level of institutionalized politics (Katzenstein, 1978). Underdevelopment, concerns about modernization, a political stand against Westernization in the name of cultural authenticity or nation-building – there are many reasons why women are left out of the process of democratization 'until later'. During this crucial period of change, women are 'assigned a place in society which [cannot] be challenged without questioning both the past and the future' (Helie-Lucas, 1991: 58). This further demonstrates the need to rethink the public/ private divide in politics.

The problem with democracy

'Democracy minus women is not democracy' (slogan of the Independent Women's Democratic Initiative, Russia).

The year 1989 was devoted to democratic change. Many walls – ideological, political and psychological – came down in Eastern Europe and the Soviet Union. What was remarkable was the rapidity and extent of this change. After years of non-democratic regimes, the people of Eastern Europe looked to the freedom that democracy would bring. 'Liberty is, in a sense, the peculiar virtue of democracy. If one is concerned with liberty as an ultimate social value, one should also be concerned with the fate of democracy', writes Huntington (1991: 28). This was also the hope of those who instigated the revolutions of 1989. Some years later the mood is no longer euphoric. Subsequent economic changes have placed their own constraints on the democratic options open to political leaderships. The harnessing of the impulse for greater democracy to the ideology of marketization and the introduction of capitalism has created a particular context for the democratization process in most post-communist and Third World states. The introduction of representative democracy into many authoritarian regimes at the same time as economic liberalization has aggravated social tensions. The pain inflicted by the economic measures is resulting in the formation of opposition groups based on ethnicity, religion, nationalism and racism, as old ideological values are repudiated. The rise of sub-nationalisms, populism and, in some cases, neo-fascism has reminded people of how painful and slow the democratization process can be.

Liberalization and/or democratization?

Making a link between economic poverty and political democracy, Huntington writes, 'Most poor societies will remain undemocratic so long as they remain poor' (1991: 315). But he continues, 'Economic development makes democracy possible; political leadership makes it real.' However, as Diane Elson (1991) argues, one of the problems with democracy is that its advance is firmly linked to the advance of capitalism. Competition, one of the most important features of democracy, is also capitalism's central tenet. The point to be made here is that this twinning of market capitalism and representative democracy has not just *happened*, but has been consciously promoted by a combination of Western governments, international financial institutions, and influential multinational economic organizations. This has resulted in some countries, notably in the ex-socialist bloc, experiencing the transition to representative democracy and economic liberalism together. In others with already established capitalist economies, authoritarian regimes have been under pressure to introduce representative democracy, as in South Africa and many Latin American countries. Still others, like India, have been under pressure to open up their economies to international capital, even when indigenous capitalism and representative democracy have functioned together for many years. In sum, the tensions that arise from the introduction of representative democracy in the context of liberalization are diverse, as are the mechanisms at the disposal of different states to deal with these tensions.

In the countries of the ex-socialist bloc where a paternalist state had ensured basic welfare and certain important women-specific rights, women are experiencing deterioration not only in their economic but also in their social and political status. Abortion rights are under threat not only in Catholic Poland but also in Hungary. A reduction in social welfare, as part of the liberalization process, has meant the closure of crèches, cutbacks on maternity leave and fewer unemployment benefits, all of which have adversely affected women's social and economic position. A new pressure of nationalism has emerged in parallel with these changes. The splintering of the socialist bloc has encouraged the resurfacing of old national tensions, and nations are becoming pro-natalist. Women are under pressure to be 'heroine mothers' again and leave the public domain to men. Because the socialist regimes formulated the 'woman question' in such an inadequate, economically determinist way, and indeed used paternalistic discourses for their own purposes, the new democracy has seen the open expression of old prejudices. As male unemployment spirals upwards, women are being pushed out of jobs, or are moving to the low-paid service industries.

It needs to be stressed here that for most women it is not a case of wanting to quit their jobs and stay at home. The element of choice is absent from the decisions they are having to make in this new era of liberty (see Rai et al., 1992). The re-emergence of civil society in the context of the pressures of the marketization of the economy has indeed led to significant attacks on women's rights. In democratizing Poland, for example, a law passed in March 1993, reflecting the growing influence of the Catholic church, made abortions possible only in cases of rape or incest, when the mother's life is endangered or when there is risk of a 'damaged' foetus. Doctors violating the law now face between two and ten years in prison. And this has occurred when polls prior to the new law showed 58 per cent of Poles in favour of a woman's right to choose, and only 8 per cent against abortion in any circumstances. In the context of limited access to contraception and practically no sex education, the coercive pressures on women are enormous. 'One of the priests' favourite questions when they hear confession from women over 30 with small families is: do they use contraception?', complained the director of a counselling centre in Warsaw (*Guardian*, 14 September 1993: 17). However, in the 1993 elections many women used the new democratic processes to protest by voting against the governing coalition responsible for introducing legislation curtailing their right to abortion.

A problem for Third World nations, and for Third World women, is that economic liberalization has been taking place on a very uneven playing field. Though the IMF and the World Bank focus on different aspects of economic restructuring, a major element of both types of reform programmes is the removal of direct controls and subsidies and a reduction in the role of the public sector. The magic of the market is seen as an essential ingredient of the economic miracle that restructuring promises. Individuation is the premise upon which markets work, so, in theory, they should empower women in the Third World nations that are opting for, or being forced into, the market economy.

However, as Elson points out, 'If most women are to gain from access to markets, they also need access to public sector services ... to lighten the burden of their unpaid work and enable them to acquire the skills they need to enter the market' (Elson, 1991: 42). With cutbacks in the public sector – a central feature of adjustment programmes in the Third World – women lose out. While shrinking public facilities largely affect urban women, reduction or cancellation of food subsidies affects the health of all poor women, whether rural or urban. Further, the abolition of subsidies on the one hand and wage freezes on the other have resulted in spiralling costs of living, deteriorating health facilities (which, because of widespread gender differentials in access to and uptake of health services, makes women particularly vulnerable), and falling educational standards (Elson, 1991: 47).

The compromises of representative politics

One of the most frequent criticisms of existing democracies is that the elected representatives routinely make politically expedient compromises and betray the confidence of their electors. However, the case of Shahbano in India illustrates both the limitations and the potential of representative democracy for women's lives. At the age of seventy-eight, Shahbano Begum was divorced by her husband and left without any means of subsistence. She took her case to the courts and, after a long battle right up to the Supreme Court, won the right to compensation. This was a hollow victory, however, as the courts in India have no jurisdiction over matters deemed personal where the Muslim population is concerned. These are within the ambit of Muslim Personal Law. The only thing the Supreme Court could do was to say that Shahbano Begum *ought* to be provided for by her husband, and urge Parliament to pass legislation to end this anomalous state of affairs where different groups of Indian citizens look to different personal laws for adjudicating family disputes.

Muslim reformers, feminist groups and the right-wing Hindu party, the BJP, took up the issue and called for a uniform civil code. These were different voices making the same demand, from very different perspectives. The Muslim clergy immediately declared the Muslim reformists misguided, even heretics, and at the same time criticized the feminists and the BJP for attacking Muslim culture in order to weaken the Islamic community in India. The call went out from the mosques that if the Congress government went ahead with legislation to bring in a uniform civil code all 'good' (i.e. authentic as opposed to deluded) Muslims should vote against Congress in the next elections. The Rajiv Gandhi government, which had been reluctant to take on this politically sensitive issue, now found it impossible to do so. The Muslim vote is sizeable, and has traditionally been pro-Congress; the Congress Party would pay dearly if it alienated this group. Hence, the attempt at reform was rapidly dropped.

Representational politics thus showed its limitations. Women lost out in a context where Islamic culture was represented as under threat from atheists, reformers, feminists and Hindus. Political parties declined to take up the challenge of the mullahs because to do so would threaten their re-election. It is also important to note how perceived group representation (the Muslim block vote) went against the interests of individual women. The complicity of a democratic state with undemocratic practices in the private sphere, in the name of recognizing (a patriarchally defined) group identity, also led to a backlash against reforming the laws from within, and the *ulema* closed ranks. However, the Shahbano story is not only the story of the betrayal of women's interests by a democratic state. What is equally important is the struggle that women's groups (and others) were able to carry on in the public arena against the state–*ulema* axis, because of guaranteed democratic rights and an established practice of democratic institutions and media in India. Women needed and used the democratic system not simply as a protector (which it might or might not be) but to gain access to a public space, in which they might mobilize in their own defence. The debate about a uniform civil code for all Indian citizens continues (see Kishwar, 1986; and Calman, 1992).

A question of priorities

Increased and equal participation of women in the economic and political life of a country is important for reasons of articulation, recognition and legitimation of their interests. In most political systems, but especially in transitional regimes, the setting of strategic public priorities is an important and involved process. Who plans and sets priorities, on what grounds and by what criteria, is crucially important. Referring to the positions that women occupied during the Algerian revolution, Helie-Lucas writes (1991: 57):

> It would have seemed so mean to question the priority of the liberation of the country, and raise issues which would not be issues any more after the liberation: we believed that all the remnants of women's oppression would disappear with independence.

Overarching state projects, whether nationalistic or developmental, make it difficult for women to challenge them, or to press for their own agenda. In the lives of developmental nation-states there is no time that is 'right' for pressing demands that do not feed into the more urgent programme of development.

We are made to feel that protesting in the name of women's interests and rights is not to be done NOW: ... not during the liberation struggle ... not after independence, because all forces had to
be mobilised to build up the devastated county ... Defending
women's rights 'now' – this now being ANY historical moment –
is always a 'betrayal': of the people, of the nation, of the revolution,
of Islam, of national identity, of cultural roots ... (Helie-Lucas,
1991: 58).

Conclusions: what does democracy mean for women of the Third World?

This brief survey of issues for democratization in the lives of
women of the Third World points to the difficulty of speaking
of democracy in any neat, coherent way. Part of the problem
is that Third World countries are themselves hugely diverse in
culture, history and their chosen future agendas. To universalize
the experience of Western liberal democracies can only lead
to intellectual and political cul-de-sacs in the Third World.
For Third World feminists too, the feminist experience in the
West does not address many of their specific problems. This
is especially the case in non-democratic regimes and at times
of transition. While they might share a scepticism about the
private/public divide with most Western feminists, their particular concerns about economic survival, political imperialism
and their place in the discourse of cultural authenticity cannot
be answered simply, either in the language of democracy or
in that of feminist consciousness.

My concern in this chapter has not been to come up with
an alternative theory of democracy that will address these
diverse and complex issues. Its agenda was more modest and
straightforward: to question the rapid movement towards democratic forms of government; to 'dis-cover' the assumptions made
in this movement and the problems that women face when
these assumptions are translated into socio-economic policy.
However, this is not to deny the importance of democracy, either
as an ideal or as political practice. The empirical material considered above provides an ambiguous and complex picture of
democratic practice and needs to be considered when we cel-
ebrate democracy.

This chapter has argued for an awareness of the complexi-
ties and ambiguities surrounding the process of democratization.

Women have at times had to make difficult choices between a general support for democratic processes and institutions and the consequences of following through the logic of the latter, as in Algeria. They have valued individual rights but have been prepared to struggle for them, sometimes within very narrow confines, as in Argentina or Chile. They have been unable to look either to the state or to civil society to protect their rights, but have negotiated between them, evolving strategies to challenge as in Algeria and Poland. Women have had to make such strategic choices in all states under all regimes. However, at times of change in regime, including democratization, women face issues which are gender-specific. While there may be an increase in pressure not to rock the boat, to postpone their particular demands for the sake of the general good, points of transition also create new opportunities for women to press their own demands. These need not be articulated in advance. Indeed, in most instances they take the form of demands only after a period of participation in the public sphere. The forms of participation are varied, depending upon the nature of the regime and the process of change. The starting points of women's participation too may be very different, and some may enter the public sphere as mothers rather than as revolutionaries in the cause of women's rights. However, shifting agendas do allow possibilities to emerge that might not exist in a period of stability (Alvarez, 1990).

Democratization, therefore, has an exciting potential for the lives of women. Whether this potential is realized or not will in large part depend upon whether and how issues arising from women's experiences in both the private and the public spheres are addressed. These include issues of choice, control and autonomy; and they need to be addressed at every level and every stage of building democratic institutions (Brenner, 1993). As to what will be the mechanisms through which this may happen, these will only evolve through the expansion, re-evaluation and contestation of existing theories and practices of democracy.

7

Concerning international support for democracy in the South

LAURENCE WHITEHEAD

Introduction

In the immediate aftermath of the dismantling of the Berlin Wall it became briefly fashionable to claim that bi-polarity would be replaced by the unqualified hegemony of global liberalism. In its strong version this thesis never seemed very plausible to those familiar with the harsh practices and cruel dilemmas characterizing the political economy of most of the South (i.e. those societies whose interests were least reflected in the bi-polar scheme of things). But like many such simplifying schemas it contained just enough insight to impress. It foreshadowed the North American Free Trade Area (NAFTA), majority rule in South Africa, and economic deregulation in India, to cite just three of the more striking examples of liberalization in the South that have recently surprised many sceptics. However, the end of bi-polarity also brought the Gulf War, abortive 'humanitarian' interventions in Somalia and elsewhere, and a softened Western stance towards the post-Tiananmen Square Communist regime in China. Thus, five years after the end of the Cold War a provisional balance sheet for the South would suggest that there has been considerably less than an unequivocal triumph for global liberalism. Admittedly five years is too short a period to give much historical perspective. Indeed, some of the most significant consequences of the implosion of the Soviet system (in areas such as international criminality, the world-wide legitimation of political parties, etc.) may only now be beginning to come gradually into focus. In any event, the disappearance of the leading centrally planned economies, and the discredit of 'actually existing' Marxist political systems, has certainly shifted the global correlation of forces in the direction of economic and political liberalization, with powerful effects both on those Southern regimes that seek to capitalize on the new possibilities, and on those that attempt to resist them. It may be too early to judge the force and consequences of the current 'liberalizing wave' in the South, but there can be no doubt that we are witnessing an international process of impressive breadth and coherence.

This chapter is concerned with just one aspect of this liberalization process – attempts to establish and consolidate national political regimes based upon conventional standards of 'democratic' government. The minimum criteria are well known (as are their limitations). Regular competitive elections, honestly counted, freedom of association, pluralism of opinions and the related liberal values and practices have long been advocated (and criticized) throughout the territories of the South. In the post-Cold War world all the major power centres now endorse some fairly standardized version of this political model. All the member states of the Organization for Economic Cooperation and Development (OECD) claim (fairly truthfully) to practise political democracy understood in this way at home, and to favour its propagation abroad. This chapter therefore aims to consider, in the light of provisional experience so far, under what conditions such international support is likely to prove sustained and effective, and how much of a contribution to the democratization of the South we can expect it to make.

As a preliminary it may be useful to report, in very broad-brush terms, on the current state of play with regard to democratic transitions in the South. Any precise exercise would lead into serious problems of definition and measurement, but it is possible to convey orders of magnitude which would secure general assent. The United Nations Development Programme's (UNDP) 1994 *Human Development Report* lists 173 countries with a total population (mid-1992) estimated at 5,450 million; 49 of them, with 1,210 million inhabitants, are classified as either 'industrial' or 'ex-Soviet bloc', which leaves us with 124 states containing 4,240 million inhabitants that are classified as 'developing' countries. All the industrial states (27, with 860 million citizens) can now be conventionally classified as liberal democracies with track records extending back at least a decade. Although their experience is much briefer and more uncertain, nearly all the 22 ex-Soviet bloc states can be described as engaged in attempts at democratization, more or less following the conventional model, and in at least half of them, covering one-quarter of the population, democratic transitions have been successfully accomplished.

In contrast, less than a third of the 'developing countries' (with about a third of the population of the South) have so far achieved democratic transitions (39 out of the 124, i.e. 1.4 billion citizens out of 4.3 billion subjects). India is, of course, the linchpin of this group and Latin America is also strongly represented. Another two-fifths (52 in all) of 'developing' countries (with about half the total population of the South) must still be classified as overtly resisting democratization. China is, of course, by far the most important of these, but the current list also includes other such major Southern states as Indonesia, Nigeria, Vietnam and Myanmar (Burma). This leaves a balance of 33 states, with about 650 million inhabitants, which are currently attempting to establish conventional democratic regimes, although it is too early to determine their success. Half of these are in Africa, with the Republic of South Africa in the vanguard; but they are also to be found in Asia – Bangladesh and Pakistan, for example; and in Latin America – with Mexico a prominent example; only in the Middle East are such attempts largely absent. In summary, then, the global trend towards democratization has yet to take root in some 55 of the 173 countries under review, or to reach some 2.3 billion people (40 per cent of the world's population).

This calculation can be cross-checked against the annual Freedom House ratings (which cover 58 dependent territories as well as 191 sovereign states, thus including the entire global population). According to their latest estimates, in January 1995 40 per cent of the world's inhabitants, or 2.2 billion people out of 5.6 billion, were 'not free'. This compares with 2.1 billion (41 per cent of the global total) classified in the same way in January 1989, before the end of the Cold War. In the immediate post-Cold War period the proportion fell as low as 32 per cent (in January 1992), but since then almost the entire gain has been reversed. Indeed, if those classified as 'part free' are added to the 'not free', then less than one-fifth of the world's population were left living in 'free' countries in 1995, according to this exercise. By contrast, five years earlier Freedom House classified almost two-fifths of the world's inhabitants as 'free'.[1] Virtually all of the 'not free' peoples in these tabulations belong to what used to be called the 'Third World', and there is an apparently good association between a country's ranking according to the 'human development' indicators developed by the UNDP and the probability of undergoing a transition to democracy.[2]

Despite the crudity of this exercise in classification it does serve to show that, five years after the end of the Cold War, the global prospects for democratic government depended mainly on as yet unresolved experiments in the South. In contrast to the countries of the OECD, and even to the ex-Soviet bloc, in the South the outcomes of these experiments seem far more uncertain, the strength of the contending alternatives more finely balanced. For this reason, it could appear that international support should prove of more decisive importance than elsewhere. However, there are three major qualifications to this view. First, if such international support flows mainly from the 'democratic' North to the 'unstable' South, it risks awakening resistances arising from the past history of colonialism and political paternalism. Second, the social and economic impediments to the establishment of an effective democratic regime may well be more intractable in the 'less developed' areas of the South than in other regions where international support for democracy has been effective. And third, the nature of the available international support also requires critical consideration.[3]

Motives for promoting democracy

Under certain conditions the international community may unite around explicit efforts to promote *either* the establishment *or* the subsequent consolidation of what can conventionally be defined as a 'democratic' regime. For example, the victorious Allies supported a wave of democratizations in Europe after 1918, and again following the defeat of the Axis powers in 1945; there was also a wave of democratizations in the 1960s associated with decolonization. Even in the throes of the Cold War, and more pronouncedly afterwards, international support for 'democracy promotion' has tended to flourish, at least at the declaratory level.

Thus, there is a long history of declaratory statements both from Washington and from most European capitals, asserting that the promotion of democracy is a major goal (sometimes even *the* overriding purpose) of Northern policy towards large areas of the South. The Alliance for Progress, British export of the 'Westminster System', sanctions against South Africa, establishment of the National Endowment for Democracy, European Parliament resolutions, etc. provide extensive testimony that even before the end of the Cold War this was a recurrent theme of Western policy. Although other Western policies pursued at the same time were either inconsistent with, or even in flagrant opposition to, these declaratory statements, and an extensive literature exists debunking them, a balanced reading of the record suggests they were spasmodically accompanied by significant elements of follow-through. Since 1989 this type of discourse has redoubled, and has spread to such hitherto ostensibly 'apolitical' financial institutions as the World Bank. Currently the Clinton administration claims that promotion of democracy provides the unifying rationale to US foreign policy in the post-Cold War era, and even the French government has shifted its official stance on francophone Africa in the direction of qualified support for democratization. We therefore need some explanation of why, despite the many evident impediments, the Northern demand for democracy promotion has proved so durable, and indeed irrepressible.

Carol Lancaster (1993:13) has argued:

> it is not just the end of the Cold War and the re-emergence of values as an influence in US aid policies that has given rise to the current emphasis in Washington on promoting democracy abroad. It is also a practical response to a variety of domestic political imperatives. The most urgent imperative is finding a rationale for a $15 billion a year foreign aid programme.

But this is too short-term and narrow a basis to account for the scale of the phenomenon, particularly since (as I shall argue below) the promotion of democracy can provide new arguments to those seeking to withhold aid as a punishment for poor democratic performance. There is, however, a broader problem facing the US administration, which is how to elicit the resources and support required to sustain a strong American presence in international affairs, when the domestic electorate is preoccupied with internal problems and there is no immediate external threat to set against that isolationist reflex. It is not just the (relatively weak) aid lobby in Washington that faces this problem, of course. Symptomatically, at the outset of the Clinton administration even the Pentagon established its own Office of Democracy Promotion, in the quest for new justifications to fend off the pressure for expenditure cuts (although equally symptomatically in mid-1994 it was renamed 'Office for Foreign Civil-Military Affairs'). No doubt similar budget-protection strategies help to account for the shifts in stance that have to be observed in the international financial institutions. However, the deeper point is that all these claimants on Northern taxpayer funds evidently believe that legislators and voters will view them more kindly if they can show that they are contributing to the cause of promoting democracy.

Moreover, success in supporting (a certain image of) democracy abroad has served to reinforce the legitimation of the democratic order at home, and to boost national pride and self-confidence. This has been particularly true for the United States, where the regime was, of course, founded on liberal constitutional principles. To take pride in one's democratic heritage at home, while denying the same values overseas, has always been problematic for American policy-makers; whilst in the current period of widespread domestic disenchantment, it has been extremely comforting and reinforcing to observe that in other parts of the world the United States' liberal democratic heritage retains a powerful appeal.

The case of the European Union (EU) is analogous, although less clear-cut. West European images of democracy are slightly different from those of the United States, and the Europeans have relatively recent experiences to remind them of the dangers (and temptations) of failing to protect liberal values. Post-war European reconciliation has been based on the painstaking construction of a liberal constitutional community which remains fragile and uncertain of its place in the world. In addition, the major European powers only relinquished their imperial ambitions a generation ago, and often under duress. Decolonization was frequently justified by reference to its democratic content, even though in most cases the resulting post-colonial states adopted authoritarian forms of government. By taking up the cause of democracy promotion in the South, the EU hopes to unite around a common project which reflects the positive aspects of its Member States' recent achievements, which compensates for their often less than liberal record in their former colonies, which puts the EU on a basis of equality with the United States, and which differentiates Western Europe from the former Communist bloc to the East. In contrast to the United States, European efforts at promoting democracy can hardly be explained in terms of budget-protection strategies, since at least in Brussels new categories of expenditure are required which compete with the EU's established spending priorities.

The Japanese case is different again and this may help to explain why democracy promotion assumes a different (and less forceful) pattern in much of Asia from that observable in Africa and Latin America. Liberal constitutionalism was imposed on Japan from without, and efforts to promote it overseas tend to be viewed as the expression of American rather than Japanese values. Promoting democracy is therefore not an instrument of legitimation for the domestic political system. Nor has the post-war reconstruction of Japan been based on an expanding multilateral constitutional system, as in Western Europe. In any case, memories of the Japanese Co-Prosperity Sphere remain sufficiently fresh in regional memories to preclude a co-operative response to democratizing initiatives from Tokyo, at least in those countries that were overrun by Japanese forces during the Second World War.

In summary, then, the underlying persistence of Northern inclinations to engage in democracy promotion in the South seems to express some quite deep-rooted political and even cultural characteristics of the established liberal democracies. Questions of ideology, legitimation and political identity appear to be more important than the relatively conjunctural issues arising from bureaucratic in-fighting in the post-Cold War setting. To the extent that such existential factors shape Northern policy-making, the various pragmatic limitations to effective action outlined at the beginning of this chapter will be insufficient to suppress the underlying thrust of policy. However, factors of this kind operate differentially within the various OECD countries, and such differences (which are often only dimly perceived) are likely to interfere with Northern efforts to co-ordinate a solid front on the democracy issue. Indeed calculations of short- and long-term national and international advantage may indicate that the promotion of democracy can be an important ingredient of regional conflict resolution; that it may, under specified conditions, also serve the objective of promoting peaceful economic development; and that the proliferation of democratic regimes could also prove of general benefit by strengthening the structure of international co-operation and dispute settlement. These are all arguments aimed at reducing the moralism in democracy promotion, and at reconciling this foreign policy goal with the more conventional aims of international statecraft. The North (at least temporarily including Moscow) seems currently to have established a fairly uniform consensus along these lines, but it remains to be seen how well this would hold up if experiences in the South were to generate repeated clashes between the objective of democracy promotion and other instrumental goals (regional stability, Southern economic development, the strengthening of international co-operation, etc.).

Thus, whether the present Northern consensus on the advantages of 'democracy promotion' survives will in no small degree depend on how well such initiatives are received both by the political elites and by the population at large in the target countries of the South. At this point we must therefore shift focus from core country motives for democracy promotion to the dynamics of democratization on the periphery. Elsewhere (Whitehead, forthcoming b) a review of the international factors contributing to the establishment of all contemporary democratic regimes led the present writer to propose a framework using four possible transmission processes: contagion, control, conditionality and consent. Whereas the first and last of these are essentially concerned with social processes and relationships at work within and between clusters of Southern countries, the second and third mainly concern North–South interactions, and the dominant process for the purpose of this volume is the third. This chapter will therefore devote most attention to recent 'political conditionality' provisions designed to encourage democratic transitions and to reinforce fragile new democracies in the post-Cold War South. However, the alternative processes also require brief consideration.

Contagion

Academic discussion of contemporary democratizations contains a growing literature on international 'demonstration effects', 'contagion' and 'waves' (see, for example, Huntington,

1991). Casual empiricism indicates that it would be unwise to disregard such explanations, however vague they may seem, and indeed they have an impressive pedigree (extending back at least as far as the succession of democratizing revolutions which broke out in Europe in 1848). One way to introduce a degree of structure into this type of analysis, and also to direct attention to the question of 'international support' for such waves or clusters, is to consider how within a given region the democratization of a major state is likely to alter the balance of forces in neighbouring but less influential countries. For example, if Nigeria democratizes it is likely to exert a substantial influence in that direction throughout West Africa. However, we need to distinguish between deliberate policies to support adjoining democratic counterparts in order to stabilize the new regime, and the more indirect, but not necessarily less powerful, influences which may spur imitations, regardless of the wishes or actions of political rulers. It is here that the metaphor of 'contagion' comes into its own.

The notion of democratic 'contagion' can be concisely presented by using the example of Paraguay (discussed in Bostrom, 1994). In 1977 the Stroessner dictatorship was completely surrounded by authoritarian military regimes. The only two remaining elected civilian governments in South America were distant Colombia and Venezuela. Thereafter, one by one, all these authoritarian regimes gave way to democracies: Ecuador (1978); Peru (1979); Bolivia (1982); Argentina (1983); Uruguay (1984); Brazil (1985); and finally even Chile (1988). Many of the influences undermining the Stroessner regime and encouraging Paraguayan advocates of political reform to press their claims derived from these external events, which were beyond the reach of the authorities in Asunción. Individual perceptions of what was possible within Paraguay were altered by the news from abroad; moreover, neighbouring regimes which had helped to suppress anti-Stroessner movements in their jurisdictions became safe havens for opposition activities, and sources of organizational support; finally, Paraguay belonged within a regional society of states and its government was therefore affected by the rise of a pro-democratic intergovernmental consensus.

Clearly, the demonstration effects and democratic 'contagion' illustrated in this example are in principle reversible. In practice, there is considerable evidence of 'snowballing' effects, whereby the success of one military coup helps trigger a succession of nearby imitations; just as the success of one democratization can have regional repercussions. Needless to say, this process only operates within certain limits which need to be further defined.

Control

It is surprising but true that the very simple notion of democracy through 'contagion' should have substantial explanatory power. Even more examples seem to fit within the framework of 'control'. After all, democracy is not just like a virus which happens to spread from one organism to another without intentionality. A more appropriate medical metaphor might be to see it as a vaccine. On this view, US forces have acted in the Dominican Republic, Grenada, Panama and (indirectly) in Nicaragua, El Salvador and Guatemala to 'inoculate' those polities from contamination by Castroism. Washington has always labelled this treatment 'democracy', and similar claims have been made for Greece and Turkey (under the Truman Doctrine). Despite the self-serving nature of such arguments, their existence could subsequently be invoked to prod US policy in a democracy-promoting direction.

The essential point is that approaching two-thirds of currently-existing democracies owe their origins, at least in part, to deliberate acts of imposition or intervention from without (acts, moreover, that were undertaken within living memory). Given this, an interpretation which excludes from consideration the roles played by external actors, their motives or their instruments of action, is bound to produce a highly distorted image of the international dimension of democratization, however good its statistical performance may seem. As always, correlation must be separated from causation. It is not contiguity but the policy of a third power that explains the spread of democracy from one country to the next.

Using the hypothesis of great-power 'control' over most democratizations, the speed, direction, limits and mechanisms of transmission of the democratization process can be accounted for more satisfactorily than under the 'contagion' approach. Thus, for example, the boundaries of democratization after 1945 were rather precisely set by the presence of US forces. This would also explain the observable sequence of changes of regime, the speed with which they occurred, and the main processes involved. Similarly, it was only territories within the British Empire that experienced attempts to export the Westminster model (e.g. after Trinidad, Barbados and St Lucia the 'contagion' skipped over Martinique to Dominica, then skipped Guadeloupe to Antigua). The order and speed of the march towards democracy was set by London's timetable for decolonization, and it was this that largely determined the processes involved. A similar analysis could be undertaken concerning the record of French decolonization in sub-Saharan Africa, where the initial idea, at least, was to promote a Gaullist/presidentialist model of democracy, which soon degenerated in much the same way as the Westminster transplants. Somewhat similar claims can be made for democratization in the Western hemisphere since 1978 (i.e. the demise of national security states within the US sphere of influence), although in this case the degree of direction from Washington was less apparent, as will be indicated in the next section of this chapter.

However, we have to mention the limitations and paradoxes of this power politics perspective. In particular, how can the relatively permissive and even altruistic act of promoting democracy be derived from the self-regarding and centralizing logic of power politics? In a small range of extreme cases these two conflicting logics may be reconciled through an act of territorial incorporation. Thus the United States has effectively both extended its power and democratized adjoining territory by adding new states to the union (Hawaii and the still not fully incorporated Puerto Rico provide two post-war illustrations). Similarly, the German Federal Republic incorporated the GDR in 1990. Another instance of significance for this chapter was the Indian invasion of Goa in 1961. Democratic South Africa's relationship with the various so-called 'bantustans' may follow a similar path. In all these cases large strong democracies incorporate adjoining weaker and more undemocratic polities, paying the costs of absorption and dictating the terms of political transformation. (The cases of Hong Kong and Macao remind us that even in the post-Cold War world it is not only democratic states that can hope to extend their power through annexation.) But such examples of democracy-through-incorporation are inevitably rare. Far more frequent have been the cases of democratization-through-decolonization.

Here we should recall that, at least in the case of British decolonization, the aim of the former imperial state was not to maximize its immediate power, but to create an international environment that would in the longer run be relatively unthreatening to a great power in decline. French, Belgian and Dutch decolonizations were similar (only Portugal took a radically different route). In international politics more broadly conceived, then, there are periods when it may be good policy for a dominant state to be permissive and decentralizing in the territories it controls, even though such a situation is hard to express in the terms of strict power politics theory. This is all the more true if we allow domestic opinion within the dominant state to affect its foreign policy.

However, sustained and effective support for the spread of democracy within a given sphere of influence will require more than just the temporary ascendancy of libertarian factions within an imperial power structure. The libertarians will have to forge and sustain a new foreign policy consensus by demonstrating that the long-run interests of the society as a whole will be best served by relaxing control over previously subordinate territories. There are likely to be two main strands to such a consensus: the security apparatus and its allies will have to be persuaded that the costs of attempting to sustain the old structures of control has become too high, and/or the probability of success has fallen too low; and the political class in general will have to be reassured that the risks and costs of tolerating democratic dissidence and uncertainty are worth bearing. It was relatively easy to achieve this consensus in post-war Britain, given the presence of the United States as a protector and in the last resort a substitute guarantor of order (the decolonization of Guyana is particularly illustrative here). This goes far towards explaining the fact that the British presided over the majority of the thirty or so democratizations-through-decolonization which scatter the world.

Of course, those democratizations which fall within the US sphere of influence cannot be analysed by reference to the strategies of great powers in decline. (The wave initiated by the Carter administration may bear some superficial comparisons with British decolonizations but these are secondary resemblances only.) During the Second World War (as in the First), Washington made the promotion of democracy a central war aim, and this contributed to America's victory in at least two important respects. It helped to engage a very broad spectrum of domestic opinion in support of the war effort, avoiding the suspicions and divisions that have hampered both earlier and later war mobilizations (e.g. some incursions into Mexico, and of course the Vietnam War). It also contributed to US success in constructing and sustaining the broad international alliances required for victory. If the European Allies had perceived the United States as just another great power engaged in empire building, the cohesion of the anti-Axis coalition would have been in jeopardy. As it was, both allies and enemies of the US-led alliance were undoubtedly influenced in their war calculations by the expectation that a victorious United Nations coalition would respect (or restore) national sovereignties and would generally favour the establishment (or re-establishment) of pluralist political institutions in the territories it liberated. If this promise was an important part of the Western Allies' political capital during the war, it held a corresponding political weight among the victors' obligations after 1945.[4]

Fortunately for Washington it proved possible to harmonize these obligations with US post-war security interests. But, although possible, this was far from inevitable, and a great deal of effort and ingenuity was required to achieve this harmonization. Moreover, Washington lacked much direct capacity for control over its authoritarian allies in the 1970s and 1980s. This was particularly evident in Southern Europe and South America. (In the Caribbean and Central America, of course, the possibility of US military action always remained part of the equation.) Nevertheless, Washington possessed substantial indirect systems of influence and support. Through the allocation of aid and other economic concessions, through gestures of political support or disapproval, and even through the dense network of military and security ties which bound it to these regimes, Washington could encourage, redirect, or resist democratizing impulses, even if it could not strongly control them.

But even in the post-Vietnam cluster of US-led transitions of regime, there are some aspects that belong under the heading of 'control'. For example, the Carter administration proclaimed a general policy of support for democracy and human rights, both within and outside the US sphere of influence. But the US sphere was very wide, and so the question quickly

emerged of where to begin (and also, implicitly, where to end).
In practice, Washington's initiatives to encourage recent democratizations within its sphere of influence have been consistently selective and contingent. Carter took the lead in the
Dominican Republic, but not in Iran; Reagan acted on Grenada
rather than Haiti; Bush backed a clean count in Nicaragua, but
not in Mexico; and so forth. Some of this selectivity was due
to variations in the strength and characteristics of the democratizing actors within individual countries, and so cannot be
classified as a product of external control. But considerations
of economic and military security, and calculations of political
and ideological self-interest, are also very evident as factors
explaining the order, rhythm and intensity of Washington's
initiatives, and to this extent the promotion of democracy has
functioned as yet another component in a world-wide system
of alliance control. Illustrations of this argument can be found
elsewhere (e.g. in Carothers, forthcoming and Lowenthal, 1991),
so it will not be elaborated on here.

Certainly the element of control has been less prevalent in
the US-led democratizations than in the decolonization-linked
processes discussed previously. It may well be that with the
ending of the Cold War, the strengthening of the European
Union, and the increasing prevalence of democratic forms of
government around the world, this factor will fade away in
future years. Perhaps 200 years after Kant's (1891 [1795]) initial contribution to the idealist tradition in international relations, his prediction that the spread of 'republican' (today we
would say 'democratic') forms of government would gather
such momentum as to bring about 'perpetual peace' (the contemporary phrase would presumably be 'the end of history')
will be realized.[5] But with regard to almost all the democratizations that have occurred since 1945, external agency has
represented a major alternative perspective that contrasts with
'contagion' in the account it provides of the international side
of democratization.

Conditionality

Following the collapse of the Soviet bloc the last major wave of
'decolonizations' has been completed. From now on, in the absence of a bi-polar power structure, and with a far larger number

of fragile states vying for external support and international recognition, continuing 'control' is likely to be replaced by intermittent 'conditionality' as the dominant feature of the North–South relationship concerning democratizations. 'Conditionality' embraces the widening range of intentional policies and structural inducements that have come into existence over the past decade or so, motivated by an avowed desire on the part of the leading developed democracies (the 'OECD countries') to reward processes of democratic transition and consolidation around the world, and to discourage backsliding. Since this new heading embraces a wide range of diverse phenomena, some of which may in practice be difficult to distinguish from 'control' or 'consent', we should begin by sketching the principles of differentiation which allow a broader scope for 'conditionality' than under the definitions implicit in much recent policy-oriented literature.

'Conditionality' refers to *international* (or at least publicly avowed) policies and incentives, and can thereby be distinguished from 'contagion'. It involves the promotion of some *minimum requisites* or *threshhold conditions*, below which defined forms of international support will purportedly be withheld, and above which they will be supplied. At least in principle this represents a contrast with 'control', in that it leaves an approved democratic regime basically unconstrained in its other policy choices (which are to be made according to constitutional and representative processes that are regarded as essentially domestic), provided that the agreed criteria for democratic performance are not violated.[6] Whereas 'control' is typically (though not invariably) exerted by a single unified source of authority, 'conditionality' implies (without strictly entailing) a process of international consultation and indeed negotiation to set standards, co-ordinate incentives and arbitrate disputed cases. 'Control' implies unilateralism; 'conditionality' implies multilateralism (even including some input from the target countries). But whereas our discussion of 'consent' will direct attention to the *internal pre-requisites* for generating authentic democratic initiatives, the notion of 'conditionality' focuses on the *international processes* through which such initiatives may be encouraged, labelled, ranked and rewarded.

All these categories involve a two-way flow of influences (even 'control' includes a dynamic of mutual adjustment) and although they may be distinguished analytically, in practice they overlap. Thus, when applying them to the analysis of particular cases we can expect to find a complex combination in play. This framework of interpretation is intended to clarify the main international dimensions of contemporary democratization processes *without*, however, overstating the contribution of international factors as compared with the domestic dynamics of democracy construction at work in each country.

The most powerful and sustained structure of international incentives favouring democratization in the contemporary period has been afforded by the European Union, when it offered the prospect of full EU membership to selected countries on its periphery (first in Southern Europe, and now prospectively in East-Central Europe) on condition that, among other things, they first achieve EU-approved standards of democratic governance. Some (Pridham, 1991; Whitehead, 1986) have argued that this form of influence worked most powerfully to reinforce regime change over the long term (i.e. to weaken and divide authoritarian regimes, and to underpin – or in one recent formulation to 'underwrite' – the consolidation stage of democratization). It is more debateable whether the EU really contributed much to the 'breakdown' and 'transition' phases of democratization in either Southern or Eastern Europe. A plausible case can be made that to exert any effective influence over such unstable episodes requires the kind of actively managed and indeed interventionist policies that only individual governments can undertake. According to this view, the United States, for example, has been more effective than the EU in attempting to mould processes of transition, whereas the European Union has more of the dispassion and staying power required to assist subsequent democratic consolidations.

The question of whether similar conditionality may be extended to certain potential new accessions from Eastern Europe (and to Turkey, which formally applied for full membership as long ago as April 1987) will put this practice to a severe test, however. Even if the EU does decide in favour of eventual further enlargement to the east, this will inevitably be a very slow process, and at least some fragile democracies will be kept waiting indefinitely. Brussels must therefore face the issue of whether it can devise other powerful instruments that will reinforce consent for democracy in those countries where accession is a distant or impossible dream. There are some limited precedents (e.g. EU support for the San José process in Central America (see Whitehead, 1992)) but their impact is very weak compared to the Union's one big prize. Full membership generates powerful, broad-based and long-term support for the establishment of democratic institutions because it is irreversible, and sets in train a cumulative process of economic and political integration that offers incentives and reassurances to a wide array of social forces. In other words, it sets in motion a complex and profound set of mutual adjustment processes, both within the incipient democracy and in its interactions with the rest of the Union, nearly all of which tend to favour democratic consolidation. Mere aid packages or political advisory missions are far less potent, no matter how well staffed or funded they may be. In the long run such 'democracy by convergence' may well prove the most decisive international dimension of democratization, but the EU has yet to prove that case fully.

According to a strong current of liberal internationalist thinking, particularly in the United States, similar processes of democracy by convergence are likely to develop in the Americas, especially as a result of Mexico's entry into NAFTA, and of plans progressively to extend so-called 'free trade' agreements from North America throughout the Western hemisphere. It is not entirely clear whether exponents of this view are committed to some notion of regional exceptionalism (i.e. the liberal republican traditions of Latin America and the strength of US influence make the region an exceptionally favourable setting for democracy by convergence), or whether the same processes are in principle expected to work in a similar manner in other parts of the South (e.g. a democratic South Africa might extend its influence northwards, stabilizing comparable regimes in Angola, Mozambique and so forth). And, even for the Latin American region, this argument involves very ambitious extrapolation from an exceedingly slender basis of experience.

In any event, the vast majority of Southern states have no early prospect of becoming members of a strong regional community of securely democratic states. So what alternative structures of international support for democratization might they tap? Over the past few years reliance has been increasingly placed on the mechanism of 'conditionality' to democratize. Loans, trade concessions, advice and support are offered selectively to those regimes which are held to satisfy internationally specified conditions of democratic performance. The conditions vary from country to country (as well they might, given the diversity of situations to be handled) and interpretations of performance standards leave much room for dispute. But in any case there seem to be some rather crucial paradoxes embedded in the notion of using 'conditionality' to 'democratize'. After all, 'conditionality' assumes that there is an international body with the authority, disinterestedness and know-how to promote the 'public good' in transitional regimes. Yet the theory of liberalization casts doubt on the very notion of disinterested public authority *within* national societies. Indeed, the more radical versions of liberal theory condemn the whole idea of purposive social engineering, which gets reclassified in terms of 'market distortion' and 'predation'. In addition, 'conditionality' can only work if there is some local counterpart to the international body which is capable of entering into, and in due course enforcing, a complex conditional contract within the territory under its jurisdiction. In other words, conditionality tends to presuppose judicial equality between contracting parties, the most indispensable of which are national states. Yet 'liberalization' often seems to be about *dismantling* states that are characterized as bloated, oppressive and obstacles to personal and economic freedom (see Lancaster, 1993).

If international financial institutions (IFIs) are to practise parity of treatment, as required by their charters, they must deal with all member states according to the principle of formal equality. Yet in practice, the reality of different starting points, different routes, different outcomes and extremely divergent state capabilities makes this principle largely a fiction, and in the post-Cold War world this artificiality is likely to become more flagrant and indefensible just when 'conditionality to liberalize' is being pressed beyond its limits. On the face of it, then, 'conditionality to democratize' might seem a self-contradictory, or at the very least highly problematic and probably unrealistic, undertaking.

In contrast to the IFIs, which are (theoretically) expected to be politically neutral, the political organs of the United Nations are not as much constrained in the same way. Since the end of the Cold War lifted the prospect of great-power vetoes in the Security Council, the UN Secretariat has become more ambitious in promoting political initiatives (backed up by the possibility of sanctions or even the use of force) to advance selected political objectives in the South. Generally, the emphasis has been on peace-keeping (or more ambitiously on peace-building) and on humanitarian relief (including the promotion of universal standards of respect for human rights), rather than on democracy promotion *per se*. Nevertheless, the holding of fair elections under international supervision has become an important ingredient in various UN peace-building programmes; indeed, the term 'peace-building' implies the provision of international support for representative institutions. Gross violation of human rights is self-evidently an extreme form of anti-democratic practice, so that policies aimed to prevent such violations may also be thought to constitute at least indirect support for democratizing tendencies.

However, the UN has inevitably tended to become drawn into those conflict-ridden parts of the South where the prospects for sustained democratization are in general least promising, and there is a distinct limit to the number of such entanglements which the international community is likely to support at any one time, particularly if the consequences of high-profile initiatives are viewed by Western public opinion as disappointing, and/or if it seems that effective UN involvement requires an excessive degree of intrusion into the domestic political affairs of member states. So far the record is mixed, and it remains possible that the UN will persist until its democratizing successes (e.g. in Namibia and El Salvador) outweigh the disappointments (e.g. in Angola, Cyprus and Somalia). It is equally possible, however, that these immediate post-Cold War bursts of UN activism will result in burnt fingers, and will be followed by a much more cautious stance. In any event, only a quite small proportion of Southern states (those least capable of defending their claims to sovereignty or, to put it more sharply, those closest to lapsing into protectorate status) are likely to be the focus of such UN initiatives.

Apart from these multilateral conditionalities, there are still substantial areas of the South where essentially bilateral relationships of dependence persist. In relation to Haiti and Cuba, for example, it is the democracy-promotion stance of the current administration in Washington that matters, almost to the exclusion of other considerations. In parts of francophone Africa, Paris still exercises comparable discretion, and India's stance on the quality of Sri Lankan democracy has on occasion in the recent past carried similar weight.

A recent study by the Overseas Development Council in Washington provides some useful insight into the US debate on the scope for using bilateral aid as an instrument for political conditionality (Nelson with Eglinson, 1992). The authors distinguish between positive and negative political conditionality; and between the use of aid to encourage respect for human rights, or the adoption of approved economic reforms, on the one hand, and its use to promote participation and competitive democracy, on the other. On negative conditionality, they note (Nelson with Eglinson, 1992: 45):

> US aid legislation has long provided for cutting off assistance in response to military coups. But the United States and other donors have not been at all consistent in this approach, nor have they normally co-ordinated their responses. The changing international setting increases the feasibility of co-ordinated donor action. A more consistent approach should be a more effective deterrent.

(Since this was written, blatantly anti-democratic conduct in Peru, Haiti and the Dominican Republic has highlighted the continuing difficulties in this area, while the US curtailment of aid to Nicaragua has shown that it is not only in the event of blatant backsliding that this weapon may be deployed.) The authors also explore the possibility of including some kind of 'democracy bonus' in a government's aid policies, concluding that any such democratic bonus 'must be carefully designed, and explicitly temporary, targeted to help the government during the difficult early period. One form a bonus might take is simply extra patience and flexibility from the donor community' (Nelson with Eglinson, 1992: 46). Here too, experience suggests that a consistent and effective application of this approach will be difficult to achieve, with the strong likelihood that more will be claimed than is actually delivered, while the real determinants of donor conduct may frequently be less noble than the official rhetoric would indicate.

The ODC study also makes an important distinction between conditionalities which are aimed at *restraining* certain undesirable forms of conduct, or at improving precisely measurable types of performance (human rights, administrative transparency, etc.), and those aimed at supporting the much more complex and imprecise processes of enhanced participation and increased political competition. The latter require 'not only enabling action by governments, but also motivation, organisation, and appropriate behaviour on the part of much of the society as a whole'. They also note that 'participation, competitive politics, and representative governments can take a multitude of forms. The institutions and procedures that work well in one country may work very poorly in another'. Moreover, 'vigorous outside intervention to encourage participation and competitive democracy can jeopardise the legitimacy of those reforms'. So they conclude that 'these contrasts counsel a much more restrained use of conditionality to promote participation and democracy than to promote human rights or improved economic governance' (Nelson with Eglinson, 1992: 43). In fact, there are good grounds for fearing that bilateral political conditionality promoted by an ex-colonial or regionally hegemonic power may be more likely to elicit unauthentic ('facade') responses by dependent clients and protégés than to entrench well-internalized locally democratic practices. Post-invasion Panama provides a vivid illustration of the risks involved here.

The West European approach to conditionality has been somewhat different, reflecting the region's distinctive post-war history. In a reaction against Nazism and Communism after 1945 the democratic political parties of West Germany sought to develop structures of political support for like-minded, fraternal parties that would not involve strong elements of hierarchy or central control. At the same time, and for the same reasons, they were highly motivated to provide effective backing to the parties they identified as their overseas counterparts. The solution which emerged was the establishment of a series of well-funded internationally oriented party foundations, which could recycle German taxpayers' money to designated Christian Democratic, Liberal, and Social Democratic organizations outside Germany, as well as providing international research and training in the general field of democratic development. These foundations contributed to the success of related party internationals, and in due course other governments came into existence (e.g. in Venezuela and later in Spain) which practised similar strategies of democracy promotion. In 1982 these European examples inspired a US response, when President Reagan created the National Endowment for Democracy, which was charged with transmitting US government funds to organizations and causes approved by a semi-official entity incorporating Republicans and Democrats, business organizations and labour unions. A decade later (and with shoestring funding) even the British government took up the model, creating the Westminster Foundation for Democracy.

Much of Africa, Asia and the Middle East has been relatively unaffected by these agencies, either because of the absence of comparable parties or because those that did exist were not close counterparts to the Western European or North American sponsoring parties. During the course of the Cold War this party-centred focus on promoting democracy seemed quite appropriate (even though cruder Cold War objectives sometimes contaminated the waters, and not all counterpart parties really espoused the ideologies or programmes suggested by their names). In the post-Cold War world, however, it is doubtful whether these ideological classifications can be sustained, or whether parties will continue to function as before. Such doctrinally-based political conditionality may therefore be on the decline, with single-issue lobbyists (promoting indigenous rights, gender equality, labour rights and so forth) perhaps providing more international support, or condemnation, than the old democratic party apparatuses.

Consent

A clear implication of this discussion of 'conditionality to democratize' is that its success will depend on the receptiveness of political and social forces in the targeted countries. This therefore brings us to the question of 'consent' (and to the related issue of the quality – the authenticity and breadth – of the democracy being constructed).

We therefore need to consider the ways in which international processes contribute to (or impede) the generation of the consent upon which new democracies must be based. There are two main aspects: (a) the territorial limits to successive democratizations and their consequences for established alliance systems; and (b) the ways in which authentic national democratic actors may be constituted from relatively diffuse transnational groupings. These two headings refer to ways in which international influences are received in particular territories, and whether such mechanisms of reception tend to favour the generation of democratic consent.

(a) Recent developments in the former Soviet Union and Yugoslavia have thrown into stark relief the question of the territorial limits to each democratization, an issue that was barely perceptible to earlier analysts working on Latin America. (With hindsight it could be discerned at least in relation to Belize, Guyana and the Falklands, but only in a muffled form.) The issue is in fact quite general. The establishment of national boundaries is an eminently international act, whereas generating consent for a representative system of government within those boundaries can be regarded as a separate, domestically driven, process. So long has elapsed in most of Latin America between the completion of the first process and the modern initiation of the second that this polarity may seem natural. In the interim powerful and sustained processes of national integration have differentiated the various adjoining polities right up to their frontiers. But in most of Europe, not to mention Africa, Asia or the Middle East, the definition of territorial boundaries and the forging of national identities have been much more recent and/or more bitterly contested, and so have overlapped with (and in many cases redirected) contemporary processes of democratization.

Consider a few examples. When Portugal became democratic this was extended to Madeira and the Azores (but not to Sao Tomé, let alone Macau, Angola or Timor). When Greece reinstated Karamanlis it was after a war in which the national aspiration for reunion with Cyprus had received a devastating setback (for some, then, this was a 'truncated' democracy). For the GDR, of course, democratization signified the total elimination of a separate East German state. The 'velvet revolution' in Prague raised issues about what democracy might signify for Slovakia. Most of the British decolonizations involved more or less strained decisions about the territorial limits of the new democracies (Antigua and Barbuda, but not including Anguilla, etc.). When the French Fourth Republic foundered it fell in Guadeloupe as much as in Paris. For that matter the democratization of Corsica remains an awkward issue in French politics, just as the democratization of Ulster plagues the British, and Sicily affronts the Italians. In short, the international processes that are fundamental for the establishment and stabilization of national boundaries also carry direct and often powerfully disruptive implications for the composition (and indeed viability) of democratic regimes within those boundaries. The disintegration of Yugoslavia may be an extreme case, but in fact it represents the tip of a very big iceberg. More optimistically, some see the interplay of Eritrean and Ethiopian nationalisms as positive for the choices of democracy in both emerging states.

A peaceful international system needs to generate consent (both within and between nations) for a precisely agreed pattern of inter-state boundaries and security alignments. Theoretically it may be that democratic states provide the best machinery for generating such consent, but at least in the transition phase of democratization there is liable to be a high degree of uncertainty about which substantive policy outcomes (including security alignments) will enjoy sustained support. The uncertainty over the future of US bases in democratizing Spain, Portugal, Greece, the Philippines and South Korea provides one good comparative illustration of this, and the prospective alignment of some newly democratizing regimes in Eastern Europe with whatever remains of the Soviet state is likely to provide another. Thus, in practice, the early phases of democratization may generate insecurity and tension through the state system, rather than the opposite; and in response the international system may generate resistance to, or conflict over, the precise forms taken by the democratization process in states with insecure national identities. This is an international dimension to the democratization process that may require considerably greater attention than it has received so far.

(b) At the outset of most democratic transitions it will be difficult to gauge which of the hastily constituted new groupings and movements is likely to emerge with real structure, support, and staying power. The origins of these emerging opposition forces typically include a substantial external component – exile clusters, for example, or social movements which enjoyed some degree of international protection through the churches, the human rights community, or from a network of fraternal parties overseas. Similar observations may well apply to the new forces emerging from the disintegrating authoritarian regime – technocrats closely associated with the IFIs, newspapers aligned with the interests of foreign investors, or possibly even CIA assets, on the one hand, or KGB nominees, on the other. In various cases elements derived from the old authoritarian regime have proved effective at invoking the cause of nationalism, and thereby turning the opportunities provided by democracy to their own electoral advantage.

In short, at the start of many transitions to democracy it can be artificial and misleading to classify all the new strategic actors as ready-made strictly 'domestic' political entities. It is only during the course of the transition itself, and in particular if consolidation proceeds well, that the 'national authenticity' of the various contending forces will become fully established. The evolution of such forces from their often diffuse and semi-dependent origins to fully-fledged and unambiguously national political status is in fact a central part of the democratization process. If it remains incomplete or is interrupted, then the transition will not proceed to full consolidation. For example, in Nicaragua the Sandinistas will have to accept the United Nicaraguan Opposition (UNO) coalition as an authentically Nicaraguan movement, not under the control of Washington, and the Chamorro government will have to reciprocate in its evaluation of the Sandinistas, in order for democratic institutions to become securely rooted in that society. (Washington would also need to adjust to this perspective.) Likewise for El Salvador, Angola, Yugoslavia, or for more peaceful experiments such as Spain and Czechoslovakia.

If this is correct, then a vital international dimension of many democratizations concerns the interactive process by which the external backers of the various contending political factions step (or are driven) back, relinquishing leverage over their protégés and lifting vetoes against their competitors. Clearly the fading of the Cold War, and the declining incentives for dominant powers to maintain tight control within their spheres of influence, discussed above, will increase the frequency of these processes. At least as important may be the proliferation of democratic regimes, offering reassurance that this kind of experimentation need not be destabilizing, and providing a denser network of cross-cutting sources of support for pluralism within each polity.

In the last analysis, what really drives this 'repatriation of political dialogue' could be the strength of the internal demand for democracy within each given society. The burden of this discussion is not to assert the primacy of international over domestic factors in the democratization process, but rather to suggest that a sharp distinction between the two categories may not be present at the outset. The distinction will crystallise, however, as consolidation progresses.

The limits of democracy promotion

Even in the apparently relatively favourable conditions of the post-Cold War era, explicit international support for democratization in the South seems likely to have no more than a fairly limited impact, confined to a select sub-set of countries. There seem to be three main types of limitation to explicit international programmes of democracy promotion, namely, those arising from: (a) great-power rivalries; (b) the resistance to democratization by stable illiberal regimes; and (c) fear of provoking disorder.

Let me take these points in order. (a) Democracy promotion efforts are likely to be inhibited wherever great-power rivalries or ideological conflicts generate distrust or disunity between leading states, since questions of alignment are likely to pollute judgements of democratic performance, block changes because of security considerations, or set narrow limits to the degree of electoral uncertainty that will be tolerated. (b) Such efforts are also likely to be muted, even in the absence of great power rivalries, in those areas of the world (and those periods of history) where non-democratic regimes appear secure and/ or successful. For in these cases most practical policy-makers will regard any but the vaguest appeals for a change of regime as futile, or even potentially counterproductive, gestures. In such conditions more modest political reforms – concerning human rights performance, labour standards, etc. – may be pressed as a substitute to unrealistic demands for full democratization. (c) Even in the absence of great-power rivalries, and in the presence of powerful local pro-democracy movements, international efforts will still be inhibited if it seems that pressures for change risk precipitating uncontrollable consequences (ethnic strife, the victory of religious fundamentalists, the collapse of state authority, the encouragement of drug trafficking or criminality, the risk of triggering a refugee flow, etc.).[7] Adding these three restrictive conditions together, it can be seen that the circumstances in which international efforts at promoting democracy are likely to acquire major salience have always been rather fleeting and exceptional. Even in the post-Cold War world such favourable circumstances are likely to remain limited and intermittent.

Whenever the democratization of large states (Russia, China, Brazil, Nigeria, etc.) becomes an issue, the cost and scale of even minimally effective action is bound to be a strong deterrent. In addition, large states are almost invariably important actors in other international arenas (arms control, trade negotiations, etc.) and so have leverage over external actors who press the cause of political reforms too far. This may help explain why first Gorbachev and then Yeltsin were embraced by the West and defined as the local champions of political reform, with scant regard for the niceties of the evidence. Stability and a pro-Western orientation were too important to be jeopardized and Western leverage over the course of events was too weak. This is in big contrast to the situation in some smaller countries, where the risks of transition are less threatening to dominant states, and where Western leverage may be far greater. For this reason much democracy promotion in the South has taken the form of 'show-case' initiatives in very small vulnerable countries where big changes may be secured at a low cost. (Central America and the Caribbean provide a particularly favourable environment for such experiments.)

Moreover, promoters of democracy are inevitably in permanent competition with market reformers, environmentalists, drug enforcement agencies, weapons exporters, and so on, for priority on the agendas of Western governments and international bureaucracies. Under favourable circumstances, and in alliance with associated NGOs and their allies in the media and academia, the advocates of democracy promotion may capture the policy initiative, at least in certain countries and for a limited period. Also under favourable circumstances, variants of democracy may be promoted which also serve some of these competing goals (e.g. in Panama and perhaps now in Haiti, democratization may be designed to serve the cause of narcotics control, or in Chile to guarantee the permanence of market-oriented reforms). But it is often difficult to convert episodic successes into a durable and comprehensive strategy that informs overall policy-making in the long run and that permanently reconciles potentially competing Northern policy objectives. This typically requires major institutional changes, such as the establishment of permanent monitoring agencies operating under the shelter of treaties, laws, and international agreements which convert promotion of democracy from a foreign policy fad into a binding structure of international obligations. Although there has been *some* movement in this direction since the mid-1980s, experiences such as the civil war in the former Yugoslavia have curbed the momentum behind this type of development. For the present, therefore, Northern advocates of democracy promotion must still bargain and compromise with rival policy currents. They can only rarely invoke a solid international mandate capable of overriding competing considerations.

These limitations to the scope and impact of explicit international pro-democracy initiatives operate most powerfully during the *transition* phase of democratization. At this point there is often great uncertainty over whether the process can stay on track, which political forces are most likely to gain (or lose) if it does, and what previous 'givens' of the political structure (foreign bases, international alignments, economic commitments) may be brought into question by a new democratic regime. Once this unsettling stage of transition has been surpassed, international support for subsequent efforts to consolidate the new order tend to be less problematic. Even cynics can be impressed by the speed with which early international vacillations can be forgotten (or at least forgiven) in the course of affirming the sanctity of the new democratic order. Thus, for example, Washington needed to be almost sure the Marcos dictatorship was doomed, before switching horses and embracing the Aquino administration in the Philippines, and Paris has sometimes been even slower to reposition itself in some francophone African transitions. What happens thereafter is that the fragile new democratic regime typically judges it wise to overlook the past, in order to shore up the future. And Western governments which had previously been tempted to stay with the status quo now have a strong interest in healing the potential breach with the new regime. In the course of endorsing consolidation of the new democracy, Western influence can also be exerted to steer it in a 'responsible' or unthreatening direction, thus helping to determine its eventual content.

International support for democracy may therefore be at its most effective (and least risky) when it is least likely to make a decisive difference to the outcome. However, as we saw in the introduction, a considerable proportion of Southern countries are far from reaching the 'consolidation' stage of democratization. Many tend to find themselves stuck in the more unstable 'transition' phase. In principle the established democracies are now committed to co-ordinated efforts aimed at stabilizing and reinforcing these new regimes, but where success is slow in coming the various limitations we have discussed seem likely to reassert themselves.

Conclusion

This chapter has focused on a range of institutions and agencies which claim to be engaged in the promotion of democracy, either through treaties, or multilateral initiatives, or 'conditionality', or perhaps even just by example. While it is impressive to note the wide variety of international actors currently undertaking such activities, we should be cautious about their staying power, or about the extent of their influence. Much may depend upon the existence of favourable conditions *within* some of the political systems on which they are attempting to act.

However, if relatively favourable conditions arise within a large number of disparate societies at roughly the same time, it is unlikely that this can occur without a certain degree of mutual influence and co-ordination. Beyond the 'demonstration' or 'contagion', and decolonization or 'control' effects already discussed (and which probably act most powerfully at the moment of *transition* to democracy), the post-Cold War world may be displaying two other more structural characteristics which will tend in the long run to reinforce the co-ordination of democratizing trends, particularly as they concern processes of regime consolidation. Thus, despite the reservations about 'conditionality' that have been stressed in this chapter, it would be wrong to end on too negative a note. There are at least two broader liberalizing processes at work, which could in some sense be regarded as generating long-term international 'support' for Southern democracies, though not of the conscious democracy promotion variety examined here. The emergence of an increasingly well-integrated 'international society' grounded on liberal values could be one such structural reinforcement. The other could be the development of a more highly-integrated and market-oriented global economic system. (The argument here would be that sanctity of contract, international factor mobilities, and increased mutual economic interdependence all militate against authoritarian forms of state organization, and therefore create a 'functional requirement' for political democracy.)

There are indeed good reasons for viewing these two underlying trends as inescapable features of the post-Cold War world, and for considering them to be at least broadly mutually reinforcing. *Prima facie*, it is also plausible to view them as generally supportive of the current wave of democratizations. However, it would be over-simplistic (possibly even teleological and reductionist) to conclude that these forces can be expected to work so powerfully and uniformly throughout the South that they decisively reinforce the prospects for democratic consolidation there. In fact, the mixed record of post-1989 UN initiatives to promote political reform in the South underscores the fragility of the post-Cold War international political consensus. Similar qualifications apply to arguments about the politically liberalizing consequences of economic internationalization. NAFTA *may* strengthen democratic tendencies in Mexico, and GATT membership *may* promote political reform in China, but the lines of causation are far from clear-cut or unilinear, and the evidence available so far is in marked contrast to much initial liberal rhetoric. The tenor of this chapter has therefore been quite cautious, highlighting the diversity of Southern democratizing experiences, and the relatively weak linkages to be found mediating between international pro-democracy influences and Southern political outcomes.

Notes

1 The annual figures from January 1981 to January 1995 are tabulated in *Freedom Review* Jan/Feb 1995: 7. They indicate a sustained trend of deterioration between 1991 and 1994.

2 The UNDP ranks all countries according to its HD indicators, and also classifies them into 'high', 'medium' and 'low' categories. Only 5 out of 53 countries classified as 'high' were not attempting democratization, compared with 25 out of 65 in the 'medium' category, and 31 out of 55 in the 'low' classification. However, as the individual country rankings made clear, a high human development index is no guarantee of democracy (Hong Kong ranks 24 and Singapore 43, but neither of them qualify) nor does a low ranking preclude the possibility.

3 Although the ending of the Cold War has confirmed the pre-eminence of democratic *forms* of government in the 'developed' or 'core' countries of the OECD,

there are substantial grounds for doubt about the *content* or *quality* of these democratic regimes. So when they claim to support democratization in the South it is legitimate to query the adequacy of their prescriptions in any setting, as well as to question the applicability of 'Northern' political models to 'Southern' socio-economic conditions.

4 Completeness requires some mention of the limitations to this doctrine, although this is not the place to explore them. Despite Western rhetoric the armed liberation of Algeria, Libya, Palestine, Persia, Indochina, Hong Kong and Korea was accomplished without any democratic accompaniment, a fact with consequences that are still unfolding.

5 'To Perpetual Peace: A Philosophical Sketch' (Kant, 1891 [1795]) was written in 1795 before the optimism engendered by the French Revolution had been completely dissipated. Sørenson (1993b: chapter 4) is a useful survey of recent studies of the claim that democracies do not go to war with each other.

6 Alex George (1992) has proposed the term 'compellance' in place of 'control', to signify that instead of continuous control international influences may be episodic. But since there are several important examples of sustained international support for democracy, I do not adopt this suggestion here. If I did, the boundary between 'compellance' and 'conditionality' would be reduced to a distinction between unilateral and multilateral sources of democracy promotion, an even more difficult distinction to sustain in practice.

7 Western democracy promoters signally failed to recognize the existence of such risks in Yugoslavia in 1991. Subsequently (e.g. in Algeria and Haiti) Western efforts have lurched back and forth as such dangers are re-evaluated.

CONCLUSION

Democratization in the South: the jagged wave

ROBIN LUCKHAM AND GORDON WHITE

A partial and contested transition

The studies in this book show that the recent experience of democratization in the South has been very variable and uneven. As Whitehead points out, the global trend towards liberal democratic systems of rule has not yet reached 40 per cent of the world's population, the great majority in the South. However, if one compares the current situation with that at the dawn of the 1980s, striking changes have taken place. Out-and-out, unrepentant authoritarian governments, such as those of China, Iraq or Myanmar, are now relatively exceptional and are under pressure both at home and abroad to move in a democratic direction. Large numbers of regimes have adopted some semblance of democratic forms, including those still ruled by authoritarian governments, such as Indonesia. Even where authoritarian regimes have been restored, as in Nigeria or Algeria, their position is contested and the pressure for democratization is mounting.

In terms of the three constellations of power introduced at the beginning of the book, all three of the general political conditions for democratic struggle still appear favourable. Unlike the era of the Cold War, international political pressures overwhelmingly favour liberal democratic over authoritarian arrangements and authoritarian recidivists face the prospect of external counter-pressures and penalties. Our case studies show the extent to which pro-democracy civil society groupings have mobilized in contexts as diverse as South Korea and Zambia, and they are likely to wish to protect the fruits of their struggle. The credibility of state elites and their capacity to resist pressure to democratize have been weakened by developmental failure or pervasive corruption and the reach of the state is being undermined by programmes of economic reform (although, as we shall argue below, this weakening of the state also stores up problems for the consolidation of democracy).

Yet in spite of these changes, it is too early to conclude that democratization in the South is here to stay. The danger of outright reversion to dictatorial rule – though real in some countries – is perhaps less than that of the erosion of democracy from within. Not only are there differences in the institutional arrangements for democracy adopted in specific countries, there is an even wider range of variation in the political substance behind them. Transitions have so far proved very variable in their success in delivering the key elements of democracy: widespread participation based on political equality, accountable political elites, open and responsive government and deep-going guarantees for civil, social and political rights. Indeed in some 'new democracies' these different elements have conflicted. In countries like Peru, Brazil or the Philippines, elected presidents or chief executives have used populist or plebiscitary appeals to mass electorates, to override constitutional guarantees of rights, or to resist accountability to legislatures.

Some observers put this conflict down to a tension between the democratic and the liberal strands in liberal democracy; others to the simultaneous presence in some polities of 'too much' and 'too little' democracy (see Weffort, 1993 for an insightful discussion). In other new democracies the main problem has been the *ancien régime*'s ability to perpetuate itself in power, as in Ghana, by co-opting the major institutions of a democratic polity: the electoral system, parliament and the executive, etc. Elsewhere, it has been the survival of important authoritarian enclaves like the military and security establishments that has created obstacles for incoming democratic governments, or limited the exercise of citizen's rights. In several countries, the capacity of governments to breathe real substance into democracy by taking decisions on behalf of the majority of their citizens has been fatally compromised through the weakening of the state that has accompanied democratization in countries like Zambia, or as a result of international constraints and conditionalities in an increasingly interdependent global political economy. Furthermore, as Rai points out, democratic institutions (in old as well as new democracies) have tended to marginalize or exclude from public life women, minorities, those without secure means of gaining a livelihood and other subordinated groups. For all these reasons claims about any particular nation's successful 'transition to democracy' should be treated with caution if not scepticism.

Although democratization in the South is still overwhelmingly a political struggle, it cannot easily be disentangled from the socio-economic constraints – poverty, illiteracy, inequality and insecurity – which may conspire to thwart its progress. As Moore points out, there is (other things being equal) a clear relationship between the presence or absence of democracy in a given society and its level of socio-economic development, even if the causal mechanisms that account for this relationship are still poorly understood. It is in the poorest societies in Africa and Asia that the impetus towards democratization has been the weakest and the chances of consolidation the least promising. Even where a credible political transition has taken place in a poor society, such as Zambia, its hold has been fragile and its substance disappointing, at least for the great majority of citizens. Conversely, where a strong impetus towards democracy has emerged in hitherto well-established and developmentally successful authoritarian regimes, such as South Korea and Taiwan, it has been spearheaded by forces of civil society which have been the consequence of socio-economic progress. There appears to be a continuing contradiction between democracy and underdevelopment, which imposes powerful conditions on both the feasibility of transitions to democracy and on the real political substance of formal democratic regimes, often exacerbated in the poorest countries by crippling external economic and political constraints. Nevertheless some poor countries like India, Jamaica, Papua New Guinea or Botswana have had relatively sustained – if not always conflict-free – experience with democratic governance. Pro-democracy movements in others, like Benin, Bangladesh or the Philippines, have struggled against the odds to bring down established authoritarian regimes and replace them with elected governments. The overall association between material prosperity and democracy has certainly not been an absolute constraint upon *changes* in a democratic direction, or even on the consolidation of democratic rule once it is in place.

Democratic outcomes are thus determined by a complex

interplay of political and developmental factors. Each country embodies this interplay in distinctive ways, so we should expect not only the politics of democratization to differ from society to society but also the particular forms of democracy which result from that process. Now that we have passed beyond the simplistic manicheanism of the Cold War era, we are becoming more aware of the variations among democratic systems in the industrialized countries, not only in their institutional arrangements but in their societal and political dynamics. Perhaps it is time for Western observers to examine the limitations and problems of democracy in their own societies before hastening to question the credentials of fledgling democracies in the South, where *a fortiori* one should expect an even greater range of variation. The South may not be eager to accept Western definitions of 'democracy' lock, stock and barrel, particularly if they are couched in relatively minimalistic conceptions of procedural liberal democracy. As Hawthorn and Rai emphasize, distinctive Southern historical and cultural contexts may give rise to innovative forms of democratic representation, accountability, participation and governance which merit respect and attention. The studies in this volume tend to suggest, moreover, that images of democracy vary according to the location of the political actor: existing political elites and international actors are more likely to settle for minimalist procedural definitions, whereas many members of 'civil society' wish to extend the conception in a more participatory direction. The politics of democratization is not merely a struggle for democracy but also about the very nature of democracy itself.

'Lessons' for democratic action

Given the above remarks about diversity, we should be very cautious about general judgements and policy prescriptions based on them. However, our studies do point to certain common elements across different contexts, and it is worthwhile attempting to draw some practical conclusions for the three groups of political actors identified in our Introduction as forces potentially promoting democratization: domestic political elites, members of domestic 'civil societies' and the international 'donor community' seeking to promote democratization through aid conditionality. The 'lessons' such groups can extract are clearly different at each stage of the democratization process. On the one hand, there may be a great deal of continuity between struggles to open democratic spaces under authoritarian rule, to bring about transition to formally democratic systems of government and to strengthen and deepen democracy within them. On the other hand, the strategies adopted to weaken an authoritarian regime, the Faustian bargains made with outgoing powerful 'interests' like the armed forces and with external donors, or populist appeals made to win over voters in the first democratic elections, can store up problems for the later consolidation of democracy.

In the context of a fledgling democracy, *democratic* politicians are not merely those who observe and manipulate the new rules and institutions in their own or their constituencies' interests, but those who are also interested in consolidating the new system. Such people can be found in many surprising places, not just in the ranks of party politicians, but also potentially amongst civil rights activists, members of the business community, or even soldiers or intelligence operatives (as in South Korea) disillusioned by the adverse impact of non-democratic government on professional standards or national development. While the need for 'constitutional' as opposed to sectional politicians is obvious, it is sensible to avoid platitudes about the need to be politically 'mature' and 'far-sighted'. A kind of democratic Machiavellianism may be more useful. There is a powerful tradition that analyses transitions to democracy as a series of bargains between outgoing authoritarian and incoming democratic elites, in which reformers within each group play a crucial mediating role in overcoming, on the one hand, the resistance of authoritarian hard-liners to any change and, on the other, the zeal of democratizing radicals for confrontation. (The seminal statements of this view are to be found in the work of O'Donnell *et al.*, 1986 a, b and c and O'Donnell and Schmitter, 1986 on transitions in Latin America and Southern Europe; they have been formalized in terms of bargaining models by Przeworski, 1991.) Though our contributions to this volume have been influenced by this approach, we would also insist on its limitations, both because it focuses largely on the point of transition, and because it tends to underestimate the broader social and political forces pushing authoritarian rulers into crisis and lending their democratic opponents the authority of history. Moreover, there are real political dangers in being too short-sightedly Machiavellian, where autocrats have been allowed to get away with reforms or even fully-fledged democratic 'transitions' that only perpetuate their own rule, as in Kenya or Ghana, or have encumbered their successors, as in Chile or Brazil, by establishing authoritarian enclaves which resist democratic accountability.

An enlightened democratic Machiavellianism remains just as necessary after power has been formally transferred to an elected government. For to the extent that democracy is not yet consolidated, even in its minimal procedural form, let alone in any maximal participatory sense, there is an ongoing political struggle in which the democratic forces may still be shifting and fragile. Democratic elites can act to strengthen the basis for consolidation in three ways: first, by striving to create a political society involving institutions (notably parties) capable not only of competition but also of credible governance; second, by seeking to accommodate to democratic forces in civil society and to build coalitions which serve to tip the overall political balance in favour of democratization and provide the social underpinning for democratic institutions; and, third, by seeking to divide, weaken and constrain potential anti-democratic forces (Luckham's discussion of how to deal with the military is instructive in this regard). The sequence of reform is also important, as Robinson argues: should political and economic reform proceed in tandem; or should the main emphasis be placed on the latter, so as to generate the conditions in which political democratization is more likely to succeed, and in which economic reform can be sustained?

Turning to political actors in 'civil society', White's analysis has shown that any specific civil society may be a complex and politically diverse entity which has anti-democratic and politically neutral as well as democratic components. Just as the latter are often crucial in sustaining what Sklar (1987) calls 'democracy in parts' under otherwise authoritarian regimes, anti-democratic groups can create severe problems for democratic institutions, all the while enjoying protection under the rules and procedures of democracy itself. And within the democratic component, some forces favour relatively minimal definitions of democracy, while others want to push the idea and the reality much further in participatory directions. Moreover, since civil societies are usually riven with conflicts of interests and belief, they carry the potential for social instability which may spell the end of a fragile democratic regime itself. Civil society is in need of 'constitutive' leaders who are willing to accommodate other political actors and social interests in favour of the maintenance of democratic institutions. Given this, political strategies may vary across contexts. Where there is a danger or a reality of 'low-intensity democracy', as in South Korea or Ghana, the role of civil society is not merely to maintain democratic procedures but to give them greater substance and range by social agitation and political pressure. Where the power of democratic forces is limited and democratic institutions are fragile, as in Zambia, the supporters of democracy should perhaps concentrate on building consensus and defending initially imperfect institutions. We would also expect that, in addition to opposing the residual forces of authoritarianism, groups in civil society would be actively involved in trying to ameliorate the socio-economic underdevelopment which militates against successful democratization (for example, through pressures to ensure that programmes of economic reform take into account their redistributive impact on poor people).

Turning to the role of the 'donor community', judgements are difficult from the outset, since, if we are referring to those actors which can influence internal political developments within developing countries through their control over resource flows such as aid, trade and finance, they can hardly be described as a 'community'. These international actors are themselves diverse and divided: between national governments and international institutions; within both these categories (for example, differences in aid philosophy between Europe, the United States and Japan, or different approaches to alleviating developmental problems between the UNDP, the World Bank and the IMF); and between governmental and non-governmental institutions (such as the international charities). We content ourselves here with some admittedly over-general remarks which will need to be fleshed out in future research. Perhaps the main message to be derived from the studies in this book concerns the need for a period of reflection. Aside from recognizing the diversity and differences in the 'donor community' and the damage which uncoordinated intervention can cause, there is also a need to recognize the systematic inconsistency inherent in previous political interventions which, during much of the Cold War period, were just as (if not more) likely to be exerted in favour of authoritarian as democratic governments.

The greatest pressures, as Whitehead emphasizes, tend to be exerted on relatively weak and vulnerable societies (for example, in sub-Saharan Africa) which are peripheral to the interests of the major controllers of resource flows. Where larger and more formidable countries are involved (China and Indonesia are prime examples), democratic conditionality tends to stay at the rhetorical level. There is double damage here. In terms of political welfare, the latter may well be the very countries where the need for democracy may be most urgent. By contrast, in the case of more vulnerable and therefore more manipulable societies, the very possibility of powerful political intervention, however well conceived or intentioned, may find its purpose defeated because of what we call the 'accountability dilemma'. To be legitimate and effective, democratic leaders in fragile democracies must be accountable to their popular constituency. This, after all, is one of the key differences between them and their authoritarian predecessors. However, if they are also heavily accountable to external agencies (for example, through a rigorous programme of economic adjustment and reform), they may be caught between conflicting pressures which undermine their credibility not merely as political leaders but as representatives of the new democratic regime. A combination of discontent caused by radical economic reform and nationalist resentment against external pressure may act both to unseat them and to undermine the regime they represent (though the risks are possibly less in countries where reforms have at least restored growth, like Ghana, than in those where reforms have yet to demonstrate their benefits, as in Zambia).

The implication here is that the exercise of both economic and political conditionality should be preceded by care, caution and knowledge. The dangers of ill-considered intervention are patent. An excessively harsh programme of economic reform imposed on a reluctant government struggling to establish its democratic credentials is one such. This would have the effect of shifting government accountability to external donors and away from domestic constituencies, and could undermine the process of democratic consolidation by weakening political consensus on economic policy. Political conditionality can backfire unless it commands strong domestic support and donors refrain from pushing for multi-party elections in circumstances where they might exacerbate deep-rooted social antagonisms. Similarly, donors trying to counteract military resistance to political reform through measures to curb arms transfers, reduce military aid and exert pressure for lower domestic military spending may risk alienating the armed forces from the new democratic government during the sensitive period of consolidation.

In general, however, positive forms of political intervention are likely to be more micro-level and indirect. For example, civil society organizations can be strengthened by encouraging and supporting 'horizontal' relationships between nongovernmental counterparts in donor and recipient countries. Political institutions can be strengthened through advice and training on legal systems, governmental organization, constitutional arrangements and other mainly procedural matters. But attempts to 'strengthen' civil society can fly in the face of established cultural traditions or social arrangements or serve to set different social groups against each other. Positive intervention needs to be based on a good deal of sophisticated understanding about the political character of the recipient society. This more modest, piecemeal approach is preferable to one which seeks to impose more comprehensive institutional models and, to be effective, needs to be conducted within the wider context of a sustained political strategy designed to generate consensus and acceptance of proposed innovations.

Democratic government and developmental effectiveness

Democratization in the South inevitably raises fundamental questions about the relationship between democracy and development. A previously influential current of opinion argued that the challenges facing governments in developing societies required some kind of politically authoritative, administratively competent and economically rational regime. Its heroes have been the authoritarianisms of East and South-East Asia as well as a number of developmental dictatorships elsewhere, for instance in Ghana and Chile. More recently, however, in the heady atmosphere of global transition, ideologues and pundits of political conditionality have turned the argument on its head and maintained that it is (liberal) democracy which is the essential precondition for successful development. Moore's comprehensive survey of the literature supports a healthy scepticism about both of these arguments: existing studies suggest that there is no consistent association in either direction between democracy and economic performance. But this does not mean there may not be more subtle relationships between democracy and development, especially if the meanings of each are broadened beyond narrow operational definitions.

Moreover, both are subject to political reinterpretation and historical change. Even those who might carry a candle for 'rational authoritarianism' as developmentally advisable, recognize that, in the light of existing domestic and international trends in the South, this is a much less feasible option than in earlier decades. Their case is also undermined by the fact that, in numerical terms at least, the majority of authoritarian regimes have not been signally successful in developmental terms, and some, especially in sub-Saharan Africa, have been developmental disasters. The star performers in East Asia have been unrepresentative of the genre, and have depended on certain conditions which cannot be reproduced easily or at all in other contexts. One also needs to factor in the heavy social and political costs of authoritarian rule, which are often passed on (in the form of high levels of political and social conflict, powerful and expensive military establishments, non-accountable bureaucracies, etc.) to the democratic successor government.

There has been increasing agreement across a wide ideological spectrum that democracy, even in its limited procedural form, is a valuable aspect of development in itself, because of the participation by people in shaping their own conditions of existence which it tries (however inadequately) to guarantee (Edwards, 1989: 116). This contrasts sharply with authoritarianism, which even in its 'rational' form has never been valued for itself (among the development community, at least), but was regarded as a means towards developmental ends which could be dispensed with when its unpleasant, but historically essential, task was completed: an argument that was not only morally dubious, but politically naive as well, because authoritarian regimes have seldom liquidated themselves voluntarily, and tend to perpetuate important authoritarian legacies under their democratic successors. The acceptance of liberal democracy has extended to include the radical Left, partly because the Leninist alternative has collapsed and never delivered much in the way of democracy in any case. Socialists of course seek to extend the notion of democracy beyond the political into the social and economic system, but now more than previously they are willing to recognize the inherent virtues of the standard model of liberal democracy (for thoughtful discussions of these issues in the African context, see Sandbrook, 1988; Mamdani, 1990).

Within this democratic consensus, however, there are varying views about the compatibility of democracy and developmental efficacy. First, there is an optimistic view, common in aid circles (particularly in Western national aid agencies and international institutions) but fading of late, that democracy is a powerful stimulus to development, basically because it provides a more conducive environment for market-led economic growth and because it carries the potential for more efficient and accountable government. This view is often incarcerated in the neo-liberal panopticon and is therefore ideologically as well as intellectually contestable, but it also carries much weight and is shared to varying degrees by representatives of other ideological and political traditions. Suffice it to say here that it is too optimistic (as Moore emphasizes) and underestimates some major problems which we shall introduce below.

Second, there is a pessimistic view which retains part of the old 'incompatibility' paradigm and regards democracy as a luxury which poor societies can ill afford. Leftwich (1993: 13), for example, argues that

> if the primary developmental objective is the defeat of poverty and misery, then liberal or pluralist democracy may also not be what many Third World or Eastern European countries need or can sustain in their present conditions.

This pessimism is also shared to some extent by some supporters of democracy who regard liberal democratic politics at the national level as sometimes developmentally unhelpful, and therefore concentrate on 'bottom-up' micro-strategies based on the democratizing and developmental potential of grassroots and community organizations (see Landell-Mills, 1992). Advocates of this position tend to list a number of seemingly insuperable post-transitional obstacles which Huntington (1991: 209–10) conveniently groups into two categories: contextual, which tend to smother the political system with unmet demands and undermine its capacity to process these demands; and systemic, which derive from the institutionalized uncertainty and conflict inherent in democratic politics. Together they can lead to political fluctuation, paralysis or disorder which weakens the capacity of democratic governments to shoulder the developmental burden, whether defined in narrower 'parametric' terms by neo-liberals or in broader versions by dirigists across the political spectrum.

The third view is what one might call the 'don't expect anything' school, typified by Huntington. He argues that the viability of democracy depends on 'disillusionment and lowered expectations'. Furthermore, 'democracies become consolidated when people learn that democracy is a solution to the problem of tyranny, but not necessarily to anything else' (Huntington, 1991: 263) This kind of view is buttressed by the argument that democratic regimes are legitimized not by their performance but by their procedures (Linz and Stepan, 1989; Przeworski, 1991). This may make sense in countries which have already achieved a relatively high level of economic development and still retain a growth momentum. But part, and perhaps the largest part, of the political fuel which propelled democratic transition in countries like Zambia was produced by popular disillusionment with economic stagnation and declining incomes under the previous regime. In such circumstances, it is probably unrealistic to assume that populations will lower their expectations and content themselves with the specific gains, important though they may be, which derive from democratic guarantees and rights. Indeed, the opposite may well be the case.

How to address this question? If we assume that some form of liberal democratic system, defined in procedural terms, is both intrinsically desirable and practically feasible in a society which faces massive developmental problems, how can such a political system best develop a capacity to tackle those problems, given the characteristic systemic problems which Huntington and others identify? Our answer should start by recognizing that some of the variations between democratic systems identified earlier depend on deeper factors embedded in the economic and social structure, in state-based and international constellations of power, or in the constitution of civil and political societies, which reduce the room for political manoeuvre. Other elements, such as the institutional design of the state, the character of the political leadership and the nature of political parties, the relative degree of organization and political access of different sections of civil society and the relations between these and state/political society, may be more susceptible to 'political crafting', to use Di Palma's term (1990).

The next questions, assuming this range of variation and some (variable) room for political manoeuvre in crafting specific forms of democracy, concern whether there are particular forms of democracy which are more suited to tackling severe developmental challenges and, if so, how they can be related to the political role of civil society. We are essentially seeking forms of 'developmental democracy', in ways redolent of Richard Sklar's call for 'political invention and improved design' of democratic institutions to confront the problems of development (Sklar, 1987: 714). Though answers will clearly vary across countries, the following avenues of 'political design' could be suggested, each of which will be more or less feasible in any given situation.

1 The institutional design of the state: there are a range of institutional alternatives in designing state institutions which may, by their impact on the internal structure of the regime and its channels of communication and access to political and civil societies, affect its degree of coherence and its capacity for developmental decision.

2 The character of political society: for instance while 'multi-party democracy' may be the current slogan, a strong argument can be made that 'multi' should ideally denote no more than two, and that the best underpinning for a developmentally effective polity is either a stable two-party system (which conventional political science used to preach as the ideal form) or, perhaps even better, a one-party dominant system. Some of the most impressive developmental performers over the past half century, notably Sweden and Japan, have had such dominant-party systems, which, in their cases at least, combined the best of both developmental and democratic worlds. The dominant party was subject to regular democratic tests at the ballot box and constantly subject to the pressures of a free civil society, while at the same time maintaining the coherence, authority and capacity for long-term decision-making which is necessary for tackling the structural problems of development (for a comparison of 'one-party dominant regimes', see Pempel, 1990). We have seen in South Korea that the political elite – with the Japanese precedent very much in mind – is trying to forge just such a regime through the amalgamation of the former ruling and some of the opposition parties, in an attempt to retain the previous developmental capacity of the state in the new political context.

3 The feasibility of the above efforts at institutional design depends

to a great extent on the constitution and action of civil society: its degree of heterogeneity, its capacity to coalesce, and the nature of its relationships with political parties and state institutions. To focus on the 'one-party dominant model', for example, this has assumed two basic forms, inclusive and exclusive. In the inclusive model, there is a form of 'social compact' based on an 'inclusive coalition' between the main segments of civil society, brokered and organized by the state and a dominant political party (in the Swedish case, the Social Democratic Party, business and labour). In the exclusive model, there is a pact involving an alliance between state institutions, a dominant political party and a hegemonic section of civil society (in the Japanese case, the state bureaucracy, the Liberal Democratic Party and big business).

But there may be dangers in pressing too far and fast down such a 'designer democracy' track. The one-party dominant model has itself been showing signs of decay (and in need of democratic renewal) in Sweden and Japan, and in developing countries such as Mexico, where a quasi-corporatist form of democracy has been in existence for three-quarters of a century. It is arguable that this kind of option might still be feasible for relatively developed and homogeneous new democracies, such as Chile (gradually moving in the direction of the more inclusive model) and South Korea (following the more exclusive example of Japan), but would be unfeasible in, say, sub-Saharan Africa. Although Botswana has been a success story, other African countries like Senegal or Zimbabwe which have followed a similar path have met with more mixed results. Much more research is needed before we can say with any precision what institutional form 'developmental democracies' might take, and in what circumstances they are mostly like to take root.

There is an even more basic problem: there is still very little clarity about *who* might be in a position to 'design' democracy, and what their relationship should be to ongoing struggles for democracy or for development, notably those at the grass roots. According to the procedural or 'don't expect anything' school, the answer is fairly clear: it is political and economic elites, together with the more 'responsible' elements in civil society, such as business or professional associations, that should both design democracy and manage development. A case in point would be Chile, where, as Arriagada Herrera and Graham (1994) observe, there has been broad elite consensus most of the way across the political spectrum about economic reform, yet (according to the polls) widespread opposition to it among voters. The implication would seem to be that democracy can be developmental only to the extent that it depresses the expectations of citizens (the Chilean polls also report increased political apathy), and insulates economic decision-making from popular pressures. Both these features may well be conducive to neo-liberal management of the economy. But it is difficult to see that they have much to do with *democracy*, especially if one takes seriously the proposition that it can play a positive role in legitimizing economic policies and mobilizing energies for development. Due to the particular circumstances of Chile's recent history, discussed by Robinson and Luckham, it has been possible for disenchantment with economic and political reforms to coexist with strong popular support for democratic *institutions*. Elsewhere in the South, one cannot be quite so sanguine. A case in point would be the Philippines, where a wide gap has opened between the political and economic elites entrenched through the institutions of a representative democracy and many of the grassroots groups originally behind the 'people's power' revolution of 1986, to the ultimate detriment of both, and of efforts to pursue a consistent and broadly accepted programme of economic reform.

What has been lacking in the Philippines and (for varying reasons) in many other 'low-intensity' democracies in the South has been a micro-level strategy of building on the social forces and grass-roots organizations mobilized, for instance, during the struggles against dictatorship, and of linking them more effectively to democratic institutions by giving them more of a voice in the design and management of the institutions by which they are governed and the economic policies that impinge on their day-to-day existence. To be sure, there are inherent difficulties in 'crafting' institutions within anything so volatile and complex as civil society; and hence a need for sensitivity about the dangers of co-opting and disempowering groups in the latter, especially at the grass roots. It would also be naive to deny that there are inescapable conflicts of interest surrounding political and, still more, economic reforms, especially when the latter are driven by the perceived need to meet externally imposed conditions, or to compete in the global market-place. But there is all the more need to design broadly-based democratic institutions and procedures through which these conflicts can be mediated, and to make sure that the voices of all those adversely affected by reform are listened to. It may be true, as Migdal (1987) has pointed out, that an over-assertive civil society can overwhelm, or undermine, the capacity of the state to provide even the minimal guarantees of personal security and freedom, let alone the benefits of a successful development strategy. But so too (though for quite different reasons) can a neo-liberal package of economic reform aimed at 'rolling back the state'. Although the ultimate ideal of an advanced liberal democratic 'civil society' hinges on an authoritative and institutionally complex state which provides the regulative and protective framework within which civil society can operate, such a state is only likely to be effective to the extent that it commands the loyalty of its citizens and can be held accountable by them. All too often in the South, a fractious, demanding and sometimes violent civil society is the Janus face of a developmentally ineffective and democratically unresponsive state. Thus in considering how to reconstitute democracy and make it more responsive to developmental needs, it is not so much the overall 'balance' between state and civil society that is important, as how best to ensure that they complement and reinforce one another.

Bibliography

Adjei, M. (1993), *Death and Pain: Rawlings' Ghana – The Inside Story*. London: Black Line.

Agosin, M. (1986), 'Metaphors of Female Political Ideology: The Cases of Chile and Argentina', WID Working Paper No. 19. Cambridge, MA: Harvard Institute for International Development.

Ahiakpor, J.C.W. (1991), 'Rawlings, Economic Policy Reform, and the Poor: Consistency or Betrayal?', *Journal of Modern African Studies* 29 (4): 583–600.

Ahn, C.Y. (1990), 'Recent Economic Transition of South Korea: Comparative Perspectives with Latin America', *Journal of Economic Development* 15 (1): 27–46.

Ahn, C.-S. (1991), 'Economic Development and Democratisation in South Korea: An Examination of Economic Change and the Empowerment of Civil Society', *Korea and World Affairs* 15 (4): 740–54.

Ake, Claude (1991), 'Rethinking African Democracy', *Journal of Democracy* 2 (1): 32–44.

Almond, G.A. (1991), 'Capitalism and Democracy', *P.S. Political Science and Politics* 41 (1): 467–74.

Alvarez, S.E. (1990), *Engendering Democracy in Brazil: Women's Movements in Transition Politics*. Princeton, NJ and Oxford: Princeton University Press.

Amos, V. and Parmar, P. (1984), 'Challenging Imperial Feminism', *Feminist Review* 17 (Autumn): 3–19.

Amsden, A. (1989), *Asia's Next Giant: South Korea and Late Industrialization*. New York: Oxford University Press.

Amsden, A.H. and Euh, Y.D. (1993), 'South Korea's 1980s Financial Reforms: Goodbye Financial Repression (Maybe), Hello New Institutional Restraints', *World Development* 21 (3): 379–90.

Anderson, B. (1991), *Imagined Communities: Reflections on the Origin and Spread of Nationalism*. London: Verso.

Andrews, G. (ed.) (1991), *Citizenship*. London: Lawrence and Wishart.

Angell, A. and Graham, C. (1995), 'Can Social Sector Reform Make Adjustment Sustainable and Equitable? Lessons from Chile and Venezuela', *Journal of Latin American Studies* 27 (1): 89–219.

Anyemedu, K. (1993), 'The Economic Policies of the PNDC', in Gyimah-Boadi (1993).

Arat, Z.F. (1991), *Democracy and Human Rights in Developing Countries*. Boulder, CO and London: Lynne Rienner Publishers.

Arriagada Herrera, G. (1986), 'The Legal and Institutional Framework of the Armed Forces in Chile', in J.S. Valenzuela (ed.), *Military Rule in Chile: Dictatorship and Oppositions*. Baltimore, MD: Johns Hopkins University Press.

Arriagada Herrera, G. (1988), *Pinochet: The Politics of Power*. Boston, MA: Unwin Hyman.

Arriagada Herrera, G. and Graham, C. (1994), 'Chile: Sustaining Adjustment During Democratic Transition', in Haggard and Webb (1994).

Ashworth, G. (1986), *Of Violence and Violation: Women and Human Rights*. London: Change.

Bachrach, P. and Botwinick, A. (1992), *Power and Empowerment: A Radical Theory of Participatory Democracy*. Philadelphia, PA: Temple University Press.

Bahro, R. (1978), *The Alternative in Eastern Europe*. London: New Left Books.

Bardhan, P. (1984), *The Political Economy of Development in India*. Oxford: Blackwell.

Barrett, M. and Phillips, A. (eds) (1992), *Destabilizing Theory: Contemporary Feminist Debates*. Cambridge: Polity Press.

Bates, R. (1977), *Markets and States in Tropical Africa: The Political Basis of Agricultural Policies*. Berkeley, CA: University of California Press.

Bates, R.H. and Collier, P. (1993), 'The Politics and Economics of Policy Reform in Zambia', in Bates and Krueger (1993).

Bates, R.H. and Krueger, A.O. (eds) (1993), *Political and Economic Interactions in Economic Policy Reform: Evidence from Eight Countries*. Oxford: Blackwell.

Bates, R.H. and Lien, D.-H.D. (1985), 'A Note on Taxation, Development, and Representative Government', *Politics and Society* 14 (1): 53–70.

Bayart, J.-F. (1986), 'Civil Society in Africa', in Chabal (1986b).

Bayart, J.-F. (1989), *L'Etat en Afrique: La Politique du Ventre*. Paris: Fayard.

Baynham, S. (1984–5), 'Civil–Military Relations in Ghana's Second Republic', *Journal of Contemporary African Studies* 4 (1–2): 71–88.

Baynham, S. (1985), 'Quis Custodiet Ipsos Custodies? The Case of Nkrumah's National Security Service', *Journal of Modern African Studies* 23 (1): 87–103.

Baynham, S. (1988), *The Military and Politics in Nkrumah's Ghana*. Boulder, CO and London: Westview Press.

Bedeski, R.E. (1992), 'State Reform and Democracy in South Korea', *Journal of East Asian Affairs* 6 (1): 141–68.

Bell, D. (1988), *The End of Ideology: On the Exhaustion of Political Ideas in the Fifties, with a New Afterword*. Cambridge, MA: Harvard University Press.

Bermeo, N. (1990), 'Rethinking Regime Change', *Comparative Politics* 22 (3): 359–77.

Bianchi, R. (1986), 'Interest Group Politics in the Third World', *Third World Quarterly* 8 (2): 507–39.

Billet, B.L. (1990), 'South Korea at the Crossroads: An Evolving Democracy or Authoritarianism Revisited?', *Asian Survey* 30 (3): 300–11.

Blair, H. (1992), 'Defining, Promoting and Sustaining Democracy: Formulating an AID Strategy for Development Assistance and Evaluation'. Washington, DC: USAID, 23 September.

Boafo-Arthur, K. (1993), 'Ghana's External Relations Since 31 December 1981', in Gyimah-Boadi (1993).

Boahen, A.A. (1989), *The Ghanaian Sphinx: Reflections on the Contemporary History of Ghana, 1972–1987*. Accra: Ghana Academy of Arts and Science.

Bollen, K.A. (1979), 'Political Democracy and the Timing of Development', American Sociological Review 44 (4): 572–87.

Bollen, K.A. (1980), 'Issues in the Comparative Measure of Political Democracy', American Sociological Review 45 (3): 370–90.

Bollen, K.A. (1990), 'Political Democracy: Conceptual and Measurement Traps', Studies in Comparative International Development 25 (1): 7–24.

Booth, D. (1987), 'Alternatives in the Restructuring of State–Society Relations: Research Issues for Tropical Africa', IDS Bulletin 18 (4): 23–30.

Bostrom, M. (1994), 'Contagion of Democracy in Latin America: The Case of Paraguay', in S.S. Nagel (ed.), Latin American Development and Public Policy. St. Martin's Press.

Bowles, S. and Gintis, H. (1987), Democracy and Capitalism: Property, Community and the Contradictions of Modern Social Thought. New York: Basic Books.

Brass, P.R. (1991), The Politics of India Since Independence, The New Cambridge History of India IV.1. Cambridge: Cambridge University Press.

Bratton, M. (1992), 'Zambia Starts Over', Journal of Democracy 3 (2): 81–94.

Brenner, J. (1993), 'The Best of Times, the Worst of Times: US Feminism Today', New Left Review 200 (July–August: 101–59).

Bresser Pereira, C.L., Maravall, J.M. and Przeworski, A. (1993), Economic Reforms in New Democracies: A Social-democratic Approach. Cambridge: Cambridge University Press.

Bruno, M. (1993), Crisis, Stabilisation and Economic Reform. Oxford: Clarendon Press.

Burnell, P. (1995), The Politics of the Revolving Door: The Ins and Outs of Zambia's Party Politics, Working Paper, The Centre for Studies in Democratisation, University of Warwick (March).

Burton, M., Gunther, R. and Higley, J. (1992), 'Introduction: Elite Transformations and Democratic Regimes', in Higley and Gunther (1992).

Butler, J. and Scott, J. (eds) (1992), Feminists Theorise the Political. London: Routledge.

Buzan, B. (1991), 'New Patterns of Global Security in the Twenty-first Century', International Affairs 67: 431–51.

Callaghy, T.M. (1990), 'Lost Between State and Market: The Policies of Economic Adjustment in Ghana, Zambia and Nigeria', in Nelson (1990).

Calman, L.J. (1992), Toward Empowerment: Women and Movement Politics in India. Boulder, CO: Westview Press.

Canovan, M. (1992), Hannah Arendt: A Reinterpretation of her Political Thought. Cambridge: Cambridge University Press.

Carothers, T. (forthcoming), 'The Resurgence of US Political Development Assistance to Latin America', in Whitehead (forthcoming a).

Chabal, P. (1986a), 'Introduction: Thinking about Politics in Africa', in Chabal (1986b).

Chabal, P. (ed.) (1986b), Political Domination in Africa. Cambridge: Cambridge University Press.

Chabal, P. (1992), 'Civil Society', Chapter 5 in Power in Africa: An Essay in Political Interpretation. London: Macmillan.

Chatterji, M., Gilmore, B., Strunk, K. and Vanasin, J. (1993), 'Political Economy, Growth and Convergence in Less-Developed Countries', World Development 21 (12): 2029–38.

Chazan, N. (1983), An Anatomy of Ghanaian Politics: Managing Political Recession, 1969–1982. Boulder, CO: Westview Press.

Chazan, N. (1989), 'Planning Democracy in Africa: A Comparative Perspective on Nigeria and Ghana', *Policy Sciences* 22: 325–57.

Chazan, N. (1992), 'Liberalisation, Governance and Political Space in Ghana', in Hyden and Bratton (1992).

Cheriet, B. (1992), 'The Resilience of Algerian Populism', *Middle East Report* 174: 9–14, 34.

Chomsky, N. (1992), *Deterring Democracy*. London: Vintage.

Chowdhury, A. (1993), 'External Shocks and Structural Adjustments in East Asian Newly Industrialising Economies', *Journal of International Development* 5 (1): 51–77.

Christian Institute for the Study of Justice and Development (1988), *Lost Victory: An Overview of the Korean People's Struggle for Democracy in 1987*. Seoul: Minjungsa.

Cohen, R. and Goulbourne, H. (eds) (1991), *Democracy and Socialism in Africa*. Boulder, CO: Westview Press.

Commission on Security and Economic Assistance (1983), *A Report to the Secretary of State*. Washington, DC.

Constant, B. (1988 [1820]), 'The Liberty of the Ancients Compared with That of the Moderns', in B. Fontana (ed. and trans.), *Benjamin Constant: Political Writings*. Cambridge: Cambridge University Press.

Cooper, D. (1993), 'The Citizen's Charter and Radical Democracy: Empowerment and Exclusion within Citizenship Discourse', *Social and Legal Studies* 2 (2).

Cotton, J. (1991), 'The Military Factor in South Korean Politics', in V. Selochan (ed.), *The Military, the State and Development in Asia and the Pacific*. Boulder, CO: Westview Press.

Cotton, J. (1992), 'Understanding the State in South Korea: Bureaucratic-Authoritarianism or State Autonomy Theory?', *Comparative Political Studies* 24 (4): 512–31.

Crenshaw, K. (1993), 'Whose Story is it Anyway? Feminist and Antiracist Appropriations of Anita Hill', in Morrison (1993).

Crook, R. (1994), 'Ghana', in R. Crook and J. Manor, *Enhancing Participation and Institutional Performance: Democratic Decentralisation in South Asia and West Africa*, Report to the Overseas Development Administration, January.

Cumings, B. (1989), 'The Abortive Abertura: South Korea in the Light of Latin American Experience', *New Left Review* 173: 5–32.

Cutright, P. (1963), 'National Political Development: Measurement and Analysis', *American Sociological Review* 28 (2): 253–64.

Cutright, P. and Wiley, J.A. (1969), 'Modernization and Political Representation: 1927–1966', *Studies in Comparative International Development* 5 (2): 23–41.

Dahl, R.A. (1971), *Polyarchy: Participation and Opposition*. New Haven, CT: Yale University Press.

Dahl, R.A. (1989), *Democracy and its Critics*. New Haven, CT: Yale University Press.

Dasgupta, P. (1990), 'Well-being and the Extent of its Realisation in Poor Countries', *The Economic Journal* 100 (400) (Supplement): 1–32.

Dasgupta, P. (1993), *An Inquiry Into Well-being and Destitution*. Oxford: Clarendon Press.

Decalo, S. (1989), 'Modalities of Civilian–Military Stability in Africa', *Journal of Modern African Studies* 27 (4): 547–78.

Decalo, S. (1991), 'Towards Understanding the Sources of Stable Civilian Rule in Black Africa: 1960–1990', *Journal of Contemporary African Studies* 10 (1): 66–83.

Decalo, S. (1992), 'Democracy in Africa: Towards the 21st. Century', in Vanhanen (1992).

Di Palma, G. (1990), *To Craft Democracies: An Essay on Democratic Transitions*. Berkeley, CA: University of California Press.

Diamond, L. (1992), 'Economic Development and Democracy Reconsidered', *American Behavioral Scientist* 35 (4/5): 450–99.

Diamond, L. and Plattner, M.F. (eds) (1993), *The Global Resurgence of Democracy*. Baltimore, MD: Johns Hopkins University Press.

Diamond, L., Linz, J.J. and Lipset, S.M. (eds) (1988), *Democracy in Developing Countries: Vol. 2: Africa*. London: Adamantine Press Limited.

Diamond, L., Linz, J.J. and Lipset, S.M. (eds) (1989a), *Democracy in Developing Countries: Vol. 3: Asia*. London: Adamantine Press Limited.

Diamond, L., Linz, J.J. and Lipset, S.M. (eds) (1989b), *Democracy in Developing Countries: Vol. 4: Latin America*. London: Adamantine Press Limited.

Diamond, L., Linz, J.J. and Lipset, S.M. (eds) (1990), *Politics in Developing Countries: Comparing Experiences with Democracy*. Boulder, CO: Lynne Rienner.

Diaz, P. and Korovin, T. (1990), 'Neo-liberalism in Agriculture: Capitalist Modernisation in the Chilean Countryside During the Pinochet Years', *Canadian Journal of Latin American and Caribbean Studies* 15 (30): 197–219.

Dick, G.W. (1974), 'Authoritarian versus Nonauthoritarian Approaches to Economic Development', *Journal of Political Economy* 82 (4): 817–28.

Dietz, M. (1992), 'Context is All: Feminism and Theories of Citizenship', in Mouffe (1992b).

Dong, W. (1991), 'The Democratization of South Korea: What Role Does the Middle Class Play?', *Korea Observer* 22 (2): 257–82.

Dornbusch, R. and Edwards, S. (1990), 'Macroeconomic Populism', *Journal of Development Economics* 32 (2): 247–77.

Dunn, J. (ed.) (1992), *Democracy: The Unfinished Journey, 508 BC to AD 1993*. Oxford: Oxford University Press.

Dunn, J. (1994), 'The Identity of the Bourgeois Liberal Republic', in Fontana (1994).

Eckert, C.J. (1990), 'The South Korean Bourgeoisie: A Class in Search of Hegemony', *Journal of Korean Studies* 7: 115–48.

Eckstein, S. (ed.) (1989), *Power and Popular Protest: Latin American Social Movements*. Berkeley: University of California Press.

Economist Intelligence Unit (1994a), *South Korea: Country Profile 1994–95*. London: EIU.

Economist Intelligence Unit (1994b), *Ghana: Country Profile 1994–95*. London: EIU.

Edwards, M. (1989), 'The Irrelevance of Development Studies', *Third World Quarterly* 11 (1): 116–35.

Eggleston, K. (1991), 'Kwangju 1980 and Beijing 1989', *Asian Perspective* 15 (2): 33–73.

Einhorn, B. (1993), *Cinderella Goes to the Market*. London: Verso.

el-Saadawi, N. (1986), *Memoirs from the Women's Prison*. London: The Women's Press Ltd.

Elson, D. (1991), 'Structural Adjustment: Its Effect on Women', in Wallace with March (1991).

Elshtain, J.B. (1981), *Public Man, Private Woman: Women in Social and Political Thought*. Princeton, NJ: Princeton University Press.

Elster, J. (1988), 'Consequences of Constitutional Choice: Reflections on Tocqueville', in J. Elster and R. Slagstad (eds), *Constitutionalism and Democracy*. Cambridge: Cambridge University Press and Maison des Sciences de L'Homme.

Evans, P. (1992), 'The State as Problem and Solution: Predation, Embedded Autonomy, and Structural Change', in Haggard and Kaufman (1992b).

Ewell, J. (1984), *Venezuela: A Century of Change*. London: Hurst.

Far Eastern Economic Review (FEER), various issues.

Farrar, C. (1988), *The Origins of Democratic Thinking: The Invention of Politics in Classical Athens*. Cambridge: Cambridge University Press.

Ffrench-Davis, R. (1993) 'Economic Development and Equity in Chile: Legacies and Challenges in the Return to Democracy', IDS Discussion Paper 316, January. Brighton: Institute of Development Studies.

Folson, K.G. (1993), 'Ideology, Revolution and Development: The Years of J.J. Rawlings', in Gyimah-Boadi (1993).

Fontana, B. (ed.) (1994), *The Invention of the Modern Republic*. Cambridge: Cambridge University Press.

Forbes, D. (1975), 'Sceptical Whiggism, Commerce and Liberty', in A. Skinner and T. Wilson (eds), *Essays on Adam Smith*. Oxford: Oxford University Press.

Fosu, K.Y. (1993), 'Domestic Public Policy and Ghana's Agriculture, 1982–89', in Gyimah-Boadi (1993).

Frankel, F. (1978), *India's Political Economy, 1947–77: The Gradual Revolution*. Princeton, NJ: Princeton University Press.

Frankel, F. and Rao, M.S.K. (eds) (1989–90), *Dominance and State Power in India: Decline of a Social Order*, 2 vols. Delhi: Oxford University Press.

Friedman, M. and Friedman, R. (1980), *Free to Choose*. New York: Harcourt Brace Jovanovich.

Frimpong-Ansah, J.H. (1991), *The Vampire State in Africa: The Political Economy of Decline in Ghana*. London: James Currey.

Fu, Z. (1993), *Autocratic Tradition and Chinese Politics*. Cambridge: Cambridge University Press.

Fukuyama, F. (1992), *The End of History and the Last Man*. London: Hamish Hamilton.

Furet, F. and Ozouf, M. (eds) (1989), *A Critical Dictionary of the French Revolution* (trans. A. Goldhammer). Cambridge, MA: Harvard University Press.

Garretón, M.A. (1989a), 'Protests and Politics in Chile', in Eckstein (1989).

Garretón, M.A. (1989b), *The Chilean Political Process* (trans. S. Kellum in collaboration with G.W. Merkx). Boston, MA: Unwin Hyman.

Garretón, M.A. (1990), 'Democratic Inauguration in Chile: From Pinochet to Aylwin', *Third World Quarterly* 12 (3): 64–81.

Garretón, M.A. (1995), 'Redemocratization in Chile', *Journal of Democracy* 6 (1): 146–58.

Gathy, V. (ed.) (1989), *State and Civil Society: Relationships in Flux*. Budapest: Ventura.

Gellner, E. (1981), *Muslim Society*. Cambridge: Cambridge University Press.

George, A. (1992), *Forceful Persuasion: Coercive Diplomacy or an Alternative to War.* United States Institute for Peace Press.

Gertzel, C., Baylies, C. and Szeftel, M. (eds) (1984), *The Dynamics of the One-Party State in Zambia.* Manchester: Manchester University Press.

Gibbon, P. (1993), 'The World Bank and the New Politics of Aid', in G. Sorensen (ed.), *Political Conditionality.* London: Frank Cass and the European Association of Development and Research Training Institutes.

Gibson, S. (1993), 'The Discourse of Sex/War: Thoughts on Catherine MacKinnon's 1993 Oxford Amnesty Lecture', *Feminist Legal Studies*, 1 (2): 179–88.

Gills, B. (1993), 'Korean Capitalism and Democracy', in Gills *et al.* (1993).

Gills, B., Rocamora, J. and Wilson, R. (eds) (1993), *Low Intensity Democracy: Political Power in the New World Order.* London: Pluto.

Goldsworthy, D. (1981), 'Civilian Control of the Military in Black Africa', *African Affairs* 80 (8): 49–74.

Goldsworthy, D. (1986), 'Armies and Politics in Civilian Regimes', in S. Baynham (ed.), *Military Power and Politics in Black Africa.* London: Croom Helm.

Gould, C.C. (1988), *Rethinking Democracy: Freedom and Social Cooperation in Politics, Economy and Society.* Cambridge: Cambridge University Press.

Gouldner, A. (1980), *The Two Marxisms.* London: Macmillan.

Graham, Carol (1994), *Safety Nets, Politics and the Poor: Transitions to Market Economies*, Washington, DC: The Brookings Institution.

Green, D.M. (1991), 'Structural Adjustment and Politics in Ghana', *TransAfrica Forum* 8 (2): 67–89.

Green, R.H. (1988), 'Ghana: Progress, Problematics and Limitations of the Success Story', *IDS Bulletin* 19 (1): 7–15.

Greenfeld, L. (1992), *Nationalism: Five Roads to Modernity.* Cambridge, MA: Harvard University Press.

Gregor, A.J. (1979), *Italian Fascism and Developmental Dictatorship.* Princeton, NJ: Princeton University Press.

Griffith-Jones, S. (1987), *Chile to 1991: The End of an Era?* London: Economist Intelligence Unit.

Guyer, J.I. (1992), 'Representation Without Taxation: An Essay on Democracy in Rural Nigeria, 1952–1990', *African Studies Review* 35 (1): 41–80.

Gyimah-Boadi, E. (ed.) (1993), *Ghana Under PNDC Rule.* CODESRIA book series. Dakar: CODESRIA.

Gyimah-Boadi, E. and Essuman-Johnson, A. (1993), 'The PNDC and Organised Labour: The Anatomy of Political Control', in Gyimah-Boadi (1993).

Gyimah-Boadi, E. and Rothchild, D. (1982), 'Rawlings, Populism, and the Civil Liberties Tradition in Ghana', *Issue: A Journal of Africanist Opinion* 12 (3–4): 64–9.

Habibi, N. (1994), 'Budgetary Policy and Political Liberty: A Cross-Sectional Analysis', *World Development* 22 (4): 579–86.

Hadenius, A. (1992), *Democracy and Development.* Cambridge: Cambridge University Press.

Haggard, S. and Kaufman, R.R. (1992a), 'Economic Adjustment and the Prospects for Democracy', in Haggard and Kaufman (1992b).

Haggard, S. and Kaufman, R.R. (eds) (1992b), *The Politics of Economic Adjustment: International Constraints, Distributive Conflicts, and the State.* Princeton, NJ: Princeton University Press.

Haggard, S., Kim, B.K. and Moon, C.I. (1991), 'The Transition to Export-led Growth in South Korea: 1954–1966', *The Journal of Asian Studies* 50 (4): 850–73.

Haggard, S. and Webb, S.B. (eds) (1994), *Voting for Reform: Democracy, Political Liberalisation and Economic Adjustment*. Washington, DC and New York: World Bank and Oxford University Press.

Halliday, J. (1987), 'The Economies of North and South Korea', in J. Sullivan and R. Foss (eds), *Two Koreas, One Future?* Lanham, MD: University Press of America.

Hamilton, C. and Tanter, R. (1987), 'The Antinomies of Success in South Korea', *Journal of International Affairs* 41 (1): 63–89.

Han, S.-J. (1989), 'South Korea: Politics in Transition', in Diamond *et al.* (1989a).

Han, S.-J. (1990), 'South Korea: Politics in Transition', in Diamond *et al.* (1990).

Hann, C.M. (1990), 'Second Economy and Civil Society', in C.M. Hann (ed.), *Market Economy and Civil Society*. London: Frank Cass.

Hansen, E. (1991), *Ghana under Rawlings: Early Years*. Oxford: Malthouse Press for African Association of Political Science.

Harding, N. (1992), 'The Marxist–Leninist Detour', in Dunn (1992).

Harriss-White, B. (1993), 'Collective Politics of Foodgrains Markets in South Asia', *IDS Bulletin* 24 (3): 54–62.

Hawthorn, G. (1991), *Plausible Worlds: Possibility and Understanding in History and the Social Sciences*. Cambridge: Cambridge University Press.

Hawthorn, G. (1993), 'Sub-Saharan Africa', in D. Held (ed.), *Prospects for Democracy: North, South, East and West*. Cambridge: Polity Press.

Hawthorn, G. and Seabright, P. (1996), 'Where Westphalia Fails: The Conditionality of the International Financial Institutions and National Sovereignty', in A. Leftwich (ed.), *Democracy and Development: Essays on Theory and Practice*. Cambridge: Polity Press.

Haynes, J. (1991a), 'Inching Towards Democracy: The Ghanaian "Revolution", the International Monetary Fund and the Politics of the Possible', in Cohen and Goulbourne (1991).

Haynes, J. (1991b), 'The PNDC and Political Decentralisation in Ghana, 1981–91', *Journal of Commonwealth and Comparative Policies* 29 (3), November: 283–307.

Haynes, J. (1991c), 'Human-Rights and Democracy in Ghana: The Record of the Rawlings Regime', *African Affairs* 90 (360): 407–25.

Healey, J., Ketley, R. and Robinson, M. (1992), *Political Regimes and Economic Policy Patterns in Developing Countries, 1978–88*, Working Paper No. 67. London: Overseas Development Institute.

Healey, J. and Robinson, M. (1992), *Democracy, Governance and Economic Policy: Sub-Saharan Africa in Comparative Perspective*. London: Overseas Development Institute.

Held, D. (1987), *Models of Democracy*. Cambridge: Polity Press.

Held, D. (1993a), 'Democracy: From City-states to a Cosmopolitan Order?', in Held (1993b).

Held, D. (ed.) (1993b), *Prospects for Democracy: North, South, East, West*. Cambridge: Polity Press.

Helie-Lucas, M. (1991), 'Women in the Algerian Liberation Struggle', in Wallace with March (1991).

Hendessi, M. (1990), 'Armed Angels: Women in Iran', a Change International Report: *Women and Society, Report No. 16*. London: Change.

Herbst, J. (1991), 'Labour in Ghana under Structural Adjustment: The Policies of Acquiescence', in Rothchild (1991).

Herbst, J. (1993), *The Politics of Reform in Ghana, 1982–1991.* Berkeley: University of California Press.

Higley, J. and Gunther, R. (1992), *Elites and Democratic Consolidation in Latin America and Southern Europe.* Cambridge: Cambridge University Press.

Hirschman, A.O. (1977), *The Passions and the Interests: Arguments for Capitalism Before its Triumph.* Princeton, NJ: Princeton University Press.

Hirschman, A.O. (1986), 'Notes on Consolidating Democracy in Latin America', in *Rival Views of the Market and Other Essays.* New York: Viking.

Hirst, P. (1993), *Associative Democracy.* Cambridge: Polity Press.

Hobbes, T. (1991 [1651]), *Leviathan* (ed. R. Tuck). Cambridge: Cambridge University Press.

Hont, I. (1983), 'The "Rich Country–Poor Country" Debate in Scottish Classical Political Economy', in I. Hont and M. Ignatieff (eds), *Wealth and Virtue: The Shaping of Political Economy in the Scottish Enlightenment.* Cambridge: Cambridge University Press.

Hooks, B. (1984), *Feminist Theory: From Margin to Centre.* Boston, MA: South End Press.

Hornblower, S. (1992), 'Creation and Development of Democratic Institutions in Ancient Greece', in Dunn (1992).

Horowitz, D.L. (1993), 'Comparing Democratic Systems', in Diamond and Plattner (1993).

Hsiao, H.-H.M. (1990), 'Social Movements and the Rise of a Demanding Civil Society in Taiwan', *The Australian Journal of Chinese Affairs* 27: 163–80.

Huber, E., Rueschemeyer, D. and Stephens, J.D. (1993), 'The Impact of Economic Development on Democracy', *Journal of Economic Perspectives* 7 (3): 71–85.

Hunneus, C. (1987), 'From Diarchy to Polyarchy: Prospects for Democracy in Chile', in E.A. Baloyra (ed.), *Comparing New Democracies: Transition and Consolidation in Mediterranean Europe and the Southern Cone.* Boulder, CO: Westview Press.

Huntington, S.P. (1957), *The Soldier and the State: The Theory and Politics of Civil–Military Relations.* New York: Vintage Books.

Huntington, S.P. (1968), *Political Order in Changing Societies.* New Haven, CT: Yale University Press.

Huntington, S.P. (1991), *The Third Wave: Democratization in the Late Twentieth Century.* Norman, OK and London: University of Oklahoma Press.

Huntington, S.P. (1993), 'The Clash of Civilisations?', *Foreign Affairs* 72 (3): 22–49.

Hutchful, E. (1979), 'Organizational Instability in African Military Forces: The Case of the Ghanaian Army', *International Social Science Journal* 31 (4): 606–18.

Hutchful, E. (1987), 'New Elements in Militarism: Ethiopia, Ghana and Burkina Faso', *International Journal* 41 (4): 802–30.

Hutchful, E. (1996), 'Organizational Decomposition and Junior Ranks' Political Action in Ghana', in E. Hutchful and A. Bathily, *The Military and Militarization in Africa.* Dakar: CODESRIA.

Hyden, G. and Bratton, M. (eds) (1992), *Governance and Politics in Africa.* Boulder, CO: Lynne Rienner.

Inkeles, A. (1990), 'On Measuring Democracy', *Studies in Comparative International Development* 25 (1): 3–6.

Jacobeit, C. (1991), 'Reviving Cocoa: Policies and Perspectives on Structural Adjustment in Ghana's Key Agricultural Sector', in Rothchild (1991).

Jaising, I. (1987), 'Women, Religion and Law', *The Lawyers' Collective* (Bangalore), Special Issue, December.

Jeffries, R. (1991), 'Leadership Commitment and Political Opposition to Structural Adjustment in Ghana', in Rothchild (1991).

Jeffries, R. (1992), 'Urban Popular Attitudes towards the Economic Recovery Programme and the PNDC Government in Ghana', *African Affairs* 91 (363): 207–26.

Jeffries, R. (1993), 'The State, Structural Adjustment and Good Government in Africa', *Journal of Commonwealth and Comparative Politics* 31 (1): 20–35.

Jeffries, R. and Thomas, C. (1993), 'The Ghanaian Elections of 1992', *African Affairs* 92 (368): 331–66.

Jilberto, A.E.F. (1991), 'Military Bureaucracy, Political Opposition and Democratic Transition', *Latin American Perspectives* 18 (1): 33–65.

Jowitt, K. (1993), 'The New World Disorder', in Diamond and Plattner (1993).

Kandiyoti, D. (1988), 'Bargaining with Patriarchy', *Gender and Society* 2 (3).

Kant, I. (1891 [1795]), 'To Perpetual Peace: A Philosophical Sketch', in W. Hastie (ed.), *Kant's Principles of Politics Including his Essay on Perpetual Peace*. Edinburgh: T. and T. Clark.

Katzenstein, M. (1978), 'Towards Equality? Cause and Consequence of the Political Prominence of Women in India', *Asian Survey* 18 (5): 473–86.

Keane, J. (ed.) (1988), *Civil Society and the State: New European Perspectives*. London: Verso.

Khilnani, S. (1992), 'India's Democratic Career', in Dunn (1992).

Kihl, Y.W. (1990), 'South Korea in 1989: Slow Progress Towards Democracy', *Asian Survey* 30 (1): 66–73.

Kihl, Y.W. (1991), 'South Korea in 1990: Diplomatic Activism and a Partisan Quagmire', *Asian Survey* 31 (1): 64–70.

Kim, C.I.E. (1984), 'Civil–Military Relations in the Two Koreas', *Armed Forces and Society* 11 (1): 9–31.

Kim, H.K. and Geisse, G. (1988), 'The Political Economy of Outward Liberalisation: Chile and South Korea in Comparative Perspective', *Asian Perspective* 12 (2): 35–68.

Kim K.W. (1992), 'The Nature and Limits of Democratisation in Korea', in Vanhanen (1990).

Kim, S.J. (1990), 'The Rise of the Neo-mercantile State: Institutional Change in Korea', *Pacific Focus* 5 (1): 111–48.

Kim Y.R. (1992), 'Korean Labour Movement and Political Participation', *Korea Observer* 23 (1): 1–18.

Kishwar, M. (1986), 'Pro-Women or Anti-Muslim? The Shahbano Controversy', *Manushi*, 32. Delhi.

Kohli, A. (1990), *Democracy and Discontent: India's Growing Crisis of Governability*. Cambridge: Cambridge University Press.

Kornai, J. (1982), *Growth, Shortage and Efficiency*. Oxford: Blackwell.

Kpundeh, S.J. and Riley, S.P. (1992), 'Political Choice and the New Democratic Politics in Africa', *The Round Table* 323: 263–71.

Kraus, J. (1991a), 'The Political Economy of Stabilisation and Structural Adjustment in Ghana', in Rothchild (1991).

Kraus, J. (1991b), 'The Struggle over Structural Adjustment in Ghana', *Africa Today* 38 (4): 19–37.

Kruks, S., Rapp, R. and Young, M.B. (eds) (1989), *Promissory Notes: Women in the Transition to Feminism*. New York: Monthly Review Press.

Kuk, M. (1988), 'The Governmental Role in the Making of Chaebol in the Industrial Development of South Korea', *Asian Perspective* 12 (1): 107–33.

Lancaster, C. (1993), 'Governance and Development: The Views from Washington', *IDS Bulletin* 24 (1): 9–15.

Landell-Mills, Pierre (1992), *Governance, Civil Society and Empowerment in Sub-Saharan Africa: Building the Institutional Basis for Sustainable Development*. Washington, DC: Africa Technical Department, World Bank (June).

Landsberger, H.A. and McDaniel, T. (1976), 'Hypermobilization in Chile, 1970–1973', *World Politics* 28 (4): 502–41.

Latin American Regional Report (LARR), various issues. London: Latin American Newsletters.

Latin American Weekly Report (LAWR), various issues. London: Latin American Newsletters.

Latin American Research Report – Southern Cone (LARR-SC), various issues. London: Latin American Newsletters.

Launius, M.A. (1991), 'State–Labor Relations in Democratizing South Korea', *Pacific Focus* 6 (1): 39–58.

Lee, C.-S. and Sohn H.-S. (1994), 'South Korea 1993: The Year of the Great Reform', *Asian Survey* 34 (1): 1–9.

Lee, C.-S. and Sohn H.-S. (1995), 'South Korea 1994: A Year of Trial', *Asian Survey* 35 (1): 28–36.

Lee H.Y. (1993), 'South Korea in 1992: A Turning Point in Democratisation', *Asian Survey* 33 (1): 34–42.

Lee S.-H. (1993), 'Transitional Politics of Korea, 1987–1992: Activation of Civil Society', *Pacific Affairs* 66 (3): 351–67.

Lee, S.J. (1991), 'Political Liberalisation and Economic Development in South Korea', *Korea Journal of Population and Development* 20 (1): 77–9.

Leffler, M.P. (1992), *A Preponderance of Power: National Security, the Truman Administration and the Cold War*. Stanford, CA: Stanford University Press.

Leftwich, A. (1993), 'Voting Can Damage Your Wealth', *The Times Higher Education Supplement*, 13 August: 11–13.

Leith, J.C. and Lofchie, M.F. (1993), 'The Political Economy of Structural Adjustment in Ghana', in Bates and Krueger (1993).

Lemarchand, R. (1992a), 'Uncivil States and Civil Societies: How Illusion Becomes Reality', *Journal of Modern African Studies* 30 (2): 177–91.

Lemarchand, R. (1992b), 'African Transitions to Democracy: An Interim (and Mostly Pessimistic) Assessment', *Africa Insight* 22 (3): 178–85.

Liddle, J. and Rai, S. (1993), 'Orientalism and Feminism: Going beyond Difference?', in M. Kennedy, C. Lubelska and V. Walsh (eds), *Making Connections: Women's Studies, Women's Movements, Women's Lives*. Brighton: Taylor and Francis.

Lijphart, A. (1977), *Politics and Markets: The World's Political-Economic Systems*. New Haven, CT: Yale University Press.

Lijphart, A. (1993), 'Constitutional Choices for New Democracies', in Diamond and Plattner (1993).

Lindblom, C.E. (1977), *Politics and Markets: The World's Political-Economic Systems*. New York: Basic Books Inc.

Linz, J.J. (1993a), 'The Perils of Presidentialism', in Diamond and Plattner (1993).

Linz, J.J. (1993b), 'The Virtues of Parliamentarism', in Diamond and Plattner (1993).

Linz, J. and Stepan, A. (1989), 'Political Crafting of Democratic Consolidation or Destruction: European and South American Comparisons', in R.A. Pastov (ed.), *Democracy in the Americas*. New York: Holmes and Meier.

Lipset, S.M. (1959), 'Some Social Requisites of Democracy: Economic Development and Political Legitimacy', *The American Political Science Review* 53 (1): 69–105.

Lipset, S.M. (1960), *Political Man*. New York: Doubleday and Co.

Lipton, M. (1976), *Why Poor People Stay Poor: Urban Bias in World Development*. London: Temple Smith.

Litwak, R.S. (1984), *Detente and the Nixon Doctrine: American Foreign Policy and the Pursuit of Stability*. Cambridge: Cambridge University Press.

Lomnitz, L. and Melnick, A. (1991), *Chile's Middle Class: A Struggle for Survival in the Face of Neo-liberalism*. Boulder, CO and London: Lynne Rienner.

Lorde, A. (1981), 'An Open Letter to Many Daily', in C. Moraga and G. Anzaldua (eds), *This Bridge Called My Back: Writings of Radical Women of Color*. Watertown, MA: Persephone Press.

Loveman, B. (1991), 'Mision Cumplida? Civil Military Relations and the Chilean Political Transition', *Journal of Interamerican Studies and World Affairs* 33 (3): 35–74.

Low, D.A. (1991), Political Superstructures in Post-colonial States', in *Eclipse of Empire*. Cambridge: Cambridge University Press.

Lowenthal, A.F. (ed.) (1991), *Exporting Democracy: The United States and Latin America*. Baltimore, MD: Johns Hopkins University Press.

Luckham, R. (1971), *The Nigerian Military: A Sociological Analysis of Authority and Revolt 1960–67*. Cambridge: Cambridge University Press.

Luckham, R. (1978), 'Imperialism, Law and Structural Dependence: The Ghana Legal Profession', *Development and Change* 9 (2): 201–44.

Luckham, R. (1982), 'French Militarism in Africa', *Review of African Political Economy* 24: 55–84.

Luckham, R. (1985), 'Militarization in Africa', *SIPRI Yearbook 1985*, chapter 9. Stockholm: Stockholm International Peace Research Institute.

Luckham, R. (1990), *American Militarism and the Third World: The End of the Cold War?* Working Paper No. 94. Canberra: Peace Research Centre, Australian National University.

Luckham, R. (1994), 'The Military, Militarization and Democratization in Africa: A Survey of the Literature and Issues', *African Studies Review* 37 (2): 13–75.

Lungu, G.F. (1986), 'The Church, Labour and the Press in Zambia: The Role of Critical Observers in a One-party State', *African Affairs* 85 (340): 394–404.

MacKinnon, C. (1993), 'Crimes of War, Crimes of Peace', in Shute and Hurley (1994).

Maier, C.S. (1987), 'Introduction', in *Changing Boundaries of the Political: Essays on the Evolving Balance Between State and Society, Public and Private in Europe*. Cambridge: Cambridge University Press.

Maier, C.S. (1992), 'Democracy Since the French Revolution', in Dunn (1992).

Malloy, J.M. and Seligson, M.A. (1987), *Authoritarians and Democrats: Regime Transition in Latin America*. Pittsburgh, PA: University of Pittsburgh Press.

Mamdani, M. (1990), 'The Social Basis of Constitutionalism in Africa', *Journal of Modern African Studies* 28 (3): 359–74.

Manor, J. (1990), 'How and Why Liberal and Representative Politics Emerged in India', *Political Studies* 38: 20–38.

Martin, M. (1991), 'Negotiating Adjustment and External Finance: Ghana and the International Community 1982–1989', in Rothchild (1991).

Meier, C. (1990), *The Greek Discovery of Politics* (trans. D. McLintock). Cambridge, MA: Harvard University Press.

Meller, P. (1991), 'Adjustment and Social Costs in Chile During the 1980s', *World Development* 19 (11): 1545–61.

Mernissi, F. (1988), 'Democracy as Moral Disintegration· The Contradiction between Religious Belief and Citizenship as a Manifestation of the Ahistoricity of the Arab Identity'.

Migdal, J.S. (1987), 'Strong States, Weak States: Power and Accommodation', in M. Weiner and S.P. Huntington (eds), *Understanding Political Development*. Boston, MA: Little Brown and Company.

Mijere, N. (1988), 'The State and Development: A Study of the Dominance of the Political Class in Zambia', *Africa Today*, 35 (2): 21–36.

Mill, J.S. (1977 [1861]), 'Considerations on Representative Government', in J.M. Robson (ed.), *Essays on Politics and Society*. Collected works of John Stuart Mill, vol. 19. Toronto: University of Toronto Press.

Miller, R.F. (ed.) (1992), *The Development of Civil Society in Communist Systems*. Sydney: Allen and Unwin.

Mohanty, C.T., Russo, A. and Torres, L. (1991), *Third World Women and the Politics of Feminism*. Bloomington, IN: Indiana University Press.

Moll, T. (1992), 'Mickey Mouse Numbers and Inequality Research in Developing Countries', *Journal of Development Studies* 28 (4): 689–704.

Montesquieu, C.L. de Secondat, Baron de (1989 [1748]), *The Spirit of the Laws* (ed. and trans. A.M. Cohler, B.C. Miller and H.S. Stone). Cambridge: Cambridge University Press.

Moore, B. Jr (1966), *Social Origins of Democracy and Dictatorship: Lord and Peasant in the Making of the Modern World*. Boston, MA: Beacon Press.

Moore, M. (1993), 'Declining to Learn from the East? The World Bank on "Governance and Development"', *IDS Bulletin* 24 (1): 39–50.

Morrison, T. (1993), *Racing Justice, Engendering Power: Essays on Anita Hill, Clarence Thomas and the Construction of Social Reality*. London: Chatto and Windus.

Morse, R.M. (1954), 'The Heritage of Latin America', in L. Hartz (ed.), *The Founding of New Societies*. New York: Harcourt Brace.

Mosley, P., Harrigan, J. and Toye, J. (1991), *Aid and Power: The World Bank and Policy-based Lending*, 2 vols. London: Routledge.

Mouffe, C. (1992a), 'Feminism, Citizenship, and Radical Democratic Politics', in Butler and Scott (1992).

Mouffe, C. (ed.) (1992b), *Dimensions of Radical Democracy: Pluralism, Citizenship, Community*. London: Verso.

Muller, E.N. (1985), 'Dependent Economic Development, Aid Dependence on the United States, and Democratic Breakdown in the Third World', *International Studies Quarterly* 29 (4): 445–69.

Muller, E.N. (1988), 'Democracy, Economic Development, and Income Inequality', *American Sociological Review* 53 (1): 50–68.

Murphy, W.F. (1993), 'Constitutions, Constitutionalism and Democracy', in D. Greenberg, S.N. Katz, M.B. Oliviero and S.C. Wheatley (eds), *Constitutionalism and Democracy: Transitions in the Contemporary World*. New York: Oxford University Press.

Nathan, A.J. (1993), 'Is China Ready for Democracy?', in Diamond and Plattner (1993).

National Commission for Democracy (1991), *Evolving a True Democracy. Summary of the NCD's Work Towards the Establishment for New Democratic Order. Report Presented to the PNDC*. Accra: The National Commission for Democracy.

Navarro, M. (1989), 'The Personal is Political: Las Madres de Plaza de Mayo', in Eckstein (1989).

Nelson, J.M. (ed.) (1990), *Economic Crisis and Policy Choice: The Policies of Adjustment in the Third World*. Princeton, NJ: Princeton University Press.

Nelson, J.M. with Eglinson, S.J. (1992), *Encouraging Democracy: What Role for Conditional Aid?* ODC Policy Essay No. 4. Washington, DC: Overseas Development Council.

Neubauer, D.E. (1967), 'Some Conditions of Democracy', *The American Political Science Review* 61 (4): 1002–9.

New Patriotic Party (1993), *The Stolen Verdict*. Accra: New Patriotic Party.

Ninsin, K.A. (1987), 'Ghanaian Politics After 1981: Revolution or Evolution?', *Canadian Journal of African Studies* 21 (1): 16–37.

Nolutshungu, S.C. (1992), 'Africa in a World of Democracies: Interpretation and Retrieval', *Journal of Commonwealth and Comparative Politics* 30 (3): 316–410.

O'Donnell, G. (1978), 'Reflections on Patterns of Change in the Bureaucratic-Authoritarian State', *Latin American Research Review* 13 (1): 3–38.

O'Donnell, G. (1994), 'Delegative Democracy', *Journal of Democracy* 5 (1): 55–69.

O'Donnell, G. and Schmitter, P.C. (1986), *Transitions from Authoritarian Rule: Tentative Conclusions about Uncertain Democracies*. Baltimore, MD: Johns Hopkins University Press.

O'Donnell, G., Schmitter, P.C. and Whitehead, L. (eds) (1986a), *Transitions from Authoritarian Rule: Comparative Perspectives*. Baltimore, MD and London: Johns Hopkins University Press.

O'Donnell, G., Schmitter, P.C. and Whitehead, L. (eds) (1986b), *Transitions from Authoritarian Rule: Latin America*. Baltimore, MD: Johns Hopkins University Press.

O'Donnell, G., Schmitter, P.C. and Whitehead L. (eds) (1986c), *Transitions from Authoritarian Rule: Prospects for Democracy*. Baltimore, MD: Johns Hopkins University Press.

Oakeshott, M. (ed.) (1938), *The Social and Political Doctrines of Contemporary Europe*. Cambridge: Cambridge University Press.

Offe, C. and Preuss, U.K. (1991), 'Democratic Institutions and Moral Resources', in David Held (ed.), *Political Theory Today*. Oxford: Polity Press.

Oppenheim, L.H. (1993), *Politics in Chile: Democracy, Authoritarianism and the Search for Development*. Boulder, CO: Westview Press.

Oxhorn, P. (1994), 'Where Did All the Protestors Go? Popular Mobilization and the Transition to Democracy in Chile', *Latin American Perspectives* 21 (3): 49–68.

Paik, Y.-C. (1994), 'Political Reform and Democratic Consolidation in Korea', *Korea and World Affairs* 18 (4): 730–48.

Panebianco, A. (1988), *Political Parties: Organisation and Power*. Cambridge: Cambridge University Press.

Parekh, B. (1992), 'The Cultural Particularity of Liberal Democracy', *Political Studies* 40 (2): 160–75.

Park, C.M. (1991), 'Authoritarian Rule in South Korea: Political Support and Governmental Performance', *Asian Survey* 31 (8): 743–61.

Park, K.Y. (1993), 'Pouring New Wine into Fresh Wineskins: Defense Spending and Economic Growth in LDCs with Application to South Korea', *Journal of Peace Research* 30 (1): 79–93.

Pateman, C. (1970), *Participation and Democratic Theory*. Cambridge: Cambridge University Press.

Pateman, C. (1989), *The Disorder of Women: Democracy, Feminism and Political Theory*. Cambridge: Polity Press.

Pempel, T.J. (ed.) (1990), *Uncommon Democracies: The One-party Dominant Regimes*. London: Cornell University Press.

Petras, J. and Leiva, F.I. with Veltmeyer, H. (1994), *Democracy and Poverty in Chile: The Limits to Electoral Politics*, Boulder, CO: Westview.

Phillips, A. (1991), 'Citizenship and Feminist Theory', in Andrews (1991).

Phillips, A. (1992), 'Must Feminists Give Up on Liberal Democracy?', *Political Studies* 40: 68–82.

Phiri, B.J. (1991), 'Zambia: The Myth and Realities of "One-party Participatory Democracy"', *Genève-Afrique* 29 (2): 9–24.

Pion-Berlin, D. (1992), 'Military Autonomy and Emerging Democracies in South America', *Comparative Politics* 25 (1): 83–102.

Pocock, J.G.A. (1975), *The Machiavellian Moment: Florentine Political Thought and the Atlantic Republican Tradition*. Princeton, NJ: Princeton University Press.

Pourgerami, A. (1991), *Development and Democracy in the Third World*. Boulder, CO, San Francisco and Oxford: Westview.

Pridham, G. (ed.) (1991), *Encouraging Democracy: The International Context of Regime Transition in Southern Europe*. Leicester: Leicester University Press.

Pringle, R. and Watson, S. (1992), 'Women's Interests and the Post-structuralist State', in Barrett and Phillips (1992).

Przeworski, A. (1985), *Capitalism and Social Democracy*. Cambridge: Cambridge University Press.

Przeworski, A. (1991), *Democracy and the Market: Political and Economic Reforms in Eastern Europe and Latin America*. Cambridge: Cambridge University Press.

Przeworski, A. (1993), 'Economic Reforms, Public Opinion and Political Institutions: Poland in the Eastern European Perspective', in Bresser Pereira *et al.* (1993).

Przeworski, A. and Limongi, F. (1993), 'Political Regimes and Economic Growth', *Journal of Economic Perspectives* 7 (3): 51–69.

Putnam, R. (1993), *Making Democracy Work: Civic Traditions in Modern Italy*. Princeton, NJ: Princeton University Press.

Rai, S. (1988), *Women of the Arab World: The Coming Challenge*, papers of Arab Women's Solidarity Conference, 1986 edited by N. Toubia, London: Zed Press.

Rai, S., Pilkington, H. and Phizacklea, A. (eds) (1992), *Women in the Face of Change: Eastern Europe, the Soviet Union, and China*. London: Routledge.

Rakner, L. (1992), *Trade Unions in Processes of Democratisation: A Study of Party Labour Relations in Zambia*. Bergen: Chr. Michelsen Institute, Department of Social Science and Development.

Ravenhill, J. (1980), 'Comparing Regime Performance in Africa: Limitations of Cross National Aggregate Analysis', *Journal of Modern African Studies* 18 (1): 99–126.

Rawlings, J.J. (1986), *The New Direction: Selected Speeches of Flight Lieutenant Jerry John Rawlings, 1 January – 31 December 1986*. Accra: Ghana Publishing Corporation.

Remmer, K.L. (1985–6), 'Exclusionary Democracy', *Studies in Comparative International Development* 20 (4): 64–85.

Remmer, K.L. (1988), *The Chilean Military under Authoritarian Rule, 1973–1987*, Occasional Paper Series No. 1. Albuquerque, NM: Latin American Institute, University of New Mexico.

Remmer, K.L. (1989), *Military Rule in Latin America*. Boston: Unwin Hyman.

Ritter, A.R.M. (1990), 'Development Strategy and Structural Adjustment in Chile, 1973–1990', *Canadian Journal of Latin American and Caribbean Studies* 15 (30): 159–65.

Roberts, H. (1983), 'The Algerian Bureaucracy', in T.A. Asad and R. Owen (eds), *Sociology of 'Developing Societies': The Middle East*. New York: Monthly Review Press.

Roberts, H. (1987), 'Editorial', in *IDS Bulletin* 18 (4): 1–6.

Robinson, M. (1993), 'Aid, Democracy and Political Conditionality in Sub-Saharan Africa', in Sørensen (1993a).

Rothchild, D. (ed.) (1991), *Ghana: The Political Economy of Recovery*, Boulder, CO and London: Lynne Rienner.

Rousseau, J.J. (1968 [1762]), *The Social Contract* (ed. M. Cranston). Harmondsworth: Penguin.

Ruddick, S. (1980), 'Maternal Thinking', *Feminist Studies* 6 (2): 342–67.

Rudolph, L.I. and Rudolph, S.H. (1987), *In Pursuit of Lakshmi: The Political Economy of the Indian State*. Chicago, IL: University of Chicago Press.

Rueschemeyer, D., Stephens, E.H. and Stephens, J.D. (1992), *Capitalist Development and Democracy*. Cambridge: Polity Press.

Rustow, D.A. (1970), 'Transitions to Democracy: A Dynamic Model,' *Comparative Politics* 2: 337–63.

Sandbrook, R. (1988), 'Liberal Democracy in Africa: A Socialist-Revisionist Perspective', *Canadian Journal of African Studies* 22 (2): 240–67.

Sandbrook, R. (1993), *The Politics of Africa's Economic Recovery*. Cambridge: Cambridge University Press.

Sangmpam, S.N. (1993), 'Neither Soft Nor Dead: The African State is Alive and Well', *African Studies Review* 36 (2): 73–94.

Scheetz, T. (1992), 'The Evolution of Public Sector Expenditures: Changing Political Priorities in Argentina, Chile, Paraguay and Peru', *Journal of Peace Research* 29 (2): 175–90.

Schmitter, P.C. (1974), 'Still the Century of Corporatism?', *Review of Politics* 36: 85–131.

Schmitz, G.J. and Hutchful, E. (1992), *Democratisation and Popular Participation in Africa*. Ottawa: North–South Institute.

Schoultz, L. (1987), *National Security and United States Policy Towards Latin America*. Princeton, NJ: Princeton University Press.

Schraeder, P.J. (1994), *United States Foreign Policy Toward Africa: Incrementalism, Crisis and Change*. Cambridge: Cambridge University Press.

Schumpeter, J.A. (1943), *Capitalism, Socialism and Democracy*. London: Unwin.

Shute, S. and Hurley S. (eds) (1994), *On Human Rights: The Oxford Amnesty Lectures 1993*. London: Basic Books.

Silva, P. (1991), 'Technocrats and Policies in Chile: From the Chicago Boys to the CIEPLAN Monks', *Journal of Latin American Studies* 23 (2): 385–410.

Silva, P. (1993), 'State, Politics and the Idea of Social Justice in Chile', *Development and Change* 24: 465–86.

Simon, W.H. (1990), 'Social Theory and Political Practice: Unger's Brazilian Journalism', in R.W. Lovin and M.J. Perry (eds), *Critique and Construction: A Symposium on Roberto Unger's 'Politics'*. Cambridge: Cambridge University Press.

SIPRI (1992), *SIPRI Yearbook 1992: World Armaments and Disarmament*. Stockholm: Stockholm International Peace Research Institute.

Sirowy, L. and Inkeles, A. (1990), 'Effects of Democracy on Economic Growth and Inequality: A Review', *Studies in Comparative International Development* 25 (1): 126–57.

Skinner, Q. (1989), 'The State', in T. Ball, J. Farr and R.L. Hanson (eds), *Political Innovation and Conceptual Change*. Cambridge: Cambridge University Press.

Skinner, Q. (1990), 'The Republican Ideal of Political Liberty', in G. Bock, Q. Skinner and M. Viroli (eds), *Machiavelli and Republicanism*. Cambridge: Cambridge University Press.

Skinner, Q. (1992), 'The Italian City-republics', in Dunn (1992).

Sklar, R. (1987), 'Developmental Democracy', *Comparative Studies in Society and History* 29 (4): 686–714.

Smart, C. (1989), *Feminism and the Power of Law*. London: Routledge.

Smith, A. (1976 [1776]), *An Inquiry Into the Nature and Causes of the Wealth of Nations* (ed. R.H. Campbell, A.S. Skinner and W.B. Wood). Oxford: Clarendon Press.

Sørensen, G. (ed.) (1993a), *Political Conditionality*, London: Frank Cass.

Sørenson, G. (1993b), *Democracy and Democratization*. Boulder, CO: Westview.

Stallings, B. (1990), 'Politics and Economic Crisis: A Comparative Study of Chile, Peru and Colombia', in Nelson (1990).

Stepan, A. (1978), *State and Society: Peru in Comparative Perspective*. Princeton, NJ: Princeton University Press.

Stepan, A. (1988), *Rethinking Military Politics: Brazil and the Southern Cone*. Princeton, NJ: Princeton University Press.

Stewart, F. (1985), *Planning to Meet Basic Needs*. London: Macmillan.

Suh, J.J. (1989), 'The Social and Political Networks of the South Korean Capitalist Class', *Asian Perspective* 13 (2): 111–40.

Sunkel, O. (1993), 'Consolidation of Chile's Democracy and Development: The Challenges and the Tasks', IDS Discussion Paper 317, January. Brighton: Institute of Development Studies.

Sunstein, C. (1991), 'Preferences and Politics', *Philosophy and Public Affairs* 20: 3–34.

Tangri, R. (1992), 'The Politics of Government–Business Relations in Ghana', *Journal of Modern African Studies* 30 (1): 97–111.

Tilly, C. (1985), 'War and the Power of Warmakers in Western Europe and Elsewhere 1600–1980', in P. Wallenstein (ed.), *Global Militarization*. Boulder, CO: Westview Press.

Tilly, C. (1992), *Coercion, Capital and European States, AD 990–1992*. Cambridge, MA and Oxford: Blackwell.

Tordoff, W. (1994), 'Political Liberalization and Economic Reform in Africa', *Democratization* 1 (1): 100–15.

Toye, J. (1991), 'Ghana's Economic Reforms and World Bank Policy-Conditioned Lending, 1983–88', in Mosley *et al.* (1991), vol. II.

Tsuru, S. (1993), *Japan's Capitalism: Creative Defeat and Beyond*. Cambridge: Cambridge University Press.

Unger, R.M. (1987), *Social Theory: Its Situation and Its Task, Preface to Politics*. Cambridge: Cambridge University Press.

Valenzuela, A. (1989), 'Chile: Origins, Consolidation, and Breakdown of a Democratic Regime', in Diamond *et al.* (1990).

Van de Walle, N. (1994), 'Political Liberation and Economic Policy Reform in Africa', *World Development* 22 (4): 483–500.

Vanhanen, T. (1990), *The Process of Democratization: A Comparative Study of 147 States, 1980–1988*. New York: Crane Russak.

Vanhanen, T. (1992), 'Conclusion', in Vanhanen (1992).

Vanhanen, T. (ed.) (1992), *Strategies of Democratization*. London: Crane Russak.

Vogel, E.F. (1979), *Japan as Number One: Lessons for America*. Cambridge, MA: Harvard University Press.

Vogel, E.F. (1991), *The Four Little Dragons: The Spread of Industrialisation in East Asia*. Cambridge, MA: Harvard University Press.

Wade, R. (1990), *Governing the Market: Economic Theory and the Role of the State in East Asian Industrialisation*. Princeton, NJ: Princeton University Press.

Wallace, T. with March, C. (1991), *Changing Perceptions: Writings on Gender and Development*. Oxford: Oxfam.

Walzer, M. (1992), 'The Civil Society Argument', in Mouffe (1992b).

Waylen, G. (1992), 'Rethinking Women's Political Participation and Protest: Chile 1970–1990', *Political Studies* 40 (2): 299–314.

Weffort, F.C. (1993), 'What is a "New Democracy?"', *International Social Science Journal* 136 (May).

West Africa, various issues. London.

White, G. (1993), 'Towards a Political Analysis of Markets', *IDS Bulletin* 24 (3): 4–11.

Whitehead, L. (1986), 'International Aspects of Democratization', in O'Donnell *et al.* (1986a).

Whitehead, L. (1992), 'The San José Process and the Identity of the New Europe', in J. Roy (ed.), *The Reconstruction of Central America: The Role of the European Community*. Miami University Press.

Whitehead, L. (forthcoming a), *The International Dimensions of Democratisation: Europe and the Americas*. Oxford: Oxford University Press.

Whitehead, L. (forthcoming b), 'Contagion, Control, Conditionality and Consent', in Whitehead (forthcoming a).

Williams, P. (1991), *The Alchemy of Race and Rights: Diary of a Law Professor*. Cambridge, MA: Harvard University Press.

Williamson, J. (1993), 'Democracy and the "Washington Consensus"', *World Development* 21: 1329–36.

Winch, D. (1988), 'Adam Smith and the Liberal Tradition', in K. Haakonssen (ed.), *Traditions of Liberalism: Essays on John Locke, Adam Smith and John Stuart Mill*. Centre for Independent Studies Readings No. 8. St Leonards, NSW: Centre for Independent Studies.

Winckler, E.A. (1984), 'Institutionalization and Participation in Taiwan: From Hard to Soft Authoritarianism?', *China Quarterly* 99: 481–99.

Wood, E.M. (1990), 'The Uses and Abuses of Civil Society', in Ralph Miliband *et al.* (eds), *The Socialist Register 1990*. London: Merlin Press.

Woods, D. (1992), 'Civil Society in Europe and Africa: Limiting State Power through a Public Sphere', *African Studies Review* 35 (2): 77–100.

Woodward, P. (1994), 'Democracy and Economy in Africa: The Optimists and the Pessimists', *Democratization* 1 (1): 116–32.

World Bank (1992a), *Governance and Development*. Washington, DC: World Bank.

World Bank (1992b), *World Development Report 1992: Development and the Environment*. New York: Oxford University Press.

World Bank (1993), *The East Asian Economic Miracle: Economic Growth and Public Policy*. New York: Oxford University Press.

World Bank (1995), *World Development Report 1995: Workers in an Integrating World*. London: Oxford University Press.

Wraith, R. and Simpkins, E. (1963), *Corruption in Developing Countries*. London: Allen and Unwin.

Zaverucha, Z. (1993), 'The Degree of Military Autonomy During the Spanish, Argentinian and Brazilian Transitions', *Journal of Latin American Studies* 25 (2): 283–99.

Zolberg, A.R. (1966), *Creating Political Order: The Party States of West Africa*. Chicago, IL: University of Chicago Press.

Index